Government and Society in Afghanistan

Modern Middle East Series, No. 5
Sponsored by the Center for Middle Eastern Studies
The University of Texas at Austin

Government and Society in Afghanistan

The Reign of Amir 'Abd al-Rahman Khan

by Hasan Kawun Kakar

University of Texas Press, Austin and London

Library of Congress Cataloging in Publication Data

Kakar, M   Hasan.
    Government and society in Afghanistan.

    (Modern Middle East series; no. 5)
    A revision of the author's thesis, University of London.
    Bibliography: p.
    Includes index.
    1. Afghanistan—Politics and government.   2. Afghanistan—Social conditions.
3. Afghanistan—Economic conditions.   I. Title.   II. Series: Modern Middle East
series (Austin, Tex.); no. 5.
DS365.K32   1979   309.1'581'04   78-31213
ISBN 0-292-72718-6

To Crystal A. Leslie

Contents

Preface

This book is the revised version of my doctoral dissertation, "Afghanistan in the Reign of Amir ʾAbd al-Rahman Khan, 1880–1901," submitted to the University of London in 1974. Major alterations have been made in the introduction, the sections on rural landlord-peasant relations and on the position of women, and the conclusion and minor alterations in other sections. In general, the whole work has been compressed, and certain sections and all appendices except one have been omitted for reasons of space. Certain sections, however, have been expanded in the light of new source materials that became available to me after the completion of my dissertation. With all this I may perhaps be excused in saying that I have not placed anything in the whole work that I did not think to be true.

When it comes to acknowledgments it is easy to know how to begin, although during my three years of uninterrupted, and before that many years of interrupted, research many persons and agencies have extended assistance to me. So my sincerest thanks go to Dr. Malcolm Edward Yapp of the University of London, under whose constructive supervision this research, before it was revised, was completed as a Ph.D. dissertation for the University of London. Without his supervision and his knowledge of modern Afghan history, this work could not have been what it is. In Kabul I am grateful to Dr. Abd al-Ghafur Rawan Farhadi for his interest in my research and for obtaining permission for me to go through the relevant sections of the archives of the Ministry of External Affairs not yet open to the public. Also, I would like to thank my former history professor Dr. Farouq Itimadi of Kabul University for lending me his copy of *Afghanistan Along the Highway of*

History by Ghulam Muhammad Ghobar. I am grateful to him for this act of bravery performed at a time when, because of its official ban, Ghobar's book was a rarity and a taboo. Professor Louis Dupree of the American Universities Field Staff at Kabul has given me continued help, enabling me to continue my research. He has shown great interest in my work. I am grateful to him, as well as to Nancy Dupree. Ashraf Ghani Ahmadzay of Kabul University has been very helpful in giving me access to his private library and putting at my disposal some rare publications on Afghanistan. I would also like to thank Norman Pritchard and Gordon Maghney for going through the text and offering valuable suggestions.

I likewise owe thanks to the following institutions and foundations: to Kabul University for granting me a long period of leave of absence; to the Asia Foundation for financing my stay for two years in the United States; to the Fulbright-Hays Scholarship Program for giving me an international travel grant; to Princeton University for granting me the status of visiting research fellow; and to Harvard University for giving me a research grant at the Center for Middle Eastern Studies and access to its rich libraries. My thanks also go to the government of India for granting me a scholarship to India in 1970.

At Harvard University a number of professors have been helpful and encouraging. I would especially like to mention Professor Nur Yalman and Professor Joseph Fletcher, both of whom showed appreciable interest in my work. They and Professor Muhsin Mahdi made possible my stay at Harvard, for which I am grateful. I also would like to thank Professor Richard Frye who went through some sections of my work and offered valuable suggestions. I would also like to express my gratitude to all those librarians who, with courtesy and ready smiles, have helped me procure research materials from some of the great centers of human knowledge of which they were the custodians. Last, but not least, I owe special thanks to all those at the Center for Middle Eastern Studies, University of Texas at Austin, as well as at the University of Texas Press who helped to bring this work to the public.

Hasan Kakar
Kabul University

Note on Transcription

Because this is a study in history not linguistics, a phonetic system of transcription for the non-English sounds of the Arabic, Pashto, and Persian terms is not adopted. A conventional system of transcription is used in which ع and ق are noted as ʾ and ض and ث are recorded as z and s. Contrary to convention, Pashto names are recorded in the singular as they are pronounced in Pashto, not in Persian. Thus *Afriday, Ghilzay, Shinwaray,* and *Hotakay* are used in place of *Afridi, Ghilzai, Shinwari,* and *Hotaki.* Terms and words not yet anglicized have been italicized, but those considered anglicized, such as *qazi, amir, mulla, sardar, khan, darbar, jehad, Shariʾa,* and others, have not been italicized. Unless it is noted otherwise, all rupees mentioned in this work are Kabuli rupees.

Introduction

Afghanistan, especially when compared with other countries in the three major regions in its area—Central Asia, the Middle East, and South Asia—is known for the variety of its physical features, climate, inhabitants, languages, religious beliefs, and modes of life. Thus, although Afghanistan constitutes a part of each of these regions, it has its own distinct characteristics.

Its habitable parts consist of both numerous long green river valleys sandwiched by lofty mountains and oases dotted in vast deserts stretching toward the fringes of the country. Being accessible almost from all sides and situated in the heart of Asia on the main ancient routes that led to these three regions, this land has been open for penetration to waves of people throughout its long history. From this fact a number of things have followed. The country has been under strong pressure from its neighbors, much as Germany has been in Europe. Its frontiers have, therefore, fluctuated over time until they were finally demarcated in the last quarter of the nineteenth century. Before the discovery of sea routes, when Afghanistan was a main thoroughfare, it was a flourishing seat of great civilizations and religions. For our purpose, most striking is the fact that Afghanistan has had three principal names each of which has lasted for centuries.

The three principal names—*Aryana* in antiquity, *Khurasan* in the medieval era, and *Afghanistan* in modern times—have distinguished this land throughout its history, although at times Herat, Bactria, and Kabul have had kingdoms of their own.

Modern Afghanistan is almost co-extensive with the land mentioned in the old Greek as Ariana, in the old Persian as Airya or Airyana, in San-

skrit as Arya-Vartta or Arya-Varsha, and in Zend as Eriene-veejo. Situated between India and Persia (Pars), Aryana was a geographical and
cultural rather than political name. Boundaries on the west and north
were imprecise, but those on the east and south were the Indus River
and Indian Ocean. Aryana's inhabitants, the Arya, were identified with
the regions in which they lived and spoke languages that "were, no
doubt, for the most part very much akin, as they were in fact natives of
one and the same country."[1] The name Aryana lasted for 1,500 years
from the Avestan period (ca. 1000 B.C.) to the fifth century of the
Christian Era.

The word *Khurasan*, signifying the "land of the rising sun" (i.e., the
eastern land), appeared in the second century of the Christian Era but
was applied to the land east of Iran in the fifth century. During the
Sasanid period (A.D. 208–561) it was a part of Eran Shahr and called the
fourth climate (*iqlim*). Later, its eastern boundary reached India.[2] The
Afghan historian, Mir Ghulam Muhammad Ghobar, writes that, "For
fourteen centuries Khurasan was applied initially to parts of Afghanistan and later to the whole country and is still in use for a small region
to the northwest of it."[3] When strong governments—such as those of
the Tahirid (A.D. 821–873), Saffarid (A.D. 867–1495), Ghaznavid (A.D.
977–1186), and Ghurid (ca. A.D. 1000–1215)—arose in Khurasan their
rulers were invariably called caliphs in Baghdad, amirs in Khurasan.
Even down to the nineteenth century the name *Khurasan*, signifying
Afghanistan, was in use along with the words *Pashtunkhwa*, and
Sarhad.[4] It was only toward the end of that century that the appella-
tion *Afghanistan* replaced the word *Khurasan* completely.

Afghanistan, however, is not a new name. It is generally believed to
have appeared with the accession of Ahmad Shah Durrani in 1747; but,
so far as is known, this word was applied in a political sense to a land
for the first time in the third decade of the fourteenth century by Saifi
Herawi in his *The History of Herat*.[5] He mentions it very frequently
along with other names, such as *Shiberghan, Turkestan*, and *Khurasan*. Apparently, Afghanistan had been independent after the onslaught
of Chinggis Khan (reign, A.D. 1206–1227) and was ruled by local rulers
of its own until they were overcome by the Kurt rulers of Khurasan in
Herat (1245–1381). All this time the word *Afghanistan* generally referred to a land situated between Ghazni and the Indus River with its
main center at Mastung (Quettar). In other words, the lowlands and
highlands of the Sulaiman Mountains where the Afghans have lived for
centuries were included in Afghanistan. Writers subsequent to Saifi
Herawi have described Afghanistan with more or less the same boundaries.

Three points must be further noted in connection with the name
Afghanistan. First, the name signified the same land even during the
height of the Durrani Empire when, in addition to present-day Afghanistan, it also included Persian Khurasan, Turkestan, the Panjab, Kashmir, Herat, and Baluchistan. Afghan historian Sultan Muhammad Durrani wrote that in the time of Ahmad Shah Durrani Afghanistan was

situated, "between India, Persia and Turkestan."[6] In 1809 Mountstuart Elphinstone observed that the Hindu Kush constituted Afghanistan's northern bulwark.[7] It was only in the second part of the nineteenth century that this name began to be applied to the land situated between the Durand Line and the Oxus River, that is modern Afghanistan. Only after all its boundaries were agreed upon and demarcated by the British government of India in agreement with the governments of Persia, Russia, and Afghanistan (much to the disadvantage of the last) did the use of the name become usual. This period also coincided with a northward migration of the Afghans who turned the provinces beyond the Hindu Kush from mere dependencies into integrated parts of Afghanistan.

The second point to stress is the fact that Afghanistan was a name employed only by non-Afghans, notably Persians,[8] until the word passed on to the Afghans themselves in the last quarter of the nineteenth century. Previously the Afghans spoke of their land either as Pashtunkwa (the homeland of the Pashtuns) or Roh (the mountain). Roh included a more extensive land that stretched as far as the Helmand River to the west.[9]

The third point to observe is that the people who principally established the Afghan kingdom were known by the names of *Afghan*, *Pashtun*, and *Pathan*.

Pathan is a comparatively recent name and was originally applied by the Indians to Afghans. Opinions differ as to how it arose. Some are of the opinion that it is derived from the word *Pashtan*,[10] while others hold that when the Afghans settled in the Pathna District of the province of Bihar in India, the Indians called them Pathans as residents of Pathna.[11] Be it as it may, since the twelfth century the name has been applied to the Afghans in India. Later, it signified the Afghans of the Sulaiman Mountains as well, and English writers tried to distinguish these Pashtuns (Pathans) from the Afghans inside modern Afghanistan as if they were two different peoples. The people, however, refer to themselves not as Pathans, but as Pashtuns.

The name *Pashtun* (or *Pakhtun*) is the original and oldest of all. It appeared for the first time in the Rig-Veda, the sacred book of the Hindus, as *Pakhtas* some three thousand years ago.[12] Later Herodotus (484–431 B.C.) used the word *Pactyan* for the residents of "the country of Pactyica."[13] Subsequent writers in general have identified the Pactyans and Pakhtas with the Pashtuns of the Sulaiman Mountains. The noted Indian historian R. C. Majumdar, for instance, writes that, "Pactyan is perhaps represented by the ethnic name of Pakhtun or the Indian Pathan."[14] Indeed, Herodotus' word *Pactyica* is to this day in use as the name, *Pactya*, for an eastern region of Afghanistan.

The word *Afghan* has an interesting history. It is linked with the Asvaka ("horse people") of Gandahara in the Mahabarata, the Sanskrit epic composed about 1200 B.C.[15] *Asvaka* and *Asvaghana* are the same compound Sanskrit word and both refer to the land of the horse people as well as its inhabitants.[16] The Sulaiman Mountains have a

very long history as a horse-breeding area, so the word *Afghan* originally signified the land as well as people. With the passage of time it
also occurred frequently in other sources: in Persian as the word *Abgan*
(also *Avgan*),[17] in Hindi as *Avagana*,[18] and in Chinese as *O-Po-Kien*.[19]
Arab geographers have invariably noted it as *Afghan*.[20] As is evident,
the name Afghan, like Pathan, was given to the Pashtuns by others.
The Afghans refused to call themselves by this name[21] until recently
when it was adopted as a national name for all citizens of Afghanistan
regardless of language, religion, and ethnic identity.

The Pashtuns are closely linked with the Tajiks, the second major
group of people in Afghanistan. Philological, anthropological, and historical research has shown that in ancient times the Tajiks and Pashtuns lived in the same geographical area. According to Georg Morgenstierne, Pashto, the language of the Pashtuns, originally belonged to
the northeastern branch of the Aryani languages, represented today by
the Pamir dialects (Shughni, Munji, and so forth), and has some features that point to a special relation to the ancient Bactrian languages
of the Surkh Kotal inscription.[22] The anthropologist H. F. Schurmann
advances the view that the kind of economy that Elphinstone has
described for the Afghans of the Sulaiman Mountains indicates an
archaic type of mixed agriculture—pastoralism of a type often found
among certain mountain Tajiks. More specifically he concludes that
the "real Afghans" form part of that vast group of mountain peoples of
Aryani stock that is best represented by the mountain Tajiks.[23] The
historian Ghobar advances a similar view. In Herodotus' times the
Tajiks (ancient Dadicae) lived along with Pashtuns in the seventh
satrapy of Darius (that is, the Sulaiman Mountains), and they "were all
reckoned together."[24] A people called Dadi, considered to be the descendants of these ancient Dadicae, still lived among the Kakar Pashtuns down to the last quarter of the nineteenth century.[25] According to
Ghobar most of these Dadicae, because of the pressure of the Pashtuns,
had much earlier left for Chitral, Badakhshan, and the lands beyond
the Oxus, as well as for Siestan, Baluchistan, and other places in central Afghanistan.[26] It is then no wonder that the Pashtuns and Tajiks,
who combined constitute most of the inhabitants of Afghanistan, have
always shown a united front to all invaders and helped to preserve
Afghanistan.

A bare sketch of the attempts made by the Pashtuns to set up states
in various lands down to the time of Amir ʾAbd al-Rahman is now in
order. Among the Pashtuns forms of elementary government can be
traced from ancient times when they appeared in Ghore and the Sulaiman Mountains. It was, however, in the tenth century of the Christian
Era that Shaykh Hamid Ludi organized his tribesmen into a state to be
able to defend the frontier district of Baluchistan against the Hindus of
India. Later, in the middle of the fifteenth century, Sultan Bahlul Ludi
established a well-structured state and an Afghan empire in India modeled basically on the state founded by Shaykh Hamid Ludi. Sultan
Bahlul Ludi was able to create a sort of Afghan confederacy by dividing

his vast empire among his relatives as amirs. Among his accomplishments were the revival of the Dehli sultanate, extension of its boundaries (Panjab to Bihar), and the rehabilitation of its prestige after years
of decline.[27] His dynasty was supreme in India for three-quarters of a
century (1451–1526). Shortly after the 1526 overthrow of the Ludi
dynasty by Babur, the founder of the Mughal Empire, Sher Shah Afghan
founded the short-lived Sur dynasty (1530–1555). As a person, Sher
Shah outshone all Afghan rulers who lived before him or came after
him. Sher Shah whose reign "proved to be one of the best India had
ever enjoyed" built "an excellent administrative system which was to
become the foundation upon which the later Mogul administration
was based."[28]

During the long period of the Mughal rule in India and Afghanistan,
Bayazid Ansari (1525–1581) initiated an independence movement, the
Roshania, among the separate tribal communities of the Sulaiman
Mountains. He brought into existence a rudimentary form of supra-
tribal organization at the same time that he waged a fierce struggle
against the Mughals. For various reasons, however, the organization
did not develop, and by 1630 the movement was crushed. Later, the
great warrior and poet Khushhal Khattak (1613–1689) and others revived the struggle for independence along nationalistic lines, but in the
end they too were unable to succeed.

The Pashtuns who in modern times overthrew foreign yokes and
organized states were the Ghilzays and Durranis. Mir Wais Ghilzay
was the forerunner of Afghan independence. In 1707 he made Kandahar
independent of Safavid Persia that had ruled it since 1622. In 1722 his
son even occupied Isfahan. At the same time the Durranis also terminated the Persian occupation of Herat and organized an independent
state of their own. Soon, however, Nadir Shah Afshar ended the rule of
both in Isfahan and Herat, as well as in Kandahar. Nadir Shah's occupation of Afghanistan also did not last long, and after his assassination in
1747 his empire collapsed. The Durranis who had returned to Kandahar chose Ahmad Shah as their king. Under Ahmad Shah they not
only made the whole of Afghanistan independent, but also established
an empire. This time the state the Durranis established proved permanent, although the empire collapsed by 1818. Ahmad Shah's dynastic rule also came to an end, mainly as a result of the wars of succession
among his numerous grandsons. Since the tradition of dynastic rule
among the Durranis had been well established and since there was a
strong desire on the part of all Muslims to have a ruler of their own
able to defend Islam in a land which for centuries had proved capable
of supporting a state, the Muhammadzay dynasty gradually replaced
the old dynasty. In 1836 Dost Muhammad Khan was proclaimed as
amir al-mu'minin (commander of the faithful). He was well on the
road toward reunifying the whole of Afghanistan when the British, in
collaboration with an ex-king, invaded Afghanistan in what is known
as the First Anglo-Afghan war (1839–1842). After some resistance
Amir Dost Muhammad Khan was deported to India. The British rule

did not last long. After the annihilation of all of the British troops
Afghanistan once again became independent, and the exiled amir was
allowed to reoccupy the royal throne in 1843. During his second reign
Amir Dost Muhammad reunified the whole of Afghanistan by noteworthy statesmanship rather than by force, usually a distinguishing
feature of Afghan politics. Perhaps the most distinguishing feature in
this period is the beginning of the consolidation of the central government in a reunified Afghanistan. His son and successor Amir Sher 'Ali
Khan, after he overcame his rival brothers in a series of bloody civil
wars in the 1860s, was even more successful in consolidating the state.
The high points of the state he instituted were a large modern army,
the establishment of the state-controlled civil and military schools, of
a consultative assembly, the expansion of the existing bureaucracy,
and the rationalization of the system of taxation. In spite of this, tribal
communities, as well as individuals, were able to preserve their traditional autonomy. The state in this period was well on the way toward modernity. The second British intervention in 1878 disrupted
this process, and the country was again plunged into a war with
the British until the accession of Amir 'Abd al-Rahman Khan
(pronounced 'Abdur Rahman Khan) in 1880.

The British, shortly after the accession of the new amir, withdrew
from Afghanistan, although they retained the right to handle Afghanistan's foreign relations. Partly because of the desire of both Russia
and Britain (whose empires by now had sandwiched Afghanistan) not
to let their empires meet in this part of the world and partly because
Afghan resistance to foreign invasion in the past had been so formidable, these two powers ultimately decided to leave Afghanistan as a
buffer state and to her own destiny. This decision by the two powers
and the fact that Britain supported Amir 'Abd al-Rahman Khan with
weapons and money during his numerous internal crises gave the amir
the excuse, leverage, and opportunity to institute a highly centralized
form of absolutist government to an extent that neither his predecessors nor his successors were able to emulate. In his reign modern
Afghanistan began to emerge.

The emergence of modern Afghanistan has two main characteristics.
First, as noted, Afghanistan's boundaries with her neighboring countries were almost all demarcated for the first time. In this demarcation
Afghanistan lost vast territories. Of particular significance was the loss
that resulted from the Durand Agreement concluded in 1893 in Kabul
between Mortimer Durand, foreign secretary to the British government
of India, and Amir 'Abd al-Rahman. By this agreement the core of the
original Afghanistan came to be regarded as within the British sphere
of influence. This loss of territory led to the rise of a strong irredentist
movement inside Afghanistan that has ever since strained her relations
with her eastern neighbors.

Second, also for the first time, the central government extended
direct control over the affairs of tribal groups and regions in a sharp
departure from the former system of administration that had allowed

various degrees of autonomy for tribal communities according to their locations and significance. In the context of Afghanistan this task was very difficult, in some ways comparable to the creation of Afghanistan in the middle of the eighteenth century. This process was the subject of my *Afghanistan, A Study in Internal Political Developments, 1880–1896.* Here only a brief sketch of the main internal political developments is given.

More than forty internal disturbances took place during the reign of Amir ʾAbd al-Rahman. They fall into three main categories: those that were the result of dynastic rivalry, those that followed the imposition of taxes and rigid administration, and those that were caused by the extension of government authority into hitherto independent regions. Of all the disturbances, those of the first group were the most serious. In this group, the amir's adversaries were his cousins, Sardar Muhammad Ayyub and Sardar Muhammad Ishaq who, like the amir, had legitimate claims to the throne since their fathers had been amirs of Afghanistan. In addition, each sardar commanded a large body of the regular army. In the case of the disturbance of Sardar Ayyub, the amir still had not firmly established his rule in June 1881 when his rival occupied Kandahar from his base in Herat. Ayyub had the support of the Durranis, who regarded the amir as an Anglophile since he had acceded to the throne in Kabul in 1880 partly with British support after eleven years of exile in Russian Turkestan. That Muhammad Ayyub was a son of Amir Sher ʾAli, who had lost his throne for his opposition to British designs on Afghanistan, and that he had defeated a British force in 1880 at Maiwand had made him a popular hero. In battle at Kandahar on 22 September 1881 Ayyub's larger army was decisively defeated, because of the amir's military skill (unlike Ayyub, the amir commanded his army in person); British support in money and weapons; and, most important, the desertion of a portion of Ayyub's army in a critical moment. It was actually only after the banishment of Ayyub in the same year to Persia that the amir was able to extend his rule over that area of Afghanistan that had formerly been ruled by his predecessor Amir Muhammad Yaʾqub, the elder brother of Ayyub, whom the British had deported to India in December 1879.

Seven years later in 1888, the second formidable revolt was staged by Sardar Muhammad Ishaq, who had been the almost autonomous governor of Turkestan since 1880. Like Sardar Ayyub, Sardar Ishaq was also popular, particularly with the people of Turkestan, but also with those of other regions, mainly for his humane system of administration that was in contrast to the autocratic rule of the amir. The popular discontent generated by the amir's rule was so strong that all troops of the amir in Badakhshan joined the rebel sardar and that a portion of the amir's army deserted to him in the battlefield. The situation for the amir was made worse by illness that made him unable to lead his army in person. Luckily for the amir, the sardar proved such an incompetent soldier that on the day of the battle in Gaznigak (27 September 1888) he left his almost victorious army behind and escaped to Bukhara. He did so because he thought that the portion of the amir's army that was deserting to his side was trying to capture him. Had Ishaq provided sound leadership to his enterprising Ghilzay-dominated army, backed by the general populace of Uzbeks and Turkmen, he might have changed significantly the course of Afghanistan's political history. His escape brought about, among many other things, a strong northward migration, mainly by the Pashtuns, who ultimately outnumbered every other single ethnic group of the area and changed Turkestan from a dependent to an integral part of Afghanistan.

The revolts that resulted from the imposition of heavy taxes were numerous. Almost all tribal groups rebelled against the government at one time or another. The Shinwaray Rising (1882–1892) is the most representative of all; but because of its wider implications the Ghilzay Rebellion will be briefly discussed here.

Concerning the Ghilzays of this period two things should be borne in mind. First, except for those who lived near Kabul and along the main roads, most Ghilzays were virtually autonomous; their elders and mullas managed their affairs for them. Second, the revenue they paid to the government through their elders was very light. In addition, the Hotakay section of the Ghilzays and certain persons, like Mulla Mushk-i-ʾAlam, who held extensive tracts of lands were exempt from paying revenue to the government. What disturbed the tribespeople themselves was the takeover of their internal administration by the central government and the imposition of land revenue in 1886 at the rate of one-third, one-fifth, and one-tenth of the produce, depending on the quality of land. Also, in the same year the government imposed on the Ghilzays, including their mullas, varieties of other taxes, although the amir in 1881 had freed them from paying poll tax (*tawan-i-sar*), which, until then, the Ghilzays had paid to the government. Other measures that stirred the tribe to action included the assessment of revenue on the hitherto revenue-free lands owned by some elders and the resumption by the state of those lands that certain elders enjoyed in lieu of their allowances. Furthermore, the imprisonment of insubordinate elders, especially those who had distinguished themselves by fighting the British during the occupation period, such as Ghazi Muhammad Jan Wardak, ʾIsmat Allah Jabar Khel, and others, disturbed the tribe to the extent that in October 1886 their elders, under the leadership of Mulla ʾAbd al-Karim Andar and Muhammad Shah Hotakay, instituted a great rising. Initially they scored victories against contingents of the armies that were stationed in Muqur and Ghazni, but they were dispersed by the army sent from Kabul in the winter of 1886. During the late spring of 1887 all sections of the tribe, including a portion of the Ghilzay in the amir's army, reassembled in large numbers in the Muqur area; but, since the tribe had little money and few weapons and since the rising did not spread significantly beyond their own territory (although other tribes refused to assist the amir against the insurgents and even a few non-Ghilzay tribes rose in their support), the large, well-armed regular army finally crushed the rising in a series of engagements that continued until the autumn of 1887. This last major rising of the Ghilzays led, among other things, to the permanent improvement of the hitherto estranged relations between the amir and parts of his own Durrani tribe and to the reimposition of revenue and other taxes on the Ghilzays, against which they had rebelled.

The pacification of the Hazaras and the conquest of Kafiristan represent the extension of government controls over areas that were, up to 1880, partially and wholly independent. The Shi'ite Hazaras who occupied the central highlands, the Hazarajat, during the period from 1229 to 1447, enjoyed a relatively high degree of autonomy until the amir's accession. This autonomy was mainly the result of their mountainous territory, although certain areas of their extensive region provided green pasture and fertile land for its inhabitants, who were said to number 340,000 in the second half of the nineteenth century. Afghan rulers in the past had gradually extended government authority over thirteen of the fifteen different tribal communities of the Hazaras. During the first decade of the amir's reign only Uruzgan had remained completely independent, whereas the rest had been brought still more closely under government control, although their religious and secular elders (sayyeds and mirs) had still retained most of their traditional power over the common Hazaras (most of the Hazara land was owned by the mirs). In 1891 even the 44,500 Hazaras of Uruzgan submitted to the amir on certain conditions. In that year, however, 10,000 troops entered Uruzgan under the leadership of a civilian governor, Sardar 'Abd al-Quddus. Soon the Hazaras of Uruzgan rose in a revolt that ultimately involved most Hazaras of the Hazarajat. The trouble started when the amir, following the entry of the army, initiated a policy of separating the Hazara elders from their tribespeople on the assumption that in the class-differentiated society of the Hazaras, where the elders had exploited the common Hazaras, the latter would not support the former. This policy, after initial success, failed utterly, mainly because of the mishandling of the situation by corrupt officials. These officials, especially the military, raped the Hazara women, took possession of their qal'as (forts), and oppressed the Hazaras without distinction; they also began disarming the Hazaras and surveying their lands for revenue purposes. The Palo section of the Sultan Muhammad tribe initiated the rising, which resulted in the destruction of the greater part of the national army. Since the Hazaras were Shi'as and were on bad terms with their Sunna neighbors the amir turned the rising into a sectarian war. He successfully enlisted the support of the Sunni tribes and of his regular army in crushing the Hazaras over a period from late 1891 to 1893 by the deployment of 100,000 troops and tribal levies. After their defeat, a large number of the Hazaras were enslaved, their land in Uruzgan was granted to the Durranis and Ghilzays, and Pashtun nomads were allowed to take Hazara pastures for their own flocks. A large number of the Hazaras migrated. The Hazara power was, as a consequence, broken to the extent that it never again challenged the government.

The last campaign waged during the amir's reign was for the conquest of Kafiristan, which had remained independent for centuries. Its inhabitants, who were known to the Muslims as Kafirs, were known among themselves by their various tribal names and spoke mutually unintelligible languages. The difficult terrain of their country had enabled them to repulse previous attempts to conquer their land by many Muslim rulers in the past. By 1880, however, the Kafirs were no match for the amir's government, owing to their small number (60,000), their primitive weapons (spears, bows, arrows, and some rifles), and the inroads of Islam into parts of their land, especially the border areas. Except for his persuasion of the Kafirs to accept Islam, the amir, until the conquest of their land in 1895–1896, largely left them unmolested, mainly because of his preoccupation with other rebellions and, to a certain extent, because of the proximity of eastern Kafiristan (the Bashgal Valley) to Chitral, which had been placed under indirect British control through the Raja of Kashmir. By 1895 when the boundary with Chitral had been demarcated and other rebellions suppressed, the amir feared that the occupation of the Pamirs by Russia and of Chitral by Britain might endanger the integrity of Afghanistan through the still independent Kafiristan. In the winter of 1895 he ordered the conquest of Kafiristan by the army and tribal levies. This conquest was accomplished relatively easily. Compared with rebellious Muslim tribes the defeated Kafirs were treated mildly, but their whole-scale conversion to Islam was stressed. This conquest increased the amir's prestige at home and abroad. After that no significant uprising took place during the amir's reign, and he concentrated on the consolidation of the state.

Government and Society in Afghanistan

Chapter I
The Central
Government: 1

The Amir

It is not known when and where ʾAbd al-Rahman, the only son of Amir
Muhammad Afzal Khan (the eldest son of Amir Dost Muhammad
Khan), was born. Stephen Wheeler believes that he was born in 1844,
and Sultan Mahomed agrees;[1] but Lepel Griffin strongly maintains
that ʾAbd al-Rahman was born in 1838.[2] ʾAbd al-Rahman's mother was
a Bangash, a daughter of Nawab Samad Khan,[3] whose tribe had little
influence with the court of Kabul. So ʾAbd al-Rahman, like his father
and unlike most Muhammadzay princes, was not fully related to his
dynasty. On the other hand, because of his Pashtun mother, ʾAbd al-
Rahman felt closer to the Pashtuns than other princes had.

The early period of ʾAbd al-Rahman's boyhood is not well known. In
1853 he arrived at Balkh, a province which his father governed from
1852 to 1864. ʾAbd al-Rahman was thirteen when he was appointed
subgovernor of the district of Tashqurghan, but later he resigned his
post on the ground that not enough authority was delegated to him.[4]
He took to hunting and shooting at the head of large groups of his servants, riders, and page boys. At the same time, he learned something of
the art of war from General Sher Muhammad, once a Christian and
then a convert to Islam, who was in command of Afzal Khan's army of
30,000.

ʾAbd al-Rahman also did the work of blacksmith and made rifles
but showed no interest in intellectual activity. In his own words: "I
was very dull. I hated lessons, and my thoughts were too much with
riding and shooting."[5] He smoked Indian hemp and drank heavily and

showed little or no concern for human life. Once during a hunting expedition he made one of his *ghulam bachas* (page boys) the target of his shooting to see whether a bullet would kill a man. The boy was shot dead; ʾAbd al-Rahman laughed.[6] His father imprisoned him for this shooting; but a year later, after the death of General Sher Muhammad, ʾAbd al-Rahman was surprisingly[7] appointed commander of the army. He was at this time probably seventeen.

ʾAbd al-Rahman enjoyed full military power and showed talent in organizing the army.[8] The test soon came when the powerful Uzbek mir of Qataghan, Mir Atalik, refused to read the khutba (Friday sermon) in the name of Amir Dost Muhammad Khan and declared himself a vassal of the king of Bukhara. ʾAbd al-Rahman, with the help of a strong army covered by sufficient artillery, overcame the mir who took refuge with the mir of Badakhshan. ʾAbd al-Rahman, supported by his full uncle Muhammad Aʾzam and another uncle Sardar Muhammad Amin Khan and reinforced from Kabul, led the army as far as Taluqan. Although Badakhshan was not overrun, its mirs were sufficiently overawed and renewed their loyalty to Kabul by paying revenue and making marriage alliances.[9] During his brief stay as governor-general of the army at Khanabad, ʾAbd al-Rahman saved a large amount of money and, by blowing depredators and rebels from guns, established order in a region that was always subject to plundering by the unruly Uzbeks, supported by the king of Bukhara.

Role in the Civil War

ʾAbd al-Rahman was probably nineteen when he became involved in the civil war in the 1860s; but his role in the war among his numerous uncles and cousins contending for the throne was among the greatest. Although in the end, he was forced to leave the country, ʾAbd al-Rahman emerged as the most formidable opponent of his reigning uncle Amir Sher ʾAli Khan. One consequence of the struggle was that it brought ʾAbd al-Rahman in close touch with the realities of political life. It was this civil war more than anything else that helped ʾAbd al-Rahman shape his political personality. During this war he learned to appreciate the power and influence of tribal elders, provincial governors, and the Muhammadzay sardars who did not hesitate to shift allegiance from one party to another and to challenge the authority of the central government when it suited them.

Specifically ʾAbd al-Rahman helped his father and uncle to the throne and defeated Amir Sher ʾAli, in conjunction with his uncle, at battles in Sayyed Abad (May 1866), Qalat (January 1867), and the Panjshir Pass (late 1867). In spite of these victories his father, while amir, did not declare ʾAbd al-Rahman heir apparent, and his hope of succeeding his father did not materialize.[10] Still, after the death of his father ʾAbd al-Rahman supported his uncle as amir against the fugitive Amir Sher ʾAli who had been driven to Herat but had not given up his claim.

During their amirates, ʾAbd al-Rahman's father and uncle made themselves unpopular, the former by his incompetence, which was probably the result of heavy drinking, and the latter by becoming a tyrant. Amir Muhammad A'zam, while amir, instead of consolidating his position with the help of his energetic nephew deputed him, probably because of fear of his influence, to the remote region of Maimana to bring about the submission of its rebel mir. Shortly afterward the people of Kandahar, who had been disgusted with the tyrannical rule of A'zam's sons, hailed Amir Sher 'Ali's son, Sardar Muhammad Ya'qub, who had marched from Herat. Thus Amir Muhammad A'zam Khan's position in the west became insecure. Subsequently, in Kabul the Muhammadzay sardars led by Sardar Muhammad Isma'il Khan seized the royal citadel the Bala Hisar for Amir Sher 'Ali Khan when Muhammad A'zam was away from the capital to fight Amir Sher 'Ali in the Ghazni area. The hasty and costly return of Sardar 'Abd al-Rahman from Maimana, which he had subdued on terms, was too late. By then Amir Sher 'Ali had been received in Kabul and Amir Muhammad A'zam had fled toward Turkestan. The last combined stand of 'Abd al-Rahman and his deposed uncle in the Bamian area in January in 1869 failed, and they then fled to Waziristan. Apparently they intended to take refuge in India; but, when the British deputy commissioner of Banu tied the grant of asylum to their settlement in a remote part of the Panjab,[11] they changed their minds and headed toward Baluchistan through the Kakar land. From there they journeyed through Seistan to Mashhad. In Mashhad they parted. While Muhammad A'zam proceeded toward Tehran (he died on the way in October 1869), 'Abd al-Rahman, declining an invitation from the shah of Persia on the ground that he was under the protection of the Czar, set out for central Asia. Traveling across the steppes of the Tekke Turkmen through Urganj to Khiwa, he finally arrived at Bukhara in November 1869. From there he went to Samarqand, where he resided for eleven years (1869–1880).

In Exile

By taking refuge first in Bukhara and later in Samarqand, 'Abd al-Rahman hoped he would be able to recover Afghan Turkestan[12] and establish an independent amirate. Confident of the support of the Uzbek mirs[13] of Afghan Turkestan 'Abd al-Rahman claimed they had invited him there. In addition, since Jahandar Shah, the mir of Badakhshan was his father-in-law, 'Abd al-Rahman was also confident of the support of the people of Badakhshan. He took his long and hazardous route, running through inhospitable terrain, in order to be near his supporters in Afghanistan,[14] but to establish himself there he also needed the support of Bukhara and Russia.

During his first flight to Bukhara in 1864, 'Abd al-Rahman had succeeded in turning the amir of Bukhara against Amir Sher 'Ali. The amir of Bukhara had made 'Abd al-Rahman his son-in-law and promised support against Sher 'Ali.[15] It was mainly because of the support of the amir of Bukhara that 'Abd al-Rahman, subsequently, occupied Balkh without opposition.[16] The support of the amir for Sardar 'Abd al-

Rahman was so well known that even in Kabul it was said that ʾAbd al-Rahman "professed to be acting on behalf, not of the imprisoned king Afzul [sic], but of the Amir of Bokhara."[17] The cordial relations of the sardar and the amir became strained, however, when the former refused to assist the latter, as he had been requested, against Russia.[18] So during the second refuge, the amir of Bukhara not only was unwilling to assist ʾAbd al-Rahman; he also placed him under mild restraint.

ʾAbd al-Rahman's approach to Russia was apparently the result of Amir Sher ʾAli Khan's establishment of a friendly relation with Britain shortly after he recovered Kabul.[19] As early as March 1869, ʾAbd al-Rahman, while in Waziristan, heard that Sher ʾAli was on his way to meet the British viceroy in Ambala. ʾAbd al-Rahman then sent a messenger to the Russian authorities to ask whether he could be allowed to enter Russian territory.[20] Praising the Czarist empire as "far more extensive than those of the Germans, the French and the English put together,"[21] and declaring that his affairs were "bound up with the interests of the territory of the White Czar,"[22] ʾAbd al-Rahman offered General von Kaufmann, the Russian governor-general in Tashkent, the benefit of his influence and connections in Afghanistan. In return, he asked Kaufmann for the support necessary for the recovery of his alleged rights.[23] He told Kaufmann that Afghanistan "has been given over to the protection of the English,"[24] and that Amir Sher ʾAli Khan was no friend to the Russians. Kaufmann, however, declined to assist him and the Russian government later declared that "when we sheltered him it was not as an enemy to England, or as a claimant to the throne of Cabul, but solely as an unfortunate and homeless man deprived of all means of supplying his own wants and those of his family."[25] An annual subsidy of 18,000 rubles (raised later to 25,000 rubles) was fixed for him. Meanwhile, Kaufmann assured Sher ʾAli that ʾAbd al-Rahman was not to "count on my interference in his differences with you, or expect any help whatever from me."[26]

But ʾAbd al-Rahman was not the kind of man to remain quiet. He was working and plotting to recover his heritage. When he failed to win Russian support, he tried to pose as a man of dull understanding in order that the Russians would leave him to his own schemes.[27] Once even he was reported to have set out for St. Petersburg to make a personal appeal to the emperor.[28] At the same time, he was perpetually intriguing with his adherents south of the Oxus. Sher ʾAli's governor of Afghan Turkestan asked Kaufmann to restrain the sardar "in order that the friendship existing between us and the tranquility enjoyed by the people, may be confirmed."[29] The Russian government assured the British government that if the sardar broke the compact he would be removed to a remote part of the empire.[30] It appeared that, because of the friendly relations existing between Russia and Afghanistan, there was no hope for ʾAbd al-Rahman to enter Afghanistan during the reign of Amir Sher ʾAli.

In Samarqand ʾAbd al-Rahman lived in a rather pitiful style, saving as much as four-fifths of his allowance,[31] in the hope of making attempts to recover the throne of Kabul. With the same object in mind, he occasionally did a little trading. He offered the wife of the French archaeologist Ijfalvy, who visited him in Samarqand, a couple of ordinary swords at an exorbitant price.[32] Occasionally he called on Kaufmann in Tashkent. Otherwise, he kept himself aloof from the Russians and amused himself by hunting and shooting. The American traveler and diplomatist Eugene Schuyler, who interviewed 'Abd al-Rahman in 1873, notes that, "He carries himself with much dignity, and every movement denotes a strong character and one accustomed to command."[33]

I have described elsewhere how Sardar 'Abd al-Rahman ascended the throne of Afghanistan;[34] but, to put it briefly, when the British invaded Afghanistan it looked as if they had established themselves in Afghanistan south of the Hindu Kush. 'Abd al-Rahman then entered Badakhshan with the connivance of the Russians. Amir Sher 'Ali had died and his son and successor Amir Muhammad Ya'gub had been deported to India. With the blessings of the Russians 'Abd al-Rahman apparently at first intended to rule over a separate domain in Afghanistan north of the Hindu Kush; but the British, because of the persistent opposition of the Afghans, decided to evacuate Afghanistan. They entered into negotiations with the sardar and he finally ascended the throne as amir in July 1880.

As a Ruler

When 'Abd al-Rahman became amir, Afghanistan was economically and politically in a state of disorder. The state machinery was nonexistent. Relations between the central government and the provinces had virtually broken down. While tribal areas had turned into autonomous regions, some elders, especially those who had fought the British, had increased their power correspondingly. Over and above this, a new dynasty had to replace the old ruling dynasty whose leading members, admired for their patriotism, were the rightful successors to the throne and were still alive in adjacent countries. Thus loyalty to the new dynasty had to be created—a task which was particularly difficult because the late amir had done away with the partisans of the family of 'Abd al-Rahman. In addition, the two most important tribal confederations of the Durranis and Ghilzays who, more than all other ethnic groups put together, could influence the course of political events had been principally attached to the family of the late amir. Of these tribes, it was said that "Tura de Ghilzo da pachaee de Durrano" (the kingdom is the share of the Durranis and courage the share of the Ghilzays). The descendants of Amir Dost Muhammad, apart from a few exceptions, either were partisans of the family of the late amir or were pro-British; and 'Abd al-Rahman was not able to rely on their cooperation. Also, the amir's long residence abroad and his sudden close association with the British were not a help to him as far as public opinion went. It was mainly because of this British association that the religious groups, as represented by the 'ulama of Kandahar, turned against him. The

British government, however, extended him much-needed assistance in money and weapons at critical moments.

Familiar with the turbulent history of Afghanistan and hoping to lay the foundation of his monarchy on a secure basis, the amir claimed that "God had made him the shepherd and supporter of his subjects."[35] Although some previous claimants to power considered "themselves to be divinely appointed,"[36] the notion that the power of the monarch derived from the Afghan jirgas (councils) was still common. The amir, with the help of the ʾulama in the capital, formulated a religious justification for the monarchy, becoming in effect the first Afghan ruler to invoke the concept of the divine right of kings.[37] From many sayings of the Prophet and Quranic quotations an elaborate doctrine was constructed, the essence of which was that the kings of religion were the vicars of the Prophet,[38] the shadow of God[39] and the shield against unbelief (kufr) and rebellion.[40] It was stated that Allah had ordained that the safeguard of the religion and of the honor of the people of Islam depended on the organization of the kingdom.[41] The obvious conclusion of this divine claim to authority, and of the amir's other similar claim that his authority and acts were in accordance with the commands of Allah and the Prophet,[42] was that those who challenged his authority intended to commit anti-Islamic acts and so deserved the hardest punishment. Thus those groups of people who had opposed the rulers in the past and who were likely to oppose him also came under the amir's criticism. In his view, the supporters of his rivals were the tribal elders, the mullas, the artisans,[43] and the sardars, the last he called "devils."[44] These elders whom he called the "middlemen" had no place in his scheme of thoughts. A nation could be built, the amir maintained, by the concerted efforts of a king as an architect, the army as masons, and the people as workmen.[45] The "middlemen" then had to be reduced or destroyed. To justify their destruction the amir declared that the tribal elders and influential persons of Kabul and eastern Afghanistan had intrigued with the British, those of Herat and northern Afghanistan were inclined to Russia, whereas the Durrani sardars and khans of Kandahar acted as pharaohs (tyrants) over the common men.[46] To the amir, the real patriots and the backbone of the country were the common men who, according to him, had opposed the enemy and protected Afghanistan[47] during the Second Anglo-Afghan War. For this, as well as their inability to intrigue with foreign powers, the amir looked on the common men as his allies.[48] He, therefore, hoped to consolidate his rule with their cooperation and believed in courting popularity with them. He leveled distinguished families,[49] waged wars on "the classes not on the masses,"[50] and punished elders severely after rebellions were suppressed.[51] It was his policy not to entrust those elders who survived with real authority. If they were given authority, the amir believed, they would ruin the state and the subjects and enrich themselves[52] as they had done in the past.[53] In theory the amir justified the killing of the few for the good of all,[54] but in practice the killing went far beyond the bounds of the "few" and reached, according to the amir himself, over 100,000.[55]

The amir's actual policy toward the various ethnic groups that collectively made the Afghan nation varied considerably in accordance with circumstances. Until the late eighties, the amir's relations with the Durranis were bad. Most of the important Durrani elders did not take part in his accession and refused to accept posts with the government or to enlist their men in the army. They were under the impression that the amir's rule would not last.[56] The amir, for his part, looked at the Durranis with suspicion because of their support for Sardar Muhammad Ayyub Khan. The Ghilzay insurgence suddenly changed all this and the amir afterwards increasingly relied on the Durranis. He then made strenuous efforts to turn the Durranis against the Ghilzays, just as he had done the opposite at the time of his confrontation with Sardar Muhammad Ayyub in 1881. After the Ghilzay rebellion it was the amir's open policy to raise the Muhammadzay clan (the descendants of Sardar Payinda Khan) to a distinguished aristocratic position similar to that which the Hotakays and Sadozays had enjoyed in the past. All members of the clan, including children and women, were given large allowances;[57] and their elders, including those who returned from exile, were given high posts with the government. By improving their economic and political status and raising their morale by calling them *sharik-i-dawlat* (partners of the state) the amir did his Muhammadzay clan a great service indeed. Consequently the Muhammadzays who, before the accession of the amir,[58] appeared to be finished as a political force once again rose to a leading position in Afghanistan.

As the Wardak had earlier been attached to Amir Sher ʾAli Khan's dynasty, so the Safays of Tagao, who had had no special relationship to any reigning dynasty in the past, were charmed by the amir. He was always lenient with them in regard to revenue matters and favored their elders. In fact they were among the first to receive the amir before his accession and assisted him afterward in fighting the Mangals, the rebellious inhabitants of Laghman,[59] and the Shinwarays. The third ethnic congregate that had had no connection to any dynasty were the inhabitants of Kafiristan whom the amir, after the conquest of their land, attached to his dynasty.

The amir's relations with the Ghilzays were good until they rose in rebellion in 1886. Only in the early nineties when the Ghilzays were no longer a threat did the amir make efforts toward a reconciliation with them because he then believed that "the bond of harmony with the Ghilzais would cement all Afghans to my cause."[60] Apart from the lenient treatment of their rebels and defeated elders, however, the Ghilzays were not shown any special favors. The amir's promise of freedom of action to the Ghilzays in the Hazarajat during the Hazara War and the subsequent colonization of parts of the Hazarajat resulted in a partial reconciliation. The amir's attitude toward the eastern Pashtuns up to the Durand Line underwent changes from the extreme harshness of the eighties to apparent mildness in the nineties; but, except for some marriage ties which the amir established with a few leading families, no special relationships were established between the monarchy and these Pashtuns.

Among the non-Pashtuns, the Tajiks of Kohistan who were the first to uphold the amir's cause were soon estranged from him, and they rebelled during his absence from Kabul in 1881. Their subsequent refusal to help the amir in the Ghilzay War strained relations still further. The amir was suspicious of the Qizilbashes and the Hazaras for their pro-British attitude during the Second Anglo-Afghan War, in spite of the fact that the Hazaras were a help to him in the occupation of Herat and the defeat of Sardar Muhammad Ishaq Khan. When the Jamshidi elders of Herat showed an inclination toward Russia, the amir became skeptical of the loyalty of the non-Pashtuns as a whole. He stated that "It was a wrong policy that up till now the chiefs of tribes other than Afghans were vested with power and authority."[61] Then he held the view that "no reliance can be placed on any other tribe than on the Afghans."[62] Thus it can be seen that the amir's internal policy was based on tribal and religious lines and favored the Sunnis against the Shiʾas and the Pashtuns over non-Pashtuns and that among the former it was the Safays of Tagao and the Durranis,[63] in particular the Muhammadzays, whom he trusted the most.

Shortly after his accession, the amir helped reconcile the Hazaras of the Qarabagh with the Ghilzays, the latter with the Durranis, and the Kharotays with the Nasirs (a subdivision of the Ghilzays).[64] This reconciliation saved the Hazaras[65] and the Qizilbashes from being massacred. When rebellions became frequent, however, the amir reversed this policy. By applying tribal forces in suppressing disturbances, the amir, in fact, revived and intensified traditional animosities between some tribes and created new ones, while at the same time he deliberately provoked some tribes against others. A major change in the amir's policy toward the tribes came in the nineties after his authority was firmly established and the fear of a foreign threat to Afghanistan was very strongly felt. Then he tried to create "a new Afghan national spirit,"[66] and for that purpose he asked his people to cooperate in "protecting our country and religion,"[67] because, as he put it, "with the two infidel powers to the north and the south, their internal disruption could be the downfall of Islam."[68] In fostering Afghan national unity, the amir invoked the "dignity of Islam,"[69] though nationalism and the creed of Islam are basically incompatible. He also instituted the *jashn-i-mutafiqqiyya-i-milli* (the national festival of unanimity)[70] on 17 August 1896 (Asad 26, 1274 H. Sh. 7 Rabi' al-Awwal 1314) and ordered its annual observance throughout the country hoping that it might "beget a feeling of unity among Afghans."[71] In this way Amir ʾAbd al-Rahman was the first Afghan ruler to make deliberate attempts to build an Afghan nation. In his concept of national unity (which consisted of a common religion, common land, and a system of intermarriages among the people and which was a concept the people of Afghanistan, according to the amir, had demonstrated that they possessed in their two campaigns against the British [72]) the Pashtuns, however, were predominant. He observed, "from here [Jalalabad] as far as Herat there are Shinwaris, Afridis, Mangals, Jajis, Waziris and etc., all forming one nation. From Herat you go to Maimana, Balkh, Shighnan and Badakhshan, these are all situated in a circle and are occupied by one nation [presumably Pashtuns]." [73]

As a Person

ʾAbd al-Rahman was a broad-shouldered handsome man of average height with a burly figure and penetrating eyes. His contemporaries have described him in different ways. To his admirers, he was "a very witty and humorous genius," [74] "and by far the most prepossessing of all the Barakzai Sirdars [sic]," endowed with "both good sense and sound political judgment," [75] and unrivaled among his contemporary rulers in Asia and with one exception (perhaps Bismarck?) also in Europe. [76] West Ridgeway draws a more balanced picture of the amir. According to him, the amir was "shrewd and quick of perception to an extraordinary degree; he has a resolute will, undoubted courage, and implicit self-reliance. Ignorant as he is, he has the instinct of a statesman, and has proved himself to be a skillful General. When not crippled by sickness, he is enterprising and very thorough in everything he undertakes; and when his judgement is not warped by vanity, he is singularly clear-headed and even reasonable." [77] He could, however, change suddenly from one mood to another. Because of this he gave different impressions to different people. The favorable comments many foreigners have written of him are largely true, but with them the amir was singularly courteous and showed his most pleasant side. He was not the same with his own people, except in times of emergency when his position was in jeopardy. At such times the amir courted friendship with his own people and tried to win them over to his side with most pleasant words and the promise of good and just rule.

Even in ordinary life the amir's changeability was obvious. When in good humor he laughed heartily; but when he was aroused to anger his face became drawn, and his teeth showed until he looked wolfish. In this state he hissed words rather than spoke them, and it was then that the least fault involved some horrible punishment. [78]

He had fixed goals in life and to reach them he employed whatever means available that did not injure his personal dignity. He was full of ideas, had initiative, and believed in hard work. He could easily impress others, especially since he had kept around him only yes-men who accepted his ideas without question. This entourage reinforced his feelings of superiority leading him to believe that "he had the monopoly of all the talents, and was the universal genius of Afghanistan." [79]

The amir had very little formal education. He was semiliterate, for he read well but wrote painfully and incorrectly. This shortcoming was, however, compensated for by his extraordinary speaking ability. His speeches normally lasted for hours on end.[80] He is, as of this writing, the last Afghan ruler to be fluent in the three most widely spoken languages of Afghanistan, Persian, Pashto, and Uzbeki. It was mainly because of his exceptional fluency that his court had, in fact, become the most important center for political propaganda in the country.

The amir had an exaggerated opinion of himself, claiming loudly that "by the grace of God, there is not a single matter I do not know."[81] He considered his own people to be an unreasonable, ignorant, short-sighted lot.[82] It was then unnecessary for him to consult them, for they were to be led and guided and not allowed to talk about state affairs. Those who did so, and whose talking of politics was reported to the authorities, were punished severely. Some were even deprived of their tongues.[83] In his opinion, "the great mistake of the former Amirs of Afghanistan was letting people talk of politics, and allowing influential chiefs to remain in the country."[84] The amir, however, did not act in a vacuum and was in touch with the mood of his subjects. By keeping contact with religious and tribal elders and disposing of the complaints of the common men he built bridges of communication with the people and acted in accord with their familiar usages and practices.[85] This type of contact was what he considered acting with the consent of the people, and he stated that "One is chief so long only as one acts with their [the people's] consent. Therefore it is necessary that nothing should be done without the consent of the people."[86] This democratic inclination was shown only in times of serious internal crises or when he was unwilling to accept a proposal made to him by the British government. In the latter case his usual excuse was that his people would not accept it.

Even from the beginning the amir was suspicious of everyone and trusted no one.[87] As time went on and thousands of people were killed by his orders, his mistrust increased. He then felt he needed an elaborate system of precaution to protect his life, and the fear of attempts being made on his life constantly haunted him. Slight irregularities in his food and beverages brought calamities on those who were in charge of them. Once a cook was thrown into a hot oven because a straw had been found in a piece of unleavened bread presented to him. Usually whatever was brought to him was first tasted by others, and everyone entering the darbar (court), irrespective of position and rank, was searched for weapons while the amir always kept himself fully armed, except when he was in India.[88] To meet an emergency, he had a mobilized cavalry regiment always on the alert near his hall. For the same reason, he held audiences at night and slept in the late mornings, while his son did the opposite. In this way a twenty-four–hour vigil was kept.

Because of mistrust, the amir refused to delegate real authority to anyone, including his sons,[89] who, together with important officials, were kept under surveillance. Once the amir accused his eldest son of intending to unseat him, telling him that "you have been giving dinners at your place, . . . so that you [might] wrest the empire from Abdur Rahman."[90] The sardar was then chained and imprisoned for a night. Similarly, when the amir, because of illness, felt unable to ward off attacks on himself personally the *mirzas* (junior clerks) were brought to him, for him to examine their accounts while they were kept with bare heads, bare feet, and their arms tied behind their backs. His favorite wife advised the amir to end scandal by killing suspect *mirzas*, but the amir argued that this would not do since, "I suspect everyone of doing harm to me, and do not consider anyone trustworthy."[91]

The amir was eager to keep abreast with current world affairs, especially concerning Russia's encroachments on the Ottoman Empire; but the British agents, whom he consulted on these matters, were not qualified to enlighten him. He relied on the information of his own news agents whom he had stationed in all neighboring lands and even in Manchester, where a convert to Islam had been employed. The reports and comments of his news agent in Lahore, Rahmat Allah, who wrote about Indian affairs, frontier problems, and, to a lesser extent, European problems, were quite informative. In the amir's view the rapprochement reached between France, Russia, and Britain toward the closing years of the century, as he called it a "tripartite alliance," was attributable to the influence of Britain. It was his prediction that if war between the great powers broke out it would be a universal war and would last for many years.[92]

The amir had a special liking for statesmen with dictatorial tendencies. In his view "the world would produce but few politicians like William, the Emperor of Germany, and Prince Bismarck, the Imperial Chancellor." He praised William Gladstone and Russia's prime minister merely as good politicians.[93] He had great contempt for liberal democracy where the opposition could speak its mind and could even come to power. In his opinion the "constitution of the British government was not good, as one time the Conservatives were in power, and at another the Liberals."[94] To him the British Parliament was like a Kabul public bath, where everybody talks and no one is listened to;[95] but he praised the British constitutional system for the smooth operation of the principle of succession.[96]

The amir had a good knowledge of political history, which he had acquired through his storytellers[97] and those who read him history books in his private council.[98] The acquisition of this knowledge was meant not to satisfy his curiosity alone, but mainly to draw political conclusions from. In his religious policy, Amir ʾAbd al-Rahman was influenced by Nadir Shah Afshar, who, hoping to bring unity to the empire,[99] compelled his subjects to adopt only the Sunni system of Islam. It was, however, the policies of his immediate predecessors that guided Amir ʾAbd al-Rahman. Since Amir Sher ʾAli and Amir Muhammad Yaʾqub had been failures, Amir ʾAbd al-Rahman followed the reverse of their policies on many major issues. For instance, unlike Amir Sher ʾAli, Amir ʾAbd al-Rahman did not let himself be influenced by his favorite wife in state affairs and to nominate her minor son as heir apparent as she had wished. Again unlike Amir Sher 'Ali, Amir 'Abd al-Rahman relied not on the Russians, but on cooperation with the British. In this he went so far as to declare that "my dynasty, owing to friendship of the English people, cannot be disturbed by anyone provided that my descendants remain obedient to the British Government."[100]

The amir believed that "revelation was nothing but clearness of mind, and the power to draw inference from the surrounding circumstances."[101] He acted in circumstances that were changeable, and with them he also adopted a flexible attitude. Accordingly, the people whom he ruled were essentially neither good nor wicked, except according to how they responded to his programs, which were the consolidation of his dynasty and the building of a strong Afghanistan. Since this entailed the curtailment of the elders' power, they turned against him. Since it was beyond his power to separate the common people from their elders and to inflict brutal punishment on the latter without instigating the former against him, the amir gradually became pessimistic and relied increasingly on force, believing that "as the people were very bad, they deserve no mild treatment."[102] Hence, he imposed on the Afghans a very tough regime and inflicted on them a wide range of inhuman punishments, which they had never experienced before and for which the amir became known as the "Iron Amir." The Afghans were so impressed by this harsh regime that they believed that "no such power exists in the world as the Amir of Afghanistan."[103] The rich and the poor trembled before him. Tribal and religious elders, the sardars, and the senior officials, including his own sons, looked upon themselves as his "slaves" and praised him with all the pleasant adjectives they could think of. Subdued public opinion, however, as expressed in the following two anonymous letters (*shabnamas*), was the opposite. "You are a tyrant, and your officials are tyrants. The people should make jehad against you and not for you."[104] Or,

❖

You have ruined Afghanistan. You have degraded the clever and experienced men and made them sit idly to gratify your vanity. You have dishonoured the members of respectable families and have elevated the meanly-born and undeserving. You have thrown into prison the wives and daughters of the innocent rayets [*sic*] and have taken their good-looking unmarried daughters to the "Pari Khana" [Fairy Palace] where both you and the Naib Kotwal have illicit intercourse with them. You have slain the leading men of all the tribes. Hold back from such tyranny, oppression and mischief.[105]

❖

The amir was a strong believer in the Sunni sect of Islam. He equally held the beliefs of the common Muslims, as was evident from his respect for saints, shrines, and religious personages[106] and from his giving alms to beggars and to the shrines. By offering alms he hoped the innocent spirits of the saints and shrines would alleviate calamities and cholera.[107] Hoping also to protect himself from what was considered the evil eye and from other calamities, he carried charms with him. The days for traveling or avoiding trips were fixed for him by his astrologers,[108] whom he also consulted before he made an important decision. He consulted his astrologers even for cutting his nails and taking a bath. In 1895 when Sardar Nasr Allah returned from Europe he was kept outside the city for nearly a week, because the astrologers had predicted that it was not a lucky hour to see his father.[109] Sunday was his lucky day and it was on that day that he usually made important decisions.[110] As directed by some Hindu fortunetellers the amir once weighed himself with *satanj* (seven different kinds of grain) to ensure good fortune.[111] It is not known whether the amir believed in any mystic order of Islam, but toward the end of his life he became a follower (*murid*) of Sahibzada Maʾsum Jan of Charbagh, near Jalalabad, who was commonly known as the Sirhind Sahibzada.[112] The amir claimed he had dreamt of the Prophet and his Companions, and that the Prophet chose him as the future amir.[113] He did not pray regularly, however, and being a king was, according to the Islamic law, exempt from observing fast. It was for his observance of Islam and of the commonly held beliefs that some Afghans called him a "saint," while others called him a "kafir" for his oppression.[114]

Unlike his youthful life, the amir's life during his amirate was mainly led indoors. His surroundings were the most luxurious in the country, as he had the best of everything.[115] He was fond of music and watched female and male dances frequently in the darbar. Music was perhaps the only thing that could soften his heart. Once he burst into tears at the excellent performance of two male dancers from Tirah. Whether in private or public, he was attended by handsome *ghulam bachas*. The amir, as well as his sons, was addicted to "unnatural sexual pleasures."[116] He had numerous wives, more than four at one time; but their company did not distract him from what he considered to be his mission. He did not live with any of them, even his favorite wife. Only in the evenings could his wives attend on him for a short while. Occasionally, he drank in his private darbar.[117] To look younger, like most Afghans, he dyed his beard and hair;[118] but he suffered from chronic rheumatism, kidney diseases, dropsy and gout.[119] Consequently, he often had headaches and complained of heaviness and heat in the head, which annoyed him greatly.[120]

Apart from hard work, what weakened him most was probably his preference for treatment by native physicians who prescribed bleeding,[121] including the application of leeches whenever he felt pain.[122] The treatment of his one-time English physician, Dr. John Gray, which had helped to improve the amir's health, was discontinued on the ground that his medicine contained spirits,[123] in spite of the fact that occasionally the amir drank alcohol in private.

During his last years the amir could walk but little and had to be carried whenever he went any distance. Near the end of his life he had to be carried even in his own room.[124] Even so, his mind was said to be alert, and, while sitting by a window overlooking people on the ground (who were kept ignorant of the amir's illness), he carried on state business as usual. Finally he reached the point when his mind failed to reason clearly,[125] and he died at midnight on 2 October 1901 at Bagh-i-Bala.[126] At first the people, who had heard rumors of the amir's death many times in the past and who were under the impression that the death of an Afghan ruler had always to be accompanied by civil wars, did not believe that the amir was dead.[127] Later, when the news was established they rejoiced.[128]

The Household

When ʾAbd al-Rahman became amir, he had a small family, consisting principally of his mother and his two sons, Sardar Habib Allah (b. 1872) and Sardar Nasr Allah (b. 1873). These sons of the amir were born of a Wakhi slave girl, Gulrez, who was a handmaid to one of his first wives, the daughter of Mir Jahandar Shah of Badakhshan.[129] Shortly after his accession, the amir married Bibi Halima (b. 1868), a granddaughter of Amir Dost Muhammad Khan, through his daughter Shams-i-Jahan. The grandfather of Bibi Halima was *mir waʾiz* (head preacher) of Kabul. Bibi Halima, by reasons of birth and her strong personal character, became the queen-sultana. As time went on, the amir married the daughters of tribal elders of Zadran, Wazir, Hazara, Qizilbash, and Bamezay. He also married Sayyed and Tajik women. Through his sons his family was also connected to the khans of Nawagai, Asmar, and Tagao; to the family of Loynab; and to Amir Sher ʾAli Khan and others. None of these women, except Bibi Halima, had any influence during the lifetime of the amir. As it was his policy to "unite tribes with the State through marriages,"[130] these marriages were political. With the attachment to the harem of a large number of *ghulam bachas* and female and male servants, most of whom were the sons and daughters of influential persons, the harem became the biggest and most important in Afghan history.

With his nearest relations, the amir also acted as a sovereign. When talking to his sons, the amir referred to himself as king not father, and his attitude toward his sons was that of a ruler to subjects rather than of a father to sons.[131] The amir was careful to see that his sons did not become a menace to him. For this reason, the amir did not appoint any of his young sons to be governors of provinces, where the temptation for a prince to defy the central government had always been great in the past. The amir kept his sons under his control in Kabul and, when he met them, made them kneel before him and to kiss his hands in recognition of forgiveness.[132] His sons looked on themselves as the amir's "slaves,"[133] and Habib Allah was once imprisoned and handcuffed for one night. The amir also imprisoned one of his wives, the mother of Sardar Hafiz Allah, for her harsh words to him. Otherwise, his wives and sons enjoyed comforts of life second only to those of the amir, although his wives were sexually frustrated and some were said to have had affairs with the *ghulam bachas*.[134] The amir's sons, whom he tried to make acceptable as princes to the people, received liberal stipends. Soon they became rich and "bought" extensive tracts of lands in Buthkhak, Bini Hisar, and other suburbs of Kabul. They were ordered to wear the most expensive clothes. Every wife of the amir was to wear a dress valued at not less than 500 rupees. Slave girls were ordered to wear white uniforms that were each valued at not less than 150 rupees. Thus, the amir's family became the paramount one in the country; but great discord existed in the domestic life of the amir,[135] and the principal actors in this discord were Bibi Halima and the amir's two eldest sons.

It was a well-known saying in Kabul that the world feared ᵓAbd al-Rahman, and he feared Bibi Halima.[136] Bibi Halima was a well-informed, generous, and ambitious lady, keenly interested in politics. Even before the birth, in 1889, of her own son Sardar Muhammad ᵓOmar Jan, it was said that in the event of the amir's death she aimed at the amirate for herself,[137] until her son would come of age. Although a woman, she thought she could succeed in this plan because Afghanistan had no fixed precedent or principle of succession. Here a few words on the considerations that help a contending prince to the Afghan throne seem in order.

Before 1880, nearly all reigning monarchs had selected as their heirs apparent their eldest sons by their principal Muhammadzay wives, not necessarily their actual eldest sons born to non-Muhammadzay wives. Since some Afghan sovereigns married four wives as allowed by the Islamic law and others exceeded the law's limit and all also kept concubines, they had numerous sons, the principal of whom contested this nomination, occasionally during the lifetime of their fathers, but usually following their deaths. This recurring contest for succession was one of the root causes of the many civil wars fought in Afghanistan, wars which were ultimately decided by the wealth, ability, and popularity of the rivals to the throne.[138] By themselves, neither the principle of primogeniture nor the nomination of a prince by his sovereign father nor the birth of a prince to a mother of the royal blood were sufficient to ensure a smooth succession. No doubt these were the added, and in the case of legitimacy the necessary, qualifications, but by far the weightiest factor in securing the throne was the personal ability of the prince and his popularity with the Muhammadzay sardars, the elders, and the army. As a keen realist Amir ᵓAbd al-Rahman, unlike his predecessors, gave priority to the training of his eldest son under his own supervision in state affairs and placed his other sons under the eldest.[139] This action put Bibi Halima in opposition to the policy pursued by the amir, who was unwilling to pass over Sardar Habib Allah in favor of her minor son, Sardar Muhammad ᵓOmar. Thus Bibi Halima and the two eldest princes, whom she looked upon with contempt because their mother had originally been a concubine, each tried to win favor with the amir and to win to his or her side important military officers. This competition in fact made it necessary for the rival parties to become active in state affairs; but under the watchful eyes of the amir, this struggle for succession did not become destructive. Rather, it helped to consolidate the amir's dynasty.

In the past the principal wives of the Afghan rulers had been active in politics behind the scenes, but Bibi Halima was the most active of all. She was the first queen to appear in public in European dress without a veil and to ride horses with armed guards accompanying her.[140] She held military exercises in the harem and trained her maids in the military art.[141] In 1888, while on the way to Turkestan with the amir her own "guard consisted not only of a body of the amir's soldiers, but of a regiment of mounted Amazons, some two hundred, the female slaves and servants of the Harem. These rode on men's saddles, were veiled, and wore on the head, over the veil, solar hamlets, or felt hats. Each was armed with a sabre and a carbine."[142] Bibi Halima made attempts to win the military officers to her side. It was reported that she was more popular with them than either Sardar Habib Allah or Nasr Allah had been.[143] She also kept one regiment of disciplined troops, led by the sons of tribal elders and by Muhammadzay sardars in service to her son.[144] In imitation of her husband, she presided over biweekly darbars attended by Muhammadzay ladies. In addition, she exercised power in government affairs by issuing *barats* (drafts or assignments of money),[145] fixing allowances for some *ghulam bachas*,[146] and interceding with the amir on behalf of senior government officials.[147] The amir's new wives were under her influence, and she beat one of them just after the newer wife's wedding when Bibi Halima found that the new bride was not beautiful enough to be worthy of the amir's harem.[148]

Bibi Halima was decidedly pro-British, disliked the amir's Central Asian associates, and tried to wean the amir from the Russians. Time and again she advised the amir to remain true to the British friendship, because, she argued, they had helped him to the throne; but the amir rebuked her for this, saying it was he who helped the British out of a difficulty.[149] Gradually, the amir deprived her of some of her power, presumably after she had unsuccessfully asked him to allow her to communicate with the British government regarding the succession,[150] had pressed him to declare her infant son heir apparent, and had beat one of her maidservants to death.[151] Still she was in a position to influence the amir, and it was on her advice that he sent Sardar Nasr Allah, not Habib Allah, to London in 1895.[152] From that time onward, however, the amir gradually delegated authority to his two eldest sons, by placing Sardar Habib Allah in charge of military and civil affairs and Sardar Nasr Allah in charge of the department of finance (diwan).[153] Further, to avoid complications in the event of his sudden death the amir, after his initial aversion to the nomination of a successor on the ground that it breeds disturbances and mischiefs,[154] in 1891 declared, "All chiefs, representatives, headmen, and tribesmen should understand that I have appointed my son, Sardar Habib Allah to be my heir apparent and successor."[155] Unlike Amir Sher 'Ali, however, ʾAmir Abd al-Rahman did not press either the British government or the Afghans to give him assurances that they would support Habib Allah after the amir's death. Instead he concentrated on training the heir apparent in the art of government, making him popular with the people,[156] and paving the way for a smooth transfer of power by disposing of the powerful men in the country.[157] The only menace left to the heir apparent was Bibi Halima, who, once, unsuccessfully tried to poison Habib Allah.[158] It was probably for this action that the amir called her "an enemy in my own house."[159] The undeclared struggle over the succession was confined to the palace but became tense whenever the amir fell seriously ill. On such occasions, Bibi Halima spent lavishly on influential people, hoping that in the event of the amir's death they might help her son to the throne.[160]

During the last days of the amir Sardar Habib Allah personally took charge of the amir's treatment in Bagh-i-Bala and kept the old ruler's illness and subsequent death secret, until he had obtained the allegiance of his full brother, Nasr Allah (to whom Habib Allah promised the succession), principal military and civil officials, and the Muhammadzay sardars, mainly through Ashik Aghasi ʾAbd al-Quddus.[161] Other reports mention that shortly before his death Amir ʾAbd al-Rahman effected a reconciliation between Sardar Habib Allah and Bibi Halima.[162] The amir warned them they would suffer and his soul would be annoyed if they quarreled.[163] Bibi Halima had no choice but to tender her allegiance, especially when Sardar ʾAbd al-Quddus and Sardar Muhammad Yusuf cautioned her against taking steps that might jeopardize the dynasty. She then vacated the palace. It was still not possible for her relations with the new amir to be good; neither did he confide in her, although he increased her allowance and appointed twelve-year-old Muhammad ʾOmar to a high position. The only incident following the death of Amir ʾAbd al-Rahman was the execution of Sardar Muhammad Naʾim Khan, a commander of the army, who was suspected of intrigues. Other than this execution, Amir Habib Allah, who was proclaimed as the "Amir of Islam,"[164] ascended the throne peacefully—the first peaceful succession in the history of Afghanistan. The new amir promised he would "walk in the footsteps of his father," because he considered the "arrangements made and orders passed by his father sacred."[165]

Also attached to the household were two groups of servants, the *ghulam bachas* and the *peshkhidmats*. They differed in origin and social background but performed similar functions. Traditionally *ghulams* (slaves) had always been attached to the courts of Afghan rulers, but in the reign of Amir ʾAbd al-Rahman their number and role increased considerably. In the past they had formed royal bodyguards (*ghulam-i-shah*) only, but during the amir's reign they were promoted to some of the highest civil and military posts in the country and were known as *ghulam bachas*. In this the amir was probably inspired by the *devshirme* system of the Ottomans under which children of the Christian subjects were recruited for training to fill the ranks of the

Janissaries (Ottoman regular infantry) and to occupy posts in the palace service and in the administration.[166] The amir hoped in this way to create civil and military officials who were independent of the tribal or regional attachments and loyal to his dynasty and to the state. They were recruited not only from among the slaves from Chitral, Badakhshan and Kafiristan, but also from among the sons of some influential Muslim families, mainly non-Pashtuns, and of senior government officials.[167] Under the general supervision of Nazir Muhammad Safar, the keeper of the amir's seal, they were instructed in public affairs and the jehad.[168] After they acquired some practical training in the darbar, where they attended the amir in various capacities, they were given high civil and military posts.[169] Thus the court became for the first time the biggest center that furnished the state with trained men. When mature, the *ghulam bachas* were married to the daughters of respectable families, mainly the Muhammadzays, and all their expenses were met by the state. The amir had the power of life and death over them and looked on them as his slaves even when they became high officials. Strict discipline was maintained in their upbringing, and those who committed homosexual acts or adultery were either thrown into the *siah chahs* (deep black pits) or executed. At one time there were two hundred of them in the court alone, most of whom were military officers.[170] The most noted of the *ghulam bachas* who held high posts during the lifetime of the amir were Parwana Khan (the Kabul *kotwal*), General Faramuz Khan (*sipah salar* of the Herat army), Nazir Muhammad Safar, and Jan Muhammad (the chief treasurer). The full impact of the *ghulam bachas*, however, was felt during the reigns of the amir's immediate successors, notably in the reign of Amir Habib Allah, when the *ghulam bachas* of the darbar, under the leadership of Wali Muhammad Badakhshani (who served King Aman Allah as regent and defense minister), played an active role as the first major reformist group in Afghanistan.[171]

The *peshkhidmats* (headservants) were recruited from among the *ghulam bachas* and also from among people of consequence in the country. The latter were kept in the darbar more as hostages than as servants. The idea was to train some people of consequence in the darbar and to attach them to the royal dynasty. The *peshkhidmats* looked after the amir's meals, entertainment, and all service related to the darbar. Since the darbar in the reign of the amir became very big and spent lavishly, a great number of *peshkhidmats* were employed. The head of every service was usually called *bashi* or *nazir* of that service, for example, *farash bashi* (head of the service in charge of the furniture) or *nazir-i-karkhana* (head of the kitchen), while the chief of all of them was called *peshkhidmat bashi*.[172] Of all the *peshkhidmats* the amir trusted Nazir Muhammad Safar most. He was placed in charge of the amir's seals and the keys of the reserve treasures, for which he was given the title of *amin-i-mohr* (custodian of the seal). The *peshkhidmats* appeared to be engaged in menial jobs; but they were, in fact, persons of great consequence. For them the darbar was field work in which they obtained practical training in the art of government and after which they were given high posts in the provinces. It is interesting to note that in spite of the amir's rigidity with his officials, Nazir Muhammad Safar was allowed to exact charges for himself from newly appointed officials when he sealed their firmans of appointment.[173]

The Court

The court was generally known as the *khilwat* (privacy), or *darbar-i-khas* (special court). It consisted of the amir, the heads of various departments, and other officials and elders;[174] but, since the key to admission was not necessarily the office one held but the amir's confidence, all heads of the departments were not included. At times, persons holding no official position under the crown were also admitted. Thus the number attending the court always fluctuated. Whatever its composition, new policies were not formulated there and those who attended it did not have collective responsibility. This lack of power was an obvious departure from the cabinet model set by Amir Sher ʾAli, who had constituted the office of prime minister and had delegated some measure of authority to its holders.[175] In the amir's reign heads of the departments or ministries attending the court were merely officials who singly or collectively had no power whatsoever. The amir alone enunciated policies and the officials just carried them out through their departments.

Although the amir was accountable to no one, he was still not an absolute ruler in the sense of being free from restrictions. Religion and customary laws were counterpoises to his authority. The ʾulama and elders, as the representatives of religion and of the general will, served as restraining influences. As head of the state, however, Amir ʾAbd al-Rahman concentrated power in his hands to the extent that no Afghan ruler had done either before or after him. In this sense he became an absolute ruler, but the title he assumed was very modest in relation to the power he actually exercised.

The Hotakay and Sadozay rulers of Afghanistan had assumed the title of shah, but Muhammadzay rulers used the title amir. The latter title was used first by Amir Dost Muhammad in 1836, at a time when the ʾulama urged him to wage a jehad against the Sikhs of Panjab, who had occupied Peshawar in 1833. Amir remained his title even when Dost Muhammad, generally known as the Amir-i-Kabir (The Great Amir), reunified most of the territories ruled by the Sadozay kings. Although Amir ʾAbd al-Rahman's rule assumed full territorial significance, in that the extent and boundaries of Afghanistan were fixed during his reign for the first time, he still used the title of amir, which, as a part of the term *amir al-mu'minin* (commander of the faithful) and unlike the word *shah*, stresses the "faithful" rather than a fixed territory. Amir ʾAbd al-Rahman also used the title *padshah-i-islam* (king of Islam)[176] and the long title Amir-i-ibn al-Amir ʾAbd al-Rahman.[177] Following the conquest of Kafiristan in 1896, the elders and the ʾulama conferred on him the title of ghazı and of *zia al-millat-i-wa al-din* (the light of the nation and religion). At this time, the amir intended to assume the more prestigious title of *shahanshah-i-adil* (the just emperor) for himself and to confer the title of amir on Sardar Habib Allah and the title of *nawab* on Sardar Nasr Allah,[178] but he soon gave up this intention for no apparent reason. At no time, however, did he use either the full title of *amir al-mu'minin* or amir in the sense of the amir of Afghanistan, as is generally but mistakenly applied to him.

Amir ʾAbd al-Rahman, despite his contempt for seeking advice, frequently sought it, although he did not consider himself bound to act on it. Often he consulted certain high officials and a few other individuals outside the state. Those who were consulted included the chief judge, the chief secretary, the *mustaufi*, the Kabul *kotwal*, the Sipah Salar Ghulam Haydar Charkhi, the chief treasurer, Zain Khan Popalzay, and a few others. In this way a select few, not all of whom were state officials, functioned as a small privy council. Except for Zain Khan, no member of this council freely discussed subjects. They only endorsed the amir's opinion so much that even he complained, saying, "no one says that on certain matters my opinion is incorrect."[179] Thus the practice of government by group and consultation that, up to the accession of the amir, had been observed by Afghan rulers in its widest form was replaced by the rule of one man. Consequently, Amir ʾAbd al-Rahman ruled Afghanistan for twenty-one years more autocratically and dictatorially than either his predecessors or successors.

As the amir refused to delegate authority to others and himself worked relentlessly even when he was ill, he had no need for a prime minister or ministers with some measures of authority to act in his absence. Only the amir's eldest son Sardar Habib Allah, when old enough, acted as a kind of prime minister and held darbar in the absence of the amir occasionally before 1891 and after that date regularly even when the amir was in Kabul. Sardar Habib Allah also exercised some measure of executive and judicial power.[180] The heads of various departments, who were not all called by such a common prestigious title as wazir, were for the most part the amir's former page boys, and *peshkhidmats*. In their official capacity these people, except for a few, were the amir's servant officials and so were more loyal to his person than to the state. These officials, in order to gain or retain the amir's confidence and, at the same time, to protect themselves from the intrigues so common among them, spied on each other and formed factions.[181] Under such circumstances it was not possible for them to become self-reliant and independent in thought. No matter how servile they were to the amir, they still acted as minor despots over their inferiors and the common people.[182]

The Council

The council, resembling a parliament, was known as the *darbar-i-ʾaam* (public court). It was composed of two bodies, the *darbar-i-shahi* and *khawanin-i-mulki*; the former was something like the upper house and the latter, the lower house. The council was composed of the sardars, the *khawanin-i-mulki* (khans with feudal privileges), the 'ulama, and the members of the court.[183]

The despotic amir never intended for the council to be powerful; and, for this reason, he held that its members were not qualified to be trusted with power because they were not properly educated.[184] The council then, in fact, became a channel through which the amir could evaluate the feelings of his subjects, especially in emergencies when he needed the support of its members and a device for keeping a sizable section of influential elders in the capital. Only those sardars, elders, and 'ulama whose loyalty to the amir had been proven beyond doubt were allowed to become members. They were no more than yes-men, who had, as was said, "neither the capacity, nor the courage to detect anything wrong in the law or the policy of their sovereign."[185] From time to time, they were consulted about the supplies for war materials and on other state affairs[186] but not about such basic issues as revenue affairs or affairs related to the army. In theory council members were supposed to express their opinions on any issue that the amir put before them, but in reality they could not dare to express an opinion different from that of the amir.[187] Since sovereignty was said to reside in the king,[188] not in the people, it was obvious that members of the council, as representatives of the people, could not claim it. Like government officials they, also, became dependent on the state represented by the amir.

Membership in the council was based on the principles of selection and election. Of the three elements composing the council the sardars were the most important. Originally, sardar was a military title (*amir-i-lashkar*)[189] bestowed only by a monarch on those individuals who distinguished themselves in wars. During the Sadozay period, heads of the Durrani clans were called sardars. Because they commanded troops under the crown and because their position was further strengthened by the wealth and splendor they derived from their situation about the crown and because they were exempt from paying taxes, their power was greater than the tribal elders' power.[190] Amir Dost Muhammad Khan further strengthened this institution by appointing the sardars, who were mainly his sons and grandsons, to be provincial governors with vast power. Because of this, it was said that in Afghanistan there were as many sovereigns as sardars, each of whom governed his region after his own fashion.[191] Thus the sardars became at one and the same time the strength and the curse of the monarchy. Most civil wars fought in nineteenth-century Afghanistan were the result of the ambitions of the sardars.

Amir Sher 'Ali partly and Amir 'Abd al-Rahman completely modified the role of the sardars by banishing and killing the more ambitious sardars and by making the rest dependent on the state. As a result, the sardars lost their former military power; and they moved permanently to Kabul without their followers, whereas in the past they had rarely visited the court.[192] By the time of Amir ᵓAbd al-Rahman's accession the role of the sardar had already undergone a change. By 1880 this title had become closely associated with the Muhammadzays, especially the descendants of Sardar Payinda Khan, the father of Amir Dost Muhammad Khan, rather than with elders of the Durrani clans. This change showed that the sardars had become identified more with the ruling dynasty in Kabul than with their tribe in Kandahar. In other words, they had acquired the characteristics of aristocratic courtiers some of whom would not hesitate to advance their claims to the throne whenever the opportunity arose. As Sayyed Jamal al-Din Afghani, who observed them during his residence in Afghanistan in the mid-eighties, has said, "like opportunistic Sufis they [the sardars] are time-servers; on whichever side they see a powerful one they quickly head their horse in that direction. . . . In vanity they are like Pharaoh and Haman and in treachery they are Satan himself."[193] During the Second Anglo-Afghan War when it appeared that the British had become supreme in Kabul those sardars who were known to the public as "Cavagnarizays" (adherents of Louis Cavagnari, the British resident in Kabul) behaved as Sayyed Jamal al-Din observed. Instead of playing their traditional role of leading the Afghans against the invading foes, these sardars actually looked to the British for allowances and official posts. Some even acted in collusion with the British in the hope of becoming amirs.

In the reign of Amir ᵓAbd al-Rahman not all sardars, but only those who held the amir's firman, were entitled to membership in the council. Also, the council was not exclusively made up of the Barakzay sardars; a few non-Barakzay sardars were also made members of it. Whatever their origin, the sardars were dependent on the state, especially after they gave an undertaking to the effect that they entertained no ambition for power or leadership and were willing to serve the state as supervisors and inspectors.[194]

The *khawanin-i-mulki* were chosen from among tribal elders and men of consequence by general acclamation. They were entitled to membership in the council only when their election was approved by the amir, and he approved of their election after it was proved that not only they, but also their fathers had been loyal to the state.[195] Then they retained their position by the amir's firman and were given honorary military ranks and allowances.

The ᵓulama including the khan-i-ᵓulum (chief justice), the qazis, muftis (advisers to the qazis), and mullas represented the religious body in the council.[196] They were influential with the people by virtue of their real or pretended knowledge of the Shariᵓa. Some of them even acted as religious advisers to the khans and the rulers and so attended the tribal and royal councils; but, as detailed in chapter 7, Amir ᵓAbd al-Rahman broke their power and made them dependent on the state. He allowed a small number of them to take their seats in the council for reasons of seniority and service.[197]

Up to the midnineties the amir summoned the council rather frequently. Thereafter, he summoned men to his private darbar, while the council was presided over regularly by Sardar Habib Allah and in his absence by Sardar Nasr Allah. Except for the ’ulama, who attended council in their white clothes and large white turbans, other members were compelled to wear expensive uniforms.[198] They occupied their seats in the council with men of their own clans not with men of their own social rank. A Muhammadzay mulla, for instance, took his seat with Muhammadzay sardars not with other mullas.

In times of national emergency, when Afghan rulers needed the support of the whole nation, the great assembly (loya jirga) was convened and presided over by the rulers in person; but the assembly only gave advice to the kings on the specific issue for which it was convened. It was dissolved as soon as the purpose for which it was summoned was achieved. Those who attended the assembly were local magnates and notables, members of the court and the council, and high-ranking military officials. It was such an assembly that chose Ahmad Shah Durrani as king in 1747. When Amir Sher ’Ali was faced with the rebellions of his brothers, he convened the great assembly and obtained its approval in suppressing the rebellions.[199] Amir ’Abd al-Rahman convened the great assembly three times in his reign: in 1885 before he paid a state visit to India in 1888 when Sardar Muhammad Ishaq rebelled, and in 1893 after the Durand Agreement was signed in Kabul.

Chapter II
The Central
Government: 2

Ministers and Secretaries

The number of ministers and secretaries increased to an unprecedented degree in the reign of Amir 'Abd al-Rahman. As with elders, so with senior officials the amir's policy was to oppose the concentration of authority in one hand. The many government departments were headed by officials who were more or less of equal standing. Senior officials were given modest titles, but the actual authority they exercised was great. Such titles as *sadr-i-a'zam*, wazir, *mustaufi*, and *na'ib al-sultanat*, which signified authority, were occasionally conferred on certain favorite officials; but they either were not used officially or were used only for a short while.[1]

The amir's relationship with his ministers was not like that of a king with ministers, but like that of a master with his servants. This fact was true of all officials whether military or civil. In the absence of laws guaranteeing or at least fixing their rights and duties, the officials in the reign of Amir 'Abd al-Rahman relied on his good will.

In the amir's reign the bureaucracy expanded to a great extent. Consequently, the number of ministers and *mirzas* (junior secretaries) increased. The amir, however, neither revived the rudimentary form of cabinet, which had been set up by Amir Sher 'Ali, nor appointed a prime minister or a minister with some measure of authority. Sardar Nek Muhammad Khan, who had incited the populace to fight the British in Charasia and who, in the reign of the amir, worked as the minister of finance for a short while, was soon imprisoned for his sympathies for Sardar Muhammad Ayyub. Similarly, Mustaufi al-Mamalik

Mirza Muhammad Hussayn was imprisoned, ostensibly for his corruption, but in reality because of the amir's opposition to the concentration of authority in one hand. For the same reason, the amir arranged to prevent his senior officials from getting together, forming friendships among themselves,[2] and talking about state affairs.[3] The amir often called his officials "bastards" and poured a variety of other abusive words on them.[4] Sometimes he obliged senior officials personally to provide amusement for him.[5]

In the public eyes, however, the image of government officials was built up. This was marked, in 1891, by granting them military titles in proportion to their civilian ranks. Sardar ʾAbd al-Rahman, the khan-i-ʾulum, was made brigadier and Diwan Naranjan Das Sardaftari, a colonel.[6] Further, senior officials were paid a high salary; but the salary was fixed for persons rather than positions. Thus Sardar Muhammad Yusuf, who was superintendent of Kabul workshops and bore the title of *sipah salar*, was paid upward of 15,000 rupees per annum, whereas Mir Abul-Qasim, head of the auditing office, who was given the title of *kumaidan*, was paid 4,000 rupees a year. Mustaufi Mirza Muhammad Hussayn was paid 20,000 rupees a year. These officials, further, had "invisible" incomes. Taken all together, their total incomes were very high, and senior officials in the amir's reign by virtue of prestige, authority, and income constituted the first major bureaucratic upper-middle class in Afghanistan.

Senior members of the bureaucracy were recruited from among the Qizilbashes, the Tajiks, the Hindus, and the Muhammadzay sardars. A few non-Muhammadzay Pashtuns and Indian Muslims also headed some departments. Gradually the *ghulam bacha* officials came to hold certain key positions, such as the *kotwali* and the treasury. Generally speaking, it was the amir's policy to give high positions in the administration to members of the smaller ethnic groups or those with no basis of power. Members of the larger ethnic groups were not debarred from the bureaucracy if it could be proved that they were loyal to the amir. No matter what their origin, most senior officials were dismissed, often disgracefully, before they became important. The commonest way of getting rid of them was to ask them to render their accounts. Since it was "next to impossible to come out safe" when the accounts of an official were questioned,[7] officials did not feel secure.[8] Even so, embezzlement was common, mainly because senior officials were allowed to keep state money with themselves and to deliver it to the treasury when the amount reached a certain limit.[9] Every official dreaded the officials of the auditing office.

Characteristic of the bureaucracy under Amir ʾAbd al-Rahman was the increase in the number of *mirzas* (a corruption of *amirzada* which means son of the amir). This prestigious title was once the prerogative of princes. (Although all bureaucrats added the honorary title of *mirza* before their names, the title was principally used by junior bureaucrats.) Their superiors, the heads of various departments, were usually called by the titles of their official positions, such as *sarrishtadar*, *sardaftari, munshi, mustaufi*. The salaries of the *mirzas* were small and their positions lower; but they, by virtue of their great number, formed the real backbone of the bureaucracy.

Before 1880 the profession of the *mirzas* was a monopoly of the Qizilbashes. In the reign of Amir ʾAbd al-Rahman they lost this monopoly, first because of their support of Amir Sher ʾAli against the party of the amir in the civil war and second, and more important, because of their alleged instigation of the Hazaras to rebellion. The policy of the amir towards the Qizilbashes is discussed in chapter 7, but it should be noted here that, although the Qizilbashes alone were unable to fill all available posts in the expanding bureaucracy, the Hazara War provided an excuse for their easy dismissal from the *daftar*. Thereafter, the *mirzas* were recruited from among the Tajiks and the Pashtuns, and among them the *mirzas* of Laghman and Herat played a significant role. The Uzbeks were also recruited as *mirzas*; but, because of their insufficient knowledge of Persian, the working language of the *daftar*, they were soon dismissed. Mullas and *talibs* (students of religious knowledge), in fact, non-Shiʾite literates, including a considerable number of Hindus, entered the bureaucracy. The exact number of the *mirzas* is difficult to assess. In Kabul alone there were fifty-two senior officials (*sardaftaris* and *sarrishtadars*),[10] each of whom had "many" secretaries (*mirzas*) under him.[11]

The education of the *mirzas* was limited to Persian composition, a smattering of the old Arabic, and the first four basic rules of arithmetic (addition, subtraction, multiplication, and division). Even in these they were far from proficient and when it came to calculating fractions they were hopelessly lost. As a distinct social group, however, they enjoyed a respectable position in the society and were very different from the rest of the population in their soft and polished manners. They wore expensive clothes, rode horses, and had many wives and female servants,[12] in spite of the facts that the average monthly pay of the *mirzas* was thirty rupees and that the amir gave "salaries to very few of the mirzas employed on Government work. He said they made money from the people whether they got a salary or not."[13]

The *mirzas* were known to be cunning and ever scheming against each other or against the moneyed people, whom they squeezed.[14] It was common practice among the *mirzas* to investigate the accounts of those of their rank or even of a higher official, on charges of having embezzled government money, and to undertake to prove their claim by going through their papers. The amir usually consented to this investigation and the result was a profit for the state from the accused's fine. If successful in their undertaking, the *mirzas* were promoted to the positions of their superiors, who were then dismissed. If not, the *mirzas* were not punished for their accusations. This practice set in motion a process that led to the easy downfall of senior officials, none of whom could hold any position for more than two or three years. The day would come when the new official himself would be treated in the same way and would be tortured, imprisoned, or killed.[15]

The *mirzas* had various ways of making money, the commonest being the collection of customs dues and various taxes. If the *mirzas* were required to give a receipt to someone for money paid or goods delivered, they would keep that person waiting for days if he gave them nothing extra, in addition to ruining him by bringing false accusations. In Sardar Habib Allah's words, "There is no one in the service from the highest to the lowest who is not corrupt. The Mirzas of Kabul . . . especially take bribes."[16]

Offices and Methods of Work

The expansion of the bureaucracy under Amir ʾAbd al-Rahman was manifested in the gradual establishment of numerous new offices in the central diwan. As the collection of revenue and taxes became the main concern of the government, the new offices were mainly financial. In the past, the central diwan had functioned under one *mustaufi*; but the new bureaucracy expanded under the direct supervision of the amir himself. Partly because of this direct supervision and partly because of the expansion of government activities, the reforms introduced into the bureaucracy were manifold.

The central diwan, generally known as the supreme diwan (*diwan-i-aʾla*), was responsible for all aspects of economic activities, tax levying and collection, customs, and government expenditures, and control of monopolies.[17] In the beginning of the reign of Amir ʾAbd al-Rahman this body was led by Mustaufi al-Mamalik Mirza Muhammad Hussayn, until he was dismissed in 1884.[18] The diwan was then divided into four departments—western, eastern, northern, and southern—each responsible for the financial affairs of one particular geographical region. The departments were placed under the charge of four officials (*daftaris*), all of whom worked under the general supervision of a higher official, Sardaftari Mirza Muhammad Zaman Kabuli.[19]

Since this new arrangement tended to give the same authority to the *sardaftari* as that previously held by the *mustaufi*, the amir subsequently separated the four departments from each other,[20] with no one official at the top. Each department was headed by a *sardaftari* who had under him many associates in subordinate positions called *sarrishtadars* and a large number of junior *mirzas*. Slowly over the years new departments (*daftars*) were added to the central diwan so that the original number increased still further. Among the first new departments was the auditing office (*daftar-i-sanjish*), which was responsible for examining and verifying financial accounts in order to prevent losses to the state.[21] Gradually this office became more important than any other in the central diwan, but the new arrangement led to a lack of coordination among the equally important *sardaftaris* who failed to prepare yearly statements of income and expenditures and to show the arrears of revenue.

Seeing the amir's dissatisfaction with the inefficient diwan, a group of six enterprising *mirzas* of the central diwan in 1890 undertook to

prepare a general financial statement and to extract the arrears that the
ra'iyyat and officials owed to the state. One condition of their request
was the exclusion from the diwan of the Qizilbash mirzas and all those
whose fathers had worked in the diwan. They anticipated that these
men could possibly sabotage the operation. This exclusion was perhaps
the biggest setback the Qizilbashes ever had in the diwan.[22] Many new
mirzas from the military offices of Kabul and the provinces were
placed under the six mirzas who came to be called sanjishiyyan. Under
the sanjishiyyan the statement of the incomes and expenditures was
still not completed; but their success was monumental in collecting
the arrears, reopening the old accounts of government officials, and
examining new ones. The auditing office under their supervision
emerged as the most powerful bureau in the diwan.

The first decade of the amir's rule was marked by an increase in the
existing rates of revenues and by rebellions and the second, by the collection of the revenue arrears (baqiyat-i-wijuh) and by squeezing government officials, including provincial governors, who had amassed
large sums of money during the first turbulent decade. With no statute
of limitations on their authority, the sanjishiyyan were able to examine any legal affair that had arisen during the amir's reign. In investi-
gating the past accounts and extracting the revenue arrears their scope
of activities was almost unlimited. Toward the end of the amir's reign,
there was probably no official who had not either directly or indirectly
felt the effects of the state auditors' authority.[23] Consequently, millions of rupees were paid to the state, which caused extreme hardship
to the ra'iyyat and to the officials. Of the six mirzas finally Mirza
Muhammad Hussayn and Mirza 'Abd al-Rauf were promoted to the
highest positions in the diwan, the former reaching the position of the
sardaftari of the auditing office. Subsequently, these two were appointed, in addition to their posts in the diwan, joint kotwals of Kabul.[24] The welding of these two positions in their hands indicated the
amir's determination to obtain the quick and forceful realization of
government money.[25]

The exercise of such extensive authority by the sanjishiyyans led to
corruption among them and to general discontent. To alleviate this in
1893, a separate daftar, the office of the signature (daftar-i-imza), was
set up. This office was required to approve only the just fiscal transactions of the officials of the auditing office. It was led by Sardar Muhammad Hasan Khan who had in the 1880s stirred the Shinwars and
the Mangals against the amir but had subsequently been forgiven.[26]

Closely connected to the increase in the revenue was the establishment of a separate land survey office (the daftar-i-paimaish-i-arazi)
within the central diwan. The actual surveying was carried out on a
regional basis and followed the establishment of the central authority
over the country as a whole. The resurveyed and reassessed land was
registered under the name of its holder, a scheme which suggests that
such lands so far had been registered under the name of either the family or the clan. The surveyors, under the supervision of engineer 'Abd

al-Subhan, a native of Jalalpur in the Panjab, also brought under assessment lands that had once been cultivated but now were lying fallow. For the administration of state land there was a separate office called the *daftar-i-khalisa*. It had been part of the central diwan before the amir came to power; but during his reign this office became still more significant, especially in Kandahar, where large tracts of lands were added to the *khalisa*. The office of *sawer*, signifying miscellaneous revenues, seemed to be in charge of incomes derived from customs dues.

Another principal office of the diwan was the *daftar-i-tashkhis*, which was responsible for paying allowances to pensioners who were not on regular active service but received allowances for one reason or another.[27] It was led by the former *mustaufi*, Mir Muhammad Hussayn, who was *sardaftari* during the whole period of the amir's reign. The *daftar-i-sukukat* (the paper office), established in 1891, issued stamps for use on papers dealing with transactions of all kinds. (After the stamped state papers were issued on a transaction plain papers were forbidden to be used.[28]) This office was intended to serve a twofold purpose: to register all cases and transactions which occurred between individuals and were settled through government agencies, and to increase state revenue. Implicit in the latter was the checking of embezzlement. All deeds required state stamps ranging in value at first between one shahi (one-twelfth of a rupee) and one ʾabbasi (one-third of a rupee) and later between one shahi and one rupee.[29] The *daftar-i-wijuhat* (office of incomes) dealt with the cash incomes of the treasury, whereas the *daftar-i-nufus* (office of population) was charged with taking census of the whole population.[30] For the civilians listed in the diwan a separate office of the living (*daftar-i-hayati*) was established. The recipients of allowances, such as feudal lords, were required to attend the office in person and to obtain the *barat* (assignment).[31] This requirement was intended to stop payment to those who had either died or fled the country but were still on the list as recipients.

The Kabul treasury (*khazana*) had two departments, public (ʾamira), and private (*khas*).[32] The latter was the amir's private treasury, where his private incomes derived from lands, trade, and so on were paid.[33] Both treasuries were supervised by the amir's trusted officials, who were mostly his *ghulam bachas* and entitled *khazanadars* (literally treasurers, but actually top officials of the treasuries). Subordinate officials of the treasuries were mainly Hindus, who were said to have been good accountants and the least likely to embezzle. Taking cash out of the public treasury, whether by individuals or as payment to government officials, required a good deal of bureaucratic procedure. Cash was withdrawn by checks in duplicate signed by either the amir or Sardar Habib Allah and countersigned and sealed by the heads and subordinates of the departments concerned. Payment was made only when the treasurer received both copies, one through the official channel and the other from the individual to be paid.

In the beginning of the amir's reign the treasury was mobile and was

taken wherever the amir went. At the same time, the amir sent cash
and valuables to Badakhshan to the custody of his most trusted lieutenant, Sardar ʾAbd Allah Tokhay, the governor of that province. It
was only after the maintenance of order and the construction of the
new palace that most of the treasury was kept in the center of the
palace.

Notable progress was made in the maintenance of a postal service
(*dakkhana*). The modern Afghan postal service was first established by
Amir Sher ʾAli and in 1872 impressed stamps worth one shahi, one
ʾabbasi, two ʾabbasis, and one rupee.[34] Disused in the Second Anglo-
Afghan War, the postal service was reestablished by Amir ʾAbd al-
Rahman and expanded to the extent that it covered the whole country,
but no impressed stamps were used.[35] At first in place of a postmark a
small piece of the letter was torn to show that a stamp had been used;
later a seal for obliteration was used.[36] The post office was led by a
sarrishtadar and was used mainly for official purposes. Private letters
were inspected and the public was not allowed to send letters except
through the post.[37] Usually posts were dispatched twice a week from
Kabul to the provinces, including Peshawar. Particular attention was
paid to making the service fast and efficient; and, to this end, a large
number of runners and horsemen were employed. During the amir's
reign Herat, the most distant city from the capital, was reached in
seven days via the Hazarajat[38] by forty-five horsemen, posted in thirteen stations. Previously it had taken nineteen days for the post to
reach Herat via Kandahar. Along the Kabul-Turkestan road, two hundred runners (*harkaras*) were employed. The post on this road took
from nine to eleven days by runners and four days by express post, presumably carried by horsemen. Along the road between Kabul and
Jalalabad runners carried the post ten miles a day, five miles in each
direction. They lived in groups in stone huts five miles from each other
along the main roads and their spears with attachments of jingling
bells were struck in the grounds outside of the huts.[39]

Reforms were also introduced in the *daftar* or register itself. Previously official entries had been made in separate unbound sheets
(*fard*), and the yearly collection of these sheets was called the *daftar*.
Thus the *daftar*, besides causing delay in work, was easily alterable
when it suited the *mirzas* without their fearing discovery. In 1892 the
amir decreed that from then on all the affairs of the diwan, except the
petitions of the individuals and the correspondence addressed to him,
would be registered only in stitched and bound volumes, whose begin-
nings and endings were to be sealed and inside pages numbered. Not
only the ruin of the book, but also the erasure of a line from its contents was punishable by the cutting off of one hand of the *mirza* in
whose custody the book had been placed. The *mirzas* were, however,
not punished for making mistakes, provided they only crossed out the
mistakes.[40] Precautions were also taken against false firmans that were
sometimes issued.[41] For a firman to be valid the amir's signature and
seal on it were no longer considered sufficient. It had to be also coun-

tersigned by the officials from whose departments it originated and to be registered in the *daftar*.[42]

For the correct registration of names, a problem arose that was peculiar to Afghanistan where so many languages are spoken; for vowels that could not be expressed in Persian written in Arabic script, the diacritical system was introduced.[43] Also for the sake of convenience and preventing fraud the *ruqumat* (numerals, that is, a system of noting numbers with letters) was replaced by the use of Arabic numbers.[44] To make the *mirzas* efficient they were provided with pens with nibs and thus relieved of the chore of sharpening the bamboo pens with which they had worked.[45] Along with these reforms the system of giving printed receipts for payments was also introduced.

Regulations were laid down for the *mirzas* in their work. Because of the lack of government buildings before the amir's reign, officials had worked in their own homes and office work had been considerably delayed.[46] The amir erected a block of government offices for the *mirzas* to work in, and these offices necessitated regular attendance and the fixing of work hours. During the winter the officials were required to work eight hours a day and in the summer ten hours.[47] Latecomers were fined by deductions from their pay. Consequently excuses of ill health became common, and the amir ordered that officials ought to attend their offices even if they fell ill. Subsequently he relaxed this ruling, but those who were unable to attend offices because of health were not paid for their absences.[48] It is not known whether the officials were entitled to yearly holidays or paid leaves of absence on social occasions, but it is known that the *mirzas*, in addition to being paid a low salary, were not paid regularly, sometimes not for three years.[49] Payment of their salary was usually made subject to their completing a project, such as the statement of incomes and expenditures. The *mirzas*, while on their way to their offices, looked pathetic and morose and their offices in the cold winter looked to them like prisons. Nevertheless, they were urged to work hard for Islam, the Muslim community, and their king[50]—an order which must have spurred the Hindu officials on. Furthermore, officials were also made to give a written undertaking to the effect that if they misappropriated state property or acted tyrannically over the people or did similar things, they would render themselves liable to death.[51] Obviously by doing so the amir intended to deter the *mirzas* from misusing their position and authority, but a number of them lost their lives for their alleged failure to comply with the undertaking.[52]

Thus, it can be seen that toward the end of the amir's reign the small bureaucracy of Afghanistan expanded to an unprecedented degree. Its well-structured central diwan contained built-in checks against the rise of an individual official to an overall powerful position; but because of the unfair structure of salary and the extremely low rate of pay for the great majority of the *mirzas* the bureaucracy was inefficient, and embezzlement and corruption became a main feature.

Outside the central diwan was the *panchayat* (commercial court) where disputes between individual merchants were settled. The majority of its members were Muslims and Hindus from Afghanistan; others were Hindus from Shikarpur in India. The *panchayat* was for a long time presided over by Dost ʾAli Shah Foshanji as *panchayat bashi*.[53] To give a national characteristic to this semi-international court, the amir removed Dost ʾAli Shah and Kashmiri and Indian members and appointed five merchants from Kabul in their stead[54] with Mir Afzal Baburi as its president. This arrangement was in line with the amir's commercial policy, which, among other things, favored the interests of Afghan merchants over those of foreign merchants. Whatever its composition, however, and whoever the *panchayat bashi*, the court did not influence the amir's commercial policy, even though its members were rich and socially important and bore the titles of mulla, sayyed, and *khwaja*.[55]

The *qafila bashi* (chief of transport) was responsible for making transport arrangements for military and civil purposes, while at the same time collecting certain taxes from the merchants.[56] In Kabul, justice was administered by the chief justice (*khan-i-mulla* or *khan-i-ʾulum*) who had under him the qazis of the appeal court and muftis (advisers to the qazis). Amir ʾAbd al-Rahman accepted the limitation of the Shariʾa on his power, and did not try to set the khan-i-ʾulum aside. Indeed, it was his policy to increase the power of the qazis in general by extending the Shariʾa throughout the country and by authorizing them to indict both those whom they thought might endanger the country and those whom they knew to be destroying property and the Muslim population.[57] Thus the authority of the qazis became almost unlimited, in spite of the fact that they were provided with manuals of instructions, *Asas al-Quzzat*, in which the extent and scope of their legal discretion and the procedure for trying cases were fixed and laid down in detail. They were required to settle cases in accordance with the Shariʾa as expounded by the great classical jurist, Abu Hanifa (d. 767). The interpretations of other classical jurists were considered to be valid only when they were found to be in agreement with those of Abu Hanifa.[58] The Hanifi system of law was applied also to cases arising among the Shiʾite population of Afghanistan.

By giving so much authority to the qazis, the amir intended to suppress crime, especially murder, which occurred very frequently in Afghanistan. The khan-i-ʾulum, however, was unwilling to pass harsh sentences unless cases were tried strictly in accordance with the Shariʾa, which required an elaborate procedure and a long time; the amir stood for quick and harsh decisions. Also, the sentences that the khan-i-ʾulum passed were usually the opposite of what the amir had expected. In 1866, for instance, when in a murder case the amir's intention was the sentencing of the accused, the khan-i-ʾulum told the amir that "the case had not been proved according to Mohammaden law." Also, when "taken to task for giving an unjust conviction in a murder case he [the khan-i-ʾulum] excused himself for not having heard the evidence correctly on account of the noise in Court."[59]

Again, the khan-i-ʾulum, contrary to the amir's view (a death sentence for a man and a woman accused of adultery), declared that an accused man had not been found guilty and he should be set free.[60] Having failed to influence the khan-i-ʾulum to settle criminal cases as he wished, the amir thereafter settled most such cases himself, without recourse to the court. He personally settled cases of adultery and usually passed death sentences on those who were accused of it.[61] He applied severe torture (fanah) in the hope of finding the truth and reducing the crime rate. The torture was so severe that many of the accused admitted to crimes that they had not committed. Mistaken judgment was then not infrequent.[62] Cases which were left to the court to settle were those arising out of inheritance of property (a major source of disputes) and property belonging to a waqf (religious foundation) and those relating to orphans and their guardians. In other words, criminal cases were settled by the amir and legal and civil cases were referred to the Shariʾa court. This division cut the jurisdiction of the khan-i-ʾulum considerably and legality lost much of its significance.

The only official whom the amir respected to a certain extent, however, was Sardar ʾAbd al-Rahman Barakzay, the khan-i-ʾulum, whose family had held the office of qazi for "several generations,"[63] that is, since the reign of Shah Mahmud Sadozay.[64] Before that time Qazi Fayz Allah of the Dawlat Shah tribe and others had held this office. At one time during the reign of Amir ʾAbd al-Rahman, besides Khan-i-ʾUlum Sardar ʾAbd al-Rahman, his sons and an uncle were the qazis of the courts of Jalalabad, Ghazni, and Kandahar. Although his brother Qazi ʾAbd al-Salam had supported Sardar Muhammad Ayyub against the amir, the khan-i-ʾulum had supported the amir and held the office of qazi without interruption until his death in 1897. In contrast to the amir, who often overrode law for political considerations, the khan-i-ʾulum observed the Shariʾa in strictest terms. Although at one time he was accused of being corrupt, on the whole, he maintained a high standard of morality. It was mainly through his scholarly modesty and strength of character that he was able to maintain the court free of outside interference[65] during a most critical period of Afghan history when it could have easily become a subordinate organ of the state.

Under Amir ʾAbd al-Rahman the kotwali (roughly similar to a ministry of interior) became far more extensive and important than it had been at any time in the past. It has remained so more or less to the present day. During the amir's reign it dealt with all kinds of civil affairs in any way connected to the security of the country. At times, even military cases were also disposed of by the amir through the kotwali. The full significance of this ministry will be better comprehended when it is borne in mind that the military operations during the first decade of the amir's reign were supplemented by a rule of terror exercised through the kotwali. The kotwali was, in fact, the department that enforced the authority of the other departments by means other than the purely military. Cases of lesser importance were decided by the kotwal (head of the kotwali), while the serious ones were presented through him to the amir.[66] In the 1880s the department was administered by Kotwal Parwana Khan and Naʾib Kotwal Mir Sultan Afshar and in the 1890s by various others, notably Mirza Muhammad Hussayn Khan and Mirza ʾAbd al-Rauf as joint *kotwals.* The most powerful and notorious of these officials was Naʾib Sultan Afshar, whose tenure of office ran parallel to the rebellions in the country. It is then necessary to briefly describe his role as a *naʾib kotwal.*

Mir Sultan was a Qizilbash of obscure parentage from Kandahar. Although only a deputy *kotwal,* his orders about security matters were obeyed throughout the country not only by the populace, but also by government officials, including the qazis. What was said to be the maintenance of security actually led to the ruin of well-to-do people, particularly those who were the well-wishers of the family of Amir Sher ʾAli. In this period no individual felt secure in his life and property. People complained that the *naʾib kotwal* dispatched the police "at the door of the house of every family which was tolerably well off."[67] By various inhumane methods he eliminated hostile elements and instituted a reign of terror previously unheard of in Afghanistan. At Kabul, the door of the suspect person was knocked on at night, and the person was disposed of by special executioners. This practice came to be called *nam girak* (name-calling).[68] Also, *naʾib kotwal* could and did offer female prisoners to friends as presents. He was, in short, said to have exercised absolute power[69] in security and criminal matters, so much so that finally discontent became widespread and senior officials informed the amir of Mir Sultan's atrocities. Some of them even believed that the *naʾib kotwal* was the root of all the disturbances and that by his removal the disturbances would be over. The *khan-i-ʾulum,* Kabul *kotwal,* and the *khazanadar* even suggested to the amir that he should be handed over to the people.[70] Sardar Habib Allah also held a similar view[71] and was determined to bring about the downfall of Mir Sultan. Nevertheless, the amir still remained exceptionally lenient toward the *naʾib kotwal,* saying, "he is a well wisher and on account of him my Government has benefitted very much."[72] That the *naʾib kotwal* was a "very wicked man"[73] and went far beyond the limits was no doubt true, but it was impossible for him to do so without the explicit knowledge and permission of the amir. To the amir[74] and his rival critics[75] the reply of the *naʾib kotwal* was that he simply carried out the amir's order. In private he expressed the fear that "if he failed to satisfy [the amir's] greed" he himself would be killed.[76] Caught up between such pressures he went on with his job until discontent reached such a point even the amir was no longer willing to protect him. Indeed, by then the program of liquidation that the amir had earlier instituted had been completed, and the *naʾib kotwal* had outlived his usefulness. The amir, then, for the first time consulted his advisers about the fate of his once most powerful official. He asked them, "This Naib Sultan is a man who has put about 60,000 persons to death. I tell you people present here that only 15 or 20 persons were sentenced by myself, and all others have been killed by Naʾib Sultan out of lust for money. I therefore ask you for an expression of opinion as to what punishment should be ordered to such a man."[77] The assembly was unanimously in favor of the death sentence. Shortly afterward Mir Sultan, once the most powerful official in Afghanistan, was publicly hanged in Paghman.[78]

Prisons and Punishment

Under Amir ʾAbd al-Rahman, imprisonment and punishment, which continued to be carried out through the *kotwali*, became a distinct feature of the administration. There is no information available concerning the number of prisons in Afghanistan before the amir's reign, but imprisonment must have been seldom practiced, since the district of Jalalabad had no jail.[79] In the amir's reign imprisonment and the infliction of severe punishment were widely practiced.

In 1882 there were "several prisons" in Kabul. By 1890 their number had increased to sixty. Still later a very large jail, accommodating nine thousand prisoners, was ordered to be built in Dehmazang, a suburb of Kabul. The most famous prisons were in the Bala Hisar (the seat of the Afghan rulers that had been destroyed in the Second Anglo-Afghan War), the Arg (the new royal palace), and the *kotwali*. Some serais and government buildings situated in various parts of the city were also used as prisons. There were, in addition, a number of *siah chahs* (dark deep pits) in the Bala Hisar and the Arg. In each provincial and district capital there were one or two prisons, enough to accommodate one hundred prisoners, the maximum number to be kept in each district at a time.[80] The city of Herat, in addition to a large prison, also had a *siah chah*.[81]

People were imprisoned for a wide range of reasons. Political prisoners included those who had participated in rebellions or were the sympathizers of the family of the late amir or were accused of spying for the British. Others included those who either had not paid revenue arrears to the government or were accused of crimes. Government officials who were accused of embezzlement or informers who had passed on false information were also jailed. As the people of Ningrahar complained to the amir, "There was no discrimination made between minor and serious offenses in terms of imprisonment awarded."[82] Members of both sexes, including children and the aged, were imprisoned. The sons and daughters of the sardars were put in separate jails, but the "unmarried and beautiful daughters of respectable people were kept in the serai of Zikrya, commonly known as the Pari Khana (the Fairy House). These last-mentioned prisoners were especially well clothed and well fed, and Sardar Habib Allah and the *naʾib kotwal* had sexual intercourse with them.[83] At times whole families and tribal sects were put in jail.

The total number of prisoners varied from time to time. In June 1882 there were fifteen hundred prisoners in Kabul, most of whom were elders from Herat, Kandahar, and other areas. Three years later their number reached ten thousand.[84] During the Ghilzay Rebellion there were twelve thousand prisoners in Kabul alone.[85] In 1890, according to an official list, there were fourteen thousand in Kabul.[86] Six years later their number was reported to be twenty thousand. Subsequently this number was reduced first to eighteen thousand and then to eight thousand, but in 1898 there were said to be seventy thousand prisoners in Kabul.[87] The last figure is doubtful. The total number of prisoners in the reign of the amir, no doubt, exceeded that limit, but it is unlikely that so many prisoners were left in prisons at any one time for three reasons: First, the daily consumption by those who were supported by the state was very high.[88] Second, there was always a shortage of accommodation,[89] so much so that at times some prisoners slept by turns at night.[90] Third, because of their intolerable conditions prisoners frequently revolted in an attempt to escape.[91]

For these reasons prisoners were regularly disposed of in many ways so that their numbers were reduced to a manageable size. To begin with, perhaps the largest number of prisoners were deported. The policy was to remove prisoners to regions away from their own. Usually those from the districts south of Kabul were deported to Turkestan and Qataghan.[92] In Qataghan a penal colony was formed. Prisoners from the north were sent south. In 1890, for instance, 1,235 prisoners from Shighnan and Chardara[93] and 7,000 members of the Shaykh 'Ali Hazaras[94] were deported toward Logar, Charkh, Wardak, and Kohdaman. In addition, 1,300 prisoners from the Shaykh 'Ali Hazaras were "distributed as slaves" among the various Durrani clans in Kandahar.[95] Conversely, in 1882 1,000 elders from Herat and Kandahar, who had been kept as prisoners, were removed to Kunduz.

A second method of disposing of prisoners was execution. Before the revolt of Sardar Muhammad Ishaq, executions were carried out somewhat secretly; only the most dangerous prisoners were put to death openly. After this revolt, however, executions were carried out openly and on a mass scale.[96] Poisoning prisoners was, however, continually practiced—sometimes at the rate of three to four,[97] or even seven a day. To this category of poisoned prisoners belonged political prisoners, in particular the elders.

Third, prisoners were released from time to time not so much because they were found innocent, as for political considerations. During the Ghilzay Rebellion, for example, when he felt he needed the support of the common people, the amir, in addition to making his rule more lenient, ordered the release of most old prisoners. Releases were also made when the amir (who sometimes made enquiry about the cases of five hundred prisoners daily) or his sons recovered from illnesses. During religious holidays prisoners were also freed. At times the release of prisoners was made conditional on the payment of fines.[98] For the release, for example, of five thousand four hundred Turkestani prisoners in Kabul a fine of two million rupees was demanded.[99] Meanwhile, a large number of Hazara prisoners were sold in free markets. With these and other methods the number of prisoners was sharply brought down within a relatively short time. For example, in 1888, out of twelve thousand prisoners previously in Kabul only fifteen hundred were left.[100] The death rate among prisoners was very high. According to an official report, a total of three hundred prisoners died in Kabul between 1 January and 30 April 1886.[101] The outbreak of epidemic diseases greatly reduced the number of prisoners at intervals. As Frank Martin puts it, "There is absolutely no thought of sanitation, and the prisoners are herded together in a house that has perhaps been used as a prison for twenty or thirty years, and never cleaned. Consequently, typhus and other diseases are common among prisoners, and typhus alone will very often sweep off seventy to eighty per cent of the men confined there, and the wonder is that all do not die."[102]

The commonest forms of punishment included the cutting off of hands and tongues, sewing up of lips, gouging out of eyes, and putting boiling oil on scalps. As a warning to others a few prisoners were put in iron cages and left to hang in public places until they perished. The famous cage that was hung on the Lata Band Pass contained a Ghilzay thief sentenced for stealing a few fowl in Kabul.[103] For hanging condemned prisoners, three gallows were erected, one in Kabul and two in Kandahar (in the Sardeh Park).[104] The nearest relations and associates of the prisoners were also punished.

Obtaining confession through a variety of tortures was widely practiced.[105] According to an observer

❖

cruelty of all sorts is common in the way of torture. Imagine a prison where the limbs which have been hacked off men were left lying about, together with the dismembered bodies of those dead, of the suffering inflicted on them, until the whole place reeks of decomposing flesh, and then consider the frame of mind of hundreds who are imprisoned without trial . . . who daily live in the midst of these horrors. If the truth about the Kabul prisons were generally known, other countries would probably unite in insisting on such barbarity being stopped.[106]

❖

By these and other similar methods the crime rate fell sharply and the amir told Lord Curzon in 1895 that fewer murders were committed in Afghanistan than in Britain. This statement was probably true; but, as Curzon observed, the paucity of crime in Afghanistan was "due neither to respect for law nor to excellence of administration, but to the reign of terror" and to the terrible tortures inflicted upon persons suspected of crimes.[107]

The Problem of the Refugees

In the eighties an unknown, but very large, number of influential people who had opposed the amir for various reasons either fled or were banished to India, Bukhara, and Persia. Broadly speaking, these people included followers of the family of Amir Sher ʾAli and of Sardar Muhammad Ishaq. Nearly all important Durrani, particularly Muhammadzay, sardars took refuge abroad. A significant number of Ghilzay and other elders also left the country for various other reasons.[108] As a result of this and of the liquidation of the remaining leading men inside the country, it was generally feared that Afghanistan could not remain independent. Mulla Najm al-Din of Hadda expressed the concern that if the British advanced on Afghanistan they were likely to occupy it without opposition. Safdar Khan of Nawagai (an ally of the amir) believed that the amir recognized the truth of the mulla's statement and was determined to recall most of the Afghan refugees in exile.[109] No doubt Safdar Khan's statement reflected the truth, but only partly. The real reason for the recall of Afghan refugees from abroad was that by the end of the first decade of his reign the amir had firmly established himself on the throne and no longer feared his former opponents. Indeed to consolidate his government the amir needed their services. Also, by recalling the refugees, he intended to weaken the position of Sardar Muhammad Ayyub and to build up at home the shaken position of the Muhammadzays under his own leadership. Actually the need for this consolidation had first been felt during the Ghilzay Revolt, which had been seen as a menace to the Muhammadzay rule. Hence, Amir ʾAbd al-Rahman recalled the most important Muhammadzay refugees in India, except for Sardar Muhammad Ayyub and the former amir, on the condition of their loyalty to his dynasty.[110] Similarly all Afghan refugees in Bukhara and Samarqand, except Sardar Muhammad Ishaq, were allowed to return.[111] It was only in the reign of the amir's son and successor, however, that all Afghan refugees were invited to come back on the promise of the restoration of their property and land, a further promise of loans (taqawi), and a temporary reduction of state revenue.[112]

The amir's reign was also distinguished from those of his predecessors by his enlargement of the darbar. The main office attached to the darbar was the secretariat (dar al-insha). That the amir's political correspondence was conducted through this office[113] and that its chief secretary acted as the amir's secretary for foreign affairs gave it its importance. The structure of the secretariat was horizontal, but the head of the Farsi section, the largest section, was its chief secretary (dabir al-mulk), who conducted the Amir's correspondence, with the assistance of many other head secretaries (mir munshis), among them a Hindu.

As in the past, so in the reign of Amir ʾAbd al-Rahman, the office of the dabir al-mulk was held by the Qizilbashes, among them Mirza Muhammad Nabi, whose ancestors had served Amir Dost Muhammad and Amir Sher ʾAli Khan in that capacity. Mirza Muhammad Nabi, a reserved, refined, and intelligent man who was well versed in Persian composition, kept himself aloof from high-level intrigues and attached himself to the amir who trusted him very much in spite of the fact that his father, Mirza Muhammad Hussayn, had belonged to the party of

Amir Sher ʾAli and on that account had left the country for Persia. The *dabir al-mulk* was present at all the high-level meetings held between the amir and the viceroy in India. The amir's version of the meetings was composed by him and published under the title of *Sawal wa Jawab-i-Dawlati*. It was probably for this service that he was awarded the title of *naʾib al-sultanat*.[114] After his death in 1892, his son was given the post but was soon dismissed and succeeded by Amir Abul Qasim, also a Qizilbash, who held the office till the end of the amir's reign.[115] The head of the English department was Sultan Mahomed, who in 1897 was succeeded as *mir munshi* by the amir's physician, Dr. Abd al-Ghani. Mulla Muhammad Khan from Laghman, head of the Pashto section, was responsible for drafting the amir's firmans and pamphlets into Pashto.[116]

The next most important office attached to the darbar was the office of the *ashik aghasi* (gentleman usher). His principal duty was to present those persons who wished to call on the amir, as well as to make arrangements for the execution of the king's judgment.[117] In particular, the significance of his office lay in his duty to invite and summon members of the council and to arrange their seats in accordance with their grades. A subordinate officer, *omla bashi*, delivered a summons to these members; and the *qabuch bashi*, another officer, introduced them to the *ashik aghasi* who, in turn, either presented them to the amir or conducted them to their seats in the darbar.[118]

Sardar ʾAbd al-Quddus, son of Sardar Sultan Muhammad by a Negro wife,[119] was the most famous of the *ashik aghasis*. He joined the amir's cause at an early date and helped him in expelling Sardar Muhammad Ayyub by occupying Herat in 1881 from his base in Turkestan. For about a year the sardar governed that province with great authority. Then he was dismissed and placed in confinement in Kabul. The reason for his sudden downfall was that he had strengthened his position by making marriage alliances with the influential families of Herat, and the amir feared a possible coalition between Sardar ʾAbd al-Quddus and Sardar Muhammad Ishaq. Only when Ishaq was expelled was Sardar ʾAbd al-Quddus restored to authority and placed in charge of the pacification of the Hazarajat. In the course of this assignment he acted strangely for a while,[120] but in 1892 he was appointed *ashik aghasi*, a post that he retained until the amir's death. Sardar ʾAbd al-Quddus was a man of little education[121] and of conservative disposition, strongly opposed to modernism.[122] During the nineties he had great influence with the amir and acted as a spokesman for the Muhammadzay sardars.

The ʾ*arz begi* (officers presenting petitions) presented the petitions, oral or written, of the individual plaintiffs by voice to the amir;[123] the *mir akhor* (head of the government stables) looked after the government transport animals. When Sardar ʾAbd Allah Tokhay, formerly governor of Badakhshan, was placed in charge of it, he was given the pompous title of chief of the *mir akhors* of the royal stable (*salar-i-mir akhoran-i-istable-i-shahi*).[124]

Other Influential Elements

Normally, the amir did not seek the advice of other people. At critical times, however, he turned to a few influential wise men. Sometimes he also sounded out his foreign employees; but at no time did he turn for advice on domestic affairs to the British. Neither did the latter choose to pressure him. In fact throughout his reign the amir was free to govern his subjects after his own fashion.

Among the first group of advisers were the amir's central Asian Muslim associates from his days of exile; these were Pashtuns, Uzbeks, and Tajiks. Among them only a few were men of high standing. The first was Mir Sora Beg, former mir of Kulab (beyond the Oxus), who had been driven off by the padshah of Bukhara. Sora Beg, however, did not show much interest in politics. At Zimma in 1880 he attended the meetings but preferred to doze off in a corner rather than to listen to the serious discussions between the amir and the British political officer, Lepel Griffin. By contrast, another person of this group, Zain Khan Popalzay, showed keen interest in politics and the amir consulted him frequently in the early years of his reign. Although he had spent his childhood in Russian Turkestan and held the rank of captain in the Russian army, Zain Khan was perhaps the most pro-British adviser the amir ever had.[125] Even before the amir was given a regular grant and while Anglo-Afghan relations had cooled, Zain Khan impressed on the amir the advisability of maintaining good relations with Britain. He assured him that the British government "have never shown so much kindness, or proved as great friend to any other Amir," and advised him to "Look upon the British Government as your patron."[126] Zain Khan, also, frequently advised the amir on internal affairs in similar terms,[127] whereas no other person was allowed to speak in such a manner. In May 1882, Zain Khan left for Samarqand to fetch his family but was not heard of again.

During the brief period of the honeymoon between the amir and the Ghilzays a few of the Ghilzay elders, notably ʾIsmat Allah Jabar Khel and Mulla ʾAbd al-Karim Andar, were consulted. The former, who was given the title of mir-i-Afghan, was especially consulted at the time of the amir's confrontation with Sardar Muhammad Ayyub; but after that, and particularly after the escape of Sardar Muhammad Ishaq in 1888, such elders lost credit with the amir altogether. Thereafter he occasionally consulted a few insignificant Muhammadzay sardars, among them Sardar Shams al-Din Khan of Besud (in Jalalabad)[128] and Mawlawi Ahmad Jan Alkozay of Kandahar. During the nineties, the amir through Sardar ʾAbd al-Quddus Khan was in close association with the Muhammadzay sardars, but there was no one among them who could influence the amir in any significant way.

From the midnineties onward, the noted umra khan of Jandol, who had taken asylum in Kabul after his unsuccessful invasion of Chitral in 1895, was frequently consulted in state affairs, presumably those relating to tribal affairs beyond the Durand Line. Although he had been the amir's main rival in the past, ʾAbd al-Rahman treated him well and conferred on him the title of *naʾib salar*. But he was not allowed, despite his request, to lead the great tribal uprising of 1897.[129]

Of the ʾulama Mulla Saʾid Muhammad, alias Mulla Khosa of Laghman, a scholar of conservative views who was given the task of examining the stipendary mullas in religious subjects, carried considerable influence with the amir. Mulla Khosa endorsed the amir's system of government, in general, and the amir enforced a strict Islamic discipline with regard to prayer, fast, and public morality. It was through Mulla Khosa that the amir tried, albeit not always successfully, to declare certain insurgent tribes and persons rebels. Other more noted members of the ʾulama, such as Mulla Najm al-Din and Mulla Mushk-i-ʾAlam, advised the amir to treat his subjects leniently, but the amir resented their advice. The result was that the amir's religious pronouncements were drafted and decisions on religious subjects reached mainly in consultation with the most conservative and the least known of the ʾulama.

Among the foreign employees of the amir a few were also occasionally consulted. Salter Pyne, a Cockney engineer from London, who helped to set up a series of arms factories in Kabul, stood high. The amir spoke of him as "a true friend of the King of Afghanistan." In the darbar to which he was frequently admitted he was allowed to occupy a seat among senior officials. Pyne, for his part, did his best to develop factories and train Afghan artisans. His sincere and successful efforts endeared him to the amir to the extent that the amir gradually confided in him in political affairs and treated him with fatherly affection. In the critical days of the early nineties before the arrival of the Durand Mission at Kabul, he carried the amir's autograph letter to the viceroy;[130] and, at the suggestion of the amir, his slow marches to India helped to postpone the proposed arrival in Kabul of a large military mission under General Frederick Roberts, whom the amir was loath to receive. Later, Pyne also carried to William Gladstone and others letters in which the amir proposed the establishment of a direct relationship with Britain. Pyne's role in creating an atmosphere of good understanding between Afghanistan and Britain was very significant. In addition, for the successful outcome of the British mission, Pyne advised Mortimer Durand that the amir "would care more for a little help in this way [military help] than for cession in Waziristan."[131] Durand wrote of him that Pyne "is a very useful man. It is amusing to feel that the mission is being personally conducted by a little Cockney trader . . . , but, though he seems to me to make a slip at times, he has done so much to improve our relations with the Amir."[132] It was probably for this service that upon return to London he was knighted.

The highly paid English geologist employed by the amir, C. L. Griesbach, was more interested in Afghan politics and mapping Afghanistan for the benefit of the British than in the task for which he was employed, discovering mineral resources.[133] By profession, he was an army officer and had fought in the battle of Maiwand. Aware of Captain Griesbach's real mission, the amir often, while playing chess with him until late at night (in the play the captain always came off worse), discussed international politics with him in the hope of inducing him to make favorable recommendations to his government. Captain Griesbach, however, followed the pro-British line so rigidly that the amir, in Griesbach's words, " accused me of only looking upon the subject from a selfish English point of view, whereas he wished to keep his country rather than save India."[134] To Griesbach's suggestion of stationing British officers along the frontiers of Herat with Russia and the necessity of the Afghan and British army fighting together against the probable Russian invading army in the area, the amir's reply was that "I consider it most unlikely that the Afghans will agree to fight side by side [with the British] against a common enemy," because, as the amir put it, by invading Afghanistan the English "have revived the old hatred, which the Afghans have been bearing them since the old war of 1840."[135] The amir's scheme was to do away with that animosity and to effect a reconciliation. He impressed on Griesbach that some principal men of both countries should get together and hold conferences either in Afghanistan or in the border areas.[136] Until the arrival at Kabul of the Durand Mission, the amir referred to this theme time and time again in his correspondence with the viceroy. On another point Griesbach's suggestion, however, impressed the amir, who modified his original plan of building forty military posts along the frontiers with Russia from Shighnan to Zulfikar to building one strong fort at Shadian near Mazar and strengthening the defences of Herat.[137]

Frank Martin, Pyne's successor, was also frequently received at the darbar; but, except for his submission to the amir of a plan for the exploitation of the mineral resources of the country (a plan which was not implemented),[138] he does not seem to have offered suggestions. Instead, the amir tried to impress him by giving him long lectures in the hope that like Griesbach he too would convey them to his government. In this case the most useful outcome was Martin's book *Under the Absolute Amir.*

Chapter III
The Local
Government

Before 1880 provincial governors had exercised extensive authority, but under Amir 'Abd al-Rahman, they lost their former role, in spite of the enlargement of the system of local government and the weakening of the position of local magnates. Also the federal type of administration characteristic of the past was replaced by a centralized form of government that, with subsequent consolidation, continues to the present day.

Historical Background

During the reign of Ahmad Shah, and even more so under his successors, a provincial governor was "rather a party in an unequal alliance than a subject"[1] and acted practically independently. All that the central government expected of him was the maintenance of peace and order in the province and the regular payment of state dues into the central treasury after he had deducted the expenses of the province.[2] In the province, only the sardar, as commander of the regular troops, was in a position to restrain the governor; but this happened rarely since the governor and sardar were usually the same person. Frequently, both offices were held by a prince who was authorized both to read the khutba and to issue coins.[3] This system gave too much authority to governors and often led to anarchy, especially after the death of a monarch. The Barakzay rulers maintained a similar system, and Amir Dost Muhammad Khan further strengthened the position of provincial governors by appointing his own sons to these posts. His governor-sons considered the provinces their own possessions and acted as "lesser kings."[4] For this reason Amir Dost Muhammad's death was followed by a protracted period of civil war among his sons until Amir Sher 'Ali overcame his rival brothers. He then directed his main efforts toward establishing central authority over the provinces and accomplished this by creating a large standing army and appointing mainly non-Barakzays as provincial governors. Amir 'Abd al-Rahman Khan developed this policy still further until the central authority was fully recognized in the provinces.

Main Features of the Local Government under Amir 'Abd al-Rahman

Amir 'Abd al-Rahman systematically split the provinces into smaller units. Only the Kabul province was enlarged; but, as it was, in fact, ruled by the amir himself, this action had the effect of increasing the authority of the central government. The Kabul province itself was divided into smaller districts such as those of Jalalabad, Kunar, Laghman, and Ghazni. These units were mostly independent of each other and each sent its revenue directly to Kabul.

Another feature of provincial administration under the amir was that no governor was allowed to wield both military and civil powers. The governors had only a small number of armed *khassadars* (militia) under them. In emergencies governors relied upon the army stationed in the provinces. Since rebellions were frequent in the reign of the amir the army ultimately increased its power at the expense of the governors.

The amir appointed unambitious and insignificant governors who had little or no tribal backing. Following the accession when he was facing strong opposition the amir appointed such important men as Sardar Muhammad Ishaq, Sardar 'Abd al-Quddus, Sardar 'Abd al-Rasul, and Sardar Muhammad Yusuf, as governors of Turkestan, Tashqurghan, Jalalabad, and Farah; but as soon as the situation warranted it they were all, except Ishaq, removed and their posts given to the amir's own men. The tenure of the governors was usually short since the amir frequently dismissed and disgraced them and confiscated their property. A few were even put to death. The amir's policy towards his governors is well illustrated by the humorous response to his appointment a governor made by a friend of the amir from his days of exile: On being told of his appointment, Kata Khan Uzbek ordered his servants to fetch all his household property. In reply to a question from the amir, Kata Khan said that "the destiny of a Governor in Afghanistan was the confiscation of his property and the loss of his life; in order to save his own [life] he preferred to sacrifice his property beforehand."[5]

The amir did not send his eldest sons as governors to the provinces, although this had been the custom and was requested by the elders of several provinces.

Administrative Units

Under Amir Sher ʾAli Khan, Afghanistan was divided into the provinces (wilayats) of Kabul, Kandahar, Herat, and Afghan Turkestan. The position of Farah was uncertain. Formerly it had been a part of Herat, but Amir Sher ʾAli made it into a separate province and placed it under his cousin Sardar Muhammad Afzal. Whether the latter paid revenue to the central government is not certain.

Amir ʾAbd al-Rahman enlarged the province of Kabul and made the others smaller. Afghan Turkestan, which in the reign of Amir Sher ʾAli had included all territories between the Oxus and the Hindu Kush, was divided into the several provinces of Maimana, Turkestan, and Badakhshan, made administratively dependent on the province of Kabul.[6] Farah, Girishk, Zamindawar, and Chakhansur, which had been dependencies of Kandahar or Herat, were similarly annexed to Kabul.[7] Later, Uruzgan and Kafiristan were also incorporated into Kabul. Thus Kabul, in spite of its loss of some territories as a result of the Durand Agreement, remained virtually a kingdom in itself.

Each province was divided into districts (tapas) whose boundaries, before 1880, were fixed more or less on tribal lines. In Ghazni, for instance, these were known as the tapas of Tajik, Wardak, Hazara, and so forth.[8] Although the amir increased the number of these districts to over ninety-seven,[9] some were still as large as provinces.[10]

Each province was ruled by a governor who was nominally the amir's lieutenant or naʾib. Except for the governor of Herat who was called naʾib al-hukuma (viceroy or naʾib of the government) the rest were called by the modest titles of hukumran or hakim.[11] The mir of Maimana still retained his traditional title of wali. The heads of districts were invariably called hakims.

Governors and Councils

As naʾibs of the amir, governors had the same subordinate officials as the amir had in Kabul. The ranks of provincial officials were, of course, lower; but the governors' darbars were the highest in the provinces.[12] Although the amir had urged governors to consult wise men, either government officials or local elders, in practice governors did not hold regular councils. Only occasionally did they feel it necessary to consult others about the affairs of the government. The amir once actually set up a council composed of government officials and some elders for the governor of Jalalabad,[13] but this was only an isolated case and it did not last long.

Among such senior government officials as the qazi and sardaftari governors acted more like the first among equals than bosses. Indeed governors were warned not to interfere in the affairs either of the court[14] or of the diwan.[15] Neither were they permitted to spend government money liberally. The qazis were even authorized to report to Kabul governors who insisted on interfering in the affairs of the court or exercising tyranny over their subjects.[16]

Notwithstanding these limitations, governors enjoyed considerable authority in matters of security and revenue. In addition, the increase in the tribal levies, the extension of the government authority to remote areas, and the amir's program of reforming some aspects of the society enhanced the authority of governors in proportion. If governors were made impotent in relation to the central government and had no control over the army stationed in their own provinces, they still acted as little despots over the populace in general. The new significance of the office of governors, in fact, lay in the unprecedented expansion of the power of the state.

Governors were, for instance, authorized to imprison both seal makers who had not obtained licenses to practice their profession[17] and forgers of documents.[18] Those who sheltered the banished refugees or their messengers or held correspondence with them or spied for them or took part in rebellions[19] were also jailed by the order of governors. They even had the permission to imprison those persons who were suspected of "intending to shoot other people" and those who uttered swearwords. In some cases, even the *khassadars* were authorized to imprison persons suspected of committing an offence.[20] Governors were also empowered to extract undertakings from elders and villagers for the safety of roads passing through their localities and for reporting to the authorities the arrival of strangers and robbers in their villages.[21] If elders and villagers failed to do these things, governors were allowed to imprison them. Similarly, in cases of abduction, murder, extortion of blood money, robbery, adultery, and even quarrels that entailed no revenge or blood money governors were given wide power.

The Qazis and the Courts

In Afghanistan, the office of the qazis, who settled cases in accordance with Islamic jurisprudence, was as old as the Islamic state. In Afghanistan the qazis functioned in the main cities. By tradition Afghan rulers permitted the qazis to sit beside them and to settle civil cases, whereas the rulers disposed of the state affairs.[22] In the countryside, where government had little or no power, justice was administered by anyone who was known to be well versed in Islamic laws.[23] Disputes were referred to local mullas, who were paid small fees for their settlement of cases. In the cities a few qazis had salaries from the treasury.[24] The scope of the function of the qazis and others who settled cases in accordance with the Shari'a was limited, however, since, in addition to the problem of few courts, a crime was referred to these courts only when it was not acknowledged by the accused. Acknowledged crimes were most frequently settled by jirgas. Taken as a whole, disputes were settled mainly in accordance with customary, rather than Islamic, laws.[25]

In the amir's reign qazis, assisted by one or two muftis[26] as advisers in legal affairs, were appointed in the districts where *hakims* presided. As a result of the extension of government authority in the Hazarajat and Kafiristan the number of qazis was still further increased. The employment of qualified qazis and muftis became a problem, and candidates were then required to pass a test in the Islamic laws.[27] Afghan graduates from foreign madrasas were regarded with suspicion and scholars from other Muslim lands were suspected of being either Wahhabis (members of a sect of Muslim puritans) or spies.[28] The posts of qazi and mufti went solely to the Sunni mullas who had graduated from the local and royal madrasas.[29] Consequently most offices of the qazis and muftis were held by Pashtuns. The amir tried to see that the holders of high offices of judgment looked dignified. They were instructed to be well dressed and to have a sober demeanor in public.[30] They were paid adequate salaries and not allowed to accept either presents or invitations from others, except their nearest relatives or the amir, although the muftis were allowed to accept presents and invitations. Both were restrained from intimidating the parties who presented their cases to them.[31] Elaborate and, in fact, impractical regulations were laid down about the mood in which the qazis were to pass judgment. They were, for instance, restrained from hearing cases or passing judgment when hungry, thirsty, riding, sleepy, lustful, or unwell.[32] They were to spend all their spare time in studying Islamic law and correcting cases in accordance with the classical authorities.[33] Like other government officials the qazis and muftis had to undertake to perform their duties honestly.[34]

The qazis had considerable freedom in the performance of their duties, and the *hakims* were not allowed to interfere in the affairs of the courts. In such cases as the registration of confiscated property or taking of undertakings from elders for security reasons the *hakims* were instructed to work in collaboration with the qazis.[35] Once a case was referred to a qazi he was free from outside interference.

The decision of the qazis was subject to reconsideration only when a party to the case appealed or the amir was informed that the case had not been settled properly. The source of the final appeal was the amir, who, advised by the 'ulama, reviewed cases brought to his attention.[36] If it was found that the qazis had misjudged they were made to pay the damage done to the wronged party.[37] Some qazis showed independence of mind and passed judgments not in accordance with the firmans of the amir when they thought that the firmans were not in line with Islamic law. Mulla Mustafa, qazi of Maimana, for instance, punished a couple of adulterers not by stoning them to death (*rajim*) as was required by the amir's firman, but by whipping them. The autocratic amir did not instantly punish or dismiss the qazi for such independence; instead he resorted to public opinion and let the people of the district know that as the qazi had on many occasions committed anti-Islamic acts, it was now up to them to say whether or not he deserved punishment.[38] Unfortunately nothing further was reported about the matter.

The proceedings of the courts were registered and the reports of the settled cases sent to the capital regularly. People were forbidden to appear armed before the courts[39] and a special day was assigned for women to appear. When the accused was a soldier the case was settled by the *qazi ʾaskar* (military judge).[40] Other than this exception defendants were tried in the courts of the districts to which the parties belonged.

The qazis were to enforce the firman of the former Afghan rulers on problems relating to the Shariʾa, as well as firmans of the Amir ʾAbd al-Rahman, only when they were in line with the Shariʾa. The decision of whether the firmans were in line with Islamic law belonged to the qazis, not the *kotwals* or the governors.[41] It is then apparent that customary laws had no validity in the courts and that the qazis were in a position to reject any ruling, even the amir's firmans, not in line with the Islamic laws. While this ability of the qazis to reject firmans increased the power of the qazis, another ruling that the decisions of the qazis must be in accordance with Islam, not their own judgments,[42] restricted their personal authority and initiative. Thus, they remained imitators of the classic authorities. The judges were instructed to delay the settlement of cases between near relatives in the hope that they might settle their disputes outside the court.[43] In other words, customary laws were still allowed to operate in spite of the fact that the amir had decreed that nobody but the government-appointed qazis and muftis was to settle legal cases. To what extent the jirgas functioned and to what extent the Shariʾa actually was enforced cannot be determined, although it is clear that during this period the Shariʾa was more extensively applied than at any other time in Afghanistan.

Elaborate regulations were laid down for court procedure. Rarely did the accused admit the claim brought against him. In the majority of cases the defendants denied the accusation and the plaintiff was required to present witnesses or, failing that, to make the accused take an oath. Thus oath-taking and witness-calling were the basic components of the court procedure and became the criteria for establishing the truth. A Muslim was required to take an oath on the name of Allah,[44] not by such phrases as "may my wife be divorced." Consequently, the Afghans made light of the name of Allah. It was then decreed that since the Afghans feared the Quran the accused should, in serious cases, swear on it alone.[45] The witnesses were required to state that they had actually witnessed the act committed by the accused, and this requirement led to the hiring of false witnesses in spite of the fact that the qazi could at his discretion find out secretly whether the witnesses spoke the truth. The qazis were also empowered to reject witnesses whom they believed to be dishonest.[46] Cross-examination was not attempted, and circumstantial evidence and inference were not criteria for establishing the truth.

The disadvantages of the system soon became apparent. Those with means and influence were able to produce false witnesses, while the poor and the uninfluential were unable to find witnesses even in genuine cases. In the Hazarajat, for example, soldiers were called to witness that Hazara girls in the possession of their fellow soldiers had been bought as slaves, whereas in fact this was not so.[47] Similarly, the Sunni population of Herat were able to pressure the Shiʾite Qizilbashes in their day-to-day dealings by the use of false witnesses. Eventually, in strict conformity with the Shariʾa, it was decreed that only those known to be honest men could be accepted as witnesses. This decree did restrict the inherent abuse in the system to a certain extent, but it is doubtful whether it was applied in all cases.

Where the poor could not obtain witnesses, culprits were able to get away with only fines[48] even for such major crimes as murder. For example the crime rate in Kandahar increased as a consequence. Also, the court procedure was so time consuming and expensive that the poor, particularly those from distant localities, abandoned their cases and went to arbitrators outside the courts for settlement. The customary ways of settling disputes still remained. This state was unwelcome to the amir, whose primary concern was to reduce the crime rate. Since he and his governors found it difficult to influence the decisions of the qazis, the amir himself then applied hasty and prompt punishment to culprits, and legality, in consequence, lost its significance.

Towns and Police

Predominantly agricultural Afghanistan had only a few small cities, but these were still big enough to require separate administrative arrangements. The amir, governors, qazis, and other senior officials lived and worked in the cities; but the men directly responsible for their administration were the *kotwals* and the *kalantars*. The *kotwals* were officials appointed by the central government, but the *kalantars* were elected by the residents of each section of the city and were approved in Kabul by the amir and in other cities by the governors. Their terms of office were indefinite, unless their constituents turned against them. The *kalantars* were paid from the public treasury but did not have separate offices under them. They were authorized to settle small disputes, but their main duties were to supervise their respective quarters and to report to the *kotwals* on a wide range of subjects. For example, the *kalantars* had to watch for banished exiles and to report the arrival of strangers and the nature of their business in the cities. In particular *kalantars* were to find out whether newcomers to villages intended to visit relatives or friends or wished to acquire knowledge in the mosques as many people traditionally did. The *kalantars* reported births and also reported deaths regularly so that epidemics could be detected and dealt with. They functioned partly as *muhtasibs* in that they had to dissuade people from smoking hashish (*chars*) and from betting and swearing. The *kalantars* were also to make reports on persons who tried to find followers in order to make themselves *pirs* (religious leaders). At the same time, they were commissioned to introduce to the darbar pious ʾulama who were the well wishers of the state, religion, and Muslims. The *kalantars* also acted as officials in that they certified the *rahdari* (travel permit) issued for travelers and traders and security deeds. The *kalantars* were also authorized to prevent people from assembling except for weddings.[49] They had to see that the streets and drainage canals of their quarters were cleaned and toilets emptied and to make house owners demolish walls that were in danger of collapsing. The Kabul *kalantars* were to be fined 100 rupees each if the streets of their quarters were found dirty.[50] Streets still remained dirty because they had neither proper drainage nor any sanitation system. In addition, the *kalantars* communicated the firmans of the amir to the public and were assigned the impossible task of preventing family quarrels. It was also their task to look after those who fell ill and the families of those who were away traveling, to persuade the unemployed to learn a profession, and to report bad characters to the *kotwals*.[51]

The *kotwal*, or *mir-i-shab* (night master), performed a variety of functions, including the administration of cities. *Kotwals* had under them the police who guarded the streets.[52] The total number of police in the cities is not known, but their number must have been high since in Kabul alone in 1887 six hundred were added to the already existing force. This increase took place in spite of the fact that cities were quiet at night, as people were not allowed to roam about between approximately eight P.M. and sunrise.[53] One consequence of this rigidity was that in cities people did not dare to converse with neighbors or to visit relations after nightfall.[54] In emergencies, residents obtained passwords from the *kotwali* and used lanterns. Offenders were taken to the *kotwals*, who punished them in accordance with the degree of their offences.[55] If the *kotwals* failed to show enough zeal in the performance of their duties they, too, were punished. Sometimes the *kotwals* were even made to offer compensation to those who, because of the *kotwals'* neglect of their duties, had lost property.[56] In this way thefts in the cities, which had occurred frequently in the past, decreased but were not eliminated. Instances of robbery in the cities were reported, but in the new circumstances robbers made the police and the *kalantars* their accomplices by taking passwords from them.[57] Taken as a whole, these new administrative arrangements led to a considerable decrease in crimes, as well as to an increase in the maintenance of order in the cities; but they also led to the association of order with force.

The Muhtasibs

The *muhtasibs* were found where people assembled for Friday prayers and ordinary transactions. They were appointed, therefore, in every part of the city to preach to common people and to advise them on religious and moral matters.[58] It is not known how many there were; but, since every city was supposed to have a chief of the *muhtasibs* and since one *muhtasib* was responsible for each section of the city, their number must have been high—an indication of the amir's program of keeping his Muslim subjects strongly moralistic.

Unlike the *kalantars*, the *muhtasibs* were appointed by government authorities and performed duties under the judiciary more than the *kotwali*.[59] Like the *kalantars* they also received payment from the public treasury. In certain respects, as will be seen, the duties of the *muhtasibs* and *kalantars* overlapped.

Theoretically, the *muhtasibs* were to be wise, just, and well informed about their profession and about what was lawful or unlawful in each denomination of Islam. In reality, most of them were ignorant and, like most government officials of the period, corrupt. Since they were authorized, among other things, to whip Muslims for small offences and since the Afghans knew very little of the religion they professed and observed its ceremonies still less,[60] the position of the *muhtasibs* was of considerable significance. They whipped those offenders who gave them nothing and let off others who bribed them. Even the *muhtasib* of the *ghulam bachas* abused his position until he was imprisoned.[61]

Broadly speaking, the *muhtasibs*[62] were to restrain people from doing what was forbidden and to persuade them to do what was lawful in Islam. Specifically, they were to persuade the Muslims to perform their religious duties and to warn those who neglected them. If a Muslim repeatedly neglected his prayers and did not observe the fast, the *muhtasib* was to administer fifteen lashes to him. Also, the *muhtasibs* were to see that the prayer leaders (*imams*) and callers for prayers (*muwazzins*) performed their duties regularly and to whip those who misbehaved in the mosques. Since the use of abusive and blasphemous words was considered anti-Islamic, offenders were punished in proportion to the social position of the individuals abused. Thus the abuse of a sayyed, a scholar, or a civic leader rendered the offender liable to twenty lashes and a fine of 50 rupees, while that of a trader or a person of similar consequence, ten lashes and 10 rupees, and that of a commoner five lashes only. Those who used blasphemous words against religion, denomination (*mazhab*), nation (*millat*), and faith were to be whipped seventy times for the first offence, imprisoned for the second offence, and executed for the third. It was up to the *muhtasib* to decide for himself whether the words were intended to insult sacred things.

The *muhtasibs* also performed duties that are taken care of today by the police and municipal committees. They were to report to the authorities the arrival in the cities of "seditious men" and the nightly movements in different sections of the cities. Also, they were to see that shopkeepers and other dealers used the correct units of measurement and weight and sold genuine goods without adulterating them. Likewise, they were to watch that the dealers sold their goods in accordance with the rate fixed by the government and did not exact higher prices. Like the *kalantars*, they were empowered to restrain people from betting and to send in birth, death, wedding, and circumcision reports to the authorities. If one person made another use intoxicating medicine without his knowledge the *muhtasibs* were to give the dispenser from ten to thirty lashes. They were also to whip and, with the order of the *hakim*, send to jail a person who lustfully kissed or hugged or touched the wife of another man. Careful directions were laid down with regard to the administration of the whip (*durrah*) with which the *muhtasibs* punished the offenders. The instrument was to be of a particular pattern; it was to be made of three strips—one each of the skin of camel, cow, and sheep; and its handle was to be made of olive wood.[63]

The Army and Local Government

Although the essential duty of the army was declared to be the defense of Afghanistan, the amir, in fact, made it an instrument to pacify the country itself. In the process the army became so much involved in politics that it extended its influence over administration. Military and civil administration, however, always functioned separately.

The increase in the role of the army was the result of the frequency of disturbances, which was a distinguishing feature of the reign of Amir ʾAbd al-Rahman Khan. Regular troops were stationed mainly in the capital of the provinces and districts and at some strategically important places. They were led mainly by generals, but in the strategically important provinces of Herat, Turkestan, and Jalalabad they were commanded by *sipah salars*. In major disturbances governors also took part and led tribal levies, but the overall command was in the hands of the army officers. The latter were supreme in provinces during war and sometimes even in peace. Generally governors were in a subordinate position to the army officers everywhere.

In the Jalalabad area the real power was in the hands of Sipah Salar Ghulam Haydar Charkhi who, as the amir's viceroy, summoned tribal elders, levied taxes, punished rebels, and by the emphatic order of the amir watched over the conduct of the governor and border officers.[64] Toward the end of the amir's reign when disturbances had been suppressed, the governors of Ningrahar and other provinces became relatively independent of the army. Still, when the people of Ningrahar complained of the misconduct of their civil governor, General Bahawal Khan, who had succeeded the *sipah salar*, was ordered to investigate the matter.[65] In Kandahar in the mid-eighties, most civil administration was carried on by officers of the cavalry regiment,[66] while the governor of the time, who was an incompetent old Muhammadzay sardar, was left only in charge of collecting the revenue. The same was true of the province of Herat despite the fact that following the expulsion of Sardar Muhammad Ayyub that province was relatively quiet. Being the most distant frontier area and exposed to the Russian threat, Herat was the station of a large army.

The relative positions of the civil governors and military commanders are best illustrated in the amir's instructions to Faramuz Khan, sipah salar of the Herat army. He was instructed that in so far as it led to the welfare of the people and to the good of the state and religion, he was to obey the governor. Should the views of the governor, continued the amir, disagree with those of the ruler regarding the affairs of the government, the sipah salar was to restrain the governor from carrying them through.[67] After the expulsion of Sardar Muhammad Ishaq, Turkestan was actually administered by Sipah Salar Ghulam Haydar Orakzay and Sardar Muhammad ʾAziz was governor in name only. Although the sipah salar's method of administering the province by referring civil disputes to elders was distasteful to the amir the ruler still allowed the sipah salar to act in a civil position superior to the governor's until Ghulam Haydar Orakzay died in 1897.[68]

The army did not take over the civil administration, however. It was left to the civil officials whose main job actually came to be the collection of revenue and the settlement of disputes between individuals and groups. Minor disturbances were left to be suppressed by governors, assisted by tribal levies;[69] but all major disturbances were suppressed by the army, as well as by tribal levies, thereby giving a military tint to the local government. Thus as guardian of order and security, the army exercised high power in the provinces. Officers, even to the rank of commander, acted as overseers of governors and arrested them when called upon to.

Rural Areas

Those directly responsible for the administration of the rural areas were the *hakims*, qazis, and, to some extent, community and tribal elders. The *hakims* as heads of districts were subordinate to governors, but their duties and power were similar to those of the governors and differed only in degree. The *hakims* had under them a few *mirzas* and ʾ*amils* (who were in charge of revenue) and enforced their authority by armed *khassadars*, whose number ranged from ten to one hundred in proportion to the size and importance of the district. Districts with towns, public markets, and large mosques had, in addition, *mir-i-shabs* and *muhtasibs*.

The amir increased the number of the *hakims* during his reign. This increase became possible, indeed necessary, when the government took over the administration of the hitherto autonomous areas, extended its authority to new territories, and split up provinces into numerous districts (*hukumats*). Unlike the situation in the past, when provincial officials had held their posts for a long time, during the amir's reign tenure of office became short. The idea was that officials should not involve themselves in local politics,[70] but the short tenure in office meant the employment and reemployment of a large number of the *hakims*. Generally the amir handled this problem personally, but governors also took care of it when they had obtained the amir's approval in advance. The *hakims* were appointed mainly from among the *peshkhidmats* of the amir's darbar and tribal elders. They were always appointed to districts far away from their own where they were unlikely to gather a following. Among tribal elders the Pashtuns, particularly heads of the Durrani clans, were preferred for this post. In the early nineties, for example, out of the sixteen *hakims* in the province of Herat, eleven were heads of the various sections of the Durrani tribe.[71]

The *hakims* and the governors performed the same kinds of duties. The former were, in fact, lesser governors with much smaller territories under their jurisdiction. They also carried out orders received from heads of various provincial departments, countersigned by the governors.

District qazis were the equals of the *hakims* and the latter were not allowed to interfere in the affairs of the court. In addition, the qazis, as well as community elders, were authorized to seal the reports *hakims* made about criminals or to take security undertakings from the criminals.[72] The *hakims* were also obliged to consult the *mirzas* in affairs concerning the *daftars* (registers).[73] The *hakims* were delegated a great deal of authority. In fact, the increasing role of the state in rural areas during the reign of the amir, as opposed to the role of the individuals and tribes, increased the power of the *hakims*, as well as that of the governors. All kinds of cases were first brought to the *hakims* who dealt with most of them in person. The *hakim* sent only the legal cases to the court, and serious ones to the provinces. Through his officials and *khassadars* the *hakim* collected government money as well as fines.[74]

Elders and Communities

The word *elder* used in this work is a loose term denoting persons who exercised various degrees of influence and power in secular affairs over either an ethnically bound group or a community composed of a mixed population. Broadly speaking, the term *arbab* was used in western Afghanistan and the term *malik* in eastern Afghanistan. In northern and central Afghanistan the terms *beg* and *mir* were common. The Arab elders of Sar-i-pul and Balkh were called *el begi*,[75] a compound Turkish term denoting the position of elders of tribes.

These elders had under them assistants called *tawachi, darugha, peradar,* and *kadkhuda.* The term *khan* indicated a much higher position, since khans usually were at the head of tribes or a larger community with many maliks or arbab working under them. Terms such as *mushr* (among the Pashtuns), *reeshsafid* (among the Persian speakers), and *aqsaqal* (among the Turki speakers) referred to aged and experienced men, whose advice was sought at critical times. Mullas, too, advised elders, especially on legal affairs.

Before 1880, elders administered their own communities with relatively free hands. Of course these communities were not politically independent but were subject to the central government, which had entrusted their internal administration to their elders. The degree of autonomy, however, differed from one community to another, depending on location, political institutions, modes of life, and the degree of inroad made by the central authority. Consequently, the position and role of elders could differ not only between ethnic groups, but also between groups within the same tribe or community. Before ʾAbd al-Rahman's policy toward these communities is discussed it is necessary to describe their composition and the role their elders played in them.

A Pashtun tribe (*qawm*) is composed of a number of groups and consists of numerous subdivisions. These subdivisions are so numerous that it is almost impossible to follow their number; the subdivisions often occupy specific areas and live in close proximity.[76] In other words, there are separate and numerous Pashtun communities, such as the Shinwar, Mohmand, Wazir, and other groups, with distinct names of their own. In spite of these divisions these groups have a shared sense of belonging based on a common descent, history, and culture. It is in this sense that the Pashtuns are collectively referred to as one nation. The Pashtuns give utmost significance to genealogy and descent. In their long and specifically remembered genealogical links, the starting figure is usually such a saint or a respected person as Abdal, the supposed ancestor of the Abdalis, or ʾAbd al-Rashid ibn Qays, the supposed ancestor of all Pashtuns. The Ghilzays, on the other hand, trace their own ancestor to one Ghalzoy, the illegitimate offspring of a Pashtun prince of Ghor and a daughter of a Persian shaykh.[77] The formation of subdivisions among the Pashtuns is extremely common, largely because in the Pashto language the descendants of a man of note (usually dead) are almost automatically known by his name in combination with either the suffix -*khel* (lineage) or -*zay* (descendants of), as in Muhammadzay or Sulaimahkhel.

Pashtun subdivisions and communities, however, do not occupy specific areas exclusively, and races and languages merge into each other while Pashto remains the common language. Members of other Pashtun subdivisions and clients (*hamsayas*), including the Hindus and Sikhs, live and seek professions with Pashtun subdivisions. Pashtun members of these communities are not necessarily connected by ties of kinship, although such ties in their ethnically composite groups remain very strong; and the client groups are united to the main body by matters of common interest. The Pashtuns are predominantly sedentary agriculturists among whom families, not clans, hold plots of land jointly. Some communities have transferred their names to the territory they occupy and these territories they call "fatherland" (*watan*), a designation also given to the country as a whole. On the one hand, this transfer reflects the breakdown of tribal organization; on the other hand, among the Bardurranis for example, the existence of a weak central authority has strengthened their attachment to their communities and the tribal codes of conduct (Pashtunwali).

Members of subdivisions are on intimate terms with immediate members of their own families, though relations between half-brothers are strained. With outsiders they are perpetually in competition or in a state of enmity. They compete with their own cousins in a game called *turburi* (literally, cousinhood, but in fact keen competition among cousins). This competition exists in spite of the practice among them of cross-cousin marriage. Members of subdivisions are at odds with members of other communities over problems arising between their communities and with the central authority because of tax impositions and the control the government seeks to impose. By contrast, they respond favorably to the call of the central authority or of the religious leaders when there is a danger to the country or the religion, to the call of their elders when there is a dispute between their community and its neighboring one, and to the call of members of their own faction (*gund*) quarreling with a rival faction within their own community. In a neatly woven web of social relations, their positions in the society are fixed and they have little or no choice about the matter.

The Hazaras are similar to the Pashtuns in tribal structure; but among the Hazaras the relatively small ruling groups, as opposed to the more numerous subordinate groups of Tajik or others of mixed origin living among them, follow a unilinear rule of descent and trace their ancestors through specifically remembered genealogical links.[78] The Dawlat Begs, and Haydar Begs of Dai Kundi, for example, claim that they are the descendants of Chinggis Khan;[79] but, even among them, there is little evidence of organization, collective activities, or group functions.[80] Also, they no longer consider themselves to be members of a Dai Kundi "tribe," but residents of Dai Kundi[81] or simply Hazaras. Conversely, among the subordinate Hazara groups, genealogies are extremely weak and their members identify themselves with their region. In this, they resemble the Tajiks among whom genealogies are unknown and blood relations are weak, hardly extending beyond secondary relations.[82]

The Tajiks, who include a number of diverse ethnic and cultural groups[83] and are scattered over extensive areas, possess no tribal organization, either vestigial or actual.[84] In this situation, nearly all elders led rather than commanded their communities, as the following brief survey will indicate.

The Tajik elders were not powerful in general. Except for the mountain Tajiks of Badakhshan and Kohistan (Nijrao, Panjshir, Ghorat), most Tajiks lived in plains in heterogenous communities, much under the sway of the central government, despite the fact that their elders were elected by the people. These elders had weight enough to settle small disputes but referred the important ones to the governor of the province or the qazi. The mountain Tajiks of Kohistan and Badakhshan were, however, almost independent of Kabul and were kept in order by their elders. The elders of the Badakhshan Tajiks acted in an absolute fashion. They were paramount elders in that of all the elders of Afghanistan they alone wielded both religious and secular power, a situation sanctioned by their religion, the Isma'ili branch of Shi'ism. Unlike other elders they bore the title of shah and received 'ushr as revenue from their subjects, who were extremely devoted to them.[85]

The Hazara political institutions were feudal and absolute and centered in the elders (mirs and begs) whose will was the law. The relation of the Hazara elders with the common Hazaras is illustrated by a statement of Muhammad Rafi⁾ Beg of Dai Zangi in 1838, when he said, "I am master of the lives of my people and if I chose to sell them to the Uzbecks [sic] no one of them would dare oppose my will." In the manner of independent rulers these paramount elders held regular darbars, enforced their authority by their armed cavalry, and received revenue, taxes, and fines from their subjects. Since among them there was a separate religious class of sayyeds and *zawwars* who also exercised "some sort of authority over the people," the scope of the elders' jurisdiction was limited.[86]

The Durrani tribal confederation, which occupied the plains of Kandahar, was governed mainly by a hierarchy of the heads of its clans. Of all elders of Afghanistan the Durrani elders were most privileged. Although after the death of Ahmad Shah Durrani elders had ceased to be the traditional commanders of the feudal cavalry, they remained powerful. Kings depended on their support because they owned extensive tracts of lands, paid only nominal revenue to the state, and obtained high official positions. Since the population of Kandahar was small in proportion to the land they occupied, they did not have feuds among themselves, and the custom of taking revenge was not common among them, their country remained, by and large, tranquil. Duties of the Durrani elders were confined to the adjustment of disputes between individuals. When these were not solved by the mediation of their elders the disputes were brought before the jirgas. Elders of the remote and unfrequented areas were, of course, more powerful.[87]

By contrast the authority of the Ghilzay elders was not as extensive. Ghilzay elders exercised only limited authority over the nearest sections of their tribe. The Ghilzays were so scattered and divided that no one khan could bring them under control. The Ghilzays near Kabul and Ghazni and along the great roads were, more or less, governed either by government officials or by their own elders; but the rest were subject to no external authority. In those areas elders kept their own families in order and left the rest to accommodate their differences as best they could until they became troublesome to the community. Neither did the jirgas among them function with any great authority, probably because their suits were settled mainly by the mullas, who carried great influence with them.[88]

The power and position of elders and jirgas among the Bardurranis or the Pashtuns of eastern Afghanistan were different from those of the Durranis and Ghilzays. In the first place, there were numerous elders, most of whom were, by tradition, first among equals. Neither were individual tribesmen subservient to them. Extremely democratic by upbringing, the Bardurranis refused to obey their elders, unless the elders were great warriors or tyrants. In the second place, the power of these elders was curbed by tribal jirgas that, among such tribes as the Mohmand, Wazir, and Shinwar, every adult male was required to attend. The more democratic the tribe the larger the jirga. As a result of this situation the jirgas were inefficient in settling disputes in spite of the coercive power of the jirgas, which included punishment in the forms of outlawry, heavy fines, or the destruction of property. The customs of revenge, blood feud and intertribal conflicts also persisted among them in an intense form.[89]

The power and position of the elders of these groups, as described, differed, but in role and function they had very much in common. They collected government revenue, retained feudal cavalry, and received allowances from the government.[90] Some were "invested with patriarchal and dynastic power" for being elders of small ruling sections (*khan khel*) or such major tribes as the Hotakay, Jabor Khel, and Dawlat Beg (called also *qawm-i-mir* and *tol-i-Sardar* "the descendants of Sardar"). As a rule maliks and arbab rose to the position of eldership by general acclamation mainly because of personal influence and character, not necessarily by hereditary right of birth and descent, although in the highly status-conscious communities of Afghanistan these were considered to be important qualifications. With the khan, as well as with the mir (among the Hazaras and Shi'ite Tajiks), the situation was a little different. Generally, the position of khan and that of mir were hereditary in a family, but any member of the appropriate family could be elected by popular consent. In times of emergency even a member of another family but of the same descent could also be acknowledged as khan upon his demonstration of pre-eminent ability and valor.[91]

It was generally assumed that whatever power the ruler of Afghanistan may acquire "its preservation can only be ensured by not infringing the rights of the tribes, and the laws by which they are allowed to govern themselves."[92] Having something like this in mind Ahmad Shah Durrani had remarked, "it would require less exertion to conquer all the neighboring kingdoms, than to subdue his own countrymen."[93] But, Amir 'Abd al-Rahman chose the latter course and the following manner.

The amir first appointed *hakims*, qazis, and other officials in the various districts near Kabul. Gradually, and particularly after the expulsion of Sardar Muhammad Ayyub in 1881, the amir sent officials to remote areas also. Governors and *hakims* were accompanied by armed *khassadars* and followed by regular troops. For the movement of the army and mule guns old roads were improved and new ones built in some regions. These officials took over the administration of the tolls collected until that time by certain elders and prevented others from raiding and committing other depredations. As indicated earlier, the amir's policy was aimed at suppressing and eliminating elders throughout the country. By 1887, in the Kabul province alone, 4,000 of them were disposed of.[94] By the early nineties, no man of influence and rank, except Sardar Muhammad Yusuf and Sardar 'Abd al-Quddus, had been left in the country.[95] Almost all tribes resented this policy and they rose over forty times in rebellion. They were suppressed by the military force as described in another book by this writer.[96]

In pacifying the rebellious communities no distinction was made with regard to race, language, or religion. The more tribes or elders resisted the government authority, the more they were suppressed. Killing of the insurgents in action was not only inevitable; it was made a duty for the army.[97] The army officers were explicitly authorized to destroy the insurgents and to seize their property by any means available.[98] *Kalla minars* (heaps of skulls) were erected from the heads of the fallen insurgents[99] and their skulls raised on spears to impress others not to follow their examples. It was a common practice to send captured ringleaders on to Kabul in chains and to keep others and their sons as hostages.[100] Crops and villages were burnt, trees cut, *qal'as* destroyed, movable property seized,[101] and new forts for the army built in the lands of the insurgents.[102] The defeated insurgents were heavily fined and women often dishonored. Such weapons as could be obtained from them were collected as part of the amir's program of disarming the whole nation. Sometimes the lands of the insurgent tribes were given to others.[103] In most cases, rebel elders, and in some cases whole tribes, were removed to other areas. Those lands of the insurgents previously not surveyed for revenue purposes were surveyed and revenue assessed on them. In addition, landowners were forced to pay revenue arrears due on them. Finally, a written document, endorsed by another tribe, to the effect that the defeated insurgents would not rebel again and would remain loyal to the amir was required of them.[104]

After the pacification of the rebellious communities an order was created in which the relations of the elders with the government and with their own districts was fixed on a new footing. The outstanding feature of this new order was the dependence of the elders on the state, but the institution of eldership itself was left intact. Indeed, the institution was reinforced, and the number of elders, paradoxically, increased during the reign of the amir. All these new elders were given allowances and visited the amir at frequent intervals.

The foremost duties of the new elders were to remain loyal to the amir and his dynasty and to make the utmost exertion for the consolidation of the foundations of the state (*dawlat*) and nation (*millat*) and for the safeguarding of the religion and the country.[105] They "gave" pledges to this effect on numerous occasions.[106] Further, the mullas and elders were expected to teach common people about their duties to their king and the merit of obedience to him.[107] Elders also undertook not to let any of the exiles, or those who had risen against the state, into their villages and to report the arrival of such people to the authorities.[108] Similarly, elders pledged themselves not to let robbers into their villages and to seize them when they were found.[109]

Elders and villagers were alike made accountable for the safety of roads passing through their locality (every village was responsible for a fixed vicinity). When unable to make the roads safe, villages were compelled to pay compensation to travelers and merchants for goods lost.[110] In practice, heavy fines, which exceeded many times the value of the lost property, were imposed. The fines were, in fact, too heavy for the villagers to pay unless they were compelled to by contingents of the army.[111] Martin notes that as a result of this policy villagers refrained from molesting travelers and that a "single traveller might go all the way from Kandahar to Kabul without being unduly troubled."[112] No doubt robbery in the reign of the amir was reduced to a lower level than ever before, but it was not stopped. In the suburbs of Herat and on some roads robbery continued right up to the end of the amir's reign. Among the new robbers were soldiers of the regular army who often went unpunished.[113]

Similarly elders and villagers were made to report to the *hakims* the incidence of murder in their localities.[114] In reality they were made accountable for the murder itself since they were forced to hand over the murderer or to accept the consequent punishment themselves. If they failed to present the murderer they were made to pay blood money that the amir had raised to 7,000 rupees. In addition, the *hakims* were, in such cases, allowed to charge villagers 10 percent of the blood money for personal expenses.[115] By these rigid administrative measures the amir reduced murder and robbery as never before in Afghanistan. Since they had been practiced over centuries, however, and since their roots lay deep in socioeconomic conditions of the country, even the Iron Amir was unable to stop them; he only suppressed them.

The power of the elders over the common people was also reduced and the former were not allowed to jail the latter,[116] as presumably they had in the past. In certain cases elders and well-to-do people were made subject to heavier punishments than those of the common people. In murder cases, for instance, they were made to pay blood money over and above the fixed rate.[117] As a result of the unprecedented expansion of administration in the reign of Amir ʾAbd al-Rahman Khan the traditional relation between the state and tribal groups weakened and, conversely, that of state to individuals strengthened. Government functionaries took over most of the functions that had until then been carried on by elders. The latter, however, did not cease to function politically altogether. The institution of eldership, though greatly modified, remained basically intact; but in the new administrative arrangements elders were subordinate to government officials. Elders derived their authority no longer solely from their own communities, but also from the government whose subsidies and recognition became significant to their positions.

Frontier Areas

Amir ʾAbd al-Rahman faced serious administrative problems as a result of the demarcation of Afghanistan's boundaries with her neighbors. The demarcation had actually begun earlier; but it was completed by the midnineties so that, in the amir's reign, Afghanistan was completely circumscribed. The boundaries were demarcated by the British, Russo-British, and Anglo-Afghan commissions. All were fixed to meet the strategic requirements of the empires of Russia and Britain at the expense of those of Afghanistan. Except for the lower and middle part of the Oxus, separating the Uzbeks and Tajiks of Afghanistan from their fellows in the Russian-controlled Bukhara, these boundaries were not natural and geographical. Being political and artificial for the most part, the boundaries were marked either by pillars and stones or simply by imaginary lines. In the east and southeast the new boundaries separated areas that had formed the nucleus of the original Afghanistan. Moreover, these lines were drawn through densely populated areas and divided communities with very strong kinship ties. Frontier areas were formed on either side of the international lines. On the British side the frontier areas were left unadministered. The government of Afghanistan found it impossible to administer its own frontier areas as it administered other areas, although these areas were in theory under the jurisdiction of the adjacent local governors. Those living in the frontier areas could easily cross the so-called international boundaries and live with their fellow tribesmen on either side. Consequently tribesmen of the frontier areas, especially the elders, in contrast to those of the other areas more or less retained their traditional autonomous positions with the government. Among other things this autonomy meant the persistence of the traditional code of conduct (Pashtunwali) especially its most destructive aspect, the *badal* or the principle of retaliation in defense of honor. Their relative autonomy also meant that, since the government authority was loosely exercised in these tribal communities, they could strike at the government whenever it was weak or it infringed upon their well-established positions. Thus, the frontier tribal communities remained an unstable factor and a potential source of threat to the government, especially when a neighboring government became unfriendly.

In general Amir ʾAbd al-Rahman followed a policy of mild repression toward these frontier areas. It took a long time to impose the governmental authority there; but administrative arrangements especially devised for these areas were by no means uniform. The case of Chakhansur may be taken as an example. Sardar Ibrahim Khan Baluch of Chakhansur, at the instigation of the Persian district governor of Qain, opposed government authority in his region for six years. Only after that time was he forced to leave Chakhansur for Mashhad. Contingents of troops were stationed in different localities [118] in Chakhansur and new progovernment *kadkhudas* were raised among the Baluches. The elder of the major Sanjarani section of the Baluch tribe was appointed *sarhaddar* (frontier officer). In addition to the allowances fixed for elders the *sarhaddar* was granted a tract of land in Charburjak as *soyurghal* (grant of land or of its revenue furnished in lieu of salary or pension) in return for furnishing the government with cavalry.[119] The Baluches, who like the Turkmen and Achakazays used to rob cattle, travelers, and caravans, were pacified by the amir to the extent that in the words of one Baluch "a child may drive a ewe-lamb along the frontier and we must all look on."[120] With other frontier communities the amir entered into agreements. The Safays of the Shali and Shungri val-

leys in Kunar, for instance, undertook that they "shall not allow anyone, who commits an offence against the ruler of Afghanistan, such as
highway robbery, murder, or theft to enter their limits." The amir, for
his part, fixed allowances for them in kind, out of the revenue they
paid to the state.[121] The Achakzays of Arghistan, who were noted for
robbery and who had rebelled, also gave a similar pledge undertaking
to hand over robbers and to make the roads safe.[122] For the safeguarding
of the frontier areas adjoining Russian territories the amir ordered the
people of Afghanistan and Turkestan to send, principally at the people's own expense, one man out of every twenty to the frontier.[123] This
force was, apparently, intended as an auxiliary against possible Russian
aggression; but, in reality, it helped administrative officials to enforce
government authority.

As a rule outposts along the borders were placed under the control of
elders of the nearby regions who were assisted by the *khassadars*. Notwithstanding these arrangements, tribesmen easily crossed the borders
in unguarded areas. This ease of crossing and the fact that there were
no agreements for extradition between Afghanistan and her neighbors [124] made the frontier areas havens for all kinds of offenders. To
deal with them the amir applied the principle of collective punishment. He made the nearest relatives or, in their absence, the villagers
of those who committed an offense suffer until they persuaded the
offenders to return. In some cases mercenaries were employed to
dispose of those who had taken refuge in places far away from the
border.[125]

Novel Ways of Administration

To make his officials and elders responsible and efficient the amir
introduced a number of new methods of administration. The petition
boxes or *sandoq-i-ʾadalat* (justice boxes) were one.

By custom individual Afghans took their complaints in person to the
ruler who received and discussed every petition. His ministers merely
brought about the orders of their sovereign.[126] Amir ʾAbd al-Rahman
followed the tradition by being accessible to the rich and the poor during the first years of his reign; [127] but later, fearing an attempt on his
life and intent upon creating a splendid image of an absolute monarch,
he gradually withdrew from the public. As a shepherd who had come
from a distant place to present his case before the amir in person remarked, "The Sardar [Habib Allah] has taken to the hunting while the
Amir has kept himself in the *ghar* [literally cave, i.e., palace]." After
this incident the amir ordered petition boxes placed in every district of
Afghanistan. The purpose of this innovation was to be that of providing
"redress for the common people" without their having to traverse long
distances and without their fearing the *hakims*. [128] People were asked
to throw in the complaints they wished to make against anyone.[129] The
boxes were sealed and guarded and sent to Kabul every six months. In
Kabul the Shahghassi ʾAbd al-Quddus opened them in the presence of

the amir and read the petitions to him.[130] The old boxes were replaced by the new and the replacement was marked by the beating of drums. This service continued throughout the amir's reign but with little effect since the common people were illiterate and did not dare speak to a third person against their *hakims*. The petitions they lodged were, therefore, about insignificant matters.[131] Also, six months was too long for petitioners to wait for redress of their complaints that had immediate concern. Furthermore, since the petitioners were later required to write their complaints on stamped petitions costing three rupees each[132] they ceased to use the boxes much. In sum, the innovation might have proved a deterrent to the *hakims*, but its benefits to the people as a whole were insignificant.[133]

Another innovation introduced in the reign of the amir was *razana-mas* (letters of contentment) obtained by the governors and *hakims* from the people. Elders periodically signed such letters stating that they were content and had no complaints to make of their *hakims*. At times even *sipah salars* obtained such letters and sent them to Kabul.[134] In many firmans the amir urged the people to make representation when they felt aggrieved. They were asked, indeed urged, to seek redress even for small injustices.[135] People usually, however, did not do so since they feared harsh repercussions if their *hakims* were not dismissed.[136] Only when the tyranny of the *hakims* caused widespread discontent were they, on popular demand, dismissed and their property confiscated.[137] On the whole, the *hakims* acted as despots over the ordinary people.[138] Neither the undertakings to perform their duties honestly, which had been taken from them, nor the strongly worded warnings that the amir frequently sent to them and other officials proved fundamentally effective.[139]

Another innovation intended to bring the country still further under the grip of the central government was the placing of restrictions on the movements of individuals and groups. Before the reign of the amir individual liberty was said to exist nowhere else in the East as in Afghanistan. Every Afghan could leave the kingdom with his family if he wished. Neither authority nor passport was required to enable him to do so.[140] In the reign of Amir ʾAbd al-Rahman all this changed. The amir, shortly after his succession, restricted the movement of individuals in Kabul.[141] Except for pilgrims from central Asia, no one was allowed to leave Kabul without a travel permit (*rahdari*). Subsequently, movements of individuals from one city to another within Afghanistan were also made subject to obtaining a permit.[142] Obtaining a permit was difficult since the applicant was required to go through many offices. Merchants, too, were made subject to this ruling, since the government maintained that they must have papers of identity to enable the government to look after them when they were in trouble abroad.[143] The merchants were also to provide security that they would return home.[144] Indeed, every Afghan, except the nomads who migrated to northern India in the winter, was required to obtain a permit by paying a fee and furnishing security to return.[145] Wherever possible—

mainly along the main roads, between cities, and across the borders on checkpoints—this ruling was strictly enforced and offenders punished. For example, two men who went from Tashqurghan to Badakhshan without a permit were imprisoned for life by the amir.[146] In remote rural areas the enforcement of this ruling was not possible, as was evidenced by the flights abroad of many individuals and groups.[147] This restriction, however, enabled the government to prevent foreigners from entering Afghanistan. Except for George Robertson and Col. W. Lockhart, Europeans in western clothes did not attempt to enter Afghanistan. A few British who had entered eastern Afghanistan in disguise were detected and expelled without being molested. Indian and central Asian Muslim informers might have entered Afghanistan, but the government refused entry to foreigners other than those who either sought refuge or came for such declared purposes as trade. Noted Muslims from Medina and Bukhara who had entered Afghanistan were expelled on the suspicion of being spies.[148] Similarly such strangers as mendicants, beggars, monkey-owners, and others who pursued a wandering livelihood in the country were expelled for the same reason. The enforcement of the permit system was further facilitated by the demarcation of the boundaries of Afghanistan. Thus, the flow of people from central Asia, northern India, and Persia who, from time immemorial, had visited Afghanistan was drastically curtailed; and the country in the reign of the amir was isolated as never before.

Another new service that became an integral part of the government was the intelligence system. Unlike the other services just noted, it was not introduced by the amir. Under the amir's predecessors a small intelligence service had been in operation; but the amir, in imitation of the king of Bukhara, expanded it thoroughly.[149]

Informers (*parcha nawis*) were employed all over Afghanistan.[150] They were also stationed in the important cities of neighboring countries.[151] In 1884, there were six hundred informers in the pay of the government;[152] gradually their number increased. Sultan Mahomed notes, possibly with some exaggeration, that "There is no country in the world, . . . where there are so many spies . . . as in Afghanistan."[153] Because of the large number of informers the amir claimed that "no person of any importance can move in Persia, Russia, India or Afghanistan, without being noticed and reported."[154] Through this service the amir hoped to protect himself and his family.[155] So the principal job of the informer became to report on the wealthy and influential people. They also reported on the provincial officers' handling of government affairs and their treatment of the common people.

Members of both sexes were employed as informers.[156] Some worked in the open; others, in secret. On informers, too, reports were made. Disguised as peddlers and beggars female informers entered the homes of the wealthy, sang songs and related amusing stories for the wives.[157] An enterprising lady regularly attended the governor's darbar in Kandahar, sat next to him, and made reports about the officials.[158] In addition to informers permanently stationed in the district who reported about the local officials, informers were periodically sent from Kabul to the provinces to report on the conditions of the common people and their treatment by the *hakims*. It was mainly through the reports of the informers that cases of corruption and mismanagement were brought to light.

The informers sent their reports directly to the amir, first once a week and later once a day. The amir showed special interest in these reports, but he was unable to go through all of them in person. A superintendent of the informers who always attended on the amir made a synopsis of the reports for him. On the basis of these reports the amir acted promptly. Those on whom adverse reports had been made were first either imprisoned or dismissed or suffered the confiscation of their property. Investigation of their cases followed later, often after a long delay and accompanied by a variety of tortures. Rarely was an accused person acquitted.[159]

The well to do dreaded the informers and, in order to save themselves from false accusations, bribed them.[160] Individuals who bore grudges against others also bribed informers to report on them to the amir.[161] To exact bribes and intimidate their enemies, some people posed as informers.[162] At times informers joined one or another of the rival groups composed of government officials and made biased reports,[163] thus inducing government officials to become informers themselves in the hope of either saving themselves or destroying their opponents.[164] The increase in the number of false reports caused a general alarm[165] and brought harsh repercussions onto the informers. Some of them were taken to the villagers in chains to repay the money they had received as bribes.[166] Others were blown from guns for their false information. The service, however, continued, strengthened, and was incorporated into the state system.

No doubt with the help of the intelligence service the amir was able to strengthen his hold over the people, but one result was to make women and men look upon each other as possible spies.[167]

Relations between Central and Local Governments

A provincial government was a remote extension of the central government. The administrative structure of the former was modeled on that of the latter. The offices in the center were superior to, and more extensive than, those in the provinces; but, to meet peculiar local requirements, provincial offices had certain divisions that did not exist in the center. Heads of all provincial offices, including the qazis, were responsible and subordinate to the heads of relevant offices in the center. Provincial officials, therefore, had to send in reports of their work to Kabul regularly. Provincial officials did not proceed on their own initiatives but received instructions from Kabul. The amir's firmans, which laid down regulations for them and initiated new policies, were also communicated to them through the relevant offices in the center.

Heads of all provincial and district offices, including governors and *hakims*, were appointed, dismissed, promoted, or demoted by the center. Except for the *kalantars* and certain elders who were, strictly speaking, not government officials, no official was elected. Throughout the amir's reign no new appointment by the center was challenged either by the inhabitants of a region or by a governor. Of course complaints were made against certain officials, but these were directed against their mismanagement not against the offices they held.

As will be discussed in the next chapter the expenses of the local governments were met from local income, and surpluses were sent to the center. Governors were merely officials who carried out the instructions they received from the amir. Once a precedent had been established on a subject governors were not supposed to ask for further instructions. In other important issues, particularly those arising out of border problems with neighboring countries, they were to ask the amir for instructions. In the beginning of the amir's reign, when the amount of discretion allowed governors was still unclear, certain governors acted in accordance with former customs and with a considerable degree of independence. Sardar ʾAbd al-Quddus, for example, treated the followers of Sardar Muhammad Ayyub in Herat leniently, whereas the amir's order had been to the contrary.[168] Also, by the order of the sardar the ears of a soldier were cut off for instigating his fellow soldiers to refuse only one month's payment. As noted this state of affairs was soon ended, and a new set of relations was established in which the complete dominance of the provinces by the center was assured. A characteristic of this new order was the dispatch of the Muhammadzay sardars from Kabul to the provinces as inspectors.[169] They were sent in groups to the provinces when complaints were made against certain officials, but they did not accomplish much since these inspecting sardars were only to make reports about the mismanagement of the officials.[170] As a result of these periodical inspections, however, provincial officials were kept under pressure. From time to time the amir summoned governors to Kabul and provided them with guidelines on the administration of their regions.[171] Whether governors were in Kabul or in the provinces, the amir was constantly in touch with them. Not only did he send them instructions in minute details, but he also treated them paternally. Most of them he addressed as his "sons" and abused when he was angry with them.[172] In a detailed letter of instruction for the benefit of frontier governors, in which they were taught how to deal with their foreign counterparts or with members of the international commissions, the amir also set them codes of behavior. Among other things, the amir instructed them to pause and to think first before they answered tricky questions, especially those asked by foreigners.[173]

As has been the case with senior officials in the center the principle of checks and balances was also applied to senior officials in the provinces. At times this principle led to factionalism, but it also successfully prevented one individual from challenging the center or dominating the others. Although the army was given power over the local government, the local government was still able to function and develop. The position of the new elders, who were more or less of equal standing, was dependent on the state. While the application of the principle of collective punishment reinforced kinship ties and tribalism, the enforcement of the *rahdari* fostered regionalism still further. The fixing of the Afghan boundaries, combined with the refusal to allow foreigners to enter the country, led to the isolation of Afghanistan for the first time in its history.

Chapter IV
The System
of Taxation

To meet the increasing expenses of the state, Amir ʾAbd al-Rahman directed full attention to the system of taxation. He modified the old system by raising the existing rates of land revenue, introducing new taxes, and bringing rent-free lands under revenue. In addition, various kinds of existing taxes on cattle, households, and the like were increased, and new ones introduced.

Various schemes were worked out for the collection of revenue. Ultimately, a system was developed that required taxpayers to pay their revenue themselves by a fixed date. The arrears were then collected by mounted troops. At the same time, the collection of certain kinds of revenue and taxes were farmed out to contractors. The responses of taxpayers to these innovations were unsuccessful revolts, flights, and finally submission.

Historical Background

Under the Sadozays land revenue was assessed on produce according to fixed proportions that varied with the nature of land and was different in different provinces.[1] The Durranis, who held most of the land in Kandahar in return for serving the state with cavalry, were exempt from paying taxes, and the Ghilzays paid only a moderate amount of taxes.[2] The Tajiks paid more revenue than the Pashtuns did;[3] and the Uzbeks paid only a small amount that was spent locally for the maintenance of the frontier province of Balkh against Bukhara.[4] Of all the provinces, Kashmir contributed the greatest amount of revenue, four and one-half million rupees.[5]

The rise to power of the Muhammadzay rulers coincided with the disintegration of the Durrani Empire and the loss of the financially rich provinces. In addition, Afghanistan disintegrated into small principalities. To consolidate their position the rulers of these principalities tried to increase their incomes. Still the principle of unequal rates of revenue paid by different ethnic communities remained the same as before. During the Muhammadzay period revenue varied according to the abundance of water that irrigated a locality or the group of people who inhabited that locality.[6] The Kandahar Durranis paid a nominal rate of revenue right up to the reign of Amir ʾAbd al-Rahman. As late as 1883, it was reported that the Durranis had always held their lands on a service tenure.[7]

From the considerable increase in the total revenue of Afghanistan in the reign of Amir Sher ʾAli it is apparent that land revenue was also increased, although it is not known what kind of reform he introduced in the system of taxation. From the revenue assessments in the districts of Jalalabad and Ghazni noted by Major William Jenkyns and Major Hastings, British officers who reported in 1879 and 1880, the main features of the revenue system in the reign of Amir Sher ʾAli can be drawn up.

In the districts of Ghazni and Jalalabad there were two kinds of assessments in operation: the *jamʾbast* and the *kot* system. The *jamʾbast* (also *jamʾ-bandi*) was a fixed quota of revenue, assessed on either a region or a specific tract of land. Originally, the whole revenue was taken in kind; but the difficulty of collecting it from the turbulent and distant tribes led, in many cases, to the substitution of a fixed amount (*jamʾbast*) in cash. The amount assessed differed from region to region, but it was everywhere lighter than even the light Muslim rate of ʾushr (tithe). Elders collected far more than they paid to the government. According to the amir, the southern Ghilzay elders, for instance, paid 8,000 rupees (80,000?) to the government while they were said to have realized 700,000 from their tribesmen.[8] The amir no doubt exaggerated the figures, but the point he tried to make is clear. In addition, the government paid elders for their services. Those communities which paid revenue on the basis of *jamʾbast* retained a high degree of autonomy and their elders were left, by and large, to administer their own affairs. The government stepped in only when the revenues were in arrears. Obviously the main benefactors of the *jamʾbast* were the elders who enhanced their incomes and became politically important.

According to the *kot* system, a fixed share of the gross produce was assessed as revenue to the government. The *se-kot* (three shares, i.e., one out of three shares to the government) was most common, although *char-kot* (four shares), *panj-kot* (five shares) and even *shash-kot* (six shares) also existed. As a rule, lands in regions where government authority was firmly established were subject to this system; but the government found it difficult to realize its exact share because it was easy for landowners to cheat the government before the crop was placed in a heap for final distribution in the presence of the agents of the government, the farmer peasant and the landowner. To prevent abuse and to reduce management expenses the government usually farmed out its share of the revenue to the highest bidder, and the government share was stored with elders. The amount needed for government expenses was deducted while the balance was disposed of by *barats* (drafts) to officials and other recipients as their salaries and allowances. The *khalisa* (crown lands), which appear to have become the property of the state at some former time because of either the failure of heirs or desertion of the land by its original owners, were also subject to the *kot* system. Government share of the revenue of the *khalisa* was high, ranging from *nem-kot* (one half) to five-sixths, and usually was farmed out.[9]

Land Revenue

The amir began his reforms in the revenue system by proclaiming a divine basis for the system. He declared that God commands people to pay the revenues in accordance with the prescriptions of the Quran.[10] The revenues belong to the *bayt al-mal* (public property). According to the amir, the king was to spend the *bayt al-mal* for the protection of the frontiers of the country and the honor of the religion and the nation.[11] This necessitated, said the amir, expenditure on the regular army and the feudal cavalry.[12] As the collector of revenue for these purposes the amir looked upon himself as the "na᾽ib of the Prophet"[13] and declared that any negligence in the payment was tantamount to the abandonment of the commands of God and that it was his duty as the ruler of Islam to see that this did not happen.[14] Since it was incumbent on the Muslims, so the amir continued, to fulfill the commands of God, they should, irrespective of position and profession, pay the revenue that was also the command of God. Therefore, he ordered that everyone, including the religious groups which until then had held rent-free lands either in return for allowances or for nothing, should pay.[15]

To increase the rates of revenue, the amir similarly based his arguments on what he considered to be the commands of God. The rates, however, were classified by the source of water for the land. In his own words, "In our holy book, the Kuran, God commands in regard to the payment of revenue by the ryots [*sic*] that on the land irrigated by a river, one-third of the produce should be realised, . . . on the land watered by a karez, one-tenth; on the land watered by spring water, one-fifth, and on the land depending upon rain, also one-tenth."[16]

In fact, not all these rates and classifications are found in the Quran or in Islamic law. Indeed, the agrarian relations in Islamic lands were not always founded on Islamic law but were mainly the result of historical developments. In the early period of Islam there were three classes of lands: (*a*) ᾽*ushri* lands, which were distributed at the time of the Muslim conquest among the conquerors as their private property (*mulk*) who paid one-tenth of the produce to the state; (*b*) *kharaji* lands, which were left to their original non-Muslim owners who paid heavier taxes than they had in former times; (c) state lands, which were employed as military fiefs,[17] that is, land granted in lieu of service.

In Afghanistan, the *kharaji* classification was not relevant, and the *mulk* was subject to taxation irrespective of who owned it, a zimmi (non-Muslim) or a Muslim. As we have seen the commonest form of land revenue in Afghanistan was the *jam'bast*, which was lighter than even the *'ushr*. The amir's claim of a divine basis for revenue was intended to do away with *jam'bast* and the power it gave to elders. The *jam'bast*, which was basically non-Islamic and the result of peculiar conditions of Afghanistan, was so common that it could not be abolished in one stroke. Even after the drastic change in the system of taxation the *jam'bast* remained in some regions, where, according to the amir "some people" still paid revenue on the basis of the "fixed scale [*jam'bast*]."[18] The method of realizing revenue on the basis of *jam'bast* was improved. An annual average, calculated from reckoning the produce of the land subject to the *jam'bast* for a number of years, was fixed and then converted into cash according to the price of the free market of the day in the same locality. Subsequently, one shahi per rupee was added, but when the fixed amount fell into arrears it was realized on the basis of the highest price during the year of the produce.[19]

The main feature of the land revenue in the reign of the amir was the shift from the *jam'bast* to the *kot* system, but the change was gradual and not uniform. It was first applied in the Jalalabad area in 1883, when the amir ordered that the gross product of the private land, if cultivated by tenant farmers, would be divided into three portions (*kots*) of equal shares among the proprietors, cultivators, and the government.[20] Actual application, however, proved difficult and took a long time because of the opposition of landowners.

Among the problems consequent upon the general shift from the *jam'bast* to the *kot* was the collection of the government's exact share. Since, according to the *kot* system, landowners were required to pay a fixed share of the indefinite amount of the gross produce of their lands, the system was open to abuse.[21] To prevent this the amir, by way of experiment, set guards to watch the crops in some areas,[22] but it was not possible to do this everywhere. Subsequently, a system was worked out in which crops were appraised before they were reaped; then arbitrary appraisals became common, a situation which increased government revenue.[23] From 1891 onward there are no available reports about the appraisal system. Presumably the system continued, though not universally, since from then on the role of government officials in revenue matters increased still further. At the same time the assessment of fixed revenue on a fixed piece of land was also attempted. This assessment necessitated the extension of the land survey that had been started earlier.

The main purpose of surveying land was to increase the revenue. The old jarib of sixty square yards was reduced by half.[24] The new jarib system had two advantages in addition to the increase it brought to revenue through resurveying. One was the detection and repossession by the state of lands that were held by landowners without legal documents. Land measurement showed that landowners were in possession of a greater quantity of lands than that recorded in state papers.[25] The second advantage of the jarib system was the assessment of a fixed amount of revenue per unit of land. This method was intended to do away with the abuses so common in the *kot* system. The system had apparent advantages but also had inherent difficulties and was applied partly in the Jalalabad area[26] and mainly in Herat. It might have been applied elsewhere also, but information to this effect is not available.

In Herat the jarib system was very complicated. There the districts adjacent to the city were called *buluks* or canals.[27] The cultivable lands irrigated by these *buluks* were divided, according to the quantity of water available for irrigation, into the three classes of *bala buluk, miyan buluk* and *payan buluk*. Each *buluk* equaled 2,427 zauj, and each zauj was divided into 60, 80, or 100 jaribs. In each of the nine *buluks* of Herat,[28] the revenue was paid per jarib partly in kind and partly in cash. In the outlying districts, collectively referred to as the *Char Wilayat* (the four districts of Obeh, Sabzwar or Isfazar, Ghorian, and Karukh), different rates of revenues were applied, but these districts were not divided into *buluks*.[29]

It is difficult to state how the state share of revenue was ascertained under the *kot* system when the jarib system was not universally applied. It would appear that the appraisal and jarib systems were simultaneously applied on lands that were subject to the *kot*, as opposed to the *jam'-bast*. Both systems required an increase in the role of government officials in the collection of revenue and this increase began in 1891. As noted earlier, before the amir's accession revenue on the basis of *jam'-bast* was collected by elders and revenue on the *kot* system was either farmed out or collected directly by government officials. By and large, government officials played a minor role in revenue collecting. In the amir's reign their role increased, and this change was made possible by the general shift from the *jam'bast* to the *kot* system and by the gradual abandonment of the contract system.

Direct collection of land revenue by government officials began sometime before 1885. The amir said, "I assess [sic] the revenue on the raiyots [sic] direct, and severed [sic] the connection of the chiefs with them."[30] Since increasing government income was one of the most important aspects of state activities, the collection of revenue, which constituted the largest item of income, was given top priority. Among other things, this priority necessitated the employment of a large number of officials. Although the effectiveness of revenue collection largely depended on the dynamism of governors, the central diwan had a substantial part to play.

Actual tax collection centered on the *hakims* who had at their commands revenue commissioners called the *'amils* and *zabits*. The former were responsible for registration work and the latter headed a large number of cavalry and infantrymen called *muhassils* (*khassadars*). Provincial officials were, as a whole, responsible not only to governors, but also to the central diwan, which audited their records and passed often irrevocable judgment on their work.[31] As a rule, the total revenue of the region over which a *hakim* presided was entered in his name by the diwan and he was made responsible for its collection.[32] Receipts were given to landowners after they paid their share of the revenue.

The focus of special attention on revenue matters led revenue officials to become overzealous and realize revenues in excess. Of this there are numerous examples. Perhaps the major one is provided by the governor of Kandahar who declared, perhaps with some exaggeration, that "every year I collect tens of lakhs of rupees more than the former revenue of Kandahar."[33] Also, although formerly revenues had been collected after the crops were reaped, under the amir they were sometimes collected in advance.[34] Moreover, since the payment of taxes had been declared a religious duty taxpayers were obliged to pay without failure. If they failed to do so revenues were realized either from their nearest relations or their tribes.[35] Sometimes, however, remissions were granted when the yields were too poor or were destroyed by natural forces.[36]

The collection of revenue by government officials led to the imposition of certain kinds of unofficial fees on the taxpayers. Previously, it had been a common practice for the *hakims*, *daftaris*, or ʾamils to exact fees (*nan-khora*) when they signed contracts with the contractors or elders.[37] The amir banned this practice, but tax collectors still continued to exact fees[38] and lived on the taxpayers until they secured the payment. Usually, they collected revenue in excess and shared with the *ahl-i-diwan* (officials of the diwan) with whom they were in collusion.[39] Such exactions were said to be even higher than the actual amount of revenue.[40] Moreover, in remote areas the *muhassils*, as a body of armed cavalry, exacted still more. In the Hazarajat, for example, they intimidated the local officials and obtained from them *barats* on the taxpayers.[41] These *barats* included such items as meat, chicken, and wheat. They also compelled the officials to issue the *barats* at a low rate but collected double the amount from the taxpayers.[42] With the help of their retinue, whom they maintained at the expense of the raʾiyyats, the *muhassils* built houses for themselves and shelters for their animals. They also took possession of lands and sold the produce at exorbitant prices to the people.[43] In Kandahar, they forced the people to furnish them rice, ghee, and meat for their food, even during periods of scarcity when the people lived on the margin of subsistence.[44] Since, for the quick realization of revenue, the amir had ordered the *muhassils* to exact 10 percent of the revenue for themselves,[45] they considered this order a license not only to use force, but also to realize an excessive amount.[46] Beating and flogging of taxpayers, even to the point of death, became common.[47] As a consequence even the *muhassils* prospered,[48] to say nothing of the revenue officials.

The increase in the rates of revenue and the excessive demands of the collectors added to the general discontent.[49] The amir did not lower the rates but tried to rationalize the system of collection. The rationalization schemes were directed at decreasing government expenditure and alleviating oppression of the taxpayers, but still nothing was accomplished. The most important concession that the amir made to the ra'iyyats was to allow them to take their revenue themselves to the nearest government station in the course of the fiscal year and to obtain a receipt for their payment.[50] In addition, to the people of Ningrahar, the amir declared,

✤

Be it known to all landlords and tenants in Afghanistan that out of regard for you I have discontinued the system of employing government servants for the collection of the Government revenue. In the future the Government revenue will be paid in three installments during the year through the headmen of each village, who will bring it to the Jalalabad Treasury. If any landlord is too poor to pay the revenue in cash when the installments fall due, grace will be allowed him to pay the whole revenue of the year before the beginning of the next year, but if he is a defaulter at the commencement of the new year he will be liable to punishment.[51]

✤

Apparently, this scheme tended to enhance the role of elders. To avoid this and, at the same time, to decrease government expenditure, the amir, in 1898, arranged for the establishment of three revenue departments (tahsils) in each province. The tahsildars (heads of the departments) and their subordinates were to be put in charge of collecting the revenue.[52] Subsequently, in a modified form of this scheme, people were asked to appoint a tahsildar and a few mirzas for every 100,000 rupees due for collection. The officials so appointed were not to receive any emoluments from the state "less they use their influence for the purpose of oppression."[53] Where and to what extent this scheme was applied is not known, but what is certain is that with these reforms paid government officials did not cease to play a role in collecting revenue. On the contrary, they became much more important than before but in the more limited field of collecting revenue arrears.

Mirza Muhammad Hussayn of the sanjish department of the central diwan periodically drew up lists of the arrears.[54] Not only were the landowners made to pay the revenue of the occupation period, but they were also required to pay their revenue on the basis of the kot system from the day of the amir's accession.[55] In 1893, the arrears of revenue in Turkestan were collected for the thirteen years since his accession. Those who, for one reason or another, had been exempt from paying revenue were also made to pay the arrears from the same date.[56] In 1890 alone 700,000 rupees were said to be in arrears.[57] The question of arrears became still more significant when the amir in 1893 set a date by which time landowners were required to pay their revenue. As before, the arrears were collected by cavalry regiments, but with a stronger sense of urgency. Periodically, royal cavalry regiments were sent from Kabul to the provinces for the collection of arrears. They were followed by commissions headed by the amir's *peshkhid-mats*. When the latter showed leniency or inability quickly to collect the arrears, they were followed by other commissions headed by the Muhammadzay sardars.[58] The arrears of revenue were registered not only in the names of landowners who had failed to pay them, but also in the names of the ʾamils and zabits who had failed to realize them.[59] For revenue officials in Herat a date was fixed by which time they were to collect the arrears. If they failed they were then to pay twenty-five qirans (one qiran is one-half of a rupee) for each twenty owed.[60] In realizing the arrears the amir officially allowed the *muhassils* to exact fees, which included cash and food for themselves and grain for their horses.[61] Grievances became common but were aired to no effect in spite of the fact that the amir had instructed Mirza Muhammad Hussayn to redress complaints.[62] In this way large amounts of arrears were collected in a comparatively short time.

The exact proportion of the *khalisa* (state lands, also called *amlak-i-sarkari* or *zamin-i-zabti*) to the *mulk* (private estate) is difficult to ascertain. In the province of Kabul alone, before 1880, there were large tracts of the *khalisa* in every district. In the amir's reign the *khalisa* was still further increased mainly due to the flights of the followers of the family of Amir Sher ʾAli and of landowners during the first turbulent decade of the amir's reign. The state, in addition, resumed lands that had been formerly assigned to elders in return for their allowances on the ground that the grant of such lands by former rulers did not mean that the state had given up its right of ownership to them. This reversion affected many people, in particular elders of the eastern Ghilzays who held extensive tracts of lands on such terms.[63] Similarly lands that had been held by individuals without legal documents were confiscated on the ground that estates that were not legally possessed were the property of the state. Also, such wild nuts as pistachios were declared part of the *khalisa*.[64] Efforts were made to sell the *khalisa* but not with much success. Apparently, people were hesitant to purchase the lands of refugees. The amir then ordered compulsory enforcement of the Islamic principle of *shafʾ* that requires the sale of land first to those landholders whose lands are adjacent to it. Neighboring landlords were then made to buy the *khalisa* adjoining their own lands. By 1888 the governor of Herat collected 15 lakhs of rupees on such sales.[65]

Obviously the government share of the revenue on the *khalisa* was higher than that on private lands. Because of the nature of the *khalisa* the state, however, did not exact the same share everywhere. Formerly, in the Jalalabad area the state took either two-thirds or one-half of the produce from the *khalisa*, depending on whether the state or the cultivators had provided the seed and agricultural implements.[66] In the Ghazni area, the state derived revenue from one-half of the produce from the *khalisa*.[67] In Kandahar the state share of the produce from the *khalisa* was either *se-kot*, or *char-kot*.[68] In the reign of the amir the latter was raised to *nem-kot*. In the Logar district of the Kabul province the state appropriated two-thirds of the produce of the lands irrigated by *karezes*, which numbered sixty-four.[69] The increased rates in other parts of the country are not known. As before, the revenue derived from the *khalisa* was farmed out.

Land revenue in the reign of the amir was realized both in kind and in cash; but unlike the situation in the past, when landowners had paid their revenue partly in cash and partly in kind, in the reign of the amir the rate of the proportion was not fixed. The proportion was determined by such changing factors as the need for old coins for melting, government expenditure, and the storage of sufficient amounts of grain for army use. The general shift from the *jam'bast* to the *kot* system meant that the government derived its revenue from whatever the land produced. Despite the problem of transportation, for the government to take its revenue in kind was direct and without much annoyance to landowners. Grain was stored in government granaries, in Kabul and the provinces;[70] but, since the quantity was large and the storage conditions poor, the grain often went bad. The storage of large quantities of grain was, in addition, partly responsible for periods of scarcity.

The collection of revenue in cash meant that the government share of the produce was first converted, by the amir's firman, into cash and then collected. The rate of the conversion was not fixed on the basis of a free market, but by the amir's firmans, which were, of course, favorable to the state. In addition, revenue officials found it easy to extract extra money for themselves when the revenue was collected in cash. In 1882 in Kandahar, for instance, they collected thirty and even forty rupees for one kharwar of grain, whereas the official rate was from twenty to thirty rupees. Subsequently when the amir began to favor the Kandaharis, one Kandahari rupee for each two maunds and ten sers of grain was realized from their landowners as revenue in cash.[71] Although cash was often scarce the amir still ordered the realization of revenue in cash when a sufficient amount of grain was stored. In 1890, for instance, the surplus revenue for the whole country continued to be sent to Kabul in large sums. For a long time pressure was brought on revenue officials to recover the arrears in cash in order to keep the Kabul demands supplied. The old coins in these cash payments were to be melted down and recirculated as new coins that were then being minted.[72]

As a whole, the system of collecting revenue in cash or kind was kept flexible, although it was not always possible to collect cash and in Kandahar in 1900 the system partially collapsed.[73] Under the amir's son the system more or less remained the same. It was changed by King Aman Allah. In his reign only cash was taken as government revenue and then on favorable terms to landowners. An average of three years of produce per jarib, a rate which was fixed by agreement between the representatives of the government and the landowners, was taken as a basis and then converted into cash. Because of inflation, the rate was subject to review every three years during the reign of Aman Allah,[74] but it was not carried out until a new system of taxation, known as the progressive system of taxation, was introduced.

Other Taxes

Other taxes included cattle, house, income, purchase, poll, artisan, and vineyard taxes and customs dues. Most of these taxes were old. Amir ʾAbd al-Rahman introduced new taxes and increased the old; some he abolished.

Under Amir ʾAbd al-Rahman taxes on the lands, mills, vineyards, and estates that yielded interest included *ʾushr*, *khums* (one-fifth), and *kharaj* up to *chehl wa yak* (one out of forty). The capital and goods of traders were also subject to taxation. All these, of course, had been subject to taxation before, but they were to be calculated anew so that what was officially described as "discrepancy, exaction, and favoritism" would be stopped.[75] In fact, this declaration was no more than an attempt to justify a fresh calculation for the purpose of increasing taxes, both in kinds and in rates. As before favoritism was shown, but exactions became still more common.

Owing to their high yields, vineyards were always highly taxed, but the rates of taxation differed from one region to another. For example, in Kohdaman and Kohistan, where the yields were the highest, one rupee per hundred vines was realized;[76] in Badakhshan a graded tax of ten, seven, and five tangas per jarib of the garden was levied.[77] In Istalif a tax of two rupees per hundred tendrils of the vines was imposed, while previously the rate had been only half of this, that is, the same rate as in Kohdaman.[78] Trees that produced fruits were also subject to taxation. Mulberry trees, which are common in Afghanistan, were made subject to a tax of one rupee per tree per year.[79] In the Jalalabad area owners of fruit trees were not allowed to pick the fruits of their orchards until these had been appraised for tax purposes.[80] In some areas this restriction led owners to cut their trees.

The rate of taxes on cattle (*zakat* or *sarghala*) was not uniform. *Chehl wa yak* was levied on the sheep and *khums* was levied on camels and cows.[81] Donkeys, goats, mares, and horses were also taxed; only cows and oxen that were kept for domestic and agricultural purposes and horses that were kept for riding were exempt from taxation.[82] For convenience and increase in taxes, cattle taxes were usually collected in cash, but the rates were not standardized. In Qataghan where large herds of cattle were maintained, two out of one hundred sheep and goats were taken, and two rupees per camel and one rupee per head of horse was charged.[83] In Badakhshan a tax of one qiran was imposed on each donkey and cow;[84] in Herat twenty qirans were realized on every one hundred goats, and fifty on every one hundred sheep.[85] Toward the end of the amir's reign the Qirghiz inhabitants of Wakhan were also made to pay *chehl wa yak* on their cattle.[86] The *kuchis* (nomads) paid four rupees on every forty sheep and goats, one rupee on each camel and on two horses, one rupee per four cows, and one rupee per six donkeys.[87] Although in every province there was a separate office in charge of the cattle tax (*shakhshumari*), the actual enumeration rested with the royal cavalry regiment.[88]

Goods were taxed to increase government incomes rather than to protect domestic products or restrict the import of luxury goods. Foreign goods were taxed on entry in the customs houses (*chabutaras*) in the cities, as well as on posts along the main roads. In Kabul alone goods were subject to hosts of small taxes, the nature of which is difficult to describe.[89] During the first decade of the amir's reign taxes on imports[90] and exports[91] were considerably increased, sometimes to rates twice as high as those in the reign of Amir Sher 'Ali Khan. Because of this and other factors that will be discussed in chapter 9, internal trade decreased and foreign trade was largely diverted. Customs duties sharply fell.[92] Only toward the end of his reign did the amir reduce the rate of charge by one-fourth.[93] On the export of fruits and raisins the tolls were reduced from thirty-two rupees per load of camel to nineteen.[94]

The introduction of a select purchase tax payable by both buyers and sellers was an innovation in the reign of the amir. In Kandahar a tax of one and a half shahis per Kandahari maund[95] on the sale of wool and of 5 percent on the sale of copper vessels[96] was levied. The sale of sheep was made subject to a tax of one anna per head.[97] Also, the sale of old and new "articles" was made subject to a tax of one anna per piece,[98] but it is not known what these articles were. In 1896 the amir decided to establish an income tax at the rate of 1 percent,[99] but no details on this are available. Earlier, however, the amir had increased the tax on profit from goods from 3 percent to 5 percent a year.[100] Those traders whose annual profit was less than one thousand rupees were exempt.[101] Another innovation was the realization of 3 percent in cash on the transfer of money abroad through government channels. Meanwhile a tax of half a rupee per hundred on cases settled in government courts was also imposed.[102]

In the reign of Ahmad Shah Durrani foreign Muslim colonists who wished to settle on the Kandahar lands as shepherds or cultivators paid the *khanadodi* or *khanawari* (capitation tax) in return for the protection the state provided them. The Durranis were exempt from this; so were the Parsiwans of Kandahar, according to one source.[103] By the time the amir came to power the *khanawari*, or as it was then called *tawan-i-sar* or *sar-i-marda*, was exacted only from the Ghilzays, at a rate of one rupee per family. Arguing that it was unlawful to exact *jazya* from Muslims, the amir abolished this tax[104] but introduced, or rather extended, house tax, which was in reality the same as the *khanawari*. At first a light rate of house tax was imposed, but in 1895 every house was required to pay ten rupees per annum.[105] In Kabul the house tax was stopped for a while, being considered unlawful in Islam.[106] Subsequently it was reimposed there and introduced, perhaps for the first time in some cases, in the suburbs of Kabul and in Kohistan,[107] Herat[108] and Kandahar.[109] In the latter province, as had hap-

pened during the reign of Ahmad Shah, only the non-Durranis, or *opras*
as they were commonly called, paid the house tax.[110] The imposition
of the house tax on the army was first held in abeyance in 1887[111] but
was resumed in 1890.[112]

Marriage tax was collected by the state before 1880,[113] but during the
amir's reign it was increased to twelve and a half rupees on the marriage of a virgin and six and a half on that of a widow.[114] This tax was
enforced throughout Afghanistan and the Hindus were also subject to
it. Further, a tax of four rupees on the birth of a male child and of two
on a female child was also enforced.[115] Burial tax in Badakhshan ranged
from three to five rupees on each dead person.[116] Whether this tax was
also enforced elsewhere is not certain. On the circumcision of a boy his
parents were required to pay twelve rupees and a felt hat to the state as
tax.[117] By contrast, the gambling tax was abolished; previously gambling and prostitution had been allowed by the state in return for
tax.[118] As is evident most of these taxes were either increased or reintroduced in 1886. Mawlawi Ahmad Jan Alkozay of Kandahar, the
one-time chief of a department in the central diwan and the famous
author of a number of manuals of instruction for government officials,
proposed that these taxes must be in line with "the political law and
the Shari'a," and the amir ordered that the taxes be enforced.[119]

Before 1880, the tax on the artisans (*asnaf*) had varied from two
rupees to seven[120] a year, but in the amir's reign it was raised to ten.
The artisans were, in addition, required to pay 10 percent of their
annual income to the state.[121] Fortunetellers and astrologers also paid
twelve rupees annually.[122] The mullas, who previously had been exempt from paying any tax, were also made subject to taxation during
the reign of the amir. They were forced to pay the house tax[123] and
also were deprived of the fees (*sadaqa* and *sarsaya*) that they had received from villagers at the end of the month of fast. These fees were an
important source of a mulla's income, and in 1892 the state appropriated them for itself.[124] Central Asian Muslims passing through Afghanistan en route to Mecca for pilgrimage were also made to pay a tax.[125]

The non-Muslim minorities (the Hindus, Sikhs, and Jews) continued
to pay *jazya* but at a higher rate. The rate of *jazya* on each of them had
been five rupees per year.[126] The amir first fixed three rates of four,
eight, and sixteen rupees on the Hindus, and presumably on the Sikhs,
in accordance with their income. Subsequently every adult—excluding
the disabled, aged, and, presumably, women—was required to pay
16 percent of his income in a year.[127] The Jews paid *jazya* at first per
family and then, in 1901, per head; but how much they paid is unknown.[128]

In 1887 the amir gave out that to meet foreign aggression Ottoman
subjects agreed to pay ten percent of their income over and above the
usual tax to their ruler the sultan.[129] The amir argued that, since the
Ottoman sultan was a Muslim, why should he (the amir) not do the
same? He then ordered the collection of an additional tax of ten rupees
a year per head from his subjects. Two senior officials, the *dabir al-*

mulk and *kabul kotwal*, advised the amir against enforcement of his order. After abusing the former and slapping the latter the amir left the order in abeyance.[130]

Tax Collection

Realizing revenue through contract or farming (*ijara*) was an old practice in Afghanistan; but the more the bureaucracy was extended the narrower the scope for contracting became. The extension of the central power in the reign of the amir might have been expected to terminate the contract system altogether, but for reasons that will be discussed shortly the system was allowed to function until it was abolished in 1901.

Under Amir Sher 'Ali all lands that belonged to villagers and were not under permanent assessment were farmed out.[131] The revenue of the lands that were subject to the *kot* system was therefore realized indirectly through contract. During the amir's reign a larger portion of the taxes and a smaller portion of the land revenue were realized by contract. As before, these contracts were taken up by the sardars, elders, and well-to-do people. Sometimes government officials, too, were given contracts.[132] In theory, a contract was open to everyone, but in practice only a few could undertake it. In Kandahar it was practically monopolized by a few.[133] The contract was neither hereditary nor for an indefinite period of time. Usually it was given for one year and occasionally for four. The annual renewal of the contract made the system subject to keen competition among the contractors (*musta-'jirs* or *ijaradars*). Whoever undertook to pay the highest amount was likely to get the contract. Only sometimes was a contract given to someone who bid a moderate amount, and then only for political reasons.[134]

Big contracts were usually given out by the amir in Kabul and by the governors in the provinces. In the past the custom had been for the *hakims, daftaris*, and *'amils* to give the contracts and to receive fees (*rusum*) for themselves.[135] The amir abolished the fee but at the same time ordered that no contract should be given without obtaining a security in advance.[136] When contractors became bankrupt the revenue was realized from their sureties and, failing that, from their relations and tribes or both.[137] In any case the bankrupt contractor was made to work, if he had been unable to abscond, in Kabul workshops until the revenues were paid in full. Sometimes the state became a contractor's partner, but only for the profit, not any loss.[138] In spite of these strict regulations there were many volunteers to take contracts. Because they were "at liberty to behave as they like in regard to the collection,"[139] the contractors normally realized more than they guaranteed. Moreover, armed with legal documents and supported by government cavalry, contractors collected taxes on items that were not included in their contracts.[140] The extent of their power can be understood from the fact that district revenue officials were made responsible to the contractors who examined their accounts.[141] It is not known whether the government paid the contractors. Only in one case was a contractor allowed to appropriate for himself 5 percent of the revenue he had undertaken to collect.[142]

Before 1880 land revenue subject to the *kot* system was usually farmed out.[143] In the amir's reign land revenue of the remote areas was contracted out, and in 1893 in Herat all sources of revenue were leased out.[144] The land revenues of Chakhansur[145] and of Turkestan were also realized on the basis of contract. The revenue of the latter province was recovered under the strict supervision of military officials for fear of absconding contractors.[146] In 1896 the land revenues of the Ghazni district were farmed out, but only as an experiment to find out whether government expenditure and exactions by officials could be reduced.[147] Reports do not make it clear whether the revenues that were realized through contract in the reign of the amir were from the *khalisa* or private land or both. Two things, however, are clear: first, the revenues that were obtained from the *khalisa* were usually farmed out;[148] and, second, from the midnineties onward, except for the experimental case of Ghazni, no land revenue was farmed out, although other taxes were. Not only was the experiment then given up, but the contract system on the non-*khalisa* revenue was replaced by a system of direct collection.

Most other taxes, as opposed to land revenue, were farmed out throughout the amir's reign. The customs dues of all provinces, except Kabul, and the customs dues of all frontier passes, except the Khyber (or, rather, Dakka?) were given out in farm.[149] Cattle taxes on the nomads traveling inside the country and on the sedentary population were also contracted, but it is not known whether the cattle taxes of the *kuchis* migrating to India were collected directly or through contract. Dues of cattle markets (*suq al-dawab*) were also leased out. Varieties of other taxes including those on silk, soap and shops[150] and taxes on the sale of postins (in Ghazni) and the sale taxes in Kabul were also given in lease. Dues on the export of wood from Kafiristan were also realized through contract.[151] The incomes of certain government offices such as the courts[152] and others were also periodically leased out.[153] Postal services of northern Afghanistan[154] and passport fees (in Kohdaman) were similarly given in contract. The *qafila bashi* tax of Kandahar was also collected through contract, but it is not known how this tax was collected in other provinces.

The overall direct consequence of the amir's policies of taxation was that after paying taxes and revenue little was left for landowners and other groups to support their families. An extreme example is provided by Sardar Sher Ahmad. According to him, the average produce of one plowland in Badakhshan in 1883 was two and a half Kabuli kharwars of grain. Out of this the government took one kharwar as revenue.[155] The share of the landowner who had cultivated the land himself, one and a half kharwars, was valued at twenty-two and a half rupees in accordance with the price of the local market of the time, fifteen rupees per kharwar. Out of this the owner paid seventeen rupees and two tangas on other taxes. Just over four and a half rupees were left to the land-owner to support his family and cattle and to procure seed for the next year.[156] In addition, the simultaneous visitation of a village by scores of government officials was not infrequent. According to one report, "In the northern district of Kandahar numerous officials collect taxes in every village at the same time: one is to enumerate sheep, the other to ascertain marriages celebrated during the past three years, the third to ascertain the amount of the effects of a deceased person, another to take census, another to collect supplies for the forces of Abdul Quddus Khan [in the Hazarajat] and another to send men to work on the road under construction from Tirin to Kandahar."[157] That was why govern-ment officials engaged in the collection of revenue were received, as the British agent put it, as a "heaven-sent calamity."[158] The cry of "It is now all over with our lives and property"[159] was frequently raised. The gulf between the government and the governed had never been so wide.

The initial resistance to the taxation policies of the amir took the form of nonpayment of taxes, an action which ultimately led to con-frontations between taxpayers and the government's forces. These have been fully discussed in the writer's *Afghanistan: A Study in Internal Political Developments, 1880–1896.* Here it is sufficient to note that wherever the *se-kot* was enforced there were risings, for this tax hit hardest small landowners who constituted the largest number of landholders[160] and whose lands were irrigated by rivers and streams, which were the most common means of irrigation in Afghanistan. When taxpayers were unable to resist or after their risings had been suppressed, they deserted their lands. Inside Afghanistan they swelled the ranks of chronic unemployment and beggary, but most flights were to frontier regions and abroad. Of the escapees probably the largest number were the inhabitants of the regions beyond the Hindu Kush: Taluqah (658 families), Baghlan, Ghuri, Qataghan, and Badakhshan.[161]

From Badakhshan alone during the first three years of the amir's rule seven hundred families absconded to Kulab, Yarkand, and Kanjud beyond the Oxus.[162] In 1888 it was again reported that "Most people of Istaq [Rustaq?] in Badakhshan" fled to Kulab. These escapees were in addition to those who fled with Sardar Muhammad Ishaq. In 1893, too, it was reported that "several thousand families" fled to Bukhara and Russian Turkestan.[163]

In eastern Afghanistan one in ten people were reported to have absconded from Jalalabad in 1887 alone.[164] Subsequently some of the residents of Kama first set fire to their houses and then fled beyond the border. Of the inhabitants of Laghman in 1899 "a large number of landlords" left to settle in the Peshawar district, Bajaur, and other areas.[165] Others were preparing to flee in the same direction. "Many zamindars of Peshbolak in the Shinwar country" also fled in 1901.

Because of these flights the amir in 1901 ordered the remittance of the arrears of revenue in Ningrahar,[166] but whether this remittance was universal is not known.

In Kandahar in 1892 a number of Zamindawaris[167] and subsequently the inhabitants of the Mashur and Bilandi villages to the south and southwest of Kandahar fled to other distant districts for revenue reasons. In Herat in 1891, 1,500 Taimani families of Ghurat[168] and in 1895 the people of Chakcharan and Anardara left their homes for various directions for the same reasons.[169] To avoid paying taxes the *kuchis* in May 1896 left India for Kashmir instead of Afghanistan.

Sometimes taxpayers took refuge in sanctuaries, hoping that the demand for increased revenue might be withheld. In the course of 1900 alone first merchants and shopkeepers[170] and then cultivators[171] took refuge in the *bast* of Gazargah in Herat, but to no effect. To meet the demand for revenue taxpayers sometimes had to sell their land, property, and even children. The difficulties in selling land were the lack of demand and the Islamic limitation that the prospective seller offer his land first to his neighboring landowner. The state did not show any interest in purchasing land. As a matter of fact, the state had the same problem in selling refugee lands to others. References to the sale of land are few: some can be found for Ghazni,[172] Sarab and Nahwar[173] and Zamindawar.[174] On these sales, too, details are wanting. Nothing else is known about them except that landowners sold their lands to meet the demands for revenue. References to the sale of cattle for the same purpose are many.[175] Reports also indicate that at times in Turkestan[176] and Badakhshan[177] taxpayers sold their daughters to pay the revenue.

Budget, Income, and Expenditure

It is not clear whether governments functioned on the basis of annual budgets showing the amount of income and expenditure before 1880. In 1857 the total revenue of Afghanistan, excluding Herat, was 4,008,800 rupees. From this, one million rupees were paid to elders.[178] The picture of the budget for the reign of Amir Sher 'Ali is relatively clear. J. Lambert, a British official, has drawn it out of the official records captured in Kabul during the Second Anglo-Afghan War. According to his list the total revenue of Afghanistan, excluding Farah, for 1877–1878 was 13,323,174 rupees and expenditure was 11,751,112 rupees. The government had a surplus of 1,482,062 rupees. Except for the province of Herat, which out of a revenue of 1,409,308 rupees had a deficiency of 125,500, other provinces provided the surplus: Kabul 1,313,323 from an income of 6,318,809; Turkestan 900,088 from 3,744,602; and Kandahar 593,994 from 1,760,298. The largest single item of the income came from the land revenue collected in cash, kind, and fodder. Of the expenditure, the biggest single item was spent on the army. It amounted to 5,640,436 rupees, or just under 43 percent of the total income; and 1,200,000 rupees were spent on the construction of the Sherpur cantonment. Payment of the police and the allowances to the feudal elders must have been a sizable item. It is difficult now to tell how great the expenditure of the darbar was and how much was paid to government officials. Other main items of expenditure were payments to religious groups and to Muhammadzay sardars.[179]

Under Amir ᾿Abd al-Rahman the revenue, as well as the expenditure, of Afghanistan increased still further. The increase in income was made possible by an increase in the rates of revenue and by the opening of nine new sources of income. First, it was usual for the amir to confiscate the wealth of senior officials, whenever they became rich. With this view in mind, the amir and his second son Sardar Nasr Allah examined the officials' accounts and struck huge balances against them.[180] Exactly how much they added to the treasury in this way is impossible to tell, but the total amount must have run to millions of rupees. Second, in addition to the expropriation of the estates of the refugees the money and the property that they had deposited, or were said to have deposited, with their relatives and with merchants were, thanks to the amir's spies, discovered and confiscated. In a firman the amir declared that if the people with whom such money had been deposited failed to produce the money and property they would be punished and their own property also confiscated.[181] Forged seals of the refugees residing in India were used to prepare letters implicating many well-to-do Afghanistan people in false charges of hiding the property of refugees; the money and property of these people who had been falsely accused were also confiscated.[182] Third, by custom, well-to-do people offered presents to government officials on many occasions, especially at the commencement of the officials' duties. The amir declared such presents to be *bayt al-mal* (public property), arguing that these grants were made to them as government officials, not private individuals, and that they received payment for serving the state.[183] Fourth, the amir expected his officials to send him presents (*nazrana*) regularly. Such presents consisted of local products, cattle, weapons, cash, and sometimes even male and female slaves.[184] When once the qazi and mufti of Jalalabad failed to offer presents to the amir after his arrival there he fined them 3,000 and 500 rupees respectively.[185] Fifth, the movable property of senior officials, including army officers, was usually taken by the amir upon their deaths. Sixth, one-fifth of the spoils obtained in the internal wars was also appropriated by the state.[186] Seventh, the government monopolized certain items of trade and became a partner with traders in others. Eighth, "for the consolidation of the foundation of the state and nation and the safeguarding of the religion and the country" the amir sought a national donation. All government employees "agreed" to contribute one month's salary[187] and traders to pay 10 percent of their annual income to the state[188] in order to purchase modern weapons. Ninth, the amir received from the British government a regular subsidy that started in July 1883 (one lakh a month) and was increased in November 1893 (one and a half lakh per month). Also, the British government offered additional grants in money and arms in emergencies in 1880, 1881, and 1887. The grants in cash amounted to over twenty-eight and a half million rupees during the entire course of the amir's reign.

In 1885 the amir provided the British government with a statement showing the income and expenditure of Afghanistan. The total figures in this statement were almost the same as they had been in 1877. The revenues of the Kabul province, for instance, in 1885 were just over 5 million Indian rupees and in 1877 over 6 million Kabuli rupees or a little more than 5 million Indian rupees. Since, as will be discussed shortly, no real budget was prepared during the reign of the amir this statement was based, with all likelihood, on an estimate with an intention to show a deficit, and for this reason income was shown to be 10,383,207 Indian rupees and expenditure 12,289,492. This exaggerated deficit, however, itemizes expenditure and appropriation for each purpose. For instance, expenditure on the regular and irregular military and paramilitary (police and *khassadars*) formed the largest item, but the total figure of 8,632,814 or 78 percent of the total national income for the army seems an exaggeration. Allowances to religious groups, elders, remission of revenue allowed to landlords according to the old custom, and expenditure on construction work were the next main items of expenditure in the list. As in Lambert's list, so in this one, payments to government officials are not noted, although in the latter payments to the collectors of revenue are computed to be 68,491 rupees a year.[189] In the reign of the amir, as before, provincial expenses were met from the local incomes and surpluses sent to the capital,[190] and the fiscal year corresponded with the solar year beginning on March 21.

By contrast reports from other sources indicate revenue surpluses in the reign of the amir. According to these reports, income and expenditure in the reign of the amir increased proportionally and expenditure was kept well within the income. A month after the amir took over, the income of Afghanistan (excluding Kandahar and Herat) for the four months from September to December was 4 million against an expenditure of 2 million rupees.[191] Three years later, with Kandahar and Herat added, this income for the whole year had risen to 13,300,000 rupees of which 6 million was derived from Kabul, 3 million from Turkestan, 2,400,000 from Kandahar, 1,600,000 from Herat, and 300,000 from Farah.[192] At that time Maimana, Uruzgan, and Kafiristan had still not been incorporated into Afghanistan and the districts of Sibi and Kurram formed parts of India. In 1889 the total income was reported to have risen to 14 million rupees[193] and in 1891 to 50 million.[194] The amir's own figures for 1889 were 50 million when he told the British agent that "I can confidently declare that the revenue will not be less than five crores of rupees."[195] By 1891 the yearly revenue in the reign of Amir 'Abd al-Rahman had increased by slightly less than four times the revenue of the last year of the reign of Amir Sher 'Ali Khan. Figures are wanting for yearly expenditure for most of the amir's reign. It may, however, be assumed that with the increase in the army in the nineties, the expansion of Kabul workshops, and the assignment of large allowances to Muhammadzay sardars the expenditure had risen correspondingly. Ghobar states that with all the exactions and increases in the income there was not much saving and that only 60 million rupees and a moderate number of valuables were left in the treasury when the amir died in 1901.[196]

Saving was the result of the accumulation of income over the years rather than of a calculation based on good information concerning annual income and expenditure. For the amir it proved easier to find new sources of income than to persuade his officials to prepare a statement showing the income and expenditure of Afghanistan even for one year. The factors responsible for the officials' failure to prepare a statement were the steady and simultaneous increase in income and expenditure; the opening of unfamiliar sources of income; the insufficient number, or rather the lack of qualified *mirzas*; the collection of revenue partly in kind; and the poor distribution of work among more-or-less equally ranked *sardaftars* of the central diwan.

This last factor was the result of the separation of the main offices in the central diwan, whose head officers followed custom and worked under the amir rather than under one financial expert, such as a *mustaufi*.

Also, the mirzas were reluctant to show the real and the net amounts of income. So despite the many increases, the yearly surplus was not considerable, mainly because of the corresponding increase in the expenditure. For their failure to prepare a statement the amir suspended the salary of the mirzas and made its resumption contingent upon their preparing the statement, but they still failed to do so. Only Mustaufi Mir Muhammad Hussayn, while in office, had arranged a statement covering the details of the first two years of his office; but his downfall (which was brought about to oust the Qizilbashes) and the rise to high offices of the junior mirzas in the central diwan led to the concealment of that statement. Among these mirzas was Mirza Muhammad Hussayn who distinguished himself as *sardaftari* of the auditing section but who, finding the preparation of the statement difficult, switched to striking balances of revenues and money that taxpayers and officials owed to the state, despite the fact that he had undertaken to complete the statement. The more basic task of balancing the budget and rationalizing the financial system to cope with the many unfamiliar problems of an expanding bureaucracy was left incomplete, and the amir let himself act as a *mustaufi*. Since the amir was not a *mirza* but was used to recourse to compulsion in the affairs of the state, his method of applying compulsion with the mirzas in the intricate financial affairs ultimately failed him.[197] Consequently, the amir ruled over the country without knowing its real income and expenditures.[198]

Chapter V
The Army

Although the army was raised to defend Afghanistan from foreign invasions, it became, in fact, the main instrument by which Amir ʾAbd al-Rahman pacified the country. The amir did not inherit the army of his predecessors but created a large, disciplined army of his own, independent of tribal control. To equip it he established factories where modern weapons were made. At the same time, he made use of the traditional feudal and tribal levies and attempted to arm the whole nation.

Historical Developments

Ever since the foundation of Afghanistan in 1747, the army had played a major role in the history of the country, but by the time of the first Anglo-Afghan War it was mainly feudal and tribal. The regular standing army was relatively small.

In the reign of Ahmad Shah the main core of the army was the feudal cavalry, but the conditions under which each tribe or group of tribes furnished horsemen differed. The Durrani horsemen were, in essence, more feudal than those of other tribes. The Durrani elders, who were responsible for furnishing the horsemen, were assigned rent-free land in return for military service. They were, in addition, paid allowances in proportion to the number of horses they retained. These and other similar privileges, which Ahmad Shah bestowed on the Durrani elders, enabled them to consolidate their position so that ultimately they became a potential threat to the monarchy, despite the fact that of the 12,559 Kandahar horsemen, the Durrani horsemen were only 5,710 and the rest were furnished by such non-Durrani tribes of Kandahar as the Tokhays, Hotakays, Kakars, Daways, and Bareches. In addition to the Kandahar were the *kara nokars*, provided by the non-Durrani tribes, particularly the Tajiks, during the Sadozay period. These horsemen were furnished by landowners in return for the remission of land revenue. In theory one man was due, without pay from the state, for every "plow" of land. In reality the tribes near Kabul furnished the number due on that principle in an emergency; but the more powerful or more remote tribes supplied a smaller proportion, and some sent none at all. The *kara nokars* were formed into groups, under their own maliks, and the maliks were commanded by the Durrani sardars.[1] In addition, for the protection of the frontier province of Balkh "an Aughaun military colony" was planted there by Ahmad Shah.[2] They were called the *kohna nokars* and were paid by assignment of land that was transferable from father to son.

In the reign of Amir Dost Muhammad elders furnished feudal horsemen throughout Afghanistan. Before Herat was pacified, the number of feudal cavalry was 38,000 out of which the Durranis provided 8,000.[3] The terms under which the elders of tribal communities provided horsemen to the state during the reign of Amir Sher ʾAli included autonomy for the elders and communities. The state in return exacted only a small quota of revenue from the people of the community through their elders. Mounted on small, but stout horses, the feudal cavalry was armed with shield, spear, matchlock, sword, pistol, and knife.

Although as early as in the reign of Ahmad Shah a separate independent force known as the *ghulam-i-shah* perhaps on the model of *shah-sevan* of the Safavid rulers, had been established, it was actually developed in the reign of Timur Shah who used it as a counterpoise to the Durrani cavalry. The Durranis were mainly excluded from the *ghulam-i-shah*. The Qizilbashes, who had retained their original military character and who, more than the Afghans, were faithful to their masters, constituted the majority of the *ghulam-i-shah*. As a standing army, the *ghulam-i-shah* were enlisted for life and received pay. They were divided into groups, and commanded by officers known as *qular aghasis*.

With the collapse of the Durrani rule in the country, the organization of the *ghulam-i-shah* disintegrated. In their place the Barakzay rulers of Kandahar organized a more efficient body of cavalry which performed the same task as the *ghulam-i-shah* had. Like the *ghulam-i-shah* the new cavalry was composed of non-Durrani mercenaries commanded by officers directly responsible to the sardars.[4]

The restoration of the Sadozay monarchy ended the military force of the Barakzay sardars and in their place a better organized corps of regular army was formed. In June 1840 William Macnaghten, British envoy in Kabul, forced Shah Shujaʾ to consent to the formation of a new force to be known as *janbaz*. The *janbaz* was commanded by British officers and received much higher pay than the horsemen had received. Three such corps, 1,200 in all, were formed in Kabul and one in Kandahar. In Kabul at the same time a similar body of 800 known as the *hazirbash* was also formed. Since the *janbaz* were paid by and were dependent on the British officers and were intended ultimately to replace the feudal cavalry, the Durrani elders in the darbar made great efforts to prevent the formation of new units in spite of the fact that the Durrani elders were, at the same time, allowed to retain a reduced number of 750 horsemen.[5]

With the collapse of the Anglo-Sadozay rule the new units also disappeared, but they had set an example for the creation of stronger systems of government by the use of disciplined forces and the training of Afghan troops that paved the way for the powerful standing army of Amir Dost Muhammad Khan with which he could extend his authority over all Afghanistan.[6]

The regular standing army of Amir Dost Muhammad during his second reign consisted of infantry and cavalry regiments, composed of eight hundred (nominal) and three hundred men. Recruitment was based on neither regular conscription nor voluntary services. Able-bodied men were seized from each district and compelled to serve on pain of imprisonment and the ruin of their family. Payment to a foot soldier, which was partly in kind and partly in cash, but often irregular, was 5 rupees a month. Strict discipline was maintained in the army. Commanded by the sons of the amir the army was distributed in various provinces and districts without being under the command of one senior officer, such as a *sipah salar*. Sir Bartle Frere held that some Afghan troops of Amir Dost Muhammad were "quite equal in armament, skill, and drill to any corps in our service."[7]

The civil war following the death of Amir Dost Muhammad led to the disintegration of the first large standing army in Afghanistan, but Amir Sher ʾAli Khan during his second reign created a larger and better army than that organized by his father. Based on the British model, it was composed of regiments of infantry, cavalry, and artillery[8] and was commanded by Afghan officers, who were subordinate to a senior officer, the Sipah Salar Hussayn ʾAli Khan Qizilbash. Such Indian instructors as General Karim Bakhsh and Sardar Ghulam Bahadur Naqshband were also employed to modernize the army.[9]

The components of the army under Amir Sher ʾAli are not known for certain, but the Ghilzays and Wardaks dominated it. Each infantryman received seven rupees and each cavalryman twice as much in cash per month. Recruited for life, soldiers wore European-style uniforms as a symbol of modernity. The army numbered 56,173 and, as before, was stationed in provincial capitals and strategically important districts, with a substantial portion in Kabul.[10] Once again, this time as a result of the British invasion of Afghanistan, the regular army disintegrated.

The third element of the Afghan army was the tribal militia called upon in an emergency. It was generally believed that the Afghans, though impatient under restraint, were born soldiers, excellent skirmishers, and experienced foragers. As soldiers they were said to possess these necessary qualifications in much greater degree than Europeans.

Against cannons, however, they felt they could not trust to the prowess that they valued so highly. The Afghans themselves believed that if other nations were, like themselves, armed only with swords instead of guns and other sophisticated weapons, Afghanistan could conquer the world. Islam further strengthened that conviction and, as Muslims, the Afghans believed that the numerous battalions of the infidels were powerless against a handful of ghazis.[11] Of the tribal militia there were three kinds, namely the *eljaris* (commonly known as *elajaris*), *dawatalab*, and the *ulus*. By the reign of Amir ʾAbd al-Rahman only the *eljaris* were called to service in an emergency. In theory the *eljaris* could form a levee en masse of the population; in reality the number raised was limited by the pay and provisions made available to them through their elders.

Recruitment of Officers and Men and Their Pay

The most important accomplishment of Amir ʾAbd al-Rahman was the organization of a large standing army. By it he intended to fulfill a twofold purpose. First, he intended to use the army to consolidate his own dynasty by eliminating his rivals and establishing an absolute government. Second, he hoped to shield Afghanistan against foreign invasion. To a large gathering of elders the amir declared,

❖

The forces I am going to raise are intended only for the protection of Afghanistan in the event of a foreign invasion.
You know your country is situated like a village between
the two governments of the infidels, each of which is ambitious to invade and take Afghanistan. You must, therefore,
be prepared for a time of emergency so as to safeguard
yourselves from invasion. If you fail to provide for such an
event, you will then have to be content with the fate of your
brethren in India, who, you know well, have no power over
their wives. You will then all become women yourselves,
with no influence over your families.[12]

❖

The amir made efforts to raise the strongest army in central Asia[13] and to make Afghanistan "one of the most powerful powers in the world,"[14] in spite of the fact that Afghanistan had limited resources and no modern technology.

In the 1880s when the amir was uncertain of the loyalty of elders he raised men of little social significance to high military posts. Accord-ing to an observer, "The company officers . . . seem far superior to the General officers, for the former do appear to have the instincts of soldiers, but General officers have had no military training whatsoever. Their appointment is merely an act of favour bestowed on any but soldiers; a slave, a surveyor, or a contractor suddenly finds himself raised to the rank of a General, and given to the command of an army, but it is the mediocre who are chosen. It is probable that a regard for his [the amir's] safety dictates this policy." [15] In the 1890s when his rule was firmly established the amir gradually recruited officers from among the sons of elders (khanzadas). As before, the peshkhidmat and slave officers remained in their positions. In fact, the number of both categories of officers increased to meet the demands of a growing army. By recruiting the khanzadas and quickly promoting them to officer rank [16] the amir further hoped that "at times of emergency the leading men having regard for the lives of their relatives would not venture to rise against him." [17]

For the modernization of the army, the amir, unlike his predecessors, neither sought the services of foreign officers nor showed willingness to accept British officers or engineers. He relied wholly on Afghan commanders, most of whom were recruited from among the landed gentry and the well-to-do people. Thus the state the amir organized became ultimately identified militarily with the elders and the well to do of the country.

The principle of loyalty was also observed with regard to the recruitment of soldiers, but with them the basis of loyalty was collective rather than individual. Within the first few months of his accession the amir recruited eight regiments on a voluntary basis principally from among old soldiers of his own. [18] The soldiers of the dispersed army of Amir Sher 'Ali were not employed at that time but were used toward the end of Amir 'Abd al-Rahman's reign. [19]

Similarly, in the beginning, the Durranis were not enlisted, because they had sided with Sardar Muhammad Ayyub. Only when the Ghilzay rebelled did the amir reverse this policy. Thereafter the Durranis were recruited in large numbers, in spite of the fact that military service was not popular with them. [20] Within the Durrani tribal confederation the Muhammadzay section was favored. From the latter a distinct and privileged royal cavalry, known as the risala-i-shahi-Kandahari, was formed.

As before, the Ghilzays constituted the principal tribal component of the regular army, in spite of the fact that during the rebellion of their own tribes some Ghilzay regiments joined the insurgents.

As a rule when a tribe was pacified recruitment was made from it. The only exceptions were the Hazaras and the Qizilbashes. In fact, after the Hazara War the Qizilbashes were dismissed from the army, [21] and only the Behsud and Jaghuri Hazaras remained in it. Such people as the Hindus who had not rebelled were also recruited into the army and police. Subsequently, the Hindus of Kabul secured their exemption in return for payment of 50,000 rupees. [22] Among the Pashtuns beyond the Durand Line a substantial number of Wazirs, Afridays, and Khattaks were enrolled, especially after the tribal uprising of 1897. Thus, although it was dominated by the Pashtuns, the army included almost all ethnic groups including the Uzbek and Aimaq.

As a rule army units raised in one region were stationed in another, apparently in order to separate the soldiers from their own people and to use them easily against other tribes when necessary. An exception

was the army stationed in Turkestan, which was said to have been recruited mainly from the local population. At the same time, soldiers
from other areas stationed in Turkestan either took their wives with
them or married local women. In this way they were said to have
been localized.[23] Regiments were organized on either a territorial or a
tribal basis. There was only one regiment that was all Pashtun in
composition.

Men between the ages of fourteen and fifty were recruited into the
army first on a voluntary basis and then by conscription. Recruitment
on the former basis continued until the country was pacified and the
amir felt that he could coerce the tribes into accepting conscription.
Among the problems resulting from the new system was the question
of the proportion of men to be enlisted, since no real census existed
and no fixed system of recruitment had been in operation before.
Various schemes were tried out until the *hasht nafari* system was
adopted. When Russian pressure on the Panjdeh built up, the amir
started recruiting men at Herat up to 15 percent of the population.[24]
Not only could the state not afford this high percentage, the people
could not provide it. In 1887 a compromise was reached whereby the
elders and mullas of Herat accepted a rate of one man out of every
twenty for enlistment in the army. In the same year, the Durranis of
Kandahar were recruited on the basis of *shash nafari*, or one out of
every six able-bodied men.[25] In 1894, in Logar and Ghazni and Ningrahar men were recruited on the basis of one man per family, a scheme
which soon became unpopular and led to the expatriation of many
people.[26] A year later enlistment on the basis of *char nafari*, or one out
of every four, was introduced[27] and in a booklet, *Nasa-ih al-Haq*, the
amir exhorted his people to keep their young men acquainted with the
tactics of war and to devote one out of every four men to state service.[28]
Finally in 1896, the select system of *hasht nafari* was introduced. By
this time, however, the regular army had probably reached its highest
number, and the *hasht nafari* was extensively applied as a system of
recruitment for tribal levies, a ready and trained reserve for the regulars
in case of emergency.[29]

Amir ʾAbd al-Rahman was not bound by any agreement to raise only
a fixed number of men in the army. Indeed, the grant the British
government gave him was said to be for the organization of the state
and the army. The creation of the army then depended on the financial
resources of Afghanistan and the personal ability of the amir. His
ability in organizing the army was very evident; indeed it was the high
point of his accomplishments.

Within three years of his accession the amir raised his regular army
to 43,000.[30] With irregulars and the *khassadars* the total number in the
same year reached 45,773.[31] In 1887 out of a total of 64,000 the regulars
numbered 44,469,[32] while in 1890 an official list showed that the total
in the army had reached 60,000.[33] From then on no reliable information about the number in the army is available; but, since the amir had
already decided to maintain his regularly paid army at 100,000 and

tribal levies at up to 70,000 and since recruitment continued at an ever-increasing rate in the nineties, the army in the last years of the amir's reign might well have reached 100,000.[34]

As in the reign of Amir Sher 'Ali, so in the reign of Amir 'Abd al-Rahman the main bodies of troops were stationed in provincial towns and largely in Kabul. By 1898 army units were also quartered in strategically important areas all over the country, mainly in the regions adjacent to India. All together throughout the country there were probably over one hundred regiments of infantry and twenty-four of cavalry.[35]

Each regiment had a paid mulla, a physician, and a surgeon. To strengthen the morale of the soldiers and the spirit of jehad among them the mullas recited passages from *Najiyya* and *Hidayat al-Shaj'an*, booklets especially prepared for this purpose.[36] In the Hazara and Kafiristan wars the mullas actually accompanied soldiers to the battlefields and preached to them. Since the soldiers were, in religion, followers either of various famous mullas or of leaders of some mystic orders, their indoctrination by the mullas to the effect that the wars were for the promotion of Islam proved effective. Soldiers were especially indoctrinated for wars against infidel armies. Like other ghazis, the soldiers were urged not to flee from the infidel army unless in grave danger, even if the enemy force were twice as numerous. This exhortation was based on the belief that in war against the infidels the Muslims were assured of victory by God; therefore, they were not to think of the infidels who, by the grace of God, were ultimately doomed and unable to oppose the Muslims. To assure victory, the Muslims needed courage and patience. The Afghan soldiers were told that in the event of their flight from an infidel army the Muslims would be doomed to some great calamity in this world and a life in hell in the next.[37]

Unlike the pay to civil officials the pay to military officers was standardized and fairly regular; it was largely in cash and only partly in kind. Military officers received much higher pay than did their counterparts in the civil administration. Also, in comparison to the pay of soldiers the pay of the officers was disproportionately high. The monthly pay of a *sipah salar* was 2,000 rupees; of a *ghat mushr* (general) and *panza mushr* (brigadier general) from 800 to 200 according to the rank; *zar mushr* (colonel) 200; *nap* (adjutant), 120; *maijir* (major) and sergeant, 40. Lower rank officers such as captain (*risala-dar* in cavalry, *sil mushr* in artillery and infantry), lieutenant (*jamadar* in cavalry and *buluk mushr* in artillery and infantry), sergeant major (*kotdafadar* in cavalry and *park mushr* in artillery and infantry), sergeant (*dafadar* in cavalry and *landakwar* in artillery and infantry), corporal (*landak hawaldar* in all) ranged from 80 to 20 rupees for cavalry and almost half of that for infantry. The soldiers each received 20 rupees in the cavalry and 8 in the infantry.[38] Pay to the Durranis was higher than that to the others. A Durrani infantryman received 11 rupees and a cavalryman in the royal regiment, 30.[39] A rudimentary scheme of pensions was worked out for the army. If military personnel were killed in battle their salaries were paid to their parents for life and to their children until they reached adulthood.[40] Also military personnel, including soldiers, were allowed to take four-fifths of the removable property captured on expedition as spoils.[41] In the expedition against the Shaykh ʾAli soldiers were allowed to take all property except the Hazaras themselves,[42] and in the Hazara War they were allowed even to possess the Hazaras as booty. The result was that officers accumulated wealth, household property, and male and female servants. Members of their families and dependents increased and military rank became a symbol of great social prestige. By comparison the situation of the soldiers was not good, mainly because of their low salaries, which were sometimes in arrears.[43]

Conditions of Service

In the reign of the amir the period of military service was not fixed. Soldiers served until incapacitated by accident or by age. Since the army was large and the age of recruitment varied between fourteen and fifty, aged soldiers in the army were not wanting. Before they became fifty soldiers were not discharged except when they provided substitutes; either the aged soldiers themselves presented young substitutes or commanding officers did so for them.[44] Discharge was also granted for those whose families were struck by such misfortunes as the loss of the father or the only guardian of the family. In Turkestan a soldier was allowed to leave on providing either two substitutes or 4,000 tangas. These new leave provisions could be considered concessions since in the past soldiers had not been able to obtain even temporary leaves of absence, and this lack had been a major source of discontent. Amir ʾAbd al-Rahman introduced the system of allowing substitutes. According to this system, which, to be sure, was still not a regular leave system, a soldier could obtain leave for as long as three months when he could produce a substitute.[45] This practice led, on the one hand, to the training of an additional number of men in the army and, on the other hand, to the possible danger of introducing inefficiency into the army through the use of unqualified men, and to the possible loss of trained soldiers. As a safety device, the amir decreed that failure of the soldiers on leave to reappear in time would make them liable to a fine of 100 rupees for a month of absence and an additional 3,500 rupees in the event of the death of their substitutes during that time.[46] Since the army units were stationed away from their own districts and since the grant of leave was conditional on providing substitutes, which was difficult if not impossible for poor soldiers, the scheme had little practical benefit to soldiers; and, in consequence, there was still much discontent among them and a good deal of desertion. To combat desertion additional strict regulations were enforced. Those who left the battlefields were either executed or forced to repay the pay they had received from the time of their enlistment.[47] In addition, their relatives were forced to provide substitutes for soldiers who had deserted.[48]

Perhaps at no previous time as in the reign of the amir was so great an effort made to maintain strict discipline in the army.[49] The main problem was the unwillingness of the Afghans to accept restraints. Homesickness, organizational restraints, and the harsh treatment that soldiers received from their officers led to disturbances among them on many occasions. Punishment in such cases was brutal, although occasionally a conciliatory attitude was adopted. For instance, in Herat in 1893 thirteen soldiers were blinded for having quarreled with their officers,[50] and in Turkestan in 1894 ten soldiers were blown from guns for having created disturbances.[51] In Kabul in 1896, however, an "extremely mild and conciliatory" attitude was adopted toward those soldiers who because of postponement of their pay and harsh treatment by their officers had become rebellious. As a rule, only noncommissioned officers were liable for such punishments as flogging, imprisonment, and dismissal. Only in extreme cases was an officer imprisoned, degraded, dismissed, or shot by the direct order of the amir or of one of the commanders-in-chief. The amir, as well as senior officers down to the rank of general, inflicted the death penalty on soldiers;[52] in no case was a penalty fixed by a jury or a committee.

Unlike penalties for groups, which varied according to circumstances, individual offenders were brutally treated. In Herat, for instance, in the days when Sardar ʾAbd al-Quddus was placed in charge of civil and military affairs a number of soldiers lost their noses and ears for demanding full pay and committing theft. Sometimes harsh treatment of soldiers brought still harsher repercussions from them. In 1892, for instance, ʾAbd al-Malik, an officer in Kabul who was a favorite of the amir, abused one soldier for having taken the wrong steps on the drill. The soldier shot him dead on the spot. Similarly it was because of strict discipline that Ibrahim Shah, a conscripted soldier from the Shevan village of Herat who was addicted to hashish (*chars*), unsuccessfully shot at the amir in Mazar in 1890.[53] While in the shooting of ʾAbd al-Malik both the murderer and General Muhammad Rustum, who was alleged to have instigated the murder, were most brutally disposed of, in the attempted assassination of the amir no one but the would-be assassin was implicated and he was killed instantly on the spot. Hashish, however, which had until then been permitted and even supplied by the government to those who used it, was forbidden because it was said to be demoralizing the soldiers. The use of other intoxicating drugs by soldiers was likewise prohibited. Gambling, though officially prohibited, was practiced nonetheless and led to frequent fighting and occasional murder. Once in the case of the murder of a soldier in a gambling dispute, five accused killers were beheaded, two of their officers blinded, and their Muhammadi regiment of 1,000 was disbanded.[54] That soldiers were sexually frustrated was a well-known fact. Strict discipline, homesickness, and sexual frustration may account for the high incidence of suicide in the army, as evidenced by four cases in Kabul alone during four months from January to May 1894.

Along with punishment, reward was also given. Promotion to a higher rank was given for distinction in war. Promotion up to the rank of sergeant (*dafadar*) was given by the generals and above that rank by the commanders-in-chief[55] and to the ranks of general, deputy commanders-in-chief and commanders-in-chief by the amir. Usually after each successful operation the amir entertained the army. Those who had distinguished themselves in the battles were rewarded. After the termination of the Hazara War eighteen thousand medals were distributed to soldiers, and five thousand *sardari* medals to the officers who had participated in the war. In addition, there were eight types of gold medals of honor, sincerity, bravery, confidence, honesty, respect, and so forth granted to officers as a reward for merit from time to time.

Weapons

The reign of Amir ʾAbd al-Rahman is marked by an unprecedented increase in the number and quantity of weapons. This increase was made possible by almost unhindered purchase from abroad, offers from the British government, and, mainly, the establishment of modern war factories in Kabul.

Weapons included swords, daggers, bayonets, pistols, rifles (jezails, Sniders, Martini-Henrys, Lee-Metfords, Lee-Enfields), and guns (machine, mountain, field, and heavy, each of different kinds and sizes). The mountain guns were the most common and varied in kind. In addition, there were muzzle-loading and smoothbore guns. Ammunition for rifles and guns was plentiful. It was said that the imported ammunition for rifles alone was sufficient for a three-month campaign and for almost indefinite guerrilla warfare.[56]

The amir was free in purchasing weapons from abroad in spite of British restrictions in his foreign policy; but, since the weapons he purchased were imported through India, the British government could embargo the shipments. In order to pressure the amir to accept a settlement of the frontier problem, the British government in 1892 held in India the guns the amir had purchased from England. At that time these guns were needed the most in the Hazara War. After the Durand Agreement the restrictions were lifted,[57] and the amir was allowed to import arms as before through his agent Buchansu Guthine and Co. from European countries, notably England and Germany. The amir purchased so many weapons that it became a source of concern to the British government, especially when it was reported that some were being sent to tribes beyond the Durand Line. In particular, the purchase of Krupp guns was distasteful to Lord Curzon. Still he considered this to "be the lesser risk" to refusing the amir's request in which case he would have probably bought guns from Russia,[58] whose rifles he had already bought on a modest scale probably through Turkmen traders of Merv.

Another source of arms supplies was grants from the British government to the amir in line with Britain's declared policy "to maintain a powerful, independent, and united Afghanistan." The quick and timely delivery of arms in critical times (in 1880, 1882, and 1887) helped the amir to overcome rebellions. By December 1905 weapons presented to, or imported by, the amir and his son and successor totalled 102 guns, 61,548 rifles, and 4,451 pistols.[59]

Most of the military's weapons, however, were made in Kabul. Workshops for the manufacture of weapons were first established in Kabul during the reign of Amir Sher ʾAli Khan. During the reign of Amir ʾAbd al-Rahman these were fully expanded. A full account of this manufacturing system will be found in chapter 8; here it is sufficient to note that varieties of rifles and guns, imitations of British and Russian weapons, were made in these workshops. Of the quantities of arms manufactured in Kabul it was said that "At the present time [1895] Afghanistan equals the European countries in manufacturing arms and other articles of war"[60] and that by 1900 the total number of arms made in Kabul exceeded the number of men fit for military service throughout Afghanistan.[61]

Regular Army

Before 1880 the Afghan regular army (sipahi-munazzam) was divided into the three branches of infantry (piyada), cavalry (sawara), and artillery (topkhana). Amir Sher ʾAli, during his second reign, introduced the British system of formation, which meant that certain large units were made to include all branches of the regular army under the command of one officer. During the Second Anglo-Afghan War this formation fell to pieces and the regular army dispersed to conduct the war on a guerrilla basis. Amir ʾAbd al-Rahman, who had a special talent for organizing the army, based his initial small army on this model. His army was composed of divisions, brigades, regiments (called battalions in the infantry and batteries in artillery), troops, and companies. Each company, which in all branches formed the basic unit, was further divided into smaller but different subdivisions. In theory, each company was to have been composed of one hundred private soldiers (sipahis), but the actual number varied between eighty-five and one hundred. Thus corresponding divisions, brigades, regiments, and troops were not the same size. With the enlargement of the army, however, the basic unit gradually approached the maximum number, and the army units were standardized. The three branches of the army met in the brigade, which was a combination of infantry, cavalry, and artillery under the command of one officer.

Infantry
As before, so in the reign of the amir the infantry formed the largest portion of the army. Its units were, in consequence, larger than those of either the cavalry or artillery. The lowest subdivision of a company in

the infantry was a *paira*, composed of from eight to ten soldiers under the command of a noncommissioned officer (*hawaldar*). Three *pairas* formed a platoon commanded by a *subadar*. While four platoons constituted a company under the direction of a captain (*kiftan*), several companies made a regiment (*pultan*) commanded by a colonel (*kumaidan* or a *karnail*).[62] The standard regiment of infantry was composed of six companies or six hundred soldiers; but there were some that were made up of eight hundred or even one thousand. By 1898, there were one hundred regiments with a total number of sixty thousand infantrymen.[63] As a rule, battalions bore the name of the territories or tribes to which they belonged. A few were named after officers. Others had such names with religious significance as the Muhammadiyya and the Charyari, the latter signifying the first four Companions of the Prophet. Still others, such as the *zardposh* and *sabzposh*, were known by the names of coats once worn. The battalions were first armed with rifles of various patterns, notably Martini-Henrys, Berdans, and Sniders (*baghalpur*). Later Martini-Henrys were issued to all in the regular army and the discarded Sniders and other rifles were distributed to the *khassadars* and tribesmen. Rifles captured from the British troops during the war and subsequently recovered by the government during the reign of the amir were also issued to the infantrymen. Every infantryman had a bayonet fixed in his rifle and a dagger (*pishqabz*). In Herat each soldier carried two pistols, a sword, and many knives.[64] Except for the guards and a few of the Kabul garrisons, battalions had no standard uniforms. Infantrymen were differently dressed since they were each responsible for supplying their own clothes. The commonest form consisted of loose trousers, shirts, and sheepskin jackets (*barak* coats) made of local woolen material. A leather belt, provided by the government, was considered the basic element of uniform. Without it a soldier was looked upon as a civilian. For headgear the turban was commonly used, although the soldiers also wore different varieties of caps and hats, and one that was similar to the Russian military peaked cap was popular.[65]

Cavalry

The cavalry regiments (*risalas*) were smaller in size and number than those of the infantry. In 1883, four hundred cavalrymen formed a regiment, although a few stationed in Herat and Kabul were made up of five hundred and six hundred each. In 1899, the cavalry regiments of Kandahar were raised from four hundred to six hundred men. There were probably forty regiments of cavalry with sixteen thousand horsemen. Cavalry subdivisions were the same as the infantry subdivisions but were commanded by officers with different titles. In the cavalry the smallest unit was made up of six horsemen, instead of the eight to ten soldiers that made up a *paira* in the infantry. Officers in the cavalry were called *dafadar*, *kotdafadar*, *jamadar*, and *risala-dar* and were headed by a regimental commander called colonel (*zar mushr* or *kar-*

nail), who, in addition, had under him such regimental staff as adjutant (*nap*), major (quartermaster and paymaster), and a sergeant. The horsemen were first armed with Snider carbines and muzzle-loading Lee-Enfields and later, at the time of general rearmament in 1898, with Martin-Henrys. The horsemen carried slightly curved swords with guardless hilts, in imitation of Cossack weapons and many other kinds of swords. A few regiments were, in addition, armed with the lance and some with pistols. The cavalrymen wore varied uniforms, principally long *barak* coats, *barak* trousers, and long boots of the Russian pattern.[66] Their horses were strong stallions most of which were bred in the district of Qataghan and were the best of their kind. Horses were branded. The Turkestani horses, numbering thirty-two thousand, were usually turned out to graze for three months in the spring. The upkeep and supply of the horses and the degree of involvement of the horsemen in them was very complicated. A tent, a pony, and a syce were allowed to every five men, including the *dafadar*. The other men cooked for the *dafadar*, ate, and lived together.

Artillery

The artillery was especially improved in the amir's reign. It was mainly with the help of a large artillery that fortifications in the country were destroyed and rebellions suppressed. The amir had almost a passion for guns. When the French engineer-designate of Kabul workshops, J. Jerom, in a bid to impress the amir, offered him a telescope to see the moon, the amir told him, "Blow the moon. What is the good of the moon to me? Can't you make a gun of the thing?"[67]

In 1891 the amir said that his army had one thousand guns of various sizes, but the British military authorities, while admitting their ignorance of the actual number of guns made at Kabul, estimated a total of eight hundred sixty.[68] The number of trained gunners was five thousand five hundred or six gunners to one gun. The artillery consisted of four major types: machine guns, mountain guns, field guns, and heavy cannon. The most famous mountain guns were the Krupp howitzers. Their latest version, which reached Kabul a year after the amir's death, was probably "the most efficient guns of their calibre in the world at that date."[66] The artillery also was divided into mobile and immobile guns. The latter were apparently not modern. The mobile guns, of which two-thirds were mountain guns, were drawn by various animals after which they were named. Those drawn by mules (*qatir*) were called *qatiri*, by elephants (*feel*), *feeli*; by bullocks (*gaw*), *gawi*. Those drawn by horses were called *jilawi*. Each of the field guns was generally drawn by six, and sometimes ten and even twelve, horses. While information about artillery formation is scanty, there apparently were six guns in a battery commanded by a captain, who had a major and a *jamadar* under him. The lowest subdivision of the artillery was a platoon, which consisted of two cannons and thirty-two crew under the command of a *jamadar*.[70] Three such platoons formed a battery (the equivalent of a regiment in cavalry and battalion in infantry). Artillerymen had no particular uniform and were, as a rule, not well dressed; but they were men of good physique.[71]

Royal Bodyguards

The task of guarding the amir and the household was entrusted to a special force composed of three infantry (*ardal pultans*) and four cavalry regiments (*risala-i-shahi*). In their formation these regiments were the same as all others, but in other respects they were different. Being the royal bodyguard, they were, in fact, a select force composed of trustworthy and socially significant elements. Also, they were better armed, better clothed, and better drilled than common soldiers. Foot soldiers of this force were armed with Lee-Metford rifles and bayonets and the cavalry with carbines, revolvers, and swords.[72] What they wore for uniforms is not known, but all sources agree that they were properly uniformed. A special body of troops of this force, the *andarun-i-khas* (household guards), were made responsible for protecting the haram and another picked company, the *hazirbashes*, guarded the amir. The *hazirbashes* were ready day and night outside the palace to accompany the amir in case there was an emergency. They were always provided with full provisions so that they might start at any moment on a journey.[73] The distinguishing feature of this force was its component elements. They were all *khanzadas* of the Qizilbashes, Tajiks (Kohistan and Herat), Uzbeks of Turkestan, Safays of Tagaw, and, above all, various sections of the Durranis of Kandahar. At a later date the Qizilbashes and others who were not *khanzadas* were removed from the force and the Muhammadzays were increasingly recruited into it, in spite of the fact that at critical moments the amir relied more on the Safays and Gardezis than on the Muhammadzays.

Sappers and Miners

A separate corps of engineers, known as the *safar mina* (a corruption of "sappers and miners"), constructed roads, bridges, canals, and serais. This corps was made up exclusively of the Hazaras and consisted of three battalions at Kabul and several detachments elsewhere in the country. It was the same as the rest of the army in formation but equipped and armed in the same manner as the Gurkha sappers and miners of India.[74] The Hazara sappers and miners possessed little knowledge of scientific engineering, but they were skilled laborers and well trained in road making, mining, and building. Since they were regularly employed, they were quite efficient in their duties.[75]

Forts, Garrisons, and Supplies

In the reign of the amir old forts were repaired and many new ones were built.[76] Forts were made with thick mud walls, containing four to six towers, and were surrounded by ditches often six yards wide and four deep.[77] In most of them guards and detachments of the regular army, including guns, were stationed. Although they were unable to stand shelling by cannons, the forts were difficult to overcome with rifle fire. They were built in places where tribes rebelled or were likely to rebel and, thus, were intended mainly for internal security. Along the border with Russia and Russian-dominated Bukhara a series of military posts (*muhafiz khanas*) were built, each forty by thirty yards long and eight yards high.[78] The forts constructed along the border with India were large enough to accommodate up to one hundred men each,[79] but no significant forts were built along the border with Persia. The fort of Dehdadi in Mazar was one of the most famous, but that of Maruchaq was the largest, occupying an area two-thirds the size of the city of Herat.[80]

The strongest fort was the citadel of Herat, which was made to be a defensive center against possible attack by Russia. This strategy fitted well with the defensive line of the government of India, which took keen interest in its fortification.[81] The Indian government contributed four lakhs of rupees to the building of the fort and sent an artillery expert to Herat to advise his Afghan counterparts. Although Herat in the nineteenth century had the strongest fortifications in central Asia and had withstood the siege lasting eighteen months by the army of Agha Muhammad Qajar of Persia in 1836,[82] the plan after the fall of Panjdeh in 1885 was to make it capable of standing a possible Russian bombardment with modern artillery. The fort, located in the middle of the city, was fortified by placing both in it and in the gates of the city thirty-one field and fifteen heavy guns[83] and storing ammunition and provisions sufficient for six thousand men for a period of nine months.[84] The British engineer suggested that all high places outside the city be leveled. This leveling was to include a small rocky hill named Talibankiyyan, considered sacred, and involved the demolition of a combination of sacred constructions composed of a mosque, a lofty hill surrounded by domes, and minarets of the *musalla* of Herat, founded by the Ghurid kings and expanded by Timur and his successors, the Uzbek and Safavid rulers.[85] The planned demolition of the *musalla*, which was decorated with Quranic inscriptions and shining painted tiles,[86] caused a debate among the ʾulama on whether it was right to keep it intact or to demolish it for protection of the country of Islam. At a time when a general rising against the planned demolition was about to take place the ʾulama of Herat (Mia Muhammad ʾOmar Sahibzada, the Mir of Gazargah, and others) issued a *fetwa* in favor of demolition on the ground that the safety of the country of Islam was more important than preservation of the *musalla*. The rising was only then averted.[87] For further fortification of the fort the moat surrounding it was deepened and supplied by water of natural springs,[88] which had the motive power of eight water mills.

The army was divided into the four divisions of Kabul, Kandahar, Herat, and Turkestan. The Kabul army, which garrisoned the regions south of the Hindu Kush up to Qalat,[89] was the largest. Although the amir was the supreme commander of the whole army, he supervised most of the forces of the Kabul division personally. Sipah Salar Ghulam Haydar Charkhi, nominally commander-in-chief of the Kabul division, actually commanded the garrisons stationed in the Easter province from 1882 to 1898. The Kandahar army[90] was the smallest of all and commanded by relatively unknown officers. The Herat division[91] was commanded by Sipah Salar Faramuz Khan (a *ghulam bacha* of the amir) from 1882 to 1901. The Turkestan division[92] before the revolt of Sardar Muhammad Ishaq had been commanded by a number of officers independent of each other. After that and until 1897 it was under the command of Sipah Salar Ghulam Haydar Orakzay, generally known as the Landay Sipah Salar.[93] Thus for the first time in Afghanistan there were three *sipah salars* at a time, each of whom commanded a large body of troops in one of the three strategically important frontier provinces.

The barracks of the soldiers were unfurnished. Except for a small number of soldiers, who slept on *charpoys* (wooden bedsteads), most of the soldiers slept on the floor. They cooked their food themselves in utensils provided by the government. For a dining table they spread a coarse mat on the ground and sat on it while eating their food.[94]

Transport animals included ponies (*yabus*), camels, elephants, and carts. The organized transport establishment was small; but, because of a large number of ponies and camels in the country, the amir could equip at short notice any force he put in the field. The Ghilzay elder Nur Muhammad, nicknamed Nurakay, was appointed as *qafila bashi* for the supply of *kuchi* camels.[95]

The army was supplied from government granaries. As a rule, one year's supply of provisions was kept in storehouses in major cities. In Herat alone, twenty thousand kharwars of barley and wheat were stored each year, out of which seven thousand kharwars were consumed by the soldiers. Such other provisions as ghee, rice, lentils, cheese, opium, and hashish were also stored. Soldiers and officers up to the rank of captain were allowed to draw forty-eight pounds of grain monthly; the cost was deducted from their pay at a low rate. A large proportion of the reserves consisted of a peculiar kind of dried bread (*talkhan*) that was said to keep for years.[96] Reserves of tents, saddlery, leather waterbags, and other articles were kept in storehouses in major cities. The animals apparently did not receive much grain and the horses were put out to graze during the summer.

Irregular Army

The military power of Afghanistan had always rested more on the strength of the irregulars (*sipahi-i-ghair-i-munazzam*) than on the regular army. It was the irregulars that inflicted severe losses on their British adversaries in all their wars. The only exception was the battle of Maiwand in which the Afghan regular army had the leading role in defeating a British force. The amir organized, in addition to a large

regular army, a large irregular force. He also made efforts to train all
the able-bodied men in the country in the art of fighting.

Feudal

Feudal cavalry (sawara-i-kushada or sawara-i-khudaspa) had always
served as an auxiliary to the regulars in both internal and external
wars. According to the amir, "When Ahmad Shah became the king of
Afghanistan . . . he levied troops from among his countrymen. . . . The
Wazirs, in the time of Shah Zaman, did away with the system of enrolling men and levied a contribution instead."[97] The Wazirs' contrib-
utory system remained open to abuse and led, according to the amir, to
the loss of the empire and even of parts of Afghanistan proper. The
amir then decided "to abolish the system of levying contributions and
to revive the old system of enrolling men and to locate them with the
regulars on the frontiers."[98]

The amir employed the irregulars extensively in internal wars. When
there were no wars feudal khans were required either to wait on the
amir or to serve in the army. Some of them were even made to work as
government officials in customs houses, warehouses, and frontier posts
in accordance with their qualifications. The idea was that, like other
paid officials, they should continue to serve the state in one capacity or
another, since they received payment from the public treasury.[99] In
this way they were incorporated into the state. Implicit in the process
was the strengthening of the institution of eldership. Since in the predominantly agrarian and tribal society of Afghanistan tribal elders
were the natural leaders, feudal khans were inevitably chosen from
among them. The only choice the amir could make was to select loyal
khans.

Feudal khans were paid by the remission of the revenue due from
them on their holdings. When such revenue was insufficient they were
paid by barats on revenue elsewhere. In no case were they granted
land or the privilege to use it in lieu of their service as had been the
custom in the past. Neither were their allowances made permanent
nor were they allowed to pass these allowances on to their sons after
their deaths. In the event of the death of a feudal khan a new firman
was needed before his allowance was given to his successor.[100] The
amir treated the khans as semiofficials. In order that they look respectable he frequently sent them dresses and presents, as he had done with
qazis and muftis.[101] To the top feudal khans, that is to those whose income per annum ranged between 1,000 and 30,000 rupees, the honorary military titles of adjutant, colonel, and brigadier up to na'ib salar
were given. They were also given the privilege of wearing the uniforms
that belonged to the titles bestowed on them.[102]

The khans were required to train their respective levies, to present
them once a year for inspection, and to keep in store sufficient rifles
and ammunition, which the government sold to them (as well as to the
khans east of the Durand Line) at a nominal price.[103] The feudal horsemen stationed along the frontiers (qarawal khana) wore army uni-

forms. Those who were stationed along the frontiers of Herat were clothed in dark brown *barak* with black sheepskin or astrakhan hats and armed with firearms of all descriptions ranging from antiquated jezails to double-barreled breach-loading rifles (*dunbalapur*).[104] In this way the feudal cavalry, which was made up of landed gentry, was given a distinct military aura, and the position of the khans was strengthened both socially and economically. Their dependence on the state was secured not only by these arrangements, but also by an increase in their number. The amir's policy was to create many feudal khans who were less likely to become a menace to the state than a few powerful khans. Most were paid allowances for retaining horsemen whose number ranged from three to fifteen.[105] While some khans were paid allowances on the basis of keeping a certain number of horsemen without being obliged to retain them,[106] a considerable number were paid allowances for retaining two and a half horsemen.[107] The fraction probably meant that the low-paid khans were to serve the state with means other than their quota of horsemen. A considerable number of other khans retained horsemen at a level of 10 percent lower than their allowances required of them.[108]

Sometimes titles that the amir conferred on certain khans did not apply. The amir, for instance, conferred the title of *mingbashi* (leader of one thousand) on the one Muhammad Nazar Toqsaba Turkman of Aqcha but instructed him to retain only four hundred cavalry under the command of four *yuzbashis* (each leader of a company of one hundred) led by a *sartip* (commander of a *bairaq* of four hundred).[109] Since this type of organization was like that of the *khassadars*,[110] it is possible that the feudal cavalry, when sufficiently large, had the same organization as the *khassadars*. Like the *khassadars* the feudal cavalry and the khans served under the direct command of their *hakims*,[111] but in major expeditions all of them served under the supervision of military commanders. From time to time feudal khans were liquidated. The old and weak among them and those who held firmans of the former amirs were dismissed and replaced by new *hazims* holding the amir's firmans.[112]

Feudal khans participated in only a few internal wars, those against the Firozkohis, the Hazaras, and Sardar Muhammad Ishaq. Feudal khans also assisted Sardar 'Abd al-Quddus in capturing Herat in 1881. The total number of horsemen retained by the khans in the reign of the amir is unknown, although it is known that in Herat province in 1886 the Durrani khans retained 996 horsemen; the Tajik, Qizilbash, and other khans, 657; the Aimaq khans, 1,101; and the Ghilzay khans, 70. Senior government officials in Herat also retained horsemen as khans did.[113] These cavalry probably included the 2,400 horsemen, generally known as the *qarawal khana* who were permanently kept along the frontier of Herat.[114] Of the Hazaras of Hazarajat many mirs and begs of Dai Kundi and Dai Zangi retained horsemen, each keeping between 20 and 40.[115] In the province of Ningrahar those whose property was valued at 20,000 rupees were ordered to keep one horse each, but it is not known whether this order was actually carried out.[116] Akbar Khan of Lalpura retained 500 horsemen and frequently took part in expeditions in the turbulent Eastern province.

Tribal

It was the custom in Afghanistan for the government to call upon what were generally known as tribal foot levies (*eljaris*), but actually were foot levies of tribal and nontribal peasants and artisans, to take part in wars under the leadership of feudal khans and other elders. In the amirs reign, *eljaris* took part in all the wars except that waged against the Ghilzays. These levies were not, and could not be, organized on a permanent basis, and after the conclusion of a war they dispersed. It was only in the course of a war that they were brought under some kind of discipline. In such times they were brought in loose groups of tens, fifties, hundreds and thousands, led by tribal leaders bearing the titles of *dahbashi, pinjabashi, sadbashi* (or *yuzbashi*), and *hazarbashi* (or *mingbashi*). They were all subject to the command of the *hakims* and governors of their regions. While they were in service the government paid for their food and provided them with arms. Presumably they were paid through their elders, since of the Durrani levies it was said that "the headmen and the Sardars of the tribe will give their wages."[117] Like the regular army, *eljaris* were allowed to take four-fifths of the booty in expeditions. This permission to loot was a novelty that left a profound social mark on the people of Afghanistan because, since almost all tribes at one time or another during the reign of the amir rebelled and since *eljaris* took part in almost all conflicts, this booty taking created new animosities and intensified old ones between tribes. It was even said that by employing one tribe against another the amir purposefully fanned the old enmities between the Durranis and the Ghilzays and that between the latter and the Hazaras. Also it was said that in this the amir's "real object [was] to excite enmity between the Ghilzais, the Shinwaris, the Khugianis, and the Mohmands."[118]

The Hazara War was the most conspicuous of all both in the use of *eljaris* and in booty taking. From 30,000 to 40,000 *eljaris* took part.[119] *Eljaris* usually preceded the regular army in battle, because they were familiar with the topography of the region. Indeed, they were a major factor in the successful conclusion of wars. On that ground the amir was pleased with them[120] and offered rewards for their elders after each campaign.

From 1894 on the amir made efforts to train what was called "a nation in arms."[121] By that time the whole country, except Kafiristan, had been pacified. The main threat then to Afghanistan was felt to be directed from abroad. In anticipation of this threat the amir, among other things, chose to arm, or rather to re-arm, the whole nation and to train able-bodied males between the ages of fourteen and fifty. The amir gave out that because his army was small he was obliged to safeguard the northern frontiers of Afghanistan [122] and the passes in general [123] by the employment of *eljaris*. The people of Turkestan were asked to provide one man out of three [124] and others one man for each thirty jaribs of land [125] as tribal levies. [126] In 1894 it was reported that ninety thousand were enlisted as tribal levies. [127] To what extent and how this project was carried out, if it was carried out at all, is not known; but this enlistment had nothing to do with the planned invasion of Kafiristan in 1895. Presumably, it was given up since subsequently the select system of *hasht nafari* was introduced.

The early reports about the *hasht nafari* system of recruitment, which followed other largely unsuccessful methods of recruitment, are contradictory and confusing. The system was said to have been initiated by elders. [128] In fact, the amir suggested it first. It was introduced at a time when elders throughout the country gave undertakings of loyalty and conferred the title of *zia al-millat-i-wa al-din* (the light of nation and religion) on the amir. Elders also pledged themselves to provide one man out of every eight between the ages of fourteen and fifty as *eljaris*. When in service their expenses were to be met by the remaining seven men, not by the government. [129] Subsequently this system was also applied to the feudal khans. It was said that "A system is being introduced in the country under which maliks and khans will maintain a number of mounted men in proportion to their rank. These horsemen will be taught drill at the nearest place where there are troops, and will report themselves to the authorities twice a year." [130]

The new system, in fact, opened the way for the government to train able-bodied men in the country and to keep them as reserves, especially after the circulation of rumors, during the tribal uprising of 1897, that the British intended to invade Afghanistan. Military centers were opened everywhere for this training. Those who lived near military cantonments were obliged to attend drills once a week. [131] Military officers were sent to teach distant villagers drilling and musketry at their own homes. [132] In this way large reserves were formed in each village and they were given uniforms and arms. [133] Subsequently, however, the issuing of rifles was discontinued for fear of their possible use by tribesmen amongst themselves. [134] The reserves could, if they wished, attend the regular army. Otherwise they were at liberty to stay at home until they were called upon. Some reports mention small pay for them also. In 1897 the number of these reserves was estimated at one hundred thousand. [135] In the meantime the feudal khans were armed and drilled in the same way. [136]

With all its apparent success the *hasht nafari* system did not proceed smoothly. "Many people" said they were ready to assist their king, but only in actual emergencies. [137] Among these "many people" were the Ghilzays, presumably southern Ghilzays, whose example was followed by "several other tribes." In Khost a rebellion broke out on that ground. In Kunar those elders who refused to enlist *eljaris* according to the *hasht nafari* were imprisoned. [138] Notwithstanding this opposition the new system was applied rather extensively in the eastern regions of the country. Also it was in this region that the amir furnished a limited number of rifles to selected elders.[139]

The Efficiency of the Army and Its Role

The major difficulty in creating a loyal and disciplined army was the social background of its components with strong regional and tribal attachments. There was no question of replacing these attachments with loyalty to the state. The amir's efforts were aimed at creating a new loyalty to the state to exist over and above the old ones. The army units were, therefore, organized tribally and territorially but abided by the new codes, transcending old loyalties. This arrangement reinforced tribalism and regionalism, as was evident in disputes between individuals of different regiments that often blew up into conflicts between their regiments.[140] Regionalism and tribalism were also evident in relations between the soldiers and officers belonging to different tribes and regions since the officers often treated the former prejudicially—a treatment which posed considerable threat to the unity and efficiency of the army but was not a threat to the state in spite of the fact that it was mainly the tribally composed army which suppressed the numerous tribal uprisings. Also in suppressing the rebellious tribes, subsections of a major tribe would take part in fighting their own rebellious tribesmen. A major exception was the Andar and Tarakay regiments in Herat that, at the time of the Ghilzay Revolt, were overwhelmed by tribal ideas against the state.[141] Against tribalism the forces of religion and concern for the larger territory (Afghanistan) and for the honor of women served as unifying bonds. Time and again the amir referred to these bonds and, in the face of fear of foreigners, impressed on soldiers, officers, feudal khans, and elders the necessity for safeguarding these bonds in concert under his leadership. These bonds contributed much toward cohesion in the army; but the different tiers of payment to holders of the same rank but different tribal origin caused resentment. Although officers were paid disproportionately highly, there is no report available to show that the soldiers resented this discrepancy. Resentment was shown against the privileged position of the Barakzays who were considered mediocre soldiers but who enjoyed concessions by virtue of their tribal origin. The amir once reprimanded the second royal cavalry regiment, which until then was made up of non-Barakzays and which had raised complaints against this unequal rate of payment: "You want to become equal to the kandaharis and the Barakzais. This will never be."[142]

The permission to the army to take plunder in expeditions made it efficient and dependable. Previously, the army had appropriated booty in external wars. In internal wars soldiers had officially been forbidden to loot, although victorious soldiers took to looting the camps of their opponents, even the Afghan people. The permission to take four-fifths of the booty, and in some cases all (including captive rebels), proved a strong stimulus for the poor peasant soldiers who showed remarkable courage in expeditions and overcame rebellions even in the most difficult terrains of the country. Discipline and compulsion also accounted for this courage, and together they proved a strong factor that until then had been lacking in the Afghan army. All these factors explain why the army, except for a portion of it which joined Sardar Muhammad Ishaq and a number of soldiers who went over to Mulla ʾAbd al-Karim in the Ghilzay Revolt, remained loyal.

The amir did not allow soldiers stationed in a region to mix with the local people; presumably he thought they might lose the fighting spirit if this fraternization were allowed. For the same reason officers were not granted lands where they were stationed as a reward for their services, although this had been the custom in the past. Indeed, soldiers posed a constant threat to the local population by committing theft and insulting women. Ill-feelings were evident between civilians and military. In Turkestan and the Hazarajat, however, soldiers were said to have lost their fighting spirit for having married local women.[143]

The internal wars kept the army almost constantly engaged in fighting. The wars gave soldiers the chance to use weapons that otherwise they could not have used on such a large scale. Above all, the wars gave the army a chance to become acquainted with the topography of the country and gave it the characteristics more of a police force, concerned with the establishment and maintenance of law and order, than of a defensive force. The many expeditions showed that the army was a terrible force against internal threats, but was it capable of defending Afghanistan against a European army?

Before the borders with the Russian empire were fixed, a number of clashes between the Afghans and the Russian forces in the frontier posts occurred. In Somatash in the Pamirs a small Afghan force refused to withdraw as had been demanded by a much larger Russian force and was destroyed. In the Panjdeh clash, the biggest of its kind, a relatively small Afghan force met a similar situation against a large Russian force and met almost the same fate. Only a small number of survivors were able to retreat. These clashes between unequal forces were not large enough to show the real fighting value of the Afghan army against a European army; but they did prove that the Afghans were willing to fight foreigners no matter what the odds were. In spite of the efforts of the amir the Afghan army probably did not reach a British or Russian standard in organization, weapons, efficiency, and professionalism of officers, although in the case of soldiers, particularly cavalrymen, this statement was not so. As one military observer put it, "without doubt, the Afghan sowar [horseman] has the making of a fine soldier in him."[144] As a whole, the people became confident of the army and were proud of it; for in the reign of the amir the people and the army of Afghanistan "were infinitely better armed"[145] than they had been ever before. In addition the Afghan authorities had more confidence in the efficiency of their army than they had had at any previous time.[146]

Chapter VI
Social Structure: 1

Rural Landlord–Peasant Relations

In Afghanistan during the time of the amir the majority of the inhabitants lived in egalitarian communities, although some lived in distinctly class differentiated communities (Hazara, Kafir, and Baluch). Even in the egalitarian communities individuals were not equal economically; rather, individuals within the same social class were more or less on the same footing and class differentiation was neither sharp nor rigid. In the agrarian communities of Afghanistan access to land determined, to a very large extent, the overall position of individuals, families, and clans. Since land was more equally divided in Afghanistan than elsewhere in the East, most Afghan communities were egalitarian. Why most of the proprietors remained small farmers and large estates and a landed aristocracy did not develop in Afghanistan is a problem worthy of discussion.

The distribution of land after the owner's death was in accordance with the Shariʾa and this system led to land fragmentation within two or three generations. More important, however, was the fact that in many areas land was originally distributed equally among families of a dominant kinship group. Probably two-thirds of the land in Kandahar (Qalat to Herat) was, for example, portioned out among the Durranis as *tiyul*[1] (or land assigned in return for military service) at the time of their general settlement in the fourth decade of the eighteenth century. In other words, in Kandahar the greater part of the land was distributed on a family basis, while the remainder was left in still smaller units with the former non-Durrani owners. A portion of the land was de-

clared state property. Of course, by the late nineteenth century some
large landholders had emerged in Kandahar,[2] but most were still small
landowners in this region with its extensive potentially cultivable
lands. In the relatively populated areas of central and eastern Afghanistan, that is, the river valleys between the Indus and the Hindu Kush,
small landholdings were the norm and large landholdings the exception. Further, even as late as the late nineteenth century in some
valleys in eastern Afghanistan, notably Bajaur, the custom of the periodical redistribution of land among families was still practiced. Only
in Herat and in the regions well beyond the Hindu Kush in the north
(Badakhshan excepted) did extensive tracts of land exist. These regions
were mostly left uncultivated, however, because of the insecurity
caused by the raids of the Turkmen and Uzbeks. Trade, especially foreign trade, which would have stimulated the development of large
landholdings, did not flourish in Afghanistan after the turn of the eighteenth century. A great setback to foreign trade was the diversion of
Indian trade toward Europe, even as early as 1803, when the British had
advanced up to Delhi and the East India Company had obtained a vir-
tual monopoly of certain items of trade. Persia and Afghanistan were
no longer the principal markets for a whole range of Indian goods (indigo, spices, and chintz) and, with India, were no longer the principal
markets for a number of Chinese goods (silk and porcelain). The Great
Silk Road passing through Afghanistan had long ceased to be a thoroughfare for large caravans. These developments caused serious disturbance in the economies of Eastern countries, and the overland trade
through Afghanistan suffered a good deal.[3] The decline is reflected in
the reduction of trading activities by nomadic "tribes" and others who
were either engaged in commerce themselves or were "hiring out their
camels to the merchants of the richer tribes, and of the cities"[4] for
transportation purposes. All of these developments hindered the accumulation of capital and put pressure on agricultural land. This
tendency was evident as early as 1809 when merchants, government
officials, and all those who had procured money in one way or another
invested their capital in land. Presumably the investment was not on
such a scale to offset the process of land segmentation significantly.
Elphinstone's 1809 statement that "The estates of the proprietors are,
of course, various in their extent, but, on the whole, the land is more
equally divided in Afghanistan than in most countries"[5] was repeated
exactly by MacGregor in 1872.[6] The changes of dynasties and the civil
wars and anarchies that usually followed the death of Afghan rulers
worked also against the formation of large landholdings. An additional
factor in the reign of Amir ꞌAbd al-Rahman was the confiscation of
large estates and their sale to landless peasants. All this may explain
why a stable landed aristocracy did not develop in Afghanistan.

The political implication of small- and medium-sized farming is
obvious: it hindered the growth of a strong central authority. When a
strong government did exist the ruler depended on the flow of tributes
from neighboring lands, especially the Panjab, or on the subsidies from

foreign powers, as did Amir ᵓAbd al-Rahman Khan. Small landholders were, at the same time, a strong bulwark against foreign domination. At all times the resistance to foreign invasion was strongest among the inhabitants of the valleys between the Indus and the Hindu Kush. The real difficulty of the British political agents during the Second Anglo-Afghan War was their inability to win over, through their customary grants of subsidies, elders of communities in the rural areas. They were too many, and none was predominant. In addition, among themselves these elders were first among equals. The gulf between landowners and landless peasants was not so wide as to make them strangers to each other, in contrast to the situation in Persia where "between the land-owner as a class . . . and the peasant there is a wide gulf," and "The landowner regards the peasant virtually as a drudge, whose sole function is to provide him with his profit."[7] The peasant situation in India was, of course, the opposite of that in Afghanistan, for in India one of the requirements of Hinduism "is the acceptance of the caste system as the structure of the society"; as a result the Hindus of the four (or five) main traditional castes are further stratified into "more than two thousand mutually exclusive groups."[8]

Class differentiation did exist in Afghanistan, as well as inequality on the basis of sex, profession, and socioeconomic standing. The point to stress is that the small proprietors constituted most of the communities. Because of this fact the small proprietors had the characteristics of a peasantry whose settlement was stable and whose lands were clearly divided. The productivity of their land was high; they had a comparatively stable surplus and a strong sense of independence. This stage in the development of an agrarian community falls historically into the intermediate period between the tribal-nomadic and indus-trializing societies.[9] Theodore Shanin's remark about peasantry in general applies to peasant farmers in Afghanistan, "The peasantry consists of small agricultural producers who, with the help of simple equip-ment and the labour of their families, produce mainly for their own consumption and for the fulfillment of obligations to the holders of political and economic power."[10] How much of the production the peasant farmers kept for themselves and how much they were to de-liver "to the holders of political and economic power" was a perennial source of contention. As elsewhere, in Afghanistan most of the sur-pluses these rural cultivators produced were transferred to a dominant group of rulers that underwrote its own standard of living and distrib-uted the remainder to other groups in society that did not farm but were to be fed for their goods and services.[11]

In the village community peasant farmers reached a level of nearly total self-sufficiency. Similar to other peasant societies, the peasant society of Afghanistan consisted of innumerable villages whose inhab-itants maintained relations with a wider society, in particular by sell-ing their partial surplus in markets. In this way they linked their vil-lages to towns, cities, and the world at large. In this respect, as well as in others, they differed from primitive societies in which people procure their food and other necessities directly by their own labor and have no contact with the outside world.[12] In the peasant commune, such as the Afghan village community, the marriage, social, and religious needs were taken care of at the village level; and the village was, therefore, the peasant's world. In this world, a common interest in commune rights, as well as in providing for productive activities, required the participation of more than one family. It generated cooperation (*ashar* among the Pashtuns), coupled with some type of grass-root democracy, as was exemplified by holding jirgas in the Pashtun communities.[13] Of course, the extent of landholding and, with it, the position of peasant farmers differed from place to place within the country, so that it is not inappropriate to speak of a mild form of hierarchy among farmers with small holdings, just as there was among farmers with large holdings. Before we turn our attention to these farmers with large holdings it is necessary to discuss the nature of landholding in Afghanistan.

The following major types of landholding can be distinguished in late nineteenth century Afghanistan. The first type, land as private property, included large estates as well as small. Both large and small landholdings had turned into commodities, subject to purchase and sale. Some owners also, as is still the custom, mortgaged their land for a definite sum of money and lost the right of using the land until the money was repaid. A second type of land was that which the state granted to others, principally courtiers, high officials, and elders, in return for military service or for payment for other services. As this was essentially state land, the state retained its ownership and treated the grantees as servants of the sovereign. Neither did the state allow the land to be inherited. The grantees in turn either farmed out the land to others or gave it directly to crop-sharing cultivators. The process did not create numerous grantees or a hierarchy of them, since the grantees, as well as those who took such lands to farm, entered directly into tenancy relations with cultivators in accordance with the conventions of centuries. In the reign of Amir Sher 'Ali Khan a significant portion of state land was granted to others, notably elders of eastern Ghilzays. In the reign of Amir 'Abd al-Rahman such lands were recovered and only a few elders were granted lands, under the name of *soyurghal*. The greater part of the state land either was sold to landless peasants or was farmed out to others.

So in Afghanistan landlord-peasant relations were relevant in the case of large private estates, although sometimes small farmers also, for one reason or another, entered into tenancy contracts with landless peasants. This type of relation was, likewise, relevant in the case of state land whether granted as *soyurghal* or farmed out. The extent of such lands, however, was smaller than that of those cultivated by landholders themselves. Also, peasants, as a rule, were free, that is, unattached to the land. In theory they were free to enter directly into tenancy relations with landowners. In reality, they could hardly refuse the offer when it was made to them. In certain areas, however, the condition of landless peasants was similar to the condition of serfs in medieval Europe in that they were attached to the land.

Unfortunately not much information is available on the social, as distinct from the economic, aspects of landlord-peasant relations in the reign of Amir ʾAbd al-Rahman Khan; but, since there is every reason to believe that such a social relation persisted for centuries, fragmentary information on other periods may shed light on the subject. A warning notice must be served here, however: since Afghanistan is a very heterogenous and ancient agrarian country, generalizations of this kind about one community may not apply to others.

Three types of relation to the land could be observed universally in Afghanistan: ownership, crop-sharing tenants, and crop-sharing laborers.

Whenever there were large estates, crop-sharing tenants and crop-sharing laborers existed; and they had more dependent ties with landlords in the plains than did their fellow cultivators in other areas. How could it be otherwise? For landlords in the plains, in addition to their ownership of land, owned mills, draft and agricultural animals, and tools and were sometimes engaged, through agents, in trade and smuggling. Their hold over landless cultivators, who sometimes possessed only agricultural tools and animals, was great if not absolute. This power enabled big landlords to maintain a rigid discipline to pressure peasants to cultivate the land to the landlords' advantage. Therefore, the social order under which they lived was hierarchical and rigid, compared with that of the democratic communities of small farmers. These big landlords, who were at the same time elders of the communities, themselves settled disputes without recourse to consultative councils and enforced their authority with armed retinues. The Baluch khans of Seistan[14] and the Hazara mirs of the Dai Zangi were (and still are) extreme examples of this type of landowner. In both areas the dominant kinship groups of Sanjarani and Dawlat Beg, respectively, constituted most of the landowning class. Generally, landowners lived near their estates in large fortified qalʾas. In Herat and Turkestan absentee landowning predominated.

Crop-sharing tenants were found in river valleys as well as in the plains, although in eastern Afghanistan they were sometimes indistinguishable from the hamsayas.[15] In the Herat region crop-sharing tenancy predominated, while in Turkestan crop-sharing labor existed as well.[16] In eastern and southern Afghanistan crop-sharing tenants were known as bazgars, as well as dehqans and, in western Afghanistan, as kishtmands. It is not correct to state, as Schurmann does, that a crop-sharing laborer "is almost universally" called a dehqan who "represents the lowest social level among cultivators."[17] Only of northern Hazarajat was this statement true, while in parts of western Afghanistan, particularly among the non-Pashto speaking population, the term bazgar signified a mere agricultural laborer. Whatever the term, crop-sharing tenants generally possessed a few animals, agricultural tools, and even shelters of their own. They were entitled to attend the jirgas,

especially when they belonged to the same kinship group as the landlords and other *bazgars*. In the latter case they claimed equal status
with landholders in spite of their economic plight. Of course, when
they entered into tenancy contracts with landlords they became the
landlord's vassals. They then became obliged to perform certain duties
for the landlords in addition to cultivating their land. In Laghman, for
instance, *dehqans* addressed their landlords as *badars* (masters). While
the *dehqan*'s wife cleaned the wheat of the master, the *dehqan* himself
carried it to the mill for grinding. In such social ceremonies as the
wedding of the master's son or daughter, as well as in emergencies, the
dehqan was expected to serve his master and to carry his rifle. On
entering the contract the *dehqan* was expected to present some ghee or
other milk product to his new master, but this was not obligatory. The
dehqan was also expected to support his master in local disputes. In
return, the master assisted his *dehqan* by extending loans, donating
secondhand clothes, providing protection, and so forth. The duration of
the tenancy was not fixed. Either party could cancel the contract at any
time, but the *dehqan* was usually allowed to stay on until the crops are
reaped.

At the bottom of the social order were agricultural laborers and
various other occupational groups. They were members either of the
formerly subdued ethnic groups or of impoverished and uprooted peasantry, living either in communities of dominant kinship groups or in
ethnically mixed communities. They might be cultivators, shepherds,
or artisans; but, whatever their occupations, they were looked down
upon and practically excluded from attending the jirgas. They occupied
this status in spite of the fact that among them some groups were
economically quite well off and integrated into the community, both
linguistically and by the adoption of certain social norms. These
groups were, as a rule, endogamous but socially not exclusive. Indeed,
thanks to the brotherly spirit of Islam and of the egalitarian society
in general, they mixed freely with others in mosques and on social
occasions. Only in Kafiristan were the client groups, especially before
their conversion to Islam, completely discriminated against.

Among the client group the biggest was the *hamsayas*. According to
I. M. Reisner, "Among the plains Yusufzais, the plains Mohmands, the
Khalilis, the Muhammadzais, the Gigianis as well as among the Dur-
ranis and the Ghilzais, the mass of the hamsayas consisted of the de-
scendants of the aboriginal population. . . . Among the Durranis and
Ghilzais, they were mostly Tadjiks, Hazaras, Kakars, and Baluches."[18]

The *hamsayas* were called by different names in different *uluses*.
Among the Shinwarays and Afridays, they were referred to as Mulla-
gorays and Tirahays. The *hamsayas* of the Yusufzays were called *faqirs*
in the early nineteenth century and later were called Kohistanis, Shil-
manis, Swatays, and other names.[19] Groups of agricultural laborers
attached to non-Pashtun *uluses* and bearing the same status as the
hamsayas were known in some places as *bazgars* (Seistan and Ghore)
and in others as *dehqan* (northern Hazarajat). Whatever the term, they

occupied the lowest level of the social order. They possessed neither land nor agricultural tools, oxen, or shelters but simply some belongings and the power of their muscles. They were, in fact, the agricultural proletariat. What Shinobu Iwamura says about agricultural laborers in northern Hazarajat applies to all: "As far as the tenant farmers are concerned the land belongs to the landowner, their homes belong to the landowner, even the livestock which they raise belongs to the landowner, the agricultural implements too belong to the landowner, in short everything belongs to the landowner. All they have left, are their bodies, otherwise nothing at all."[20]

It is held that the *hamsayas* were the aborigines who were, in the course of time, reduced to a state of dependency by the more powerful groups of newcomers.[21] It is in this sense that, after the spread of the Pashtuns in the west, the Aimaq and Parsiwans were regarded as "a conquered people."[22] It was held that since the Pashtuns were a people of war and plunder, they left trade and cultivation to the conquered people.[23] "Directly an Afghan receives a concession of land from his chief," wrote Ferrier in the 1850s, "he places it and a few oxen in the charge of a Parsivan, who tills, sows and reaps it for him."[24] This statement implies that the *hamsayagi* is exclusively a Pashtun institution; Reisner clearly holds this to be so.[25] My position is that the *hamsayagi* is sociological in content and common to all communities in Afghanistan to various degrees, irrespective of ethnicity. Even in Elphinstone's time non-Durrani Pashtuns were reduced to this status. "Afghans who join an Oalooss," he writes, "after quitting their own property, are considered Humsauyehs, but are treated with more regard than the rest of the class."[26] Further, as noted earlier, the *hamsayagi* as an institution has also developed in non-Pashtun *ulus*. Indeed, the word *hamsaya* itself is Persian and literally means "some one sharing the same shade," or "neighbor." In number, however, the *hamsayas* do differ from one *ulus* to another, and proportionally there are perhaps more *hamsayas* in the Pashtun *uluses*. Generally, *hamsayas* do not make up a majority of the people in the *ulus* in which they live, except among the Yusufzays of whose *hamsayas* it is said that "The fakeers are much more numerous than the Eusofzes."[27] This fact may explain why the Yusufzays, conscious of their small number, have reduced their *hamsayas* to a very low degree of servitude,[28] whereas among the Durranis the *hamsayas* are "in a situation rather to profit by their hospitality, than to suffer by their rapacity."[29] Everywhere, however, they are protected against injuries from outsiders.

Of all the *hamsayas* the artisans and shepherds were economically better off, but socially still further down the scale than other *hamsayas*. Generally, tradesmen—weavers, dyers, masons, blacksmiths, carpenters, *doms*,[30] drummers, silversmiths, and so forth—were permanently attached to a *ulus*. They lived in market towns and large old villages. Most were paid a proportion of the crops for their services. Some were paid for specific services which they rendered to individuals. They worked for free only for the *ulus* in which they lived. Some

among these tradesmen—such as Handkees, *doms*, and drummers—
were darker in color and Indian in origin. Why *hamsayas*, even the
fair-skinned weavers among them, were handicapped socially is difficult to tell. Their low status could possibly be the result of the static
technology of the time and its exclusiveness to them or of the influence of the caste system of India.

Of the same category as the agricultural laborers, but on somewhat a
different dimension, was another group of poor seasonal laborers
known as the *gharibkar*. These impoverished members of a community temporarily left their locality with or without their families for
casual short-duration labor in other areas on the land or in cities.
According to Schurmann, "Gharibkari is any form of crude urban labor
performed by immigrant peasants from the interior or by city prole-
tarians."[31] *Gharibkari* is seen by Schurmann as one-way traffic toward
cities, but Ferdinand has dealt with it exclusively as a rural phenomenon in reference mainly to the impoverished nomads.[32] In fact, historically *gharibkar* migration has occurred between the rural areas and
urban centers and between one rural area and another. *Gharibkari*, as
well as *hamsayagi*, has been the result of agricultural crises and den-
sity of population and has been found more in the river valleys than in
the plains, mainly because in the river valleys, hemmed in by mountains, the reclamation of new land has been insignificant, if not impossible. That *gharibkari* has been a historical process Schurmann also
suggests. According to him, "the permanent agricultural crisis, which
lies at the basis of *gharibkari* is a relatively old phenomenon, and not
of recent origin."[33] Elphinstone has made numerous references to men
in eastern Afghanistan who went to places in northern India in search
of casual labor, although he does not call them *gharibkari*. The
Hazaras, by way of contrast, provided an example of city laborers even
before their pacification in the late nineteenth century. After their
pacification they migrated even more toward cities, especially Kabul.
To quote Schurman once again, "Gharibkari is largely responsible for
the great migration of Hazaras to the cities of eastern Afghanistan. The
Hazaras form the principal proletarian element in the eastern cities.
Insufficient agricultural production drives the poorer peasants into the
cities for work. Most of them intend to return when they have accumulated sufficient cash to buy land."[34] The *gharibkari* of the Kabul
region, on the one hand, went (and still go) in the winter to the warmer
regions of eastern Afghanistan, especially Laghman, to work as wood-
cutters, construction laborers, fuel and manure carriers, and the like.
On the other hand, the *gharibkari* of eastern Afghanistan, including
the impoverished nomads, went up in the summer to the high regions
of Kabul to harvest crops and pick grapes.[35]

As seasonal laborers the *gharibkari* wandered singly or with their
families. In the latter case, they lived in shelters provided by some
notables and were provided for as the *hamsayas* were. In any case, the
gharibkari worked in loose groups without any form of organization.
They were temporary laborers and most returned to their original

homes after they had saved a little. These savings added to their status, especially when they bought a piece of land.

Gharibkari has resulted in rather extreme population fluctuations, a constant coming and going between areas. Just as it is said that in Afghanistan there have been seen "so many notables in rags" because of a change in their positions, there have also been instances, at least in some ethnically mixed regions, when even members of the blacksmith groups have become religious scholars and government officials. From an early date, this type of mobility, though on a modest scale, has been slowly but steadily undermining tribalism and regionalism in Afghanistan. Simultaneously it has contributed to the stratification of the society. Yet, the process of proletarianization and stratification has, at no time, become a threat to the community in times of crises. Although such an action was clearly to their disadvantage, landless peasants, *hamsayas*, and the socially disabled artisans have defended the status quo in critical times, if not with the same zeal as the small and large farmers, at least with enthusiasm. Instances are numerous in which, instigated by landowners, landless peasants have risen against the government, but there are none in which they have risen against the landlords. A policy of Amir ʾAbd al-Rahman Khan was to divide the two, but in almost all of the over forty uprisings that occurred in his reign,[36] landless peasants stood by the landowners. Landless peasants and agricultural laborers had still not entered history as an independent class. As was said of the French peasants in the middle of the nineteenth century, the Afghan peasants were "incapable of enforcing their class interest in their own name."[37]

Nomads and the Problem of Settlement

Nomads in Afghanistan included those who were partly settled, partly pastoral, or wholly pastoral and dependent for their living on flocks or their production and trade. They followed regular patterns of seasonal migration in search for grass and water and lived in portable dwellings, tents. In Afghanistan of the period under discussion portions of the Pashtuns,[38] Char Aimaq, Uzbeks, Qirghiz, Arabs, and Hazaras were either wholly or partly nomadic. Among the sedentary population a few Tajiks also lived in tents. The Kafirs were wholly sedentary but owned large flocks also.

Portions of the Durranis and Ghilzays were either nomadic or semi-nomadic. Eastern Pashtuns were almost wholly village-dwelling agriculturalists. Exceptions among them were two sections of the Upper Mohmands, who moved in the spring with their flocks to the upper parts of the Helmand in Khurasan.[39] Portions of the Safays and Shinwarays were also nomadic. The larger part of the Wazirs lived in either black tents or movable hovels of mats and spent the warm part of the year in nearby hills. A small part among them, as well as a few of the Afridays, lived in caves.[40] The following pages will cover aspects, first, of the Ghilzay and Durrani nomads and, then, of other nomads in conjunction with the problems relating to their settlement in the period under discussion.

Of all the Pashtuns, indeed of all the ethnic groups of Afghanistan, the Ghilzays were the most nomadic. Among the Ghilzays, the Kharotays and Nasirs were true nomads. The nomadism of the former was apparently the result of overpopulation and insufficient arable land. Their fields were so hemmed in by steep mountains that it was impossible for them to extend cultivation. Also, their mountains were covered with pine trees that did not permit the growth of any herbage suitable for the maintenance of flocks. In addition, the land of each person was divided posthumously among the sons according to the Shari'a and the portion that fell to the share of each was soon too small to maintain a person. With the natural increase in their population many of the Kharotays abandoned their lands to their brothers and dedicated themselves to pasturage.[41] Probably by a similar process portions of the Shinwarays, Safays, Kakars, Niyazays and Ludin, whose habitats resembled that of the Kharotays and who, together with the Ghilzays, constituted the major nomadic group of Afghanistan, turned to nomadism also. This process indicates that Pashtun nomadism, like nomadism in general, is a postagricultural phenomenon. Generally Pashtun nomads, as well as other nomads in Afghanistan, traveled along fixed routes between their winter and summer quarters, and these they considered their territories.

The Nasirs also had no land and like other Pashtun nomads lived in black tents and depended entirely on their herds. All Ghilzay nomads were engaged in long transhumance between the Hotakay and Tokhay lands in the spring and from the Hotakay land to Daman up to the upper Sind in the winter, passing through the hostile Waziri land in transit.[42] The Sulaiman Khel Ghilzay were, however, not so pastoral in the nineteenth century. At that time only a few shepherds among them moved to Gomal and Daman. Even among these shepherds men often quit the pastoral life for that of husbandmen, but seldom was the reverse the case.[43]

Among the Sulaiman Khel Ghilzay the Ahmadzays, who grazed their flocks in the winter in the regions extending up to Jalalabad, were pastoral. In the early twentieth century, however, of the three hundred thousand *powindas* or *kuchis* (terms commonly given to the nomads of eastern Afghanistan)[44] who entered India in their annual migration, the Sulaiman Khel were the greatest in number.[45] Not all Sulaiman Khel had become pastoral, but the opening of the Hazarajat had led to the development of pastoralism among the *powindas*.

The economy of the *powindas* was adapted to moving life. Their tents, which were invariably black, were small and light. They carried few belongings with them. While men among them tended the animals and handled the outward relations in trade and politics, women did the major part of daily work. The *powindas* were, however, not self-sufficient but were dependent on wandering Pashtun weavers for making their tents and sacks and on the city bazars for their kitchen utensils, clothes, and, above all, their main item of diet, wheat. Their own products were few and consisted of milk products, felts, woolen ropes, tanned-skin sacks, and thread.[46] Thus, in spite of the division of land between the settled population and the *powindas*, the two groups were not far from each other and a sense of strong symbiotic relation was apparent between them.[47] Their relations, however, were not always friendly.

The main source of the *powindas'* antagonism with the settled population was grazing pastures and the frequent raidings of the former on the crops of the latter. On that ground they were at odds with the Hotakays and Tokhays in whose lands they camped in the summer. They were also at war with the Zadrans and Formulies,[48] but their bitterest enmity was with the Wazirs through whose land, especially that along the Gomal River, they passed twice a year.[49] Among themselves the *powindas* were also at loggerheads. The Sulaiman Khel feuded with the sons of Turan, that is, the Tokhays, Hotakays, Kharotays, Nasirs, and others. Smaller sections of the *powindas* joined one or the other of the other groups according to circumstances, but all of them made temporary alliances against common danger.[50]

In ordinary times the *powindas*, who were impatient of control not only by government but also by their own elders, gave little authority to their tribal leaders. When elders were authoritative it was because they possessed strength of character, wealth, numerous relations, influence with government, and, last of all, high birth.[51] Only in an emergency did the *powindas* give special power to their elders. For instance, when passing through the Waziri land the *powindas* elected special magistrates called *chalwaishtays*, or groups of forty, led by an authoritarian mir. The *chalwaishtays*, in fact, resembled military governments formed in emergencies.

On entering India in their seasonal migration by way of the Gomal, Kundur, Dhanasar, Tochi, Kaitu, and Kurram the *powindas* were divided into three distinct groups. First, those who took their families with them and established themselves in fixed camping grounds (*kirris*) in Daman (Sind) where they sought pastures for their flocks. Second, those who went down with caravans as merchants with or without their families. Third, those who possessed no belongings and went down to India as unskilled laborers (*charras*).[52] The merchant *powindas* carried goods between Afghanistan, Bukhara, Persia, and India. The hawkers and moneylenders among them went as far afield as Burma, Assam, Bengal, and Nepal. From Afghanistan they carried wool, ghee, almonds, pistachio nuts, dried fruits, and crude vegetable drugs, and from India they brought cloth, shoes, sugar, salt, and tea.[53] As discussed before, the merchant *powindas* were losing ground in international trade during the period under discussion. Still, by the very nature of their calling they came into contact with peoples of various cultures and were exposed to outside influences.

Many *powindas* were fluent in Urdu as their second language, and some spoke Persian. It was by no means rare to meet *powindas* who spoke Burmese, Assamese, Bengali, and Panjabi. They were strict Sunni Muslims and, like most Afghans, they followed the Qadiriyya and Chistiyya orders. It was also not unusual for them to seek the blessing of the *pirs* who led the Suhrawardiyya and Chistiyya orders. The Sulaiman Khel and other tribes followed the Naqib Sahib of Charbagh and the Hazrat Sahib of Delhi, who represented the Qadiriyya order and the Naqshbandiyya order in Afghanistan.[54]

The pacification of the Hazarajat opened a new region for both flock-owning and merchant *powindas*, providing pastures for the first and "virgin market" for the second.[55] Previously, the Hazarajat was an isolated area and only caravans touched its outskirts. As far as the *powindas* were concerned they could graze their flocks in the pastures of the Ghazni and Behsud Hazaras; but the nomads had to fight their way, since the latter opposed them.[56] Because they had helped the amir in the Hazara War, the *powindas* found their opportunity when the Hazarajat was pacified and divided into nine districts. First, they forced their way into Malistan.[57] Unable to oppose them the Hazaras sought redress. To the Hazaras' satisfaction, a commission appointed to settle the dispute fixed a boundary line passing through Nahur, Kadanay, and Ajaristan. The *powindas* undertook to pay a fine of 20,000 rupees if they crossed these fixed borders.[58] Subsequently, however, with the connivance of government officials the *powindas* did.[59] On the repeated complaints of the Hazaras, unsuccessful attempts were made to restore their rights. The *hakim* of Malistan even upheld the cause of the Hazaras; but, against the forceful entry of the *powindas*, he found himself powerless. The *powindas* ultimately occupied the pastures of Dai Zangi, Dai Kundi, Behsud, Nahur, Malistan, Ajaristan, and other interior areas[60] and turned them into their summer camping grounds. This forceful possession was shortly afterward reinforced by their obtaining legal rights to the pastures. First, according to a firman, all pastures throughout Hazarajat, which had been commonly held by the Hazaras, were declared state property. Subsequently the lands were sold to the *powindas*[61] on a tribal basis.[62] The *powindas*, thus, became a permanent restraining influence on the Hazaras but did not show any inclination either to settle in the Hazarajat or to mix with the Hazaras. The two groups, however, collaborated on many levels; and this collaboration "made life easier for the Hazaras," in spite of the conflict between these "two fully intact nations with different culture and language."[63]

The loss of pastures by the Hazaras led to the destruction of their flocks. "Most poor Hazaras" abandoned their fields and lands. Since the Hazaras had marketed the products of their flocks in Afghanistan, the loss of their pastures and the destruction of their flocks brought about a shortage of meat and inflation in the country. In addition, their dispossession led to a permanent feud between them and the *powindas*, especially as the latter, in an effort to increase grazing lands for their flocks, over the years slowly acquired legal rights to the land in the central upland.[64] Among the Hazaras trade was based on the barter system and sugar and salt were much in demand; to meet this need the impoverished Hazaras accepted credit on exorbitant terms from the *powindas*. For some *powindas* these activities developed to such an extent that animal breeding lost much of its importance and they became traders *(tejar)*.[65]

Not only were the *powindas* unwilling to settle in the Hazarajat; they also showed no inclination to settle in Turkestan and Herat in spite of the efforts of the amir to force them to. In the early years of his reign when the amir made conciliatory efforts between the hostile tribes he also persuaded the Sulaiman Khel, Kharotays, and Nasirs to give up enmity among themselves. Accordingly, in 1883, elders of these tribes, who had in their own words, "Never desisted from entailing loss of life and property on one another," entered into what was called "perpetual friendship with one another."[66] Agreement or no agreement, in 1887 these tribes fought one another, but only the elders of the Nasirs declined to present themselves to the amir when summoned. Instead, they fled to India.[67] They had already refused to pay tithes as tax to the state[68] and, after that refusal they joined their Ghilzay kinsmen in rebellion in spite of the fact that the amir had earlier advised them against it.[69] The amir then tightened his earlier order forbidding the entry of the Nasirs into Afghanistan altogether.[70] They were told that because of the great numbers of the nomads, shortage of pastures, and the fact that the Nasirs remained for the greater part of the year in India, their presence in Afghanistan caused harm and friction.[71] In response to their repeated pleas the amir proposed to them the following: "Come all of you. I will provide you with a large quantity of land and good pasture grounds near Balkh and Herat. If you will not accept these proposals you should not enter Afghanistan."[72] Their elders accepted the proposal, but most of their tribesmen opposed it. The position of the Nasir elders was similar to that of the elders of Shinwar who were amenable to a compromise settlement with the government during their rebellion in the 1880s but were not strong enough to carry their tribesmen with them. We see that even when the amir subsequently expressed willingness to accept hostages and 10 percent of the Nasirs for settlement in Qataghan[73] in return for their unimpeded entry into Afghanistan,[74] the Nasir tribesmen, in opposition to their elders, turned the proposal down.[75] Anticipating the forceful entry of the Nasirs, the amir instructed the Sulaiman Khel to fight them. As a precaution, Ghazni was also reinforced with the regular army.[76] For their part, the Nasirs, who found India and even Kashmir unpalatable in the summer, "had no alternative but to enter Afghanistan." In the summer of 1889 a group of ten thousand families of Nasirs entered Darwazagay and Lwargay[77] in the Kandahar area, not in Ghazni, as had been anticipated. Seeing their great number and hearing the sturdiness of their reply to his warning, the governor of Kandahar asked them to send a deputation of their elders to the amir. They did so, and the amir, in return for their payment of 'ushr and a tax on their commercial goods,[78] revoked his earlier order and permitted their unimpeded entry into Afghanistan as had been allowed before.[79]

Pasturage was more extensive among the Durranis than among the eastern Pashtuns. The two groups used black tents of slightly different types. Unlike the Ghilzays, the Durranis were not at war either among themselves or with others. Also, they covered much shorter distances during their transhumances, moving in the summer from their low desert land to the highlands of Siahband in Ghor and Toba in the Achakzay land. Their camps were also smaller than those of the Ghilzays, consisting of from ten to fifty tents. Another feature distinguishing them from other nomadic groups was that the Durranis, while camping, held festivities and hunted with hounds, known in the western world as Afghan hounds or simply "Afghans." Also, unlike *powindas*, the Durranis were not wholly nomadic, for they combined agriculture with pasturage. They cultivated their lands themselves and in their absence their *hamsayas*, who were mainly the Tajiks, Aimaq, Ghilzays and Kakars, took care of the lands. The combination of agriculture with pasturage made the shift from one to another rather easy for the Durranis. When, for instance, a *karez*, an underground irrigation channel upon which cultivation depended, dried up, the seminomadic Durranis became wholly pastoral. Because of the abundance of grass in their extensive land, the Durranis maintained large flocks that consisted, in descending order by number, of sheep, goats, camels, bullocks, and asses. In the spring they hired shepherds for grazing their herds. It was because of their keeping large herds that they were known as *malders* (cattle-owners), rather than *kuchis* or *powindas* as the Ghilzays nomads were called. Sometimes they were simply called Kandaharis, after the place from which they came. The settled and the nomadic populations among the Durranis were not sharply separated, as they were among the Ghilzays. Another notable difference between the *powindas* and the Durrani pastoralists was the division of work between men and women. The Durrani women, unlike the *powinda* women, worked mainly indoors and wove tablecloths. Also, unlike the *powindas*, the Durranis, except the Achakzay section, did not carry on trade. Unlike the *powindas*, who were in contact with many culturally and linguistically different people, the Durranis were in touch mainly with the Persian-speaking Taimanis. Nevertheless, the Durranis were more open to the influence of others than the Ghilzays were. As has been already noted, some of the *powindas* spoke other languages without giving up their own; they also influenced many Hazaras to speak Pashto.[80] By contrast, as Ferdinand observes, "A considerable number of Pashtun nomads in Western Afghanistan have lost their native tongue and become Persian-speakers." He also states that because of the absence of "cultural and ecological obstacles" between the pastoral Durranis and the Aimaq (as Ferdinand calls the Taimanis in this context) and the fact that the Durranis have purchased irrigated lands among the latter, it is probable that in the long run the Durrani pastoralists among them will be "Aimaqized,"[81] as the Nurzay Durranis have already been "Persianized."

Except for the Arab *kuchis* of Jalalabad who migrated in the summer to Paghman and Betut,[82] most nomadic groups, such as the Char Aimaq, Uzbeks, and Hazaras, covered short distances between their summer and winter camping grounds. These seminomads had much in common. To begin with, their tents were round dome-shaped felt yurts, which were also used among the Turkish-speaking nomads (Turkmen, Uzbeks, and Qara Qirghiz) and Qazaqs.[83] They called their tents by various names. In the early nineteenth century the term *khirgah* was commonly used.[84] In the period under discussion the Firozkohis and Jamshidis called their tents, in which they lived all year, by the name *siahkhana*, signifying the black felt from which their tents were made.[85] They also lived in reed huts. In 1885 they applied the term *yurt* not to the tents, but to the land they occupied[86]—a usage which suggests their attachment to their territory. The Sariq Turkmen of Herat and all the Uzbeks of Maimana in the late nineteenth century adopted as their tents Russian *kibitkas*, which like *khirgah* were round dome-shaped structures.[87] Among the Hazaras the term *khirgah* was still in use in the late nineteenth century.[88] Whatever the term, the structure of these tents was the same and their distribution in Afghanistan corresponded roughly to the zone of dome-shaped mud houses.

Another common denominator among these seminomadic groups was the short distance between their summer and winter quarters. Perhaps the most important feature that distinguished them from, say, the Ghilzay nomads, was their participation, though on a small scale, in agriculture. All the Aimaq were agriculturalists, though poor ones who raised crops that were barely sufficient for their subsistence. They kept large herds and pursued a mode of life that enabled them to move about to places where the best pasturage was found.[89] The limited size of their agriculture was compensated for by the abundance of pasture in Herat, especially in the rolling hills of Badghis, where even the settled population grazed their cattle for seven months every year. Herat was, in fact, more pastoral than agricultural,[90] since it had extensive tracts of good grass.

Perhaps over one-sixth of the Uzbeks of Maimana also led a seminomadic life, wandering in the summer in the hills nearby and camping in the winter outside the city of Maimana, not inside it as they had done before it was garrisoned by the army.[91] Most of the Hazaras led their sheep to the summer camping grounds on the grassy uplands from which they returned in the autumn to reap their harvests round their small villages in which they would then spend their winter and early spring. During the winter months when most of their country was under snow the Hazaras engaged themselves in spinning, weaving, making clothes, and leatherwork. A large number of them went to major cities in Afghanistan, especially to Kabul and Kandahar, and to India to work as coolies.[92] Unlike the Pashtun *kuchis* who had a symbiotic relationship with the settled population these seminomadic groups were self-sufficient and not dependent on the settled population.

The Turkish term *aimaq*, meaning a tribe or a section of a tribe, was applied to a number of seminomadic tribes residing mainly in the dependencies of Herat. Originally, the word included the Taimanis, Hazaras of Qal'a-i-Nao, Taimuris, and Zuris (a section of Taimanis). Hence the compound Turco-Persian word *char aimaq*, meaning four tribes. As time went on the word *aimaq* was, in addition, applied to tribes such as the Firozkohis, Jamshidis, Durzays, and other groups.[93]

The Uzbek inhabitants of the village of Charshanba in Maimana called themselves Dwazda Aimaq, or twelve tribes.[94] In the period under discussion the term *Char Aimaq* was in common use and included the Jamshidis, Firozkohis, Hazaras, and Taimanis, who were seminomadic, Sunni in faith, and Persian speaking. They had, in addition, some broad political interests in common, notably exemption from taxation[95] and the collection of 60,000 rupees as annual allowance in return for their serving the state with feudal cavalry. Among themselves, however, they had no spirit of common concern, perhaps because they were of mixed origin.[96] The political institutions of the Char Aimaq, unlike those of the *powindas*, were authoritarian, and their elders ruled their autonomous communities in absolute fashion.

Of the Char Aimaq the Hazaras were the wealthiest, the Firozkohis the most numerous, and the Jamshidis the most important. The Taimanis were known for their lack of courage. The significance of the Jamshidis arose from their historical connection with the Turkmen, particularly the Sariq Turkmen of Panjdeh, for whom the Jamshidis acted as intermediates with the government. Because of this connection, the Jamshidis pictured distinctly in the amir's colonizing program for the northwest frontier region of Herat and in the complexities of the Panjdeh crisis.

The northwestern regions of Afghanistan were the most unstable and insecure of all for the following reasons: In that part of Afghanistan large sections of the frontier regions were undefined. They were, also, the least populated and most vulnerable to occupation by Russia. The depopulation of the frontier regions of Herat and Turkestan was essentially the result of the dichotomy between the settled and nomadic modes of life that was so pronounced in this part of the world. In the early 1880s the frontier regions of Herat had been subjected to repeated pillage by the predatory Turkmen and the fertile region of Badghis had been desolated.[97] Similarly, the Turkmen ravaged the northern region of Turkestan and Maimana. In Maimana even the settled districts along the high roads suffered.[98] The wide stretches of cultivable grounds between Aqcha and Tashqurghan had also been laid waste.[99] While the Tekke Turkmen of Merv used to raid along the frontier regions of Persia and Herat, the Sariq Turkmen of Panjdeh and of Yulatan and, to a lesser degree, the Kara and Arsari Turkmen from the bank of the Oxus of Bukhara laid waste the border regions of Maimana.[100] In Turkestan, moreover, local communities had been weakened and depopulated by a long series of internecine wars and by cholera epidemics and the Persian Famine of 1872.[101] During the first decade of the amir's reign the northern provinces, as a whole, lost much of their population to Bukhara because of the increase in the taxation and the rebellion of Sardar Muhammad Ishaq. As one observer put it, "the western portion of Afghanistan . . . wants nothing but the population to cultivate it."[102] The methods used by the Turkmen in carrying out raids had some similarity to those of the eastern Pashtuns; but, while some sections of the latter—the Achakzays and Baluches— only supplemented their living by robbing caravans, the Turkmen had made raiding a way of life.[103] They carried away cattle, sheep, and women not only from the timid Uzbeks, but also from different sections among themselves. Whereas such raids among the Kafirs of Kafiristan resulted in enmity that lasted for generations, among the Turkmen these raids did not lead to intratribal feuds. At any rate the lack of security was the most important factor that caused these vast and potentially fertile stretches of land in northwestern Afghanistan to remain uncultivated. In the amir's reign much-needed security was provided, and consequently these vast stretches of potentially fertile lands were populated by people from areas south of the Hindu Kush.

The Colonization of Northwestern Afghanistan

In late 1882 the amir decided to settle nomads, as well as sedentary population from the densely populated regions, in the depopulated northwestern areas. The purpose of the colonization program was essentially defensive, but increase in government revenue, the prosperity of the land, the decrease of pressure among the inhabitants of densely populated areas,[104] and finally the weakening of tribal power were also goals. At first nomadic and settled populations from different regions and different ethnic groups were invited or compelled to migrate. The number of resettled Pashtuns increased when the non-Pashtuns in the border area became suspected of disloyalty. This migration became the beginning of a northward movement that has continued over the years until recently.

In January 1883 the Jamshidis, who occupied Kushk in Herat, were invited to settle in Badghis, where one thousand families of Sariq Turkmen had settled after the defeat of the Merv Turkmen by Russia.[105] The Jamshidis were given priority over other tribes because their elder, Yalantush Khan, had assisted in the occupation of Herat in 1881 and because the Sariq Turkmen were on friendly terms with the Jamshidis. It was hoped that the frontiers of Herat would thus be secured, the raids of the Tekke and Qara Turkmen stopped, and, above all, the Afghan control over the Sariq Turkmen of Panjdeh consolidated. Yalantush Khan and his brother Amin Allah were one after the other appointed the *hakims* of Panjdeh. Portions of the Firozkohis and Hazaras were also allowed to settle there. The program of colonization proceeded slowly, because of shortage of funds and supplies and the rise of disputes among tribal elders; but, by the beginning of 1885 some two thousand families had settled in Bala Murghab.[106] This program, however, had an immediate setback.

The decisive blow to the colonization program came from the occupation of Panjdeh by Russia in March of 1885. The Hazaras and Firozkohis left their new homes in the midst of the crisis. Among the Jamshidis two factions appeared, one wishing to submit immediately to the Russians and the other intending to wait and see.[107] W. D. Merk, who as a member of the boundary commission was in Badghis at the time, held that the Jamshidhis, who saw that their former profitable position as middlemen on the frontiers of Herat was now gone forever, turned "against the Afghans and in favour of a European ruler."[108] Meanwhile, Yalantush Khan, who had already established correspondence with Col. Alikhanov, the Russian governor of Merv, received messages from him urging the elder to visit him and to accept the governorship of Panjdeh. Apparently the Russians tried to influence the Jamshidis inside Afghanistan through the Sariq Turkmen of Panjdeh, just as the amir had tried to do the opposite. The Sariq elder ʾIwaz Khan, as newly appointed governor of Panjdeh, made several overtures to the Jamshidis. In the background were, of course, the former unfriendly relations between the Afghan officials and the Jamshidis. In the 1830s Yar Muhammad Khan Alkozay, then governor of Herat, had suppressed a rising of the Jamshidis and a large section of them had migrated to Urganj under the leadership of ʾAbd Allah.[109] In 1880 the most celebrated leader of the Jamshidis, Khan Agha, had been executed by the order of Sardar Muhammad Ayyub for his collaboration with the British, in spite of the fact that he was the father-in-law of the sardar. It was against this background that, subsequently, the amir imprisoned Yalantush Khan and ordered the removal of the Jamshidis from Kushk and Bala Murghab and forced them to settle in the Herat districts of Obeh, Shafilan and Ghorian.[110] Thereafter, the amir began to settle loyal tribes, particularly the Pashtuns, along the border, saying, "It is proper that as the king is an Afghan, his tribesmen, the Afghans should guard the frontiers."[111]

In this second attempt at populating Badghis, Durrani nomads, in particular the Ishaqzays of Pusht-i-Rud and Farah, were invited to settle in the region; but the Alizays of Zamindawar refused migration, and other Durranis expressed willingness to migrate but only without families.[112] This condition was unacceptable to the amir, who then encouraged the Ishaqzays to occupy Badghis and the Achakzays of Zamindawar to occupy Qalʾa-i-Wali.[113] By mid-September 1886 about five thousand families of the Barakzays, Nurzays, and Ishaqzays were settled.[114] Some Ghilzays of the Obeh district and other places from Farah were also settled there. The newcomers were provided with transport carriages, *taqawi* (a loan), and some cash. The *taqawi* was to be paid back after two years, and revenue on the newly cultivated land was due to start after three years.[115] The following summer, however, the Barakzays and Ishaqzays began to abandon their new area, following an attack made on them by the Firozkohis, who were moving to their traditional summer grounds in Ghor, and the inhabitants of Bab-i-Ilahi. A number of people were killed on both sides and many animals of the *malders* plundered.[116] But Taju Khan Ishaqzay, elder of the *malders* in Badghis, spoke only of the mosquitoes and flies that, in his view, made it impossible for flockowners to settle in the region. In seeking royal permission to return home Taju Khan, in fact, insinuated that the region was unsuitable for settlement; but the amir asked him how, if his people could not protect themselves from a few Firozkohis, they could possibly defend the frontiers against Russia? "Go to any place," said the amir, "where flies do not trouble your camels and fleas do not molest yourself."[117] The Badghis settlement program again failed, but this time not completely since the Musazay Ghilzays, Achakzays, and others who were pleased with their new lands remained there. Such factors as exceptional dryness that summer and bad supervision might have contributed to the failure of the second attempt as Nancy Tapper suggests,[118] but the most important single factor responsible for its failure was the lack of security, as was evident from the hostility of the Aimaq. Indeed, when immunity from insecurity was ensured by the discontinuation of the raids of the Turkmen from the Russian side and those of the Aimaq from inside Afghanistan, the amir's third attempt, though not so zealously pursued, met largely with voluntary responses. It is not known how and when newcomers, or rather those who had been in the region before but returned in the third attempt at colonization, volunteered; but by June 1890 some eight thousand families of the Kandaharis, among them some from Naozad, and Zamindawar had settled in Bala Murghab.[119] To these were later added sixty families from Logar,[120] thirty-six Shaykh 'Ali Hazara families and two hundred families of Salu Lang, Shinwarays, and Mohmands.[121] The number of newcomers was still increasing, in spite of the fact that the program of colonization was so mishandled by corrupt officials that some Ishaqzays migrated to Panjdeh to spend the winter under the "infidel" Russians and the summer in Mashhad under the Shi'ite Persians. As one Ishaqzay *malder* told Muhammad Taqi in Kandahar, "Were you to be subjected to the tyranny and oppression which we experienced at the hands of our Hakims every day, you would not pay great heed to religion and race."[122]

The amir was not as successful in populating the regions of Maimana, Turkestan, and Khanabad with the nomads. Some of the Ishaqzays who had abandoned Badghis began to roam between Maimana and Pusht-i-Rud through the Hazarajat and Turkestan under the leadership of Saif Akhundzada.[123] Unwilling to settle they collided with the local population, in particular the Hazaras of Dai Zangi and Dai Kundi.[124] Their wandering, however, opened the way for future waves of migration. Schurmann holds the view that the subsequent migration of the Pashtun nomads to the north and the pacification of the regions north of the Hindu Kush were not as important in this migration as was the difference between the black-tent culture of the Pashtuns and the round-tent culture of the non-Pashtuns. The Pashtun nomads were relatively more mobile and were used to long journeys, while the non-Pashtuns were not. With the natural growth of their population and livestock and the relative suitability of the Turkestan regions for nomadization they penetrated the northern regions. Were it not, the same author continues, for the existence of the Soviet boundary the Pashtun nomads would probably be ranging deep inside the Soviet territory today.[125]

The amir was, by contrast, more successful in populating northwestern Afghanistan with the sedentary population. After the Russian occupation of Panjdeh he began to establish a kind of military colony in Turkestan. The nucleus of this colony consisted of two thousand Garo Khel Ghilzay who were assigned lands in return for military service.[126] This settlement was, in fact, based on the model of the *kohna nokar*. The amir soon reinforced the nucleus by sending five thousand families of other Ghilzays and three thousand families from Deh Afghanan in Kabul.[127] The identity of these people from Deh Afghanan is not known, but all were provided with free food and transportation. The strongest among them were settled in Maimana on the state land, but the terms for their settlement were not as attractive as were those for the newcomers in Badghis. The immigrants in Maimana were allowed to take one-third of the produce for themselves and were required to give the rest to the state.[128] This fact suggests that they were to settle on the state land as cultivators, not owners. Nevertheless, the prevailing food scarcity in Kabul in 1885 made this large migration necessary and the amir warned the people that the produce in Kabul was insufficient for their upkeep.[129] Subsequently, the amir offered other prospective immigrants better terms. In addition to providing them with road expenses and animals for transport purposes, the amir gave the new settlers in Turkestan a three-year tax exemption on the lands they were assigned. After that period they were to pay the tax at the same rate the inhabitants of Turkestan paid.[130] The new settlers were probably also provided with *taqawi*. At any rate, these terms indicated that the new settlers were given the land in perpetuity. The amir repeatedly urged the people of Kabul and the Ghilzays from the distant areas to migrate to Turkestan saying that "The Kafirs [Russians] are coming and this country [Turkestan] shall go out of our hands."[131] Consequently, in view of the scarcity and the favorable terms offered settlers an influx of new immigrants took to the roads to Turkestan. Reports vary as to their number, but by the summer of 1886 over eighteen thousand families were settled in Turkestan.[132] Of these eighteen thousand persons were reported settled in Kunduz.[133]

Shortly afterward the amir decided to establish a penal colony in Baghlan to which he expelled prisoners from Kulman, Laghman, and Kunar. In 1890 a total of 1,150 prisoners, among them Sulaiman Khel Ghilzays, with their families were added to them. During the rebellions of the Ghilzays and of Sardar Muhammad Ishaq a pause in immigration toward Turkestan occurred, but after that the amir, thinking that the area needed more population than it had, decided to send to Turkestan one family out of every four from the densely populated areas,[134] that is, from Kabul and the eastern parts of Afghanistan.[135] At the same time he banished 155 families from the suburbs of Kabul and other areas [136] and 102 families of Garo Khel and from Laghman.[137] Similarly, some Nasirs, Zurmutis, and Shaykh ʾAli Hazaras were deported to Khanabad and Turkestan.[138] In reverse, about 12,000 families of Uzbeks from Turkestan were deported to Kabul and Jalalabad.[139] With the outbreak of the Hazara War, northward migration was suspended and not taken up again in the amir's reign.

Cities and Towns

In the amir's reign, except for Kabul, the cities were not developed significantly. As before, the few cities of Afghanistan were heavily dependent on the countryside for the necessities of life. All were surrounded by thick walls and deep ditches, and each had several gates.

Kabul

Since the city of Kabul had been the capital of many kingdoms in the past and since it was an important commercial center at all times, an adequate background on its development is needed.

Kabul is a very ancient name. In Sanskrit it was called Kubha. The classic Greek writers called it by such different names as Kophen, Kophes, and Koa. The Persians and Aristotle named it Khoaspes, while the famous Chinese traveller Hieun Tsang noted it as Kaofu. The name (or names) was first given to the river of Kabul, as the name Hari was first given to the Hari Rud in Herat. As time passed the name *Kabul* came to be applied to the whole region between the Hindu Kush and the Sind, which was also called Kabulistan. Later, the name was also given to the city, but it is not known who founded the city of Kabul or when. At any rate, since the region called Kabul includes numerous fertile river valleys in which men have lived for centuries and had been, before the discovery of the sea ways, an important thoroughfare linking central Asia with the subcontinent of India and China with the Middle East, the city was the seat of many empires, notably the Great Kushans and Kabul Shaban.

For centuries before and after the Christian era, Kabulistan included many separate states of which Kapisa was the main one. These states coincided with the land that came to be known as Afghanistan. Basing his conclusion on the Chinese writers, Alexander Cunningham writes that Kaofu was probably the name of one of the five Yuchi or Tukhari tribes and that this tribe gave its name to the city when it occupied it in the second century B.C. This supposition seems likely since before that century the Greek writers of the Alexander period made no mention of Kabul. They, instead, called the city Ortospana, meaning "a high place." This name corresponds exactly to the compound Sanskrit

word Urddhastana, which has the same meaning and was applied to
Kabul. Later, Ptolemy called it Kabura, the center of the Paramisadae.
Apparently, Ortospana was the main seat of the region that, after the
Greek domination of the area, gave its place of importance to Alex-
andria. Later the Hindu and Scythian princes rebuilt the city of Kabul,
but it was subsequently abandoned for Opian when that city became
the capital seat of Kapisa. This situation obtained up to the invasion of
Chinggis Khan in the first quarter of the thirteenth century A.D. After
the destruction of Kapisa and, later, of Ghazni, Kabul once again came
into prominence.[140] In modern times Kabul came to prominence after
it became the capital of the kingdom in 1776. At that time Kabul consisted of semiattached houses situated between the right bank of the
Kabul river and the Bala Hisar, along the Sher Darwaza Mountain. The
first significant development of the city took place during the reign of
Amir Sher ʾAli, when Kabul expanded northwestward beyond the left
bank of the river called Sherpur. This expansion became more extensive during the reign of Amir ʾAbd al-Rahman, when he built a new
royal palace, and people of consequence settled in and expanded the
small village of Deh Afghanan. Also, the construction of Kabul workshops along the left bank of the river stimulated the development of
the city toward the west.

Originally there were six large gates in Kabul, namely, the Kandahari, Safid, Sardar Jahan Khan, Bayat, Guzargah, and Lahori. By 1880
only the Lahori Gate to the east remained. Kabul had many bazars.
Chief among them were Shore Bazar and Darwaza-i-Lahori Bazar. The
first bazar extended parallel to the Sher Darwaza Mountain from the
Bala Hisar to the shrine the Ziarat-i-Baba Khodi and the second from
the Lahori Gate to the New Bridge over the Kabul River. The western
portion of the New Bridge was the site of the *Char Chata* (Four Arcades), at one time the most significant bazar in Afghanistan. The
bazar, ascribed to ʾAli Mardan Khan, the Mughal governor of the Kabul
province (Soba) during the reign of Shah Jahan (1628–1657), was handsomely laid out and greatly embellished with paintings. Four covered
arcades were separated from each other by open squares, originally
provided with wells and fountains. The structure was destroyed by the
British when they demolished almost the whole city in revenge for the
annihilation of their entire army in the First Anglo-Afghan War. Portions of Kabul bazars were assigned for the manufacture and transactions of articles of the same categories. Here and there, particularly
at the end of the streets, were located markets of charcoal, grain, wood,
cattle, and dried and fresh fruits.[141] Of its many mosques, the principal
ones were the Masjid-i-Safed, Masjid-i-Bala Chouk, Puli Khishti, and
ʾId Gah, built by Timur Shah, Babur, Shah Shujaʾ, and ʾAbd al-Rahman
respectively.

Kabul was an irregular and unplanned city. Most of its houses were
one-storied, but some were two-storied. Each house had a separate
courtyard (*haram serai*), surrounded by a wall. Houses were made of
either mud or sun-dried bricks with much wood used in them. Wood

was used to make houses relatively secure from the frequent earthquakes but was a breeding ground for insects of all descriptions, which made life unpleasant, especially in the summer. The seclusion of the houses indicated the prevailing sense of insecurity and of the men's dislike of women in their families being seen by strangers. Compactness was the other peculiarity of the city. Blocks of houses were separated by narrow and occasionally covered alleys. Effort was needed to cross these streets in the snowy winters, especially when the snow from the flat roofs was thrown into them, as was the custom. In the cold season people warmed themselves in traditional *sandalis* (heating system) in their houses. Turkish baths (*hamams*) were commonly used. People used water both from wells dug inside their houses and from the narrow streams running along the streets. This impure water was the source of many diseases and prolonged epidemics. Crowding and the lack of a drainage system made the city extremely dirty; but the many wandering dogs, which were a source of irritation for passersby, decreased the refuse considerably. Toward the end of the amir's reign a system of latrines was introduced, and cultivators from the suburbs carried away the waste by donkeys for use in their fields.

People of various origins lived side by side in the city. Only the Qizilbashes lived exclusively, occupying the walled and fortified Chindawal and Murad Khani. The great majority of the city population consisted of people called "Kabulis," the detribalized inhabitants of the city. They differed in origin very much, but the Persian speech and the common habitat gave them a common identity, which in the eyes of the people of the countryside was synonymous with cowardice. By profession the Kabulis were either artisans, traders, or shopkeepers. The second main group of the city inhabitants were the Pashtuns (Durranis, Ghilzays, and Safays), who had begun to adapt to the city ways of life without abandoning the traditional ways of the country. The non-Muslim inhabitants of the city, Hindus, Jews, Armenians, and Sikhs, all engaged in trade and money lending. Socially the 150,000 inhabitants of Kabul in the reign of the amir might be grouped, beginning at the top and going down, as members of the amir's family, senior bureaucrats, page boys, Durrani courtiers, tribal elders, ꞌulama, merchants, artisans, mendicants (*darweshes, qalandars,* and *malangs*), beggars, bad characters, and the Hazara laborers.

The great majority of the city people were illiterate. A special group of scribes (ꞌariza nawis) wrote private and business letters in return for fees. All of the city dwellers were fond of music and dance. Musicians rose from among them frequently, but they employed dancers from India and Herat.[142]

Kandahar

The city of Kandahar was an almost regular quadrilateral, fortified, surrounded by high walls, and protected on the outside by a shallow ditch. It had six gates: Kabul, Bardurrani, ꞌId Gah, Shikarpur, Herat, and Topekhana. From each of these led a thoroughfare that took its name from the gate it left and together these roads divided the city into many quarters, each known by the name of a certain tribe or group of people that occupied the section. Other streets bore the names of either famous persons or sacred shrines or certain professions or trades. Four of the main thoroughfares, along which shops were built, met at a circular space in the center of the town, known as the *charsu*. It was here that proclamations to the public had been made in the past. Situated between the rivers of Arghandab and Tarnak, not far from the old city and Nadir Abad (built by Nadir Shah Afshar), the new city was built by Ahmad Shah Durrani in accordance with a plan. Ahmad Shah named it Ashraf al-Bilad (the Noblest of the Cities), but this remained only its official name and was not used generally.

A large majority of Kandahar's population was drawn from various sections of the Durranis, who were settled there on a tribal basis by Ahmad Shah. The non-Durrani Pashtuns of the city included the Ghilzays, Kakars, and Bardurranis. Qizilbashes, locally known as Parsiwans, formed its second largest group. The Hindus formed a sizable portion of the population. Arabs, Kashmiris, Turks, Baburis, Babis, and Jews were also found among them. No author has mentioned Hazaras living in the city. Only Tully spoke of "Moghuls," who supplied the local markets, particularly the main one (*ganj*) with fresh skins, fruits, and dyes.[143] Most probably these people were Hazaras, whose number increased when the Shaykh ʾAli Hazaras and others were added to them. In the early nineteenth century when the metropolis of Kandahar was the largest city of Afghanistan some Jews, Baluches, Uzbeks, and Aimaq also settled there.[144]

As a trading center linking Herat and central Asia with Kabul and India, Kandahar had many caravanserais and was always prosperous. Its Hindu inhabitants traded with India, and the Parsiwans traded with Herat and Mashhad. The Durranis of Kandahar were also engaged in trade. In the late nineteenth century Kandahar had 3,700 shops, and 300 "general merchants."[145] Like the tribes, who lived mainly in separate portions of a quarter, the different classes of merchants and shopkeepers occupied separate streets or portions of streets in various quarters.[146] In this respect Kandahar differed sharply from Kabul.

In proportion to its Sunni population of 20,000, Kandahar had a large number of mosques, 180[147]—an indication of the religiousness of its Sunni population. This devotion explains why the mullas carried great influence with the Kandahar Sunnis. Surgeon Tully, who supervised the British hospital during the occupation period, stressed this influence too much, however, when he observed that "their inclinations for good and evil are entirely controlled by their priests or mullas."[148] Also, in Kandahar the animosity between the Sunni and Shiʾite populations was not as pronounced as it was in Kabul and Herat, perhaps because the Shiʾas of Kandahar were Pashto speakers and, thus, linguistically integrated into the community. Kandahar was noted for the shrine of Ahmad Shah and the cloak of the Prophet where grieved persons took refuge (*bast*). Perhaps more than other cities Kandahar was a male city. Women were confined to their homes, except when they had to visit their relatives, or to *hamams* where they could go inside in veil. Like other cities Kandahar, too, had many public *hamams*, but the Durrani sardars had *hamams* of their own in their large houses with wide courtyards surrounded by high walls.

The inhabitants of Kandahar were keen on learning and Arabic. Having given rulers and emperors to the country, they were very proud but had poor fighting spirit. They were known for homosexuality and many were addicted to hashish.[149] Amidst the affluence of Kandahar, poverty was visible. Angus Hamilton observes, "Mendicity is to be seen in its most loathsome and repulsive forms. The blind, the maimed and deformed, ragged and unspeakably squalid men, women, and children not only stand on and sit but lie grovelling in the dust or mire under the feet of the crowd."[150] During the British occupation period a latrine system, supervised by the *kotwali*, was introduced into Kandahar; but it was soon disused, and the city remained as dirty as ever.

Herat

The city of Herat was more fortified than any other city in Afghanistan. The city was watered by a river and stood in a fertile plain crowded with villages and covered with fields of corn.[151] From its five gates known as the Qutubchak, Malik, Iraq, Kandahari, and Kushk, ran four main streets, which met at the *charsu*, here a domed square covered with beams.[152] Crooked, narrow, and roofed lanes branched off from these thoroughfares. Pools of stagnant water left by the rains, piles of refuse thrown from the houses together with dead cats, dogs, and the excrement of human beings mingled in them.[153]

Herat was a center of early human settlement. Its ancient name was Areia or Hari, derived from Hariva or Arius (modern Hari Rud). Later Arab geographers called it Herat. It was founded, according to Horace Wilson, "By Lahrasp, extended by Gushtasp, improved by Bahman, and completed by Alexander."[154] According to tradition the nucleus of the present city was a place called Shumairan, where the present citadel stands. Shumairan was subsequently abandoned for a nearby city, named Hazar Jarib because it occupied a space of one thousand jaribs. Finding their city unattractive the inhabitants of Hazar Jarib gradually settled around Shumairan and expanded it.[155]

Perhaps no city in central Asia has been destroyed and reconstructed so many times as has Herat. It has invariably risen from its ruins, if not always with renewed splendor, at least with a vigor that is without parallel.[156] The intensive agriculture and elaborate canal systems of the region, which have made Herat known as "the granary of Asia," have probably been the essential factors in the rebuilding of the city. In the period under discussion, Herat, like other cities of Afghanistan, was on the decline. In the thirteenth century Chinggis Khan leveled it to the ground and it ceased to be a dwelling place until one of his sons rebuilt it later. Thereafter many Chinggisids resided in Herat and their offspring are still to be seen there.[157] In the nineteenth century the Persians twice contested its possession but failed to occupy it. A consequence of this invasion was a considerable decrease in the city's Shi'ite population who, because of their intrigue with the Persians, were subsequently sold to the Turkmen by Yar Muhammad Khan Al-kozay. In the anarchy that followed his death and the second siege by the Persians the city again lost many of its Shi'ite inhabitants. The raids of Turkmen also did much the same. By 1885 the city was, as a consequence, declining and had a population of 17,623.[158] Of these over 10,000 were "Parsiwans," over 6,000 Afghans, over 1,200 Jews, and 60 Hindus. There is no mention of whether Tajiks also lived in the city. Presumably Parsiwans and Tajiks were mixed in the listing. Hamilton adds Hazaras, Taimanis, and Jamshidis to the city dwellers.[159] Like other cities, Herat also exhibited more striking diversity than the surrounding countryside.

Herat had a large number of shrines, among them those of Khwaja 'Abd Allah Ansari and Mawlawi 'Abd al-Rahman Jami. Of its buildings the public mosque (Jam' Masjid) adorned with gildings, carvings, and mosaics was perhaps the most significant structure in central Asia. There were several caravanserais in the city, but it had scarcely any trade and was no longer the great central market between India, Persia, and central Asia that it had been. During the reign of the amir the city still had a number of native craftsmen who worked in silk, metals, leather, and wood; but there were few opportunities for their skills to develop and no money with which to pay them.[160] Many inhabitants of the city, unlike those of Kandahar, were reluctant to perform their religious duties, but they showed keen interest in reading and writing and in taking clerical jobs with the government.[161]

Smaller Towns

Unlike other cities in Afghanistan, the city of Ghazni, the once famous capital of the Ghaznavid empire, was built on top of a mound. It was, like the other Afghan cities, surrounded by a wall in part natural and in part artificial. It had three gates: Miri (also called Kabuli), Kinuk, and Bazri (also called Kandahari). The city was divided into the three sections of Kunjuk, Bazar, and Miri. Blocks of houses in these sections, which were separated by narrow alleys, were built of mud and only occasionally had domed roofs. Ghazni was famous for its numerous shrines, which were said to have numbered 197. The most famous were the tomb of Emperor Sultan Mahmud, two minarets built by him, and the tombs of Bahlole the Wise, of Hakim Sanai the poet, and of Shams.

The population of Ghazni fluctuated with the season and the amount of trade passing into India. It rose to eight thousand in the summer and fell to about three thousand in the winter and was largely drawn from the Ghilzays, Durranis, Tajiks, Hazaras, and Hindus. The Hindus traded with India, the Hazaras brought wool, *barak*, ghee, and carpets from their region to the market of the city. The only articles manufactured in the city were saddles, postins, and shoes.[162]

Jalalabad, built by Emperor Jalal al-Din Akbar in 1570, had no more than two thousand summer inhabitants in the period under discussion. In the winter their number increased tenfold when tribesmen from the surrounding hills flocked into the town because of its warmer climate. Its location on the main route between Kabul and Peshawar was advantageous to trade; but Jalalabad was still a small squalid town of no particular interest. The frequent visits of the amir, however, gave some significance to it.

Notable towns in the north were Balkh, Mazar, and Maimana, where, as in Herat, cross-shaped bazars, many of which were roofed, tended to predominate.[163] Balkh, which had been known as Bactria and Umm al-Bilad (the Mother of Cities) in the past, was, in the late nineteenth century, reduced to a town of two thousand people, including a small colony of Hindus and seventy Jews.[164] Up to the 1830s it had retained some of its former position, since it was still the capital city of the province of Balkh that took in the territory between the Oxus and the Hindu Kush and Badakhshan and the Khwarazm land. The Uzbeks traditionally allowed whoever possessed Balkh the right to assume the title of their paramount lord. In the 1830s the city of Balkh still had a bazar, two caravanserais, and one madrasa and some dwelling houses. The ruins of the ancient metropolis were extensive.[165] The attacks of intermittent fever, caused by the surrounding marshes, and the Uzbek raids reduced the city considerably. In the reign of Amir Sher ʾAli Khan its public mosque, which was a renowned center for learning, had become the residence of mendicants (*darweshes* and *qalandars*), who were probably members of the Sufi orders. Viceroy Muhammad ʾAlam Khan, himself a Timurid Shiʾite of Herat, reduced the city still further when he transported the bricks of its mosque to improve the tomb of Mazar, believed to be that of Caliph ʾAli.[166]

Situated on an elevated place in the middle of a flourishing district, the city of Mazar was surrounded by a wall with five gates; the gates were named Nazargah, Zanjirgah, and Charbagh, and two were called Qasim Khani. In the late nineteenth century it had three thousand households. Originally, Mazar was the site of a Zoroastrian fireplace converted subsequently into a mosque called Khwaja Khairan. According to tradition, during the reign of the Seljuk emperor, Sultan Sanjar a certain man (some say the sultan) dreamed that close to Khwaja Khairan lay the body of Caliph ʾAli. The *sayyeds* of the region supported the dream, but a mulla objected to it, stating that the Caliph had been murdered at Kufa and buried at Najaf in Iraq. The next night ʾAli miraculously appeared and reprimanded the mulla in a dream for his disbelief. Everybody was then convinced of the truth of the dream. Soon, by the order of Sultan Sanjar, a building was erected over the grave in A.D. 1136. The building, but not the grave, was in the next century destroyed by Chinggis Khan but was built anew in A.D. 1481 by the order of Sultan Hussayn Baiqira. Each of the subsequent Uzbek rulers added to it such things as wells, mosques, and shops. Expansion of Mazar took place during the viceroyalty of Naʾib Muhammad ʾAlam

Khan who also made Mazar the capital of the province, which it has remained ever since.

Mazar is as sacred to the Shiʾas as Ghazni is to the Sunnis. Shrines in both are visited by the faithful. In Mazar "thousands of the halt and the maimed and the blind collect every April in the hopes of miraculous cure, and the failure to get it is simply put down to want of faith on their own part."[167] The faithful never question the potency of the shrines.

The outside and surroundings of the shrine to the Caliph ʾAli were filthy in the extreme and visitors were besieged by beggars at the gate. In the spring when the annual fair, called Gul-i-Surkh, was held in Mazar the dirt and crowding were tremendous. Inside at the entrance of the shrine was placed a huge copper pot in which donations from a bit of bread to large sums of cash were collected. These donations and the *waqf* attached to the shrine were managed by its guardian (*mutawalli*), who, next to the mir of Kunduz, was the wealthiest man in Turkestan. In the 1830s its guardian was Shujaʾ al-Din, who commanded great influence in the councils of the local elders. In the reign of Amir ʾAbd al-Rahman the *waqf* of the shrine and, probably, its other incomes were taken over by the state.[168]

There were, in addition, a large number of market towns in Afghanistan, differing from villages by the occupations of the inhabitants of the towns; most of them functioned as full-time nonagricultural specialists. The inhabitants of these market towns, in contrast with those of villages and hamlets, displayed many urban traits.

Linguistic Groups

Some thirty-two languages are spoken in Afghanistan, and they belong to the four main linguistic groups of Indo-Aryan, Turkic-Mongolian, Semitic, and Dravidian. In the eighteenth century when the Afghan empire was at its height it included Baluchistan, Kashmir, and other areas. During this period when Brahui, Balti (Tibetan), and Burushkashi (of unknown origin), in addition to several Indian languages, were spoken within its borders, Afghanistan was actually the linguistic center of Eurasia, and nearly all the chief language families of the area were represented in the empire.[169] This plurality of languages may be explained by the fact that Afghanistan throughout history has been a thoroughfare for repeated waves of migration that have introduced new languages to the country and by the fact that even up to modern times inhabitants of remote and inaccessible mountain valleys have retained their peculiar cultures in relative isolation.[170]

Probably at least four-fifths of the population of Afghanistan speak Iranian languages. The term *Iranian* is used here to denote the whole of the western branch of Indo-Iranian, or Aryan languages, through Persia and Afghanistan, with a small offshoot on the Chinese side of the Pamirs. In ancient times Iranian languages were also spoken in the steppes of southern Russia, as well as in many parts of central Asia.[171]

Among the Iranian languages spoken in Afghanistan, Pashto and Persian, which belong to the Indo-Iranian branch of the main Indo-European languages, are the most important. Pashto, or Pakhto, the language of the Pashtuns, on the one hand, has preserved many ancient words and, on the other hand, like other languages, has undergone changes by having adopted numerous words from neighboring Indian languages, as well as from Persian and Arabic.[172] It has numerous dialects, notably the Kandahar or "soft" dialect, spoken in Kandahar and Waziristan and the "hard" spoken among the rest of the eastern Pashtuns. Some Ghilzay dialects are intermediate between the two.[173] The Wanetsi dialect of Pashto, spoken in the Harnai-Shahrig region of Baluchistan, occupies a rather independent position. According to Georg Morgenstierne, the Wanetsi dialect must have split off from the rest of Pashto earlier than other dialects.[174]

Strangely enough, the Pashtun rulers of Afghanistan adopted Persian, not Pashto, as the language of the court and of administration. Even the Pashtuns Ludi and Suri sultans of Delhi, in the fifteenth and sixteenth centuries, adopted Persian as the language of administration. Although Pashto as a literary language had developed considerably during the course of the seventeenth century, it was only in the reign of Amir Sher 'Ali that Pashto began to find its way into administration, when Pashto titles were adopted for senior officials and the words of commands for the Pashtun-dominated army were adapted from English. Under Amir 'Abd al-Rahman, Pashto was used in the army as before, and, in addition, the amir's firmans addressed to the eastern Pashtuns were in Pashto. A number of official publications also made their appearances, perhaps for the first time, in that language. The systematic development of Pashto as part of the official policy, however, was a thing for the future.

The present Persian language is, according to Morgenstierne, based on a dialect of the southwest (Fars) type, although it has absorbed numerous elements of northwestern and northeastern Iranian origin.[175] As a literary language Persian emerged in the ninth century in Khurasan in competition with Arabic, which had been introduced by Islam. The basis of this ninth-century Persian was middle Persian, itself based on the old Persian of the same family as Avesta.[176] This transformation from middle Persian to ninth-century Persian was probably caused not so much by invasions or immigrations on a general scale as by continued infiltration and absorption of earlier languages spoken in Badakhshan in the Pamirs, among the originally Mongolian Hazaras, and in many districts of Afghanistan south of the Hindu Kush. Only in the west, in the Herat region, is there a direct contact between Pashto and the Persian language of Persia and a certain merging into the dialects of Persian Khurasan.[177] By and large, the Persian dialect of Afghanistan, even when spoken by educated people, is rather different chiefly in phonology, vocabulary, and, to a lesser extent, morphology, from the modern "Irani" of Persia.[178] It is probably for this reason that the Persian spoken in Afghanistan is now once again called Dari, meaning "court language," as it was when spoken in Balkh and Khurasan before and after the conquest of Islam.[179] In Afghanistan, Persian had always been the language of the court and of the administration and was spoken by the Tajiks, Hazaras, Qizilbashes, and Char Aimaq. A significant factor in the promotion of Persian in Afghanistan has been its adoption by the originally Pashto-speaking ruling dynasties. In particular during the reign of 'Abd al-Rahman Persian made much progress because of the extension of administration.

Galcha, or the Pamir, languages, spoken by the mountain Tajiks of Badakhshan and the Pamirs, include Munji (with its offshoot of Yidgah in Chitral), Sanglechi, Ishkashmi, Wakhi, Shughni, and Roshani. These are, in fact, the northeastern dialects of the Iranian group of languages. Another dialect, Sarghulami, which was recorded by Zarubin, a Russian scholar, and which was spoken in a valley east of Fayzabad in Badakhshan, has now died out.[180] Among other Iranian languages are Baluchi spoken by Baluches in Farah and Seistan; Urmuri spoken in Logar; Kanigram, in Waziristan; and Parachi, in Nijrao and Shuttal.

Of the Indic group of languages spoken in Afghanistan, the most prominent is the Pashaee, which has several widely divergent and mutually unintelligible dialects and is spoken on the fringes of Nuristan (formerly Kafiristan). Other languages of the Indo-Aryan group are Gowarbati spoken in a few villages in Kunar; Savi, in Sao; Tirahi, in a village of Ningrahar; and Gujuri spoken by the Gujur nomads travelling in the summer in the valleys of eastern Afghanistan. The Jats, or gypsies, of Afghanistan speak Jati. The Hindki language, or Lahnda, is spoken by the Hindus in and north of Kabul. Some Hindus might have remained in this area after its conversion to Islam, but in their present form their languages represent the speech of later immigrants from India. Of still more recent origin is the Panjabi spoken by the Sikhs.

The languages spoken in Nuristan are neither purely Indian nor Iranian but represent a third, originally independent, branch of Indo-Iranian, called by their traditionally established name, Kafiri. These languages are probably derived from the languages of the early wave of Aryan invaders from central Asia toward the plains of India. The ancestors of the later Kafirs were then probably pushed back by the stronger and more numerous successors into the remote and, until recently, inaccessible valleys. The Kafiri languages must have split off from Indo-Aryan in pre-Vedic times.[181]

The Kafiri languages are divided into northern and southern groups, the first consisting of Kati and Prasun and the second, of Waigali and Ashkun. Kati, spoken in Ramgal, Kullam on the headwaters of the Alingar and Bashgal rivers, is numerically the most important of the Kafiri languages and in many respects the most archaic one. While Prasun is spoken in the Parun valley, Waigali is spoken in Waigal. It has several dialects, one of which, Gambiri, is still largely unknown. West of Waigal, between the Pech and Alingar valleys, Ashkuni, with its related dialect Wamai, is spoken. Kalasha and Khowar are possibly spoken within Afghan territories also.[182]

The main Turkic-Mongolian languages are Uzbeki spoken by the Uzbeks; Qazaqi spoken in the northwestern part of Afghanistan; Uyghuri spoken in the villages of Arghu and Abibarik in Badakhshan; Qirghizi, in the Pamir; and Afshari (a variant of Azerbaijani), in the Afshar quarter near Kabul.[183] Mongolian is still spoken by the Taimanis about Rudi Gas and Adraskan near Sabzwar and possibly by those between Maimana and Herat.[184] It is also spoken by the Mongols of the Herat region in Kundur, Karez-i-Mulla, and Dorudi and possibly in Ghor; but the major Mongolian ethnic group, the Hazaras, have long since adopted dialects of Khurasan Persian, sometimes known as "Hazaragi." Among the Hazaras of Behsud and the Mongols of the north of Maimana, words with Mongolian origin are still heard.[185]

Arabic, which was spoken in many towns in Khurasan in the early centuries after the introduction of Islam, is now spoken only in a few villages (Khushhalabad in Dowlatabad, Sultan Aregh in Aqcha, and Hasanabad near Shiberghan). The only vestige of the pre-Vedic languages is Brahui, spoken among a few thousand tribal shepherds of that name living with the Baluches from Shorawak to Chakhansur.[186]

From these linguistic patterns, it can be concluded that Afghanistan has been an extension neither of Iran proper nor of India proper, but, by and large, of Indo-Iran.

Chapter VII
Social Structure: 2

Religion, Religious Groups, and Minorities

Islam has long been the acknowledged religion of the overwhelming majority of the inhabitants of Afghanistan. Hinduism, Sikhism, Judaism, and Christianity have been practiced only by small minorities. Like most Muslim countries, Afghanistan, too, has had representatives of the Sunna and Shi'ite faiths, but the great majority of the Afghan Muslims have been Sunnis. Amir 'Abd al-Rahman strengthened the Sunna still further but weakened the position of the 'ulama, whom he incorporated into the state. Also, with a view towards bringing unity to the country, he forced the Shi'as to observe the Sunna only.

The Sunnis of Afghanistan, who adhered to the Hanafi system of Islam, included all Muslims except the Qizilbashes; the Hazaras; the mountain Tajiks; the inhabitants of Kada in Seistan;[1] most of the Kayanis of Herat and Kandahar; and the Tajiks of Chora,[2] Gizao, and Bamian[3] who were Shi'as. Other Shi'as were the Turis of Kurram, some Bangash, and the Orakzays. On the other hand, the Hazaras of Qal'a-i-Nao, half of the Shaykh 'Ali Hazaras,[4] the Tirahis of Ningrahar (who were formerly Shi'as),[5] the Rikas of Kabul and Ningrahar were Sunnis. The Sunnis had no division among themselves, but the Shi'as were divided into the "Twelvers" and "Seveners." The former lived in the Hindu Kush and in the regions to the south of it, and the latter mainly to the north of it; but the Twelvers were more numerous. The Seveners, or Isma'ilis, were generally known as Mawlais or Agha Khani Muhalati (after the Agha Khan who originally resided in Muhalat, a little to the south of Tehran, and in 1840 went to Bombay where he became the acknowledged leader of the Khwojas of India). In Badakhshan proper and in a district near Balkh they were also known as the followers of Sayyed Ja'far. In other parts of Afghanistan they were known as Muftadis. Among "many Pashais of Laghman and adjacent valleys" were Isma'ilis who called themselves 'Ali Ilahi.[6] The Isma'ilis observed no fast, performed no prayer, and claimed they had little in common with other sects. In place of the Quran they used a book in Persian called *Kalam-i-Pir* (*The Word of the Pir*), compiled by an anonymous Isma'ili author.[7] The Twelvers and Seveners were on bad terms with each other, as is evident from the insulting term *ghalati* (those in error) by which the Isma'ilis were known to the Twelvers, or the Imamis. To both sects, unreserved and unhesitating obedience to Caliph 'Ali, called the Imam and Sahib al-Zaman, was obligatory.[8]

The Agha Khanis were extremely poor and showed unbounded devotion to their religious leaders (*pirs*), some of whom they called shah and to whom they paid 'ushr through their representatives (*khalifas*). The shahs spent some themselves and sent the rest to the Agha Khan in Bombay.[9]

Among the Twelvers or Imamis only the Qizilbashes prayed in mosques. The Hazaras, who were ignorant of their faith, neither had mosques nor observed the *muharram* ceremonies in their *takya khanas* (enclosed places where the Shi'as commemorated the martyrdom of Hussayn during the month of Muharram). In Herat alone there were forty-one *takya khanas*. Like the Sunnis who paid visits to Mecca, the Twelvers, but not the Seveners, visited Karbala and the shrine of Musa Raza in Mashhad. Through these pilgrimages they kept in contact with the Shi'as in Persia and remained open to influence from the mujtahids (interpreters of the Shari'a) whom the Shi'as were obliged to believe and follow in accordance with their faith.[10] Consequently, followers of both groups of Shi'as paid religious allegiance to persons outside Afghanistan: the Isma'ilis to the Agha Khan of Bombay and the Imamis to the mujtahids of Persia. Sunnis and Shi'as alike believed in ghosts, demons, fairies, *dajal* (Anti-Christ), fortunetellers, and, particularly, shrines, numerous all over Afghanistan.

Among the zimmis (non-Muslim inhabitants of Afghanistan) the Hindus lived mainly in urban centers and rural areas in eastern parts of the country. Although not ahl al-kitab (people of the book), as the Jews and Christians were, the Hindus were tolerated in return for *jazya* they paid to the state and were allowed an undisturbed exercise of their religion in their own temples. Also, they had schools where their children were brought up in their own religion. Before 1880 their most sacred shrine was located in Panjsher. By the amir's order it was brought to Kabul where it was embedded in the Asmaic Mountain for which the Hindus were grateful. Among themselves the Hindus were divided into the four groups: Brahmans, Kahtars (most numerous of all), Roxes and the "Travellers."[11]

The Hindus settled their disputes with the Muslims according to the

Shari ᵓ a but those among themselves in accordance with their own laws (Dharma Shastre). The amir, who ruled his Muslim subjects with an iron rod, treated the Hindus leniently, punishing their corrupt officials in accordance with their own mild laws.[12] In the amir's reign many Brahman Hindus were given high positions in the bureaucracy. Naranjan Das was even made a honorary brigadier. A council composed of five Hindu elders was set up to investigate all suits, claims of interest, and questions relating to Hindu laws, before they were to be submitted to the amir for his instruction.[13] In disputes between Hindus and the Sikhs favoritism was shown to the latter, but all felt humiliated by being obliged to wear only yellow turbans and pay the *jazya*. Occasionally, some of the Hindus gave up their religions for Islam, but they were in no way converted forcibly. Because the Hindus were treated mildly in Afghanistan, many Hindus from Jammu in Kashmir volunteered to enlist in the Afghan army, but their request was turned down for their reported misbehavior toward their neighboring Muslims.[14]

Groups of Jews have settled in Afghanistan at various times. The first Jewish emmigrants were said to have come to Afghanistan from Baghdad around A.D. 900. About half a millennium later the second and third waves established colonies in Herat, Mazar, and Ankhui. Subsequently, some of these moved to Kabul. In 1944 there were 3,350 Jews or 440 families settled in Herat, Kabul, and Balkh.[15]

All Afghan Jews were of the old Hebrew Safarji sect. As zimmis they were free to practice their religion in their synagogues, of which they built six in Kabul, four in Herat, and two in Balkh. Each Jewish community had a rabbi who, as head of the community, administered its affairs. Relations among the Jews were regulated according to their own customs, while those between the Jews and Muslims were subject to the Shari ᵓ a. Each Jewish community had, in addition, one representative for what was called "external affairs," that is, dealings with the government. The Jews had adopted some local customs, eating Afghan food and veiling Jewish women in public at the same time that they traded in alcohol.

Like most minorities elsewhere, the Jews in Afghanistan were engaged in trade, especially between Herat and Merv. About half of them were small shopkeepers, selling cotton piece goods, fancy goods, tea, and candy. Others were servants of the well-to-do Jews or brokers in a small way. A small number owned land, mostly around Balkh. The old and unemployed among them were supported by a common fund.[16]

In the reign of Amir ᵓAbd al-Rahman the Jews suffered financially, not religiously. The introduction of state monopolies deprived many Jews of trading activities. Also, the use of alcohol, which until the amir's reign had been marketed openly, was prohibited. This last hit the Jews hard. It was officially, though misleadingly and with much exaggeration, stated that "All the Jews were forced into exile and the consumption of wine was prohibited so that now it can not be procured even for medicinal purposes."[17] The fact was that the Jews were not expelled at all; but, as zimmis and traders, they were made to pay an increased sum to the state as taxes. Most probably Muhammad Yusuf Riyazi refers to these measures when he states that all the Jewish inhabitants of Afghanistan (he calls them a "Jewish nation") were made subject to new regulations as a punishment for their intriguing and creating troubles between the army and the inhabitants of the cities.[18]

A small colony of Armenians was planted in Kabul by Nadir Shah Afshar, and later a church was built for them.[19] In Kabul, they became related to the royal family when Amir Muhammad A'zam Khan married a daughter of Timur Khan. Sardar Muhammad Ishaq was a son of this marriage. During the Second Anglo-Afghan War their church was destroyed by their fellow Christians, the British, and the Armenians later drifted away to India or Persia.[20] This exodus took place after the revolt of Sardar Muhammad Ishaq. Before that, in 1886, the Armenians of Kabul were ordered to settle in Mazar where "a large number" of them were said to exist. Before the final expulsion of the Armenians to Peshawar,[21] the amir had invited some twenty Armenian families of Calcutta to settle in Kabul and to take jobs with the government, mainly as interpreters,[22] but nothing more was heard of them.

The Sunnis performed their prayers in mosques (*masjids*) built in hamlets, villages, and cities. They prayed, in fact, wherever a community of Sunnis could be formed. They were allowed to pray inside or outside the mosques collectively or individually. In the former case they were led by imams, who were mullas, or by any Muslim who was able to lead them in the prayer. Only Friday prayers, during which the khutba (Friday sermon) was read in the name of the sovereign, were to be performed in large mosques, where large gatherings were possible. Because such gatherings were politically significant, they became, during the amir's reign, the subject of discussion among the 'ulama regarding whether prayers were to be held in any mosque or only in certain mosques. The official historian Fayz Muhammad notes that the 'ulama, after a long discussion, issued a *fetwa* saying that Friday prayers were permissible anywhere where "large gatherings" were possible and that the amir endorsed this *fetwa*.[23] Numerous other reports, however, indicate that by the amir's order "the religious observances on Fridays should be held only in the principal mosques of the city, and not in any other villages, where neither Qadis nor officials are present."[24] By this restriction the amir intended "to put a stop to the gatherings of the people at large villages . . . so as to lessen the opportunities for discussion."[25] Notwithstanding this restriction, the amir's contribution to the spreading and consolidation of the Sunna was the greatest of all the rulers of Afghanistan.

By the amir's order all mosques in the country were repaired and maintained at state expense and were provided with necessary supplies and equipment.[26] Allowances were fixed for imams and callers for prayers (*muwwazins*); also, *khatibs* (preachers) were appointed to preach Islam in large mosques. In addition, roving mullas were commissioned to educate the Muslims of the rural areas, who were considered ignorant of their faith, in the fundamentals of Islam.[27] For that purpose, they were provided with booklets, which the ʾulama compiled from Islamic works on jurisprudence and theology for the benefit of common Muslims.[28] Vigilance was kept to see that Muslims observed fast and performed prayers regularly. The qazis and *muhtasibs* were empowered to fine those who failed to pray five times a day, as required by Islam.[29] Blasphemy was punished and the Shiʾas accused of it were stoned to death.[30]

The amir's most noted service to Islam was the conversion of about sixty thousand Kafirs of Kafiristan. The inhabitants of Kafiristan, who were called Kafirs by their Muslim neighbors and were known among themselves by the names of the tribes to which they belonged, believed in a form of idolatry with a mixture of ancestor worship and some traces of fire worship. They had numerous gods and goddesses in a hierarchical order, who were expected to protect the Kafirs and their crops from calamities.[31] On the eve of the conquest of their land in 1895, however, their religion had weakened, and Islam had already made considerable inroads in Kafiristan, as is evident from the work of Sir G. S. Robertson, *The Kafirs of the Hindu Kush.*

Even before Kafiristan was conquered, the amir had made efforts to introduce Islam into the area, through a series of deputations of Kafir elders, who visited the amir in Kabul. Large-scale conversion was attempted after Kafiristan was overrun, but in a society that was still basically Kafir it proved difficult. The mullas were given the task of educating the Kafirs in every village and hamlet in the fundamentals of Islam; but, because of the resistance of the Kafirs and their occasional violent opposition, the mullas were to be protected by armed *khassadars.* The mullas themselves were also armed. Resistance to conversion was offered partly because some mullas took Kafir women, and in some cases previously married women, for their wives and partly because some Kafir elders were still attached to their idols, despite their outward manifestations of devotion to Islam.[32] At the same time, some Kafirs were imprisoned for their unwillingness to accept Islam.[33] Coupled with other causes, religious questions led to a rising among the Katirgullis, who killed some mullas and *khassadars.* The rising was suppressed, the number of mullas was progressively increased, and more and more mosques were built. By 1901 over three hundred mullas were stationed in Kafiristan, twenty of whom were killed in one night.[34] Still, persuasion accompanied by occasional intimidation remained the official policy with regard to the conversion. By and large it succeeded, but the complete replacement of the Kafir religion by Islam was still to be a matter of the future. In early 1901 several Kafir elders offered sacrifices at their shrines, on the rumored death of the amir.[35]

In general it was said that most Afghans followed one mystic order or another (*tariqa*). In Turkestan the majority of the people adhered to the orders of the Chishtiyya, Qadiriyya, and Naqshbandiyya.[36] Also, there are numerous references in literature to *darweshes, qalandars,* and *faqirs*, who were probably the followers of one order or another, and to *takya* and *khanaqa*, which indicated cells.[37] As a strict Sunni, the amir was opposed to these orders, especially when their followers supported Sardar Muhammad Ishaq against him. It was probably because of support of the rebel sardar that the amir discontinued allowances to those persons who maintained *khanaqas*, where they fed the poor; he argued that granting allowances to such people was permissible only when the country was safe from the threats of infidels and there was surplus in the treasury.[38] The amir did, however, permit and pay allowances to the descendants of Sufi Islam of Karrukh in Herat to preach to his followers out of his own respect for their ancestor, the Sufi, who had sacrificed his life in declaring jehad against the Persians for their attack on Herat.[39] Sufi Islam had actually come from Bukhara and he founded the *khanaqa* of Karrukh where he taught the Naqshbandi order. Herat had been a center of many Sufi orders, including the Naqshbandiyya, which had survived the Safavid persecution. In fact, various branches of the order have survived there to the present day, with their influence extending across the Persian border to include the Sunni population of Khurasan.[40]

Religious groups consisted of the mullas, qazis, muftis, sayyeds, *sahibzadas*, *khwajazadas*, and *faqirs*.[41] The learned among them, the 'ulama, consisted of the mullas, qazis, and muftis. As the highest body among the Sunnis the 'ulama issued *fetwas* on subjects concerning religion and the state. Further, they served as a protective shield against the tyranny of the secular rulers over the general populace.

Compared with other Muslims the Muslims of Afghanistan were "a liberal and a tolerable people."[42] Zimmis lived among them unmolested not only in cities but also in remote villages and were allowed the private exercise of their religions. "The very presence of these Hindus [says C. C. Davies] and the religious toleration they enjoy is a proof that we often overestimate the fanatical propensities of Muhammadans and fail to realize that on the subject of Islam and Toleration much biased history has been written."[43] The Europeans before the British invasion of Afghanistan were said to have been "so popular" with the Afghans, but afterwards they became "a hated race."[44]

The mullas, drawn from all groups of Muslims, were closely associated with the people whom they led in prayers. They performed functions which in other religions were placed in the hands of the priesthood; but there was no hierarchy among them as there is among the priests of many other great religions. At times, however, they have formed secret organizations in which a leader called a "king" had lieutenants called "wazirs," with members tied together by codes and aims the purposes of which were to enforce through their bands of students (*talibs*) the precepts of Islam and silence those who were considered heretics. For the performance of religious services the mullas were paid rather handsomely. Their main income came from the rulers of the country and through alms and the hospitality of the people who offered them cash and goods on many occasions. Every landlord paid them a basketful of the produce of the land under the name of *haq Allah* (God's right).[45] They also received rewards for the advice they gave to the rulers and khans and for their settlement of disputes in rural areas.[46] As living repositories of the religion of the people and by the force of public opinion, they exercised a weighty influence over the Muslims; but they possessed no political power, and their influence was entirely moral. Those who had the reputation of extreme piety were supposed to possess the power of working miracles.[47] The main reason for the influence of the mullas in Afghanistan was that the common Muslims were ignorant of the religion they professed, and because of this influence Afghan rulers made full use of the mullas when Afghanistan was threatened by a danger. In such times the mullas felt it to be their duty to raise the cry that Islam was in danger. Indeed, they were always ready to issue the verdict of unbelief (*kufr*) against anyone who said anything against their wishes. That was why in Sayyed Jamal al-Din Afghani's opinion "their harm is greater than their benefit, because they make many inroads and numerous changes, on their own account, in the laws of God, and they promulgate many orders from their personal desires."[48] The position of the mullas was strengthened very much in the nineteenth century, especially during the Second Anglo-Afghan War when some mullas for the first time in many centuries emerged as leaders of the campaigns and in many cases offered more sound military opposition to the British than either the sardars or tribal elders did.[49]

The amir's relations with the ʾulama were strained from the very beginning. In 1881, the Kandahar mullas, under the leadership of Mulla ʾAbd al-Rahim and ʾAbd al-Ahmad Akhundzada supported Sardar Muhammad Ayyub and issued a *fetwa* to the effect that the amir, for his association with the British, was an "infidel." When the conflict was over the amir personally executed Mulla ʾAbd al-Rahim after he had forced the mulla out from his refuge in the *khirqa*. After this execution all the mullas were angry with the amir.[50] The opposition of Mulla Muskhk-i-ʾAlam to the amir's treatment of his subjects was, in fact, an indication of this estranged relationship. The mullas refrained from giving moral and religious support to the amir for his suppression of rebellions. For his part, the amir, distrusting the mullas "as leaders of the people,"[51] declared that "I . . . dislike those who, under the pretence of religion, meddle with the politics of the kingdom."[52] In his view the mullas were only "to preach for the religion and welfare of Islam" and to refrain from "criticising their Sovereign who was the representative of God."[53] The critical point came in 1883 when in the Mangal Rebellion the amir, because of the unwillingness of the mullas to endorse his proceedings, complained of them, saying, "The mullas of this country enjoy allowances amounting to lakhs of rupees. These cuckolds do not exhort the people. Why do not these mullas denounce them [the Mangal] as 'Kafirs,' because they are fighting against the king of Islam?"[54]

The amir then determined to weaken the position of the religious leaders in general by doing away with some mullas, stopping or reducing the allowances (*wazifas*) of others, and giving allowances to those who were willing to serve the state. The amir never sought to weaken Islam but rather to strengthen it and fully integrate it into the state.

The reported imprisonment of seven hundred mullas and three hundred qazis is most probably untrue, but of far-reaching consequence was the setting up of a commission, under the chairmanship of Mulla Sa'id Muhammad, alias Mulla Khosa of Laghman, to test the stipendary mullas in religious knowledge. In a firman the amir declared, "Every mulla who passed a certain test shall receive a royal diploma and wear a white turban, but a mulla who has not reached up to the above mentioned standard, shall wear a coloured turban, and every mulla whose whereabouts, nationality and parentage are not known shall be expelled from the country, so that no stranger may come and foment disturbances."[55] It is not possible that all the points in the firman were enforced. No mulla would agree to wear a colored turban, which would make him look like a non-Muslim; but they found it increasingly difficult to conceal their identities, as they had done in the past when they had been known to the local people by the names of the regions from which they came, not by their personal names. Not disclosing their identities was one way for the mullas to escape when they were wanted by the authorities. The question of testing the mullas was stressed further when many mullas under the leadership of Mulla 'Abd al-Karim led the Ghilzay Rebellion in 1886. After the first easy victory of the army over the rebels the amir declared, "Now I will make them return the allowances they have received during the last seven years. I will sell their daughters and wives to realise the amounts. . . . I will now settle their affairs properly."[56] The amir went so far as to declare that the mullas were "Wahabis, atheists etc. and hostile to the religion."[57] It is significant to note that the amir was still unwilling to stop their allowances by his own order but tried again to stop them through a commission. The tradition of paying state allowances to the 'ulama was so strong that the mullas considered it their right; they told the amir, "You are the ruler of Islam, and according to the Mohammadan law, all Mullas should be supported by you from your treasury."[58]

The examining commissions were sent to several provinces, and deputations of mullas from provinces were summoned to Kabul from time to time. In Kandahar most of the mullas did not appear before the commission for testing. The amount of their allowances, in consequence, fell in a year to 24,000 from 140,000 rupees.[59] Similarly, most of the Herat mullas did not go to Kabul, as they were asked to do, and their allowances were stopped.[60] In addition, like everybody else the mullas were required to pay taxes from which they had so far been exempt.

The Ghilzay Rebellion in early 1887 immediately upset the amir's program for dealing with the mullas. He felt that he needed their support in denouncing the Ghilzay as rebels. The subject was put to a discussion among five hundred mullas from Logar, Laghman, and the neighborhood of Kabul. Mulla Khosa actually drafted a *fetwa* in which he declared that it was lawful to wage a jehad against the rebel Ghilzays. The great majority of the mullas, however, told the amir that "he had killed all the chiefs who could help him, that he could expect nothing from them, except prayers, and that he was justified in fighting those who were most dangerous to Islam."[61] Disappointed by most of the mullas, the amir sent deputations of his partisan mullas with copies of the Quran to the people so that they could become of one mind because, as he put it, "the infidels were approaching from two directions and were gaining power."[62] At the same time he confirmed the allowances of the Herat mullas.

After the suppression of the risings of the Ghilzays and of Ishaq, the amir opened up the question of the mullas once again. By that time no influential mulla, except Mulla Najm al-Din, was left in the country. In both of these risings the mullas had played a significant role, and additionally in the Turkestan rising, the amir believed that the mullas and sayyeds were the instigators.[63] Also the amir held that the *faqirs* "solemnly meditated and dreamt dreams and told Ishaq that God had given him Afghanistan, India etc."[64] Still, the amir was unable to obtain a *fetwa* from the mullas to declare lawful and necessary a contemplated levying of a tax of two rupees per head for war purposes.[65]

Testing of the mullas continued as before. In Mazar only two mullas (out of possibly hundreds) passed. The amir, then, ordered the dispatch to Turkestan of stipendary mullas from other parts of the country, apparently to educate the Uzbeks who were considered backward in religion but in reality to separate the mullas from their own communities.[66] Whether this order was enforced is not known, but from this time on the question of the ᵓulama was basically solved in a rather different way. When the influential mullas had been liquidated the amir considered it inadvisable to alienate the rest of them from the state. Instead he tried to make them dependent on the state and make them serve it, as the elders did. The amir held that the mullas might receive their allowances, provided that they were ready to serve the state in return. Presumably they were willing since subsequently a large number of them performed various functions, such as collecting taxes and taking censuses, in addition to persuading the people to join in a religious war when it was declared by the amir and to pay their taxes.[67] In return for the allowances the mullas were required to pay the state *sadaqa*[68] and *zakat*[69] which they had received from the people. Whether they actually paid these is questionable since it was next to impossible for the state to assess them even if the mullas consented to pay them. At any rate, the sectarian turn of the rising of the Hazaras; the necessity caused by the conquest of Kafiristan of employing many mullas as qazis, muftis, and instructors; and the alarmist pronouncements of the amir about the danger to Afghanistan caused by the approach of the infidel powers were all factors causing the mullas to rally round the amir and finally to give him a *fetwa* to the effect that whoever made excuses to avoid serving the king of Islam was, according to the Muhammadan law, an infidel.[70]

Special attention should be paid to the relationship between the amir and Mulla Najm al-Din, who was generally known as the Hadda Mulla and, like Mulla Mushk-i-ʾAlam and the former Akhund of Swat, had influence with the people of eastern Afghanistan in general and with the mullas in particular. The Hadda Mulla was said to have had more than one hundred thousand followers; [71] but his influence was the result of piety and learning not of private wealth, although through the charity of his followers he was able to entertain sometimes one thousand people a day. Most people considered him the saint of the time (*qutb-i-zaman*).[72] In the beginning, the amir apparently respected him but in reality placed no trust in him, saying, "A man like him can raise disturbances whenever he likes."[73] After failing to obtain a *fetwa* through the agency of Mulla Daʾud to the effect that the Hadda Mulla was a Wahhabi, the amir asked the Hadda Mulla to exhort the Ghilzays to desist from fighting. He accepted the task provided that the amir would agree to treat his subjects mildly and to realize revenue from them of not more than what they had paid during the reign of Amir Sher ʾAli Khan.[74] Disliking the proposal, the amir is reported to have arranged to have the Mulla killed secretly, but the intended victim anticipated the plot and escaped from Kabul to Shinwar.[75] Thereafter he lived on the fringes of eastern Afghanistan beyond the reach of the amir.

Expecting the Hadda Mulla to lead them in their struggle against the amir the Shinwarays offered him the title of Padshah; but, considering himself "a humble mendicant" the Hadda Mulla made it known that he did not intend to enter politics.[76] Shortly afterward he took up residence in Jarobi in the Mohmand country where he instructed his disciples and preached to the public. His relations with the amir up to the time of the demarcation of the Durand Line were apparently strained. While denouncing the amir "as one of the most oppressive rulers who was hated by the people of Afghanistan,"[77] the Hadda Mulla continued reading the khutba in this ruler's name. At times he dissuaded the Mohmands from obeying the amir, alleging that "the Amir was an infidel, and the Mohammadans were only to obey the orders of such kings who were just and true Musulmans."[78] In addition, in his view the amir interfered "with the religion of the people by bringing in Europeans"[79] and he concluded that "no amount of money could have done as much for the British Government as the tyranny and oppression of the present Amir of Kabul, which have exceeded all bounds and are quite unbearable."[80] For his part, the amir made attempts to persuade the Hadda Mulla to come to Kabul "to promulgate the Mohammadan law afresh." In a letter of invitation to him the amir stated, "I consider the presence in my Durbar of men like you, who are perfect in devotion and religion, as a means of success and guidance for eternity."[81]

He did not come to Kabul, but on the question of jehad against the infidels which he had made his favorite theme, the mulla could not do without the amir. To be able to lead his followers in a jehad effectively he needed a legal justification for the war. This requirement meant the declaration of jehad by the amir, especially since his archrival Mulla ꞌAbd al-Wahhab, alias the Mulla of Manaky, initially opposed the jehad against the British on the ground that there was no Muslim ruler in Swat. What actually went on between the amir and the Hadda Mulla before the tribal uprising of 1897 is shrouded in mystery, but the indications are that, through Sipah Salar Ghulam Haydar Charkhi, the monarch encouraged the mulla to think that jehad would be declared. After the failure of the rising the mulla took residence, first, in Jarobi and, later, in Charmang and denounced the amir for having sold the Muslims to the British government for money. To neutralize these utterances, which had gained considerable credence among the people, the amir, in a booklet that was intended also to reach the British authorities declared that "the first condition of a jehad is the cooperation of the King of Islam. It is curious that the King is on friendly terms with the English, and (yet) you are making a fuss about jehad."[82]

On purely religious matters the Hadda Mulla was at odds with some other noted mullas. His disputes with them reflect the state of religious outlook in Afghanistan at the time. Apparently, the Hadda Mulla intended to introduce some reforms on orthodox lines and preached against smoking tobacco and using snuff. A sensation was created among the mullas of eastern Afghanistan when the Hadda Mulla preached what became known as the doctrine of *ishara*, or raising the forefinger during prayer, because it was an innovation for the orthodox mullas. The Mulla of Manaky opposed this doctrine, for which the Hadda Mulla denounced him as a kafir and instructed his followers who were imams in the mosques of Laghman, Kunar, and Ningrahar to expel from these regions imams who followed the Mulla of Manaky.[83] A kind of civil war between the mullas of eastern Afghanistan was about to take place, especially when the amir declined to intervene in the dispute on the ground that the leading mullas lived outside his domain, although he had imprisoned those imams in his kingdom who followed the Hadda Mulla. On the suggestion of the Hadda Mulla both leading mullas, accompanied by their followers, assembled in Gandao in the still independent territory of Mohmand to reconcile their differences; but their followers quarreled over the use of snuff and two followers of the Manaky Mulla were killed and the rest robbed of their property and expelled.[84] Finally the amir came out against *ishara* and took security from the imams in eastern Afghanistan that they would not preach it.[85]

For the amir it did not prove difficult to dispense with the allowances of the sayyeds and others. They were paid allowances not because they were knowledgeable about Islam, but because they were, or believed they were, the descendants of the Prophet. It appears that the stipendary sayyeds had received allowances from the days of the Mughal emperors, because they were told to produce documents from the time of these emperors before they could be paid.[86] Perhaps they did so, for the amir subsequently ruled that he was willing to pay only those say-yeds who held firmans from the Afghan rulers. Perhaps they presented these firmans also, as the amir declared, "I am tired of these Soyids [*sic*]. How is it that the Soyids are found in such large numbers every-where? I can not accept the geneological table of any of them."[87] To restrict their number the amir then made the payment of their allow-ances conditional upon their serving the state.[88] What services, if any, they performed is not known.

The opposition between the Shiʾas and Sunnis is a well-known story to the students of Islam. In Afghanistan, two additional factors had a pronounced bearing on this enmity.

Amir ʾAbd al-Rahman was the first ruler to pursue a systematic anti-Shiʾite policy in Afghanistan. He left the Ismaʾilis unmolested because they were few and, unlike the Imamis, were unsupported by a foreign power; but he compelled the Imamis to abandon Shiʾism for the Sunna, with a view toward bringing unity to his subjects. For the same reason he tried to sever religious ties between the Shiʾite population of Afghanistan and the mujtahids of Persia, who had interfered in the politics of Afghanistan through these Shiʾas. The amir began with the Qizilbashes, who had arrived in the cities of Herat and Kandahar in small numbers during the Safavid period. Later, Nadir Shah Afshar planted a military colony of them as rear guards (*chindawel*) in Kabul, and, still later, Ahmad Shah brought some more of them to Afghani-stan. From then until the reign of Amir ʾAbd al-Rahman the Qizil-bashes played a role as clerks, traders, and, especially, royal bodyguards that was out of all proportion to their small numbers. Their principal tribal divisions were Jawanshir and Afshar with such important sub-divisions (*uluses*) as Bayat, Kacharlu, Shahmansur, and Kurt. The Qizilbashes, as Shiʾas and a minority of Turkish origin, were on bad terms with their Sunni neighbors and relied heavily on the ruling dynasty that they served faithfully. They cooperated for the same reasons they had cooperated with the Persians during their invasions of Herat in 1836 and 1856 and with the British in both Anglo-Afghan wars. By the reign of Amir ʾAbd al-Rahman the animosity between the Qizilbashes and their Sunni neighbors had assumed many dimensions.[89]

Still most of the Qizilbashes lived relatively undisturbed in the eighties, except for over one hundred families of the Kandahar Qizil-bashes who, out of fear, left for Mashhad in 1882,[90] and sixty families of Kabul Qizilbashes[91] who were expelled to Peshawar.[92] According to Isfahani, the amir was mild towards them so long as Sardar Muham-mad Ayyub was in Tehran, since ʾAbd al-Rahman feared that Nasir al-Din Shah of Persia might assist the sardar against the amir if he mal-treated the Qizilbashes.[93] As will be seen, facts do not support this view. Even before the Ghilzay Rebellion the amir told the Kabul Qizil-bashes either to prove that they were Shiʾas, in which case they had to wear black turbans marked with red spots,[94] or to be prepared to pay a poll tax.[95] A little later he ordered them all to leave for Turkestan or to go to either Persia or India. This intended deportation was attributed to their past cooperation with the British,[96] but nothing was done because of the outbreak of the Ghilzay Rebellion. In fact, the amir raised leading Qizilbashes to the status of feudal khans because they provided cavalry to the state. All of the Qizilbashes were also ordered to provide men for the regular army and the royal cavalry.[97] As before the Qizilbashes continued to serve in the bureaucracy. Only when the Hazara War broke out did the amir reverse this policy, because the Qizilbashes carried strong influence with the Hazaras for, among other things, their common faith, their common speech, and their visitation of the shrine of Musa Raza in Mashhad, where every year about one hundred thousand pilgrims from both groups[98] came together and communicated with the mujtahids of Persia.[99] During the Hazara War the amir gave out that both the mujtahids of Mashhad and the Qizilbashes were instigators of the war because, said the amir, the former distributed books among the Shi'as of Afghanistan in which the Companions of the Prophet had been insulted and the Shi'as had been instructed to disobey their Sunni rulers.[100] The causes of the Hazara War were complex and the amir oversimplified them in order to justify his persecution of the Shi'as.

This persecution was pursued on religious lines, and the subject of blasphemy was taken seriously. The amir declared that every one who blasphemed a Companion of the Prophet would be stoned to death in accordance with the Shari'a.[101] The pronouncement was general, but it was commonly understood that it was intended against the Shi'as, a few of whom were accused of blasphemy and sentenced to death.[102] In all cases the accusers were tried, and the sentences issued by the qazis and muftis.[103] Qazi Shahab al-Din, a famous Qizilbash scholar, was accused of refusing to acknowledge the first three caliphs as lawful successors to the caliphate, and the court found him guilty of this charge. Before a sentence was passed on him, however, a certain Sardar Khurram Dil murdered him.[104] The sardar was released after a short imprisonment and Sardar Habib Allah, who had been influenced by his Sunni advisers,[105] declared that "every Mohammadan has the right to kill any man who should speak irreverently of the Caliphs."[106] Similarly, four Qizilbashes (including a woman) among whom was found a manuscript in which "'Ali was likened like God and the other three Caliphs abused"[107] were burnt in the Hindu Suzan sector of Kabul. These were probably copies of the book called *Hayat al-Qulub*, which, according to the amir, had been compiled by Mulla Muhammad Baqir Majlisi, a famous Shi'a.[108] According to Muhammad Yusuf Riyazi, whose mother was a Shi'a, this book was made up by Muhammad Sa'id at the request of the amir.[109]

Meanwhile, the amir, first, stopped the Muharram ceremonies and, later, restricted them only to three *takya khanas* and denied outsiders permission to watch the traditional dirge, as had been the custom.[110] After this first phase of the persecution, however, the amir favored a reconciliation between the Sunnis and the Qizilbashes so that in the future they would "serve the religion of Islam with a united heart."[111] With this goal in mind the amir married a Qizilbash, a daughter of Mir Abu Talib.[112] The Qizilbashes were relieved and gave a bond of fidelity to the amir,[113] but this time of good feeling did not last long. A son of Mulla Yusuf Ali (a former mujtahid of the Qizilbashes) of the royal cavalry was seized while armed and proceeding toward the amir's apartment. The boy was of unsound mind and was set free, but the amir lost confidence in the Qizilbashes.[114] Thereafter the persecution was stepped up still further.

The Shiʾas were then urged to "grasp the true facts of a true religion,"[115] which meant that they should observe Islam in the same way as the Sunnis did. Precedence was given to religious appearances and conversion by conviction was expected to follow. The Shiʾas were ordered to attend the mosques with the Sunnis and to let their *takya khanas* be used as mosques. Mullas were appointed as supervisors to see that the Qizilbashes attended the mosques and were given liberty of action in cases where the Qizilbashes refused. The use of extreme measures did not become necessary against the Qizilbashes since they did not resist. In 1896 the leading Qizilbashes and Hazaras of Kabul informed the amir that they had become Sunnis.[116] They agreed with the amir that he was at liberty to do what he liked if they were found to be practicing in accordance with the Shiʾite faith rather than the Sunna.[117] It is doubtful whether they really became Sunnis. Apparently they professed conversion in order to avoid persecution in accordance with their doctrine of concealment (*taqqiya*), which allowed them conversion in times of danger. At any rate they complained of their women who, according to them, resisted conversion. Some among the Qizilbashes wore red turbans to fit their names and to live distinctly as Qizilbashes. A few Qizilbashes bribed their instructing mullas for which they, together with the mullas, were put into *siah chahs*.[118] The Qizilbash army regiment had been disbanded already. Attempts to convert the Hazaras of Dai Zangi were not successful.[119]

The Kandahar Qizilbashes attended the mosques and obeyed the order of the amir regarding their conversion to Sunna,[120] but their contact with their kinsman Mirza Muhammad Taqi, who worked as a newswriter for the British, brought calamity on them. The amir feared that by contacting the mirza the Qizilbashes would jeopardize his relations with the British. By the amir's order the property of some leading Qizilbashes was confiscated and one hundred of them were imprisoned on the allegation that they were "causing a misunderstanding between His Highness and the British Government."[121]

In Herat the compulsory conversion of the Qizilbashes created such excitement that it threatened to disrupt order in the city. Many Qizilbashes were rounded up and brought on a Friday to the public mosque to perform prayers in accordance with the Sunna. Had it not been for the timely intervention of the *sipah salar* and the foresightedness of Qazi Muhammad Hussayn and Mulla Muhammad ʾOmar (supervisor of the Kodal madrasa) a communal collision of the worst kind would have followed.[122] Subsequently, however, their numerous *takya khanas* in Herat were turned into mosques,[123] and many cases of blasphemy were reported to the court.[124] Over one thousand of the Qizilbashes left for Mashhad[125] and the amir instructed the *sipah salar* not to prevent them from proceeding if they were unwilling to accept the Sunna,[126] because, said the amir, they had originally come from Persia.[127] Those who remained behind were forced to attend mosques regularly.[128] In Mashhad the mujtahids, under the leadership of Shaykh Muhammad Taqi, took up the cause of the Qizilbashes and began to inflame anti-Sunni feelings and to seek protection from the Russian government, until finally he was dissuaded by the shah of Persia.[129]

Expelled from the army and bureaucracy and reduced throughout the country to five thousand families,[130] the Qizilbashes lost their former position in Afghanistan. They took to shopkeeping, commerce, and agriculture. Their position improved in the reign of King Amam Allah who, unlike his immediate ancestors, treated his Sunni and Shiʾite subjects alike.[131]

Education

Mosques were the traditional centers of education in Islamic countries where the mullas taught children the basic teachings of Islam[132] and the ʾulama instructed higher-level students in madrasas attached to the principal mosques. The curriculum was mainly religious and included subjects on the fundamentals of Islam, Islamic jurisprudence, formal logic, and Arabic. In urban centers private tutors (*nazims*) taught students in Persian literature and in the basic rules of mathematics to enable them to take bureaucratic posts with the government. The mass of the populace, however, was illiterate, and this illiteracy accounted for the importance given to oral communication and instruction as exemplified by the existence of story tellers, town criers (*jarchi*), news carriers (*khabarchi*), and scribes who composed personal and official letters. Among the upper layers of society, especially in cities, a minute portion, mainly men, were fortunate enough to read and write. Most schools on the elementary level were supported privately rather than publicly, but madrasas were publicly financed. In both levels of learning stress was placed on reciting Arabic texts, the meaning of which even many of the instructors themselves could not comprehend. Generally, the curriculum glorified and perpetuated the dominant norms of society and religion and was not meant to develop intellectual curiosity or creative thinking.[133] Taken as a whole, the education system of nineteenth-century Afghanistan was, as a result of the cultural and economic stagnation of the country, in a bad state.[134]

The amir believed that "Our deterioration is owing to our want of knowledge and learning; men without science and art can never progress and prosper."[135] Still, he took no noteworthy steps in education. In the background was a general unwillingness to learn about, even opposition to the acquisition of, modern science and learning, which were associated with the *feringees* (Europeans). The Second Anglo-Afghan War further hardened this attitude, and led to an atmosphere in which people mistrusted things and men associated with the *feringees*; they even suspected Afghans who had acquired traditional education in Turkey, Medina, India, and Bukhara. The long period of disturbances gave the amir and others no chance to promote the status of learning, even if they had wished to. On the contrary, the isolationist measures that the amir took with respect to his administration, the new buffer status of the country, and its peculiar landlocked position combined to place it away from the mainstream of modern science and culture. All of these factors and the fact that in this period a great number of the men of learning were either expelled from the country or liquidated hindered the development of modern education in Afghanistan.

The amir's only contribution to education was the opening of the royal madrasa in Kabul where two hundred students were provided with free lodging and education, which consisted mainly of Islamic law.[136] This madrasa had many cells or classes and one mulla was put in charge of seven. The task of instruction was given to the Sunni mullas, among them Mulla Ahmad Jan Tokhay and Gul Ahmad Ahmadzay, who were known for their piety and knowledge of Islamic classicism and rationalism.[137] Such subjects as mathematics and geometry were taught for their application in the construction of canals and in mining,[138] and the study of jehad was made a major part of the curriculum because the amir, by establishing the madrasa, intended "to use the mullas thus educated in exciting the religious feelings of the subjects."[139] The graduates of the madrasa were appointed qazis and muftis.

Stress on religious education was supplemented by the appointment of roving mullas for teaching Muslims the fundamentals of Islam and by the authorization of the *muhtasibs* to prosecute those who failed to observe the basic commandments. It is not known whether madrasas in other parts of the country, notably in Herat,[140] were subsidized by the state, even after the state took over the *waqf* out of which some madrasas had been financed.

No steps were taken to improve the existing system of primary education during the amir's reign, except for the opening in 1898 of a school for the poor and orphans and the amir's instruction to elders to encourage the people to send their sons to local schools to become literate and to acquire religious knowledge.[141] There were no public libraries; neither was there a paper industry. Indeed the paper imported was limited in quantity, bad in quality, and expensive. A large lithographic press was set up in Kabul, but only official publications were printed there. No newspaper or periodical was published, but a considerable number of pamphlets, including manuals of instruction for government officials, booklets on jehad, and bound volumes for office use, were printed. Consequently, the lack of books, among other fac-

tors, made the flow from India of books in Pashto and Persian and on
varieties of superstitious subjects attractive.[142]
Meanwhile the establishment of Kabul workshops, where a number
of Englishmen were employed, made it necessary for Afghans to have
some knowledge of English. For this purpose William Tasker and a Mr.
Tanner of the workshops were assigned to teach English to twenty
boys,[143] who probably made up the first group in Afghanistan to be
taught the English language. Previously some Hindu and Armenian inhabitants of Afghanistan had learned English in India. Because of this
deficiency the rulers of Afghanistan had always employed Indian Muslims to conduct their correspondence in English.

Public Health

Afghanistan is an arid and semiarid country, and its barren mountain
ranges; steppes and deserts; light alluvial, permeable soils found in
most of its fruit oases; fast-flowing mountain streams; and the high
degree of evaporation and abundant sunshine are unfavorable to the
spread of many infectious diseases. The natural features of the country
provide epidemiological conditions that are distinct from those in
humid tropical lowlands. Afghanistan, therefore, cannot be termed a
"country of epidemic diseases,"[144] but the Muslim fatalism and belief
that running water is pure, the ignorance of the native physicians
(hakeems) about modern medicine, and, above all, the public ignorance
of hygiene were, and still are, among the factors that account for the
frequent occurrence of diseases and a high rate of mortality. On the
other hand, Islamic requirements that Muslims make ablutions five
times a day, take baths regularly—especially after sexual intercourse—
and, in general, keep themselves clean were positive hygienic factors
among the poor peasant population of Afghanistan.

In Afghanistan, as in other countries of the Middle East, many features of folk medicines have survived to the present. An obvious example of these practices is the talismans or amulettes given by the
mullas to avert, or even cure, diseases and deter evil spirits.[145] Other
popular medical concepts current in Afghanistan were probably attributable to Greek origin. The basic Empedoclean qualities of cold, hot,
damp, and dry were, and still are, used in Persian, as well as Indian,
medicine. In Afghanistan the concepts of cold and hot (sard wa garm)
were significant for diseases, as well as foodstuffs and medicine. All
nonsurgical cases were classified as cold or hot and treated accordingly.
Thus with warm fevers no warm medicine was accepted, whereas the
warm drug was eagerly taken in such cases of cold fevers as malaria
with shivering cold.[146] Little was known about the medicaments handed out by native physicians, but the drugs used in folk medicine were
called Greek. The traditional medicine itself was also called the ancient Greek medicine. Native physicians were guided by authority,
without recourse to the study of the disease in the living subject.[147]

They were ignorant of anatomy, physiology, and pathology and prescribed medicine, mostly purgative mixtures, from old books. While
dressers dressed wounds and ulcers and broken limbs, barbers bled
their patients for fever, dyspepsia, gout, headache, or any other feeling
of malaise. Malaise and rheumatic troubles were believed to be caused
by wind in the body vessels—a belief which may be of Greek or Indian
origin. Cauterizing cones, which, according to Hippocratic notions, are
the ultimate therapy, were applied in cases of chronic diseases.[148] For
the cure of snakebites and lunacy, patients were taken to certain
shrines. The shrine of the Caliph ʾAli in Mazar was said to cure blind-
ness, deafness, and sickness in general.[149] Thus, here at the "crossroads
of Asia," the meeting point of several cultures, a folk medicine containing Greek, Indian, and, possibly, Arabic elements, was, and is still,
practiced.[150]

Amir ʾAbd al-Rahman's contribution to medicine, though modest, is
noteworthy. He may even be considered the pioneer of modern hospitals in Afghanistan, although the British opened their hospitals to
the inhabitants of Afghanistan during the occupation period. In Kandahar for instance, during the first quarter of 1881 no less than 3,371 out-
patients from all over Afghanistan attended and received medicine
and advice, while twenty were treated in the British facility.[151] Before
the employment of Europeans the amir had opened a hospital in the
military cantonment where civilians were also treated. It had two dis-
pensaries, one for native and one for European drugs,[152] and the latter
was full of "patent medicines warranted to cure every disease under
the sun."[153] Native physicians and Indian assistants were put in charge
of the hospital. Later the amir employed a number of English profes-
sionals, among them two physicians (John Gray and Lady Lillias
Hamilton), a veterinarian (Clements), a registered nurse (Mrs. Daly),
and a surgeon-dentist (O'Meara). In 1895 the first public hospital in Afghanistan was opened in Kabul and a few rudimentary military hospitals were added to the existing ones. Vaccination against smallpox
was introduced under the supervision of Lady Hamilton, who compiled
a pamphlet that was translated into Persian and was probably the first
textbook on modern medicine in Afghanistan. In addition, with the introduction of public latrines in Kabul and the manufacture of soap in
large quantities in Kabul workshops, health standards were considerably improved during the amir's reign.[154]

The inhabitants of Afghanistan were not altogether receptive to
modern medicine, but their responses differed from one group to another. The mullas were opposed to modern medicine on religious
grounds, arguing that a "Feringhi doctor" "by the help of the Powers of
Evil, has in this world the gifts of knowledge, skill, and health, but . . .
in the next life must inevitably be consigned to eternal torment.
Doubtless with his deadly poisons he can cure diseases if he wish, but
it is not wise, and, indeed, is scarcely lawful, for a sick man to make
use of him."[155] The Hadda Mulla, Mulla Najm al-Din, reflected this
opposition when he accused the amir of interfering with religion by

bringing Europeans to Afghanistan. The native physicians, who looked on modern medicine as a menace to their position, began to frighten rich people, saying, "Europeans use deadly poisons in their medicines, which are just as likely to kill as to cure."[156] Consequently, the rich and more educated people were not so ready to avail themselves of modern medicine. By contrast "Eager to be cured by him,"[157] "the peasants, and hillmen, the soldiers and the townsfolk trusted themselves, when sick, to European skill."[158] They tried to obtain medicinal tablets, even when they had no complaint, for use during future probable illnesses. They welcomed Dr. John Alfred Gray "by every sign of gratitude"[159] and thronged to the hospital, coming to it from distant villages where there were no native physicians and people either went untreated or treated themselves.[160]

The lack of preventive medicine, coupled with public ignorance of germs as the source of certain diseases, accounted for heavy tolls during epidemics, notably of smallpox, chickenpox, and cholera, diseases which were usually virulent and spread rapidly in the urban centers, but not in the rural areas. In 1889 inoculation against smallpox was introduced into Kabul and parents were urged under severe penalty to inoculate their children.[161] During the spread of cholera certain pills were distributed in the city, but casualties were still heavy. To lessen possible incidence of infection at such times, government offices and shops were closed and soldiers were distributed into the country and, prevented from eating fresh fruits, were allowed to eat only dried, cooked meats. As a remedial measure, city people were urged to pray in mosques and portions of the Quran were distributed among them in the hope that the quotations "may protect them from the prevailing epidemic and other diseases."[162] The amir and his family, however, at the appearance of the first signs of an epidemic would take refuge in nearby hills, notably in Paghman where no one from the city, except those with special passes was allowed. Communications with the amir were maintained through heliograph. In Paghman the amir's only preventive measure against the disease was the burning of sulphur, gunpowder, and tobacco for purification of the air.

Law

In Afghanistan, laws, as regulators of relations between individuals on the one hand and between the state and individuals on the other, were based on the Islamic and the customary laws. Before 1880 the latter type was more widely practiced than the former, but in the reign of the amir many new laws were made that were based mainly on the Islamic laws.

The application of a unified system of laws, whether customary or statutory or both, in any given society is a manifestation of the extension of the authority of the central government over the country as a whole. In Afghanistan this extension and unification happened in the reign of the Amir 'Abd al-Rahman Khan. Previously, the Shari'a was accepted as the general law of the country, but in rural communities customary laws prevailed. Each of these communities, where little was known of the Islamic laws, had its own peculiar customary laws.[163]

Pashtunwali, the code of the Pashtuns, was applied to criminal cases, among others. It was founded on such principles as could be supposed to have evolved and prevailed before the institution of a central government. The opinion was still strong among the Pashtuns that it was every man's right and duty to do his own justice and to avenge his own injuries, and the right of society to restrain even the reasonable passions of individuals and to prevent them from taking redress of wrongs and the punishment of crimes into their own hands was still imperfectly understood. This attitude must have had its origin in a time when government afforded no protection to individuals, who consequently considered it lawful and even honorable to seek private redress. Injured parties considered themselves entitled to retaliation (*badal*) against the aggressors. Retaliation caused feuds and assassinations that became, in consequence, part of a vicious circle and lasted for generations. To discourage murder resulting from a blood feud, elders of the community levied compensation or blood money to be given to the injured party or to his relatives. The Wazir Pashtuns further restricted retaliation by permitting the vengeance of a murder on the person of the murderer, but not on one of his relatives or kinsmen as was the practice among other groups.[164] Only in some cases did elders levy some fine for the state in addition; by and large it was not thought that society had been injured or that it had any right to punish for the sake of example after the actual sufferer had been satisfied.[165]

The Islamic laws practiced in Afghanistan, as well as in India and in Bukhara and Ottoman Turkey, belonged to the Hanafi system of laws, one of the four principal surviving schools of law in the Sunni Muslim world, the others being those of Maliki, Shafi'i, and Hanbali. Each school was known after its founder, 'Abu Abd al-Malik, Muhammad bin Idris Shafi', Ibn Hanbal, and Abu Hanifa. The legal systems of the Ismai'li and Imami Shi'as were not recognized in Afghanistan, thus the Imami Shi'as mujtahids, who as living interpreters of the law in the absence of the Imam were responsible for applying and interpreting the law,[166] were not allowed to function in Afghanistan.

In no other period as in the reign of the Amir were so many laws made in Afghanistan. The general belief was that in cases of conflict with customary laws Islamic laws were to prevail. In this way Islamic laws made inroads into the domains of customary laws. Only in cases where there were no clear prescriptions in the Islamic laws did the amir make rules of his own; these were ultimately based upon Islamic laws, the opinion of the people, and the amir's own personal views.[167] Also, as a ruler he believed he had the right to define how Islamic laws were to be applied. In the criminal and political domains he made laws based mainly on his own views.[168] It was through the laws in criminal and political matters that the amir exercised unlimited power since as the sovereign he felt free to determine what behavior constituted an offence and what punishment was to be applied in each case. This concept was based on the principle of Islamic *ta'zir* (deterrence) for the purpose of deterring others from similar conduct. Whereas most jurists restricted the *ta'zir* punishment to flogging or imprisonment not to exceed the prescribed limit (*hadd*) of one hundred lashes or one year's imprisonment,[169] the amir observed no limit for punishment and frequently applied the death penalty in cases of murder, treason, apostasy, and even adultery.[170] Sometimes he also sentenced to death criminals convicted of smaller offences.[171] Here the amir in effect followed the Maliki principle of punishment that required that the punishment should fit the nature of the crime and the character of the offender, including the death penalty in certain "suitable cases."[172]

Among the main categories of laws made during the amir's reign was one regarding reducing crime, notably murder. As noted, revenge murder was very common among some tribes, particularly the eastern Pashtuns.[173] Revenge involved not only individuals against individuals, but in many cases families against families and even tribes against tribes. In 1880 the amir ruled that "no tribe or private individual should seek justice except through the law."[174] Apparently, this ruling did not prove effective and the amir subsequently raised the blood money (*diya*) to seven thousand rupees for the life of any adult[175] from the twelve rupees for the life of a woman and fifty and three hundred rupees for the life of a man, as had been required before the amir came to power.[176] By and large this increase led to a decrease in the rate of murder, but, among certain tribes, it prolonged rebellion against the amir. The Mangal, for instance, during their rebellion, argued that they were unable to pay this exorbitant sum[177] and insisted that it be reduced.

The laws on theft, in the broadest terms, implicated in the crime the nearest relations and friends of the person or persons suspected of having committed the act. The hand of a person caught thieving was to be cut off according to the law. In addition, the person's face was blackened, and the person was ridden on a donkey through villages to impress upon others that such would also be their lot if they stole.[178] When the actual person who had committed the act could not be traced, the people in whose vicinity the act had been committed were made responsible for it.

On the question of women, a major source of conflict in Afghanistan, many laws were introduced. Notable among these was one that required severe punishment, including the death penalty, for adulterous women, in spite of the fact that in the Quran the penalty for fornication is only flogging after the act had been legally proven.[179] In other respects the position of women was improved by the law in the reign of the amir. In Afghanistan it had been customary for the parents and guardians of girls to betroth them while they were still infants. The girls had no choice but to consent to the eventual marriage even if they were opposed to it. The amir ruled that girls on reaching puberty were at liberty to repudiate such marriages. Also by custom, women in

Afghanistan had been tied to the households of their husbands. After
the death of their husbands women were remarried to brothers or other
near relations of their deceased husbands. Failure of widows to consent
to such compulsory remarriages often caused feuds between families
and tribes. In 1883 the amir decreed that all such claims were to be
illegal and that widows were free to remarry those whom they
wished.[180] Another law fixed the amount of *mahr* promised at the time
of marriage contract by husbands to be paid to their wives in accordance with the Shari᾽a. Previously, the amount had not been fixed, and
parents' demands of exorbitant sums to be paid to their daughters was
a major source of conflict. Another novel law decreed that all marriages
be registered with the government. Previously, marriages had been
only rarely recorded in writing, and none were officially; this lack was
another source of frequent disputes.[181] Also, laws of inheritance and
personal property were laid down in detail and in strict conformity
with the Shari᾽a.

Another novel law made residents of a village through whose locality a road passed accountable for the safety of travelers, goods, and
caravans.[182] Slavery was also abolished by law, but its end was accomplished only gradually. Another law required fair treatment for home-
born slaves (*khanazad*). Also, by law any master who killed his slave
was made liable to the same punishment he would have received if he
had killed a free person. Similarly, parents were forbidden by law to
sell or kill their children.[183]

Administrative laws entailed severe punishment for officials if they
worked dishonestly. A law required the cutting off of the hands of an
official who took a page out of the official book placed in his custody.[184]
The new rates of revenue on land, cattle, and other items were also
said to have emanated from the Shari᾽a, and the rulings about these
therefore had the force of laws.

The legislative process needed to create these laws did not require an
elaborate procedure. The amir would read a proclamation or make a
speech on the points of law or changes that were required in the existing law of the country before the council of the sardars (*khawanin-i-
mulki*) and the ᾽ulama; and then he would ask their opinions. They
would invariably approve his changes. He also made laws without recourse to the council.

The texts of the amir's speeches or proclamations were prepared in
consultation with the ᾽ulama or were the work of various heads of the
governmental departments. Only rarely did members of the council
initiate proposals that would become a part of the law after they were
approved by the sovereign. The laws existed in the shape of books and
scraps of papers (firmans), and all were sealed and signed by the amir.[185]

Efforts were made to see that the laws were strictly adhered to. When
a case between a powerful and a weak party was tried the presumption of the amir's laws was in favor of the weak unless proved otherwise. There were neither exemptions nor special laws for the highest

officials of the crown or the nearest relatives of the amir.[186] In fact, if any official or courtier exceeded his jurisdiction he was liable to severe punishment.

The overall effects of these laws were that for the first time the inhabitants of Afghanistan began to learn how to obey a sole monarch and a uniform set of laws, although the notion that personal rights stood before state rights still prevailed.[187]

Manners and Customs

Some manners and customs were common to all ethnic groups in Afghanistan and these will be discussed now. Manners and customs peculiar to one particular group of people will not be covered.

Throughout most of Afghanistan, wherever possible, the use of personal names was avoided. People of social status were called by some such rank, title, or designation as *malik sahib, khan sahib, arbab sahib, mulla sahib*, and so forth. Elders, whether related or not, were called *baba* (father), *kaka* (paternal uncle), *mama* (maternal uncle). Persons of the same age addressed each other by personal names, or as brother or sister. Younger people were called by their personal names, usually with the added suffix *jan*, as a term of endearment.[188] Government officials were addressed by their official titles with the added *sahib*. The use of surnames or family names was still not in vogue. Persons were known by the names of the tribes or the regions to which they belonged. Only writers and poets used to adopt titles (*takhallus*), such as Tawwaf, Wasil, Tarzi, Shaiq, and so forth, adding them to their names as surnames. Persons greeted each other without introduction even though they were not acquainted. People of all ethnic groups wore long loose trousers and shirts with belts around their waists. Their costumes differed in turbans, footwear, tunics, and waistcoats. In Kabul during the amir's reign the traditional costumes had just begun to be replaced by clothes of European cut. The process started when the amir employed a number of Indian tailors under the supervision of an English master tailor, Mr. Walter, who introduced European-style clothes. There was no tangible resistance to this innovation; rather, seeing that the amir, members of his family and of the darbar, and senior military and civil officials had adopted uniforms of European fashion, the well-to-do inhabitants of the city followed suit. Indeed, the more a person rose in social scale the more he became Europeanized in costume.[189] This Europeanization happened more generally in Kabul than in many parts of India, though the latter had been open to European influence for centuries. Consequently, tailoring flourished in Kabul where tailors were clever enough to imitate the English style sufficiently well to satisfy their patrons, who were ostentatious in appearance and saved most of their incomes for new clothes. For the same reason they also dyed their hair and beards a deep black. There were many old men who were seen with black hair and beards.[190]

Of all the customs those relating to marriage were socially the most important. Except among well-to-do people, marriage took place relatively late because of the high bride price and the enormous expense involved in marriage ceremonies. Parents betrothed their daughters fairly early but refused to allow them to marry unless they received a larger sum than had originally been agreed upon. In 1884 the amir fixed a very low figure of thirty rupees as a bride price and declared that should a man's wedding be pending for want of money he should borrow the fixed amount from the state treasury.[191] Apparently this ruling was not enforced, since high bride prices were still demanded. This demand was deep rooted and, possibly, linked with the seclusion of women,[192] a significant factor in Afghan society. Polygamy, which was permitted by the Shariʾa, had become only an upper-class phenomenon. Also, the rise of parallel cousin marriages and the custom of bride exchange (*badal*) between two families, which were common in Afghanistan, were probably a consequence of the demand for a heavy bride price.[193] In both cases marriage expenses were lowered to the minimum level. Marriage expenses were so high that many families seeking brides for their sons became impoverished.[194] Neither custom nor religion was against intermarriage; people preferred to marry within their own tribes, particularly their nearest relations. The Pashtuns frequently took wives from other ethnic groups, but the reverse was rarely the case.[195] Until the amir's reign the marriage contracts drawn up by the mullas in accordance with the Shariʾa were not registered. The amir made it a law that they should be registered in government documents. Also, he fixed the amount of *mahr*, as distinct from the bride price, payable by husbands to wives. In reality, wives rarely demanded this sum. Originally it had been an indefinite amount of property but by the amir's time had risen to a disproportionate sum. The amir in 1883 decreed that the *mahr* for members of the royal family should be between three thousand and twelve thousand rupees, of the nobility between one thousand and three thousand, and of the ordinary people between three hundred and nine hundred.[196]

In theory both husbands and wives under certain circumstances had the right to seek divorce. In practice, however, they rarely did so, mainly because divorce was considered a social disgrace.

Since the society was dominated by males and since the line of descent was reckoned in the male line, the birth of a son was received with the greatest joy, while that of a daughter passed unnoticed. Similarly, the circumcision of a boy, carried out usually at the age of seven, was made an occasion for great rejoicing.

Burial expenses, like those of weddings, were very high. In addition, among the well to do it was the custom to assign reciters (*qaris*) to read the Quran over the graves of the deceased for several days after their death; the amir abolished this practice. The amir also prohibited the use of hashish, which was common among the inhabitants of Badakhshan and Herat. In the city of Herat alone, at one time sixty-eight persons, including some elders who had smoked it, were imprisoned for life and their release was made conditional upon their abandoning its use.[197]

Position of Women

Traditionally in Afghanistan the position of women was (and still is) inferior to that of men. In some respects Amir ʾAbd al-Rahman made women still more subservient to men, but in others he improved their condition.

In Afghanistan, as in other agrarian societies, the position of a woman varied according to the woman's age and the norms of the social and ethnic groups to which she belonged. Everywhere, however, women's position economically and legally was inferior to that of men. To begin with, except for elderly widows, women did not dispose of property, even their own, although they were entitled to do so by law. In addition, women could not own much. According to the Shariʾa, daughters, for instance, inherited only half the amount received by the sons on the death of their father. This sum, too, they usually left to their brothers on whose line alone the continuation of the family depended. Widows inherited less than their daughters.

The other major source of women's property, beside inheritance, was the *mahr* they were assigned by their husbands at the time of their marriage contract. In practice, however, they seldom, if ever, laid claim to *mahr*. Men, however, were absolutely responsible for the support of women in their families, and women enjoyed a far greater degree of security than did men. Only when men failed to support their wives or when they proved impotent were women entitled to seek divorce, whereas it was much easier for men to divorce. Nevertheless, divorce happened very rarely. Usually marriages lasted for life, contributing greatly to the stability of family and of society. Some peasant women helped their husbands in the fields, and others served the well-to-do households for payment. In general, however, women were not expected to earn a living, as this work was considered a slur on their husbands. A Pashto saying illustrates this well: "To hell with a woman's earning, and a donkey's load." The economic dependence of women on men was complete.

From the fact that a woman received half of man's share in inheritance and because two female witnesses were equivalent to one male witness in the Shariʾa court, there had arisen the belief that two women were equal to one man, in the same way that Pashtun males held that one Pashtun equalled ten Hindus in strength. This false consciousness, reinforced by the beliefs that women were intellectually inferior (*naqis-i-ʾaql*), were weak by nature, and were open to temptation, made men deny them positions outside their homes. The term "woman" had been assigned such a low position in society that when a man intended to insult his opponent he simply called him a "woman." Nevertheless, in their homes women had great influence over their children as well as over their husbands. Within these bounds men greatly respected them, although they expected them also to be dutiful and obedient. Women were expected to look after the needs of their husbands, whom Pashtun women referred to as *khawand* (lord). Some upper-class women received a little education, but in the main women occupied themselves in cooking, sewing, milking cows, weaving, spinning, rearing children, and so forth. Servants to some extent freed well-to-do women from this drudgery, but even rich women still remained inside the walls of their homes. Like other women, the well-off called upon their relatives on social occasions only. Occasionally, women went to local shrines for entertainment, but, here as elsewhere, women were separate from men. According to a recent writer the division of the females and males into separate worlds is more pronounced in Afghanistan than in many other parts of the world.[198] To an extent this division had been true of the unmarried females of the urban middle classes, but it would be incorrect to assume that it was universal. Women did enter the men's world; but, when they did most of them, especially those of the upper classes, veiled themselves.

Women were more secluded in urban centers than in rural areas. Indeed, among some people in the rural areas, for instance among the Hazaras,[199] women were not secluded at all. Some of them, however, sold their wives for asses.[200] Among the Pashtuns, particularly the Ghilzays and more particularly the *powindas*, women were less secluded. The Uzbeks, however, shut their women out of view with jealous solicitude.[201] According to Schurmann, division of labor more than anything else accounted for the seclusion of Afghan women.[202]

Kafir women were neither secluded nor veiled before their conversion to Islam. Unlike women among other ethnic groups in Afghanistan, Kafir women had considerable freedom. If caught in adultery, their partners were fined, but the women themselves were neither beaten nor abused. Unmarried women were said to have little or no restriction on their having sexual intercourse with the opposite sex, and the Kafirs received their fatherless grandchildren with no apparent contempt. The condition of the women, however, was deplorable, since they were overworked, underfed, and treated by men with a tolerant contempt far worse than actual ill usage.[203] In spite of their conditions, Kafir women provided a contrast to members of their sex in other ethnic groups, where women were regarded as a source of pleasure for men in addition to their generative functions.[204]

In time of war women in Afghanistan carried supplies to men in the battlefields. In the Kabul area many of the women during the Second Anglo-Afghan War used to go out at night after a battle and mutilate the bodies of the dead and kill the wounded and the dying.[205] It is generally held, though historically not established, that the Afghan victory over the English at Maiwand was largely the result of the encouragement of the reluctant ghazis by a maiden called Malalay. Her story has become widely known, and she has become the symbol of female courage, as the following popular couplet indicates:

✢
Lover! if you were not martyred in Maiwand
By God, then they want to keep you for a disgraceful life.
✢

In the reign of the amir, a large number of women lost their husbands in wars or had husbands and guardians who were expelled from the country or were employed by the government and lived away from their families for most of the time. Consequently, among other things, adultery became frequent. The amir considered adultery the worst sin, and to deal with it he punished both parties to the act with death. Women who were accused of adultery were often put in sacks and exhibited.

The amir inflicted these severe punishments on adulterous wives because like other Afghans he believed that "the honour of the people of Afghanistan consists in the honour of their women." [206] It was the slight of this "honor" by Alexander Burnes which, according to the amir, ignited the First Anglo-Afghan War. [207] According to the amir the religion of Islam entitled men to control their wives and to kill them if they were unfaithful. [208] Among other things the men's control of women meant that the latter were not allowed to go out of their houses without the consent of their husbands. Time and again the amir impressed on his subjects that the Christian powers would if they occupied Afghanistan deprive them of their hold over their wives because, said the amir, "according to their laws women enjoy liberty" [209] and "under them no husband has any control over his wife." [210] In the amir's view, the occupation of Afghanistan by the British had emboldened the women and it was his duty to see that they kept the honor of their husbands.

With regard to the right to property of women and their right to support by their husbands, the amir applied the prescription of Islam by compelling husbands to grant freedom to their wives if they were unable to support them. [211] Also, he compelled husbands to give their divorced wives the *mahr* that had been agreed upon at the time of the marriage contract. [212] Further, as noted, the amir, in accordance with the Shari'a, improved the conditions of women by the restoration of their hereditary rights in the property of their deceased husbands, [213] by granting freedom to adult women to repudiate their betrothals made when they were infants, and by emancipating widows from compulsory remarriages to brothers of their deceased husbands.

Slavery

The sale of both Muslims and non-Muslims obtained by kidnapping was, on a limited scale, practiced in Afghanistan in the nineteenth century, but slavery as an institution was dying. Slaves were only attached to families and were treated well. In the reign of Amir 'Abd al-Rahman, the sale of slaves ended; but those Hazaras, who had been sold into slavery, remained in bondage as domestics.

With the inability of the rulers of Afghanistan to wage wars against the non-Muslims of India and to obtain slaves as did their predecessors before the nineteenth century, there began a marked shrinkage in the source of slaves, which, in accordance with the Islamic law, were birth in slavery and capture in *dar al-harb*.[214] Thereafter, slaves were obtained from Kafiristan, Hazarajat, Badakhshan, and Chitral, although a number of Abyssinian slaves also were brought to Afghanistan.[215] In other words, the Kafirs of Kafiristan, the Shi'ite Hazaras, the Shi'ite Tajiks, the Sunni Chitralis, and the Shi'ite inhabitants of southern Persia who had been enslaved by their Baluch neighbors,[216] were kidnapped and sold as slaves in the city markets of Afghanistan and central Asia. At the same time the "people of Baluchistan" were also made subject to kidnapping and selling; as late as 1884 the men in the service of the *hakim* of Shorawak did this.[217] A year before that the amir had advised the Shinwarays, "Do not sell any person among you into slavery."[218] This warning suggests that in eastern Afghanistan, too, individuals, other than the Kafirs, were kidnapped and sold into slavery, but this practice soon ceased, as we can see by the fact that in 1887 a woman failed to sell as a slave a girl whom she had captured in Laghman. Since, according to the Islamic law, only the Kafirs among the above categories of slaves could legally be reduced to slavery, it was no wonder that slavery as an institution was fast dying in Afghanistan. The end approached more quickly after the Kafirs of Kafiristan were converted to Islam and the amir prohibited their sale as slaves under severe penalty.[219] For this reason European powers did not bring any pressure to abolish slavery to bear on Afghanistan as they did on other Muslim countries in the nineteenth century, in spite of the unfounded allegation of the Anti-Slavery Society that in Afghanistan "slave hunts are carried out on a very extensive scale."[220] Instances of the sale of Hazaras and Kafirs, however, were reported right up to the end of the amir's reign.

Slaves were obtained through kidnapping, sale, and gift in Afghanistan. Those who obtained slaves by kidnapping were usually the tribes located around the Hazarajat and Kafiristan. The Firozkohis,[221] Turkmen, and Jamshidis, for instance, captured the Hazaras and sold them in the markets of central Asia, especially Bukhara, where they took them by way of Bandar and Charsada. As late as 1899 the Jamshidis occasionally carried females from the Berber Hazaras to the Turkmen in Panjdeh even though they were usually arrested there by the Russian authorities. Although the Pashtuns held slavery in detestation[222] and called the Uzbeks who had sold slaves by the derogatory term of *adam firosh* (man sellers),[223] the Tarakays used to capture the Hazaras of the Qarabagh and sell them in Kandahar[224] and the Yusufzays enslaved the Kafirs of Kafiristan. The Hazaras themselves, when compelled by hunger, offered their children as slaves in markets.[225] Also, some elders among them were so powerful that they sold fellow Hazaras as slaves.

Among the Kafirs the sale of *baris* (craftsmen who were treated as slaves) was common. *Baris*, who were either domestics or artisans, were sold in and on the fringes of Kafiristan. It was probably among these *baris* that Colonel A. Durand, while British agent at Gilgit, noted that in Kafiristan wives were separated from their husbands and sold at Yarkand and small boys were exchanged for sporting dogs and horses.[226] Similarly the mirs of Shighnan and Roshan sold the children of their followers and also offered them as presents to the rulers of Afghanistan.[227] Such presents formed the main source of slaves for the amir, although his officials also bought slaves for him. From time to time the amir's officials in Badakhshan, Sipah Salar Charkhi, the mehtar of Chitral, khans of Dir and Bajaur, and the noted Mulla Paiwanda offered slaves to the amir. The Kafirs themselves, when harassed by their zealous Muslim neighbors, offered slaves to the amir, even before their country was invaded.

Slaves, who were usually young females (*keniz, surati*) and males (*ghulam*), were attached to the amir's *haram* and to the well-to-do families, where they served as concubines and servants. Since the children of the slave girls by their master were considered free, they enjoyed full status like the master's other children. Most probably Sardar Habib Allah and Sardar Nasr Allah were the sons of such a slave girl, who was called Gulrez and was from Badakhshan. In the family atmosphere the slaves were not subject to harsh treatment. Like the sons of elders who were attached to the darbar, some of the more talented of the slaves were trained in the art of government. In Afghanistan for the first time in the reign of the amir some of these slaves, who were called *ghulam bachas*, were raised to high military and civil positions. Previously slaves formed mainly the royal guards. Also they worked on their masters' fields as free tenants worked, but the slaves neither were attached to the soil nor received any share in the crop.[228]

In the amir's reign owners had the right to sell their slaves, as the Mughal Khan of Goshta did when hard pressed for money in exile;[229] but they did not have the right to kill them. Any owner who did so was treated as if he had killed a free-born person.[230] In 1890 a sardar of Kandahar, who had enjoyed full authority over the lives of his slaves, was sent to court for trial for gouging out the eyes of his slaves. In addition, the amir confiscated his property. Certain people called *kanjars* bought Kafir girls and used them as prostitutes in Jalalabad.[231] Still, the number of slaves in the reign of the amir was not high because even in the Hazara War when slaves became plentiful their price was considerable, in spite of the fact that the price paid for the Hazaras was generally the lowest. In 1892 the amir fixed one hundred rupees as the price for a young male or female Hazara slave, fifty for a boy or girl twelve years of age and thirty for boys under twelve.[232] Subsequently, however, the increase in the number of the Hazara slaves lowered their prices and then almost every well-to-do family owned one or more of them as slaves. At this time friends and government officials made presents of Hazaras to one another frequently.

One of the first laws the amir passed was to the effect that there should be no more selling of free persons into slavery and that only captives taken in war or the offspring of those who were already slaves were to be considered slaves.[233] Since slavery was so deep rooted, however, it was difficult to put a stop to it at once. In 1884 the amir again issued a firman prohibiting the sale of the Hazara and Panjshiri women,[234] but during the Hazara War the amir himself reintroduced slavery by allowing the enslavement of the Hazaras who, up to 1894, were "sold in exactly the same manner as cattle and sheep."[235] In that year, on the recommendation of a qazi and a mufti, the amir issued an order "for the stoppage of further traffic in the sale of the Hazaras other than those obtained in the war."[236] Subsequently, when Kafiristan was occupied and the amir ordered that no Kafir was to be enslaved slavery in Afghanistan was doomed, but instances of the sale of the Hazaras, by the Jamshidis in particular, were still reported. It was because of these instances that in 1899 the governor of Panjdeh asked his counterpart at Herat "to stop Afghans selling slaves in Panjdeh."[237] In 1901, General Bahawal Khan, the successor of the Sipah Salar Charkhi at Asmar assured some Kafirs that he would recommend to the amir that "slavery should be abolished throughout the whole of Kafiristan."[238] The general gave this assurance to sixty families of slaves from the Bashgal valley who had requested their emancipation. With all probability they were the *baris* who were still treated as slaves by other tribal Kafirs. The amir, as well as his sons, continued to receive slaves as presents as he had before.[239] King Amam Allah gave the final blow to slavery in Afghanistan when he emancipated all those who worked as domestic slaves, among whom the Hazaras were the highest in number.

Jehad

The tradition of jehad in Muslim Afghanistan, lying as it does on the border of Hindu India, was always strong; and the rulers of Afghanistan frequently invoked the principle of jehad against their non-Muslim adversaries. Amir ʾAbd al-Rahman, seeing that Afghanistan was sandwiched between two Christian powers, extended jehad more than any other ruler had done, as a means of mobilizing not only the army but also the public at large against the possible invasion of Afghanistan and the ruin of Islam by the Christian powers.

The amir threatened jehad whenever he wanted to warn his subjects that because of the approach of the British and Russians their country, women, and religion were in danger. Briefly, jehad was set in motion after the Russian occupation of Panjdeh in 1885. In times of severe internal crisis the amir, in order to divert attention to external dangers and to bring about a sense of unity based on fear among his subjects, also intensified his talk of jehad. It was during the most critical period of the amir's reign and shortly afterward that the most important treatises on jehad, namely *The Words of the Amir of the Land toward* the Encouragement of Jehad (1886), Ghaza (1887), and The Calendar of the Religion (1889) were published. The beginning of activities by the British government along the eastern borders of Afghanistan, which were in line with that European power's Forward Policy, intensified the movement of jehad. Although subsequently the signing of the Durand Treaty weakened this intensification, the problems arising from the demarcation of the Durand Line, the British occupation of Chitral, Russia's approach to the Pamir, and the Russo-British rapprochement in the midnineties became factors that led the amir to carry on this ideological struggle with full force. This intensity of jehad had a great deal to do with the tribal uprising of 1897 in which not only the eastern Pashtuns beyond the Durand Line became directly involved, but also the amir's own subjects along the border as far as Laghman and Tagao, in spite of the fact that the amir had not overtly declared jehad.

The movement of jehad that the amir started was intended to serve many purposes. Although mention was occasionally made of the words of God and sayings of the Prophet, "O, Muslims, fight the infidels so long as there is infidelity,"[240] actual stress was placed on the safeguarding of the "land of Islam" and the "frontiers of Islam"[241] from the encroachment of the infidels. While the spread of Islam beyond the frontier of Afghanistan was not stressed, both the strengthening of the religion of Islam[242] and the duty of "the Muslims in general and the people of Afghanistan in particular"[243] to safeguard their country against a supposed third invasion by the infidels were equally stressed.[244] This and many similar pronouncements gave a defensive character to the jehad movement, and the classic notion of jehad, which consisted of military action to expand Islam, an objective itself based on the universality of Islam,[245] was apparently given up as a declared policy. Among other things, this change of emphasis led to the expansion of the doctrine of rabat, that is, the safeguarding of the frontiers of Islam,[246] to include not only invading foreign countries, but also preventing the entry of the infidels into the country of Islam and their occupation of the cities of Islam. This expansion of the doctrine of rabat, which was thought to be highly meritorious, led to the stationing of one man out of every twenty in the country as feudal cavalry in forts along the Russian frontiers following the report that Russia intended to invade Afghanistan.[247] Similar arrangements were made along the frontiers with British India. In time of war, however, when the sovereign declared jehad, it was incumbent (farz-i-ʾayn) on all able-bodied Muslims to defend the frontiers and the land of Islam themselves or to support the ghazis with property,[248] for the jehad was in essence nothing else than extreme exertion of self and property in the cause of God[249] in return for what amounted to the reward of spoils in this world and a most comfortable life in the next.[250]

Another major point which time and again was stressed was the connection of jehad with the ruler in Islam. Although the jehad was declared to be a continuous process[251] no one but the imam and khalifa, or on occasions *padshah* (king) and sultan, was entitled to declare it.[252] The necessity of organizing the state and the obedience of the Muslims to their kings was stressed. Only when the kingdom of the people of Islam was organized was war and peace with the infidels possible, and a kingdom without a king was said to be open to invasion and destruction.[253]

Curiously, in the treatises on jehad the Wahhabis were also vehemently denounced; but apparently the disciples of Muhammad b. Abd al-Wahhab (1703–1787), whose general aim was to do away with all the innovations later than the third century of Islam,[254] were not meant. Rather the treatises were aimed at the followers of Sayyed Ahmad of Rai Bareilly (1786–1831), the founder of the so-called Wahhabi movement in India, whose Islam was "more comprehensive, richer and more flexible and retained a marked Sufi coloring."[255] While the amir denounced them from time to time, in general terms the ⟩ulama took specific issue with them, but the one-sided polemic they started actually dealt not with the Wahhabis but with the views expounded by Mirza Ghulam Ahmad of Qadian (b. 1839) in the period running almost parallel to that of the amir's reign. These "Wahhabis," that is, the Ahmadiyyas (followers of Ghulam Ahmad), were denounced as Kafirs for their rejection of the notion of the seal of prophecy,[256] although whether their founder claimed to be a *nabi* (prophet), and, if so, what he meant by the term is still disputed between the two groups of his followers that were divided after his death.[257]

The movement of jehad that the amir started and that continued afterward had significant bearing on the minds of the Muslims of Afghanistan. Since what was preached was based on the Quran, the sayings of the Prophet, and the views of the great mujtahids, the early notions of Islam and the tradition of authority as the source of the truth were strengthened. In addition, topics for pamphlets on jehad were selected because they suited the amir's position. Expression of any view that ran counter to the views of the amir was suppressed. A mulla who preached that since, like the Muslims, the Christians were ahl al-kitab (people of the book) "Mussulmans must regard Christians as brothers"[258] was stoned to death. The significant thing about this death was that at first a jury of twelve ⟩ulama absolved him from punishment for the views of which he was accused. Since the preaching of the notion of brotherhood among the ahl al-kitab tended to undermine the movement of jehad, the amir wanted the mulla to be declared guilty. Despite this wish, in the second trial only two members of the jury approved the death sentence, which was, however, instantly carried out.

The movement of jehad with its particular anti-infidel hysteria, which was directed this time against the Christians, not Hindus, created a sense of solidarity among the Muslims of Afghanistan. Also, it consolidated the xenophobia that had been the result of the Anglo-Afghan wars. Consequently, the Muslims of Afghanistan looked on those who were not of their religion and country as their enemies[259] and lived in fear of the Christians the sight of whom became especially "obnoxious" to them.[260] With the suppression of the Shiʾas and the expansion and consolidation of the Sunna the movement of jehad made the Afghan society still more conservative and its inhabitants more religious and inward looking. These were the changes that accounted for much of the resistance offered to the liberalizing efforts of King Aman Allah in the nineteen twenties and that finally led to the downfall of the amir's dynasty.

Chapter VIII
Economic Structure: 1

Population

Before 1880 the total number of inhabitants of Afghanistan was not known. Approximations were, however, many and conflicting. In 1892 a census of the population was officially attempted. Mainly because of the recurrent epidemics and high rate of mortality among children the growth of population was extremely low.

There are numerous reports on the number of tribes and inhabitants of different localities in nineteenth-century Afghanistan. These were written by foreigners and based on approximations; in addition, the authors were mainly concerned with showing the fighting strength of tribes rather than the population and its different age groups. Also, their figures were strikingly and abruptly at variance with each other, which makes it impossible to discern the rate of growth from them. To gain an idea of the population Charles M. MacGregor averaged these figures (a curious approach in itself) and put the total population (from the Oxus to Peshawer) at 4,901,000 souls.[1]

In the beginning Amir ʾAbd al-Rahman did not know how many people he ruled. Yet he quoted conflicting figures according to circumstances. Early in 1882, for instance, in response to a request for military assistance by Makhdum ʾAli, the ousted ruler of Merv, the amir, at the suggestion of the viceroy of India, excused himself by asking how he could possibly come to the deposed ruler's assistance when he was the monarch of a country with only "two million" people. On the other hand, to boost the morale of his own subjects the amir later in the same year declared that the English numbered only "ten million" and the Afghans outnumbered them by two lakhs. Five months later in March 1883 in a firman the amir proclaimed that the population of Afghanistan was thirteen million.[2] In private, however, in 1888, the amir said that the population of Afghanistan was 4,345,000, a figure that agreed closely with the generally accepted figures in the nineties.

As early as 1884, the amir felt the necessity of knowing the number of his subjects in order, he said, to prevent people from evading taxes and to distribute the produce of lands to children, old men, and women. The real purpose, however, in taking the census was military. In a firman the amir declared, "in the event of my country being invaded by any foreign enemies, I may be in a position to know how many fighting men, Mussulmans, I can command for the purposes of waging a religious war."[3] In particular, the registry of those between the ages of fourteen and fifty was stressed, since it was within this age limit that people were drafted into the army.[4]

How the census was taken is not known. The task of enumeration was given to qazis and 'ulama, in particular the mullas whose enumeration of the female population, which was also to be included, was least likely to provoke the public. In some regions revenue officials also took the census. Whether the whole population was enumerated is not known, although according to certain reports the census of the population up to the Hindu Kush was completed. According to the amir's courtiers the total number of population in 1894 was eight million, but Lord Curzon estimated it to be five million.[5] Qazi 'Abd al-Qadir, who had an intimate knowledge of Afghanistan and under whose supervision the census of the city of Kabul was taken during the reign of Amir Sher 'Ali in 1876, maintained that the population of Afghanistan, excluding the Kafirs and Arabs, was 4,004,000.[6] The writer of the article on Afghanistan in the third edition of the *Gazetteer of Afghanistan*, however, held that "Some of the Kazi's figures do not agree with more recent and perhaps more reliable information, and in a general way should be accepted as under rather than over the mark, the total population subject to the Amir probably amounting to not less than 4,500,000 souls."[7] The last figures appeared in many of the subsequent publications of the government of India until the appearance in 1906 of the *Military Report of Afghanistan* that put the total number at 6,100,000.[8]

For the city of Kandahar reliable figures are at hand, for from 1880 to 1891 census was taken three times. From these figures the trend in growth of the urban centers is discernible. Surgeon E. Tully's figure for the city of Kandahar, which was probably taken sometime before the battle of Maiwand in July 1880, is 29,400.[9] By October of the same year it had increased to 30,000.[10] Ten years later, in August 1891, it reached 31,514. The population of the city of Kandahar, thus, increased by 7 percent in eleven years, or by an average of 0.636 percent in each year. This trend in growth, which is extremely low, shows the growth in population of a flourishing urban center in Afghanistan. Yet it almost corresponds to the lowest rate of growth of an agricultural society, which is said to vary between 0.5 and 1.00 percent per year.[11] Presumably, the rate of growth in the rural areas was still lower than that of the urban centers in Afghanistan.

The question requiring discussion is why the rate of population growth was so extremely low. The answer can be sought in the supposition that like every other social phenomenon this slow growth is complex and the result of a hierarchy of causes. In the background are the financial situation and the customs that had a marked bearing upon marriage and reproduction in Afghanistan. As was discussed in the preceding chapter, because of high bride price and marriage expenses, marriage among the low-income people took place late in life; but after marriage reproduction occurred at frequent intervals and pregnancies were said to occur once every two years or so. At the same time, the frequency of pregnancy involved risks for women in childbirth. The result was a high rate of mortality among child-bearing females. To combat this, women usually prolonged lactation as long as possible, the usual period being two years.[12] In contrast, among well-to-do people the rate of reproduction was high, since marriage among them took place relatively early and polygamy was common. The well to do could form large families. The average among the Taimanis of Herat and in Seistan was four and one-half a family.[13] In Afghanistan the wealthier the man the larger the family. The Muhammadzays, who multiplied greatly during the nineteenth century, became a conspicuous example of this tendency. One reason why they retained power, in spite of the numerous civil wars, was their relative numbers. On balance, one is tempted to suppose that the tendency toward a high rate of reproduction among the wealthy was outweighed by the reverse tendency among people with low incomes, since the latter outnumbered the former.

Perhaps the most significant factor that curtailed the growth of population was the high rate of infant mortality. During the amir's reign probably one-half of the children born in Afghanistan died before reaching the age of three years.[14] Among the diseases responsible for high infant mortality were smallpox, chickenpox, and cholera. Although the custom of inoculation, as distinct from vaccination, by rubbing the crust of a sore from a smallpox patient into an incision of the person to be inoculated was at one time almost universal in Afghanistan, the smallpox that resulted, though usually mild, was sometimes so severe as to cause the death of the patient.[15] During the smallpox epidemics the rate of mortality was particularly high. In Kabul, for instance, in December 1886, according to a report, "most children" who caught smallpox died of it. In Herat, during the same month in the next year deaths from smallpox among children from two to eight years of age were fifty to sixty per day. During the cholera epidemics casualties were highest among children and the aged. Preventive medicine and the vaccination of children against contagious diseases on a mass scale were still things of the future, although a beginning had been made in the reign of the amir.

The disease that struck all age groups in large numbers and that occurred at frequent intervals and curtailed population drastically was epidemic cholera. While endemic diseases might also have checked the growth of population, there is no information available on this. Cholera in Afghanistan, however, was of a worse type than that in India. In Afghanistan it spread rapidly, and only a few persons attacked by it recovered.[16] In its virulent form, however, it did not last long. During the reign of the amir cholera occurred in epidemic form five times; in 1885, 1889, 1891, 1892, and 1899. Every time it appeared in major cities its outbreak in the countryside was also reported. One would suppose, however, that because of crowding the casualty rate would have been highest in cities, although the Persian Famine of 1872 that was followed by cholera was said to have depopulated several districts in Herat and Turkestan.[17] During the amir's reign the severest cholera epidemic was the one that occurred in 1892. In that year in Kabul alone 14,000 people died of cholera and 150 houses were closed up because all of their inhabitants had died.[18] This number means a loss of 10 percent occurred in a population of 140,000, which Kabul was presumed to have had in 1876. At this rate the total of victims in the country could be estimated at 500,000 out of 5 million people. Since the casualty rate in the rural areas was not supposed to be so high, the figure of 100,000, which according to the amir was the total number of victims throughout Afghanistan, is probably near the mark.[19] Whatever the real nature of the epidemics, children and aged people were their main victims. One can, therefore, conclude that after each outbreak the population remained relatively adult rather than young. In other words, the potentiality for reproduction was proportionally not affected much. This trend was probably balanced, more or less, during the first decade of the amir's reign when there were so many war casualties and expulsions among the adults.

Among the minor factors that contributed to the curtailment of population were wars and slavery. During the nineteenth century civil wars in Afghanistan were frequent, but in the amir's reign they were more numerous and casualties were higher in civil disturbances than in the two Anglo-Afghan wars put together. Like wars, the custom of blood feud also led to the destruction of the adult population. The blood feud was, and still is, a deep-rooted institution which prevailed with full force among the eastern Pashtuns. Among them a Pashtun was required by custom to wipe out an insult with an insult (*badal*).[20] This led to a blood feud, which as a general rule had its origin in *zar*, *zan*, and *zamin* (gold, women, and land). Because of strong family and tribal cohesion a dispute between two individuals involved their respective families, clans, and tribes. Under this system murder begot murder and the greater the bloodshed the greater the probability of a long duration of the feud. Women, children, and mullas were exempt from these disputes; but blood feud among the Pashtuns was not the sole cause of internecine wars, for the tribes were also traditionally split up into political and religious factions. These factions, which among some Pashtuns were known by the names of *ghar* and *samil* and among others *speen gund* and *tore gund*, were said to have originated from two of their ancestors.[21] At any rate, they perpetuated the blood feud and so led to the curtailment of the adult population.[22]

When slaves were sent out of Afghanistan, slavery also led to a decrease in the population, but the number of slaves carried abroad, especially to central Asia, was small. In the amir's reign this kind of slavery came to an end.

To a limited degree homosexuality also checked the growth of the population. Homosexuality existed in various degrees here and there in Afghanistan, but among the Tajiks of Badakhshan it was conspicuously prevalent and was practiced perhaps to a larger extent than elsewhere in Asia. Probably this predilection and the lack of cultivable land made Badakhshan poor.[23] The average family there numbered three and three-quarters, as opposed to four and one-quarter elsewhere in Afghanistan.[24] It is interesting to note that among the Jews of Afghanistan an average family numbered between six and seven and that, because of the strong sense of solidarity among them, the extended family was the norm. By contrast, among the Kafirs of Kafiristan families were small because the women worked so hard that, unlike women in other communities, they did not bear many children.

The city of Kandahar in 1880, perhaps because of the war, had more females than males. In 1891 this relation was reversed to 16,064 males and 15,450 females. Owing to the lack of information, nothing can be said with any degree of certainty about age groups. In the amir's estimate men and women each made up half of the population in Afghanistan. Half of the males, according to him, were the aged, children, and boys under age. Basing his estimate on a population of twelve million for the whole country, the amir's figures were for cultivators and laborers, one and one-half million; for mullas, faqirs, and the unemployed, seven and one-half lakhs; for the sick and diseased, three and one-half lakhs. There remained four lakhs who, according to the amir, were sound and able bodied and fit for enlistment in the army.[25]

There are also no figures available to show life span, but considering the high rate of infant mortality and the extremely low rate of growth in general, life span in Afghanistan was probably similar to the shortest in traditional agricultural societies, where it averaged between twenty and thirty-five years.[26] In Afghanistan, however, a person sometimes lived a long life, as did, for instance, a certain man who, in 1884, was "proved to be 200 years"[27] and the famous Mulla Mushk-i-ʾAlam who died at the age of ninety-three.

The Agricultural System

In dry Afghanistan, arable land constitutes a small portion of the total area. Even this small portion is subject to differing and rather uncertain courses of water supply, which ultimately depend on rainfall and account for different types of farming. This variety, in turn, accounts for different types of land tenure.

In Afghanistan the combination of the mountainous character, the heavy snowfall on the high mountains, and rain on the plains brings about conditions that permit irrigated, as well as dry, farming for the agricultural population and perennial grasses for the herds that belong to nomads.[28] This situation is rather unfavorable to agriculture, which has to adapt itself to a considerable degree to the source of the irrigation, that is, rainfall.[29] Under these conditions grain is not in surplus but in shortage, and whenever rainfall is low or a natural disaster occurs frightening scarcity is the result.[30]

Basically, there are two types of farming, *abi* and *lalmi*, that is, land irrigated by surface water and by rain; these terms signify irrigated and nonirrigated dry farming. Generally, irrigated farming produces two crops in a year and nonirrigated only one in a year and in some places only every two or three years. In addition, since nonirrigated farming is dependent entirely on the rainfall, its crops are less certain. In the nineteen twenties both types of farming were said to be in use on almost equal acreages of land, each having 500,000 hectares of land,[31] whereas tilled acreage constituted no more than 2 percent of the whole territory of Afghanistan.[32] Irrigated farming was, of course, more productive, and its extent was increasing. It constituted, therefore, the principal type of farming.

There are three principal types of irrigation: source irrigation, river irrigation, and *karez* irrigation. Source irrigation, which is characteristic of hilly regions, consists of diverting the waters of mountain springs by running small streams onto the fields, which usually lie at the foot of a mountain gorge or slope.

River irrigation is perhaps the most widespread system of irrigation in Afghanistan. Water is diverted, with or without damming, from a river or stream at a point above cultivated fields. River irrigation systems vary from simple channels, which irrigate given villages or settlement nuclei, to relatively large-scale systems, which irrigate entire oases. In the mountainous areas where narrow valleys prevent any lateral extension of the fields, settlements are usually spread in long lines along the banks of the river. Thus a given village nucleus tends to have its own irrigation system that is independent of those to which other village nuclei are attached. By contrast, in the larger oasis areas the irrigation systems reach a certain degree of complexity. Here the individual settlements are bound up with an extensive irrigation system that is based on a number of main primary irrigation canals, such as, for example, on seven canals in Herat, eighteen in Balkh (known as *hazdahnahr*), three in the Logar area, and several in the Jalalabad area. Damming techniques, even on the larger rivers, are not fundamentally different from those used in the mountain areas. Dams are built of stones thrown across the river to block the current.

Karez irrigation is common in southern and western Afghanistan. A *karez* is an undergroud man-made channel that draws water from adjacent mountains and diverts it onto the fields. It is made by boring wells at intervals of two or three meters and connecting them at the bottom. But the wells and underground channels must be kept clear constantly. In addition to the great expenses involved in its construction, a *karez* requires unremitting work and attention. Since the *karezes* irrigate fields that cannot be irrigated by either source water or rivers, they are constructed and maintained occasionally at the expense of government or a wealthy landlord, but more generally at the expense and cooperation of a large number of small landowners among whom the cost and the use of the water is equally or proportionally divided. Some *karezes*, for instance the one in Ghazni said to have been constructed by the order of Sultan Mahmud, have supplied a constant amount of water for ages.[33]

Agricultural Products
Because of differences in elevation, the climate of Afghanistan, its scenery, and products are varied. The first place in cultivation is occupied by wheat, the second by barley, the third by rice; then follow other grains and the legumes, especially peas, beans, common lentils, and, in the regions adjacent to India, maize. The intensive type of farming in the valley of Hari Rud, especially near Herat, is characterized by a diversity of field crops and more than one hundred crop plants are cultivated. In Afghanistan, also, a great variety of fruits, vegetables, nut trees, and animals abound.[34]

In the nineteenth century fields in Afghanistan were tilled with various primitive tools. The most important was the wooden plow tipped with iron, which was drawn generally by oxen but in some regions (for example, Turkestan) by horses and in others (among them, Seistan and Shorawak) by camels. In a few places asses were also employed.[35] In Kafiristan slaves and also women drew the plows. To smooth the roughly plowed fields, break up the surface, and prevent the soils from becoming too compacted, a smoothing board (*mala*) was drawn by draft animals or humans in the same manner as the plow. Various hand shovels were used mainly for cleaning the network of ditches and for the distribution of water.[36] Fertilizer, which was used extensively, was composed of dung and straw, the mud of old walls and various other substances. To thrash the cereals rollers were mainly used. On irrigated land there were two harvests in a year, one sown at the end of autumn and reaped at the end of spring and the other sown in the summer and reaped in the autumn. The harvests were named for the seasons in which they were reaped: *bahari* was reaped in the spring and *tirmahi* in the autumn.

Grain was ground, principally, by water mills and, to some extent, by windmills and hand mills. Windmills were not generally used, except in the west where a steady wind would be relied on for a good portion of the year. Hand mills were used principally by nomads and only in some parts of the country.

Land Tenure and Rent

As noted in chapter 6, land in Afghanistan, compared to land in other countries in the East, has been fairly equally divided among the land-owning population. Small landholdings were the predominant feature, although big landholdings also existed especially in western Afghanistan.

In Afghanistan, then, most of the land was cultivated by landowners themselves assisted by their families and, occasionally, by hired laborers. Elsewhere landowners supervised lands cultivated by crop-sharing tenants or laborers. How, and on what basis, landowners and tenants shared the crops depended on the extent and nature of the lands and water, and on the provision of the seeds, draft animals, and labor. Since these varied from region to region there was no uniform system of tenure. In Ghazni if the tenants provided the cattle for the plow and half of the seed they received one-third of the produce, but if these were provided by the landowners the tenants received only one-fourth.[37] In the Jalalabad area, where the *se-kot* system was generally in operation, the division was more or less the same as in Ghazni. There the cultivators were either mere laborers (who received food and clothing and a wage of grain at the harvest time) or tenants. Sometimes, landowners supplied all of the seed, cattle, and implements of husbandry; in other cases, some of these, probably draft animals and the implements, were provided by tenants.[38] As a rule, tenants there took one-third of the produce.

In Ghor, where small landholding was common, tenancy conditions ranged between the opposite extremes. In some cases, when tenants provided only labor, they received one-tenth of the produce; and in others, when they provided everything and in addition took responsibility for paying the taxes, they received four-fifths of the harvest.[39] In the Hazarajat, where relatively large landholding existed and where class differentiation was exceptionally sharp for the mountain people,[40] the landlords as a rule took three shares of the produce out of every four. In some areas they took four shares out of five and even five out of six.[41] In Dai Kundi, where big landholdings existed and where the Beg family controlled villages and laborers, the latter resembled the serfs who, according to one observer, "in fact, belong to the soil, from which they can not by the law of usage be severed."[42] In all these cases landowners provided the seed, agricultural implements, and cattle and tenants only the labor. In Mazar where the greater part of the irrigated lands and the best nonirrigated lands belonged to private individuals and the state, tenants worked for a low share of the harvest. They received one-tenth share of the produce; their landlords not only provided seeds, but also furnished monetary aid that the tenant did not have to repay. In Maimana the proportion of the produce that the tenants received was greater than it was in Mazar: one-seventh to one-fifth. The Maimana tenants, however, shared the paying of taxes with landowners and received less monetary aid than their fellows in Mazar.

In the regions between Qataghan and Badakhshan, where big landlords prevailed, the share of the tenants was among the highest we know of. The tenants provided everything necessary for raising the crops without receiving monetary aid from the landlords. There the tenants' share was more than half of the crops (the exact proportion is unknown). Because of the relatively favorable terms for tenants in this area their conditions might have been expected to be better than those of their fellows elsewhere, but the Soviet scholar Monic, who visited the area in the 1920s, came to the opposite conclusion and said that, "The concentration of landownership and the pauperization of the peasantry have in no way brought about either a capitalistic plantation economy with improved techniques of agriculture, nor [sic] an arny [army] of wage earners."[43] In Badakhshan, where the most ancient form of agriculture existed and where small landholding was the prevalent feature, landowners tilled their lands themselves.

Apart from landowners, tenants, and the government, others received a portion of the harvest. If the crops were cut by hired cutters, they received their wages from the still undivided and unthrashed crop, usually at the rate of one heap of produce out of every twenty. When the crop was ready for distribution a basketful of it was given to the *imam* as *haq Allah* (God's right). The origin of this and other dues given to the religious class goes back to early Islamic times, when it was an established practice to give alms at harvest time.[44] From the still undivided heap of crops a considerable portion was set aside for cleaners, weighmen (whose dues were called *tarazodari*), watchmen, the elder of the village (*malikana*), *hakim* of the district (*shaykhdari*) and the accountant official (*qalamana*). W. Jenkyns notes that such tradesmen such as carpenters, blacksmiths, and, presumably, barbers received their portions exclusively from the share of the tenants as fees for their services,[45] but he appears to be mistaken because today when the share of the government is fixed these tradesmen receive their portions from the common heap.

The Agrarian Policy of Amir ʾAbd al-Rahman Khan

Agriculture was badly hurt during the reign of the amir. Its deterioration had actually started during the two years of the Second Anglo-Afghan War; but in the reign of the amir the seventeen years of civil war, the imposition of heavy taxes, the frequent outbreaks of epidemics, and the creation of a large standing army considerably decreased agricultural production. Although this decrease was accompanied by a relatively small loss of population through deaths (in civil wars and epidemics) and expulsion, for agricultural Afghanistan, which did not produce enough crops even for home consumption, it increased the number of those who lived on the border of subsistence.

These factors caused many canals and *karezes* to dry up and large tracts of cultivable land to remain uncultivated. In addition, some landowners were unable to till their land because of the lack of funds and seeds. In Herat, for instance, two hundred such landowners were imprisoned for their inability to pay government revenue.[46] In Ningrahar people complained against conscription into the army on the grounds that there were not enough people left to cultivate lands.[47]

In the absence of data it cannot be determined what percentage of the approximately one million hectares of irrigated and nonirrigated land that was cultivable at the time was fallow and what percentage of agricultural production decreased, but the effects of scarcity were evident everywhere. Scarcity became common even at times when there were no wars or natural disasters. The following examples were selected to describe this situation. During the Hazara War when large quantities of grain were taken to the soldiers in the Hazarajat most of the people of Kandahar were "merely subsisting on green fodder."[48] In 1896, in Kabul two hundred men, who had, for one reason or another, come from the rural areas to lay their grievances before the amir, were reported to be "dying fast of starvation."[49] A youth who had been caught in theft for the second time told the amir that "he was compelled by hunger to do so, and that he did not fear death."[50] Winter months were usually bad as far as food was concerned, but in the winter of 1885 it was reported that "the people fight over flour when [it is] brought to market for sale. The soldiers take it by force and the people find it difficult to get any."[51] One reason why conditions in cities became so bad was that lack of work in the countryside drove many people from their lands to work as coolies.[52] In some parts of the country poor people had no food and lived on mulberries that they dried for consumption for the winter.[53] Because people were "yearly getting poorer,"[54] their purchasing power became so low that some of them were unable to buy even a piece of cloth (*kafan*) in which to wrap their dead for burial.[55] Even among the wage-earning population of the Kabul workshops it was not infrequent for people to starve.[56]

To deal with this situation the amir followed both short-term and long-term programs. In times of crisis speculators and profiteers were compelled to bring grain to markets, but often they would not bring it. Indeed, in Kabul in 1885 the speculators had run short of grain in their stocks. On such occasions the government sold its own grain, but for "much profit."[57] Large amounts of grain (27,000 kharwars in 1886) were always stored in Herat for fear of shortages in times of national emergency. When the governor of this province, on his own initiative, sold some grain to alleviate the shortage, the amir reprimanded him, saying, "Such supplies when stored should never be sold; if they go bad throw them away or destroy them."[58] Beggars, whose number was reported to be "very high," were fed by the government during scarcities. In 1898, for instance, in Kabul 32 maunds of cooked rice were daily distributed to the poor. A year later, one thousand registered beggars were fed during the month of fast.[59] The amir also sent money for distribution among the poor throughout the country.

The goal of the amir's long-term program was to make Afghanistan economically independent of other countries by ensuring "that every thing should be produced in Afghanistan."[60] This was, of course, a lofty ideal that the amir, for obvious reasons, could not accomplish; still he made efforts to do it. First, *taqawi* was advanced to destitute landowners, on the condition that until the loans were paid back half of the produce of their lands was to be paid to the government. Loans were also advanced to those who undertook to bring waste lands under cultivation.[61] The loans were advanced first in 1888 to the landowners of Kandahar and by the end of the amir's reign all landowners were invited to obtain them.[62] How much money was actually advanced, how many landowners took advantage of the loan program, and to what extent it improved agriculture is not known.

Second, large tracts of uncultivated *khalisa* were declared open for lease to cultivators on favorable terms. Such leaseholders were, then, given the option of purchasing the *khalisa* that they had cultivated.[63] Among other things this policy had the effect of increasing the number of small landholders.

Third, a considerable number of new canals for irrigation purposes were constructed and some old ones were improved. In 1889 the Patab Canal of Kandahar was completed. Also, the existing canals of Mazar were deepened and widened. In addition, a new canal, the Royal Canal, which was said to have been constructed by the "voluntary service" of the people of Turkestan and which was thirty thousand steps long brought "large tracts of lands" under cultivation.[64] Near Kabul, in Bagram and Tutum Dara, where all attempts in the past to construct canals had failed, new canals were constructed.[65] Also, some canals from the Panjsher River and near Raig-i-Rawan were constructed. As a result, the desert of Bagram as far as the hills of the Safays was settled with people from Turkestan. The two new canals in Ghori and Baghlan (the latter known as Ajmil) brought one thousand and seventy *jufts* (yokes of oxen, a measurement of plow land) of land under cultivation.[66] Similarly, the two large deserts of Baharak and Khayirabad in Badakhshan were made arable by widening and reconstructing disused old canals.[67] Presumably the new lands thus brought under cultivation were turned into the *khalisa* as was the case with one hundred *jufts* of land near Khwaja jungle in Taluqan that were made arable as a result of the construction of a canal.[68] By contrast, except for a report to the effect that all *karezes* in Kandahar were to be inspected for the purpose of irrigation of additional land, the amir made no attempts either to construct new *karezes* or to improve the existing ones.

Fourth, the amir made extensive efforts to introduce new types of plants and animals into Afghanistan. In 1888 sugar cane, indigo, and henna from Lahore were cultivated on government lands in Kandahar and Farah; but the first was abandoned because of poor results. The attempts to introduce American cotton, much superior to the local type, into Jalalabad and Laghman were relatively successful.[69] Also, introduced into Afghanistan were horses from Persia, millet from Samarqand, donkeys from Bukhara, sheep from Australia and England, and grain from Europe; the imported sheep did not last. Inside the country fruit plants and mulberry trees were moved from one province to another.[70] The crops, as before, were subject to frequent attacks by pests, but the amir sometimes ordered his troops to kill the locusts damaging the crops.

The Industrial System

Manufactured articles, including varieties of woolen and cotton fabrics and weaponry, were made by hand looms and power produced by water mills. The artisans used metals by melting them in furnaces for making utensils and other implements. In the reign of Amir ʾAbd al-Rahman steam power was introduced and a complex set of factories set up, where weapons of European standards and some necessities of modern life were made.

The principal industrial products in Afghanistan consisted of products of silk, the manufacture of felts, postins, carpets, cotton fabrics, rosaries, metal utensils, and agricultural implements. They were made by private individuals and artisans who were helped by members of their families and apprentices. Because these articles were made, by and large but not exclusively, for domestic consumption there was no need felt for either the concentration of large capital or the existence of large-scale organization. Human hands and hand looms (the latter made mainly of wood with some iron) were the principal manufacturing tools that were helped by power obtained from either water or small furnaces.

Felts were extensively used by both the settled population and nomads as carpets, cushions, bedding, and similar items. These felts were made of wools, usually a mixture of wool with the hair of goats and camels. Unlike carpets, felts were easily made by rolling and unrolling a wet mixture of wool for a long time until the fibers were firmly interwoven after which they were soaped and watered and color patterns were attached to them. Peculiar to Kandahar was a kind of long coat (*kotzay*) made of thick, but light, felt that was waterproofed and lasted for a long time.[71] By contrast, great skill was required for the manufacture of carpets made in Herat and Turkestan in looms operated by six or eight persons (mainly women). The main features of the carpets at the time were their smallness and repetitive design.[72] The wool was always dyed before it was spun into thread, a practice which was said to make the carpets keep their color much longer.

Also complicated was the manufacture of varieties of postins made of sheepskins, mainly in the cities of Kabul, Ghazni, and Kandahar. Their manufacture required a long process of curing and dyeing sheepskins that, because the postins were used extensively, provided occupation for many hundreds of families, especially after these clothes were adapted as winter dress by the British army in the Panjab.[73] In Kafiristan the use of goatskin was common among the general populace, but the well to do wore cotton fabrics. The latter were perhaps not very common in Afghanistan, as cotton was grown only scantily in some districts before 1862.[74] The amir's introduction of American cotton into Afghanistan must have stimulated the cotton industry since by the 1920s the industry had become so widespread that in some regions whole districts were occupied in manufacturing the so-called *karbas* (coarse handwoven cotton cloth) for use by the poorest part of the population. For its manufacture a weaver loom of the type found all over the East was used.[75]

In the manufacture of wool for clothing the Hazaras were self-sufficient. The *barak* they made of the wool of lamb and sheep and the hair of camel was famous.[76] The chogas (*chapans*) which were generally used throughout the year, but mainly in the winter in northern Afghanistan, were made of different kinds of wool and were often ornamented with embroidery of gold lace and sold at high prices.[77] Silk was still produced in large quantities despite the great skill and time required. In Kandahar it was produced in the villages near the city, but in Herat silkworms were reared in almost every home. The silk made of worms whose eggs started hatching usually at the end of March was used for export, especially to Bombay, and for ornamental embroidery at home.[78] Kandahar was also known for rosaries of all kinds made of soft crystallized silicate of magnesia mined from the hill of Shah Maqsud.[79]

Artisans, who worked largely in cities, were of various trades. In Kabul they were divided into thirty-two trades,[80] the largest number in a single city. Among them the coppersmiths, goldsmiths, silversmiths, jewellers, and leather artificers were the most important. Each trade had one elder (*kalantar*). The artificers (*ustads*) were assisted by apprentices (*shagirds*) who were usually young boys. To become an artificer a boy had to work years for a small wage. Artificers followed their trades until they became old. They passed their skills on to apprentices in a relatively short time only when the apprentices were near relations; thus, in effect, they had a monopoly of their trades, which was formed by certain families, the Tajiks and Kabulis. In the Kabul copper bazar, where domestic utensils were produced, the ceaseless tapping of countless hammers was heard from early morning until sunset. These workers of metals were known for their extraordinary patience and exactitude; but the business transacted in their stalls was out of proportion to the labor involved, and sales were arranged only after many days of protracted dealings and bargainings.[81]

Weapons and Workshops

In the past such weapons as swords, daggers, lances, matchlocks (*dahanpur*), and guns were made by hand in Kabul, Kandahar, and Herat. Notable progress in weaponry was made in the reign of Amir Sher ʾAli Khan when he established workshops (*karkhana-i-sultanat-i-Kabul*) where modern weapons were made on a large scale. The Afghan artisans made brass guns before Amir Sher ʾAli Khan obtained new guns (a mountain battery) from the British government. Apparently, the number of brass guns cast at this time was very high, as could be guessed from the exaggerated quotation from an artisan of the time that one fully workable gun was made every day in the reign of Amir Sher ꞌAli.[82] After the introduction of iron batteries the old brass guns lost their significance. This change occurred when Amir Sher ꞌAli sent Dost Muhammad, a skilled Kabuli artisan, to Peshawar to learn how to cast guns as the English did. An attempt to cast guns in this manner in Kabul had already failed. Dost Muhammad was allowed by the government of India to visit the arsenal and to see how rifled guns were made. Upon his return to Afghanistan he was also given wooden models of guns with complete drawings of their details. Thus equipped with new knowledge in weaponry and money and equipment made available to him by Amir Sher ꞌAli and assisted by other such skilled artisans as Sulaiman and Muhammad Ibrahim who had learned the art from masters in Isfahan, Dost Muhammad was finally able to turn out four or five guns a month.[83] Iron for the guns came principally from India. A small quantity was procured from Bajaur and Zurmut. The guns were bored out by the machinery at the water mills of Deh Afghanan. The machinery for these mills had been set up by a Hindustani, who had been trained by Muhammad Ibrahim Isfahani (when the latter had returned from Persia to be in the service of Sultan Jan, the late governor of Herat). The old ordnance was broken up and new guns were cast in the Bala Hisar, the boring and polishing being done at the Deh Afghanan water mills. In these guns a larger percentage of copper than was necessary was used.[84] In the reign of Amir Sher ꞌAli the workshops in Kabul did not replace other workshops and in Herat brass guns were made as before.[85] Just before the Second Anglo-Afghan War there were 379 guns of various sizes and kinds in Kabul of which 256 were captured by the British and 123 remained in the country.[86]

The manufacture of rifles in the reign of Amir Sher ꞌAli was not such a success. In addition to the old rifles (*dahanpur*) new Sniders (*baghalpur*) were also made. Martini-Henrys (*panahpur*) were under construction when the war broke out.[87] In addition, rifles of different patterns, including the French, with abundant gunpowder and many percussion caps were found in government magazines in the Bala Hisar. Before the arrival of the British forces at Kabul the Afghans carried off many rifles from the arsenal, but munitions sufficient to have supplied all Afghanistan were still left behind.[88] These workshops were totally destroyed, however, by an explosion in the Bala Hisar during the war. Most of the guns and rifles were carried to India and the rest captured by the Afghans.[89] Amir ꞌAbd al-Rahman did not inherit many of these weapons. When they evacuated Afghanistan the British returned only a few light guns to the amir, and these were said to be unworkable. The amir subsequently recovered some rifles from his own people.

Following his accession, Amir ꞌAbd al-Rahman, who claimed to be an engineer as well as a practitioner of a number of professions,[90] started factories for making rifles, gunpowder, and artillery guns. This much, however, was not satisfactory to the amir, who intended to have factories run by steam power for the manufacture of weapons on the modern European system. For that purpose the amir in 1885 employed M. Jerome, a French mechanical engineer and provided him with money to purchase machinery and to employ Indian mechanics. Jerome did so, but he was not heard of again. Possibly the government of India, preferring to see its own "expert-agent" at the Afghan court, prevented the Frenchman from proceeding to Kabul.[91] After this fiasco, the amir turned to the British whose employment he had initially avoided probably for political considerations. He decided to approach them because he believed that unless he "had the same sorts of guns, rifles and other war materials that were used by other nations, it would be impossible to keep the integrity of my Government intact, and to protect the country from the attacks of foreign aggressors."[92] At the recommendation of his agent at Calcutta the amir then employed Salter Pyne, a Londoner, who became the chief instrument for introducing western military technology into Afghanistan and, in addition, played an important role in effecting a settlement between the governments of India and Afghanistan in the early nineties. On 7 April 1887, the day of the foundation of what soon became a complex set of factories (curiously known as the Kabul workshops or *mashin khana*), the amir told Pyne, "This is the happiest day of my life. I have today seen the foundation of what is to be a great event in Afghanistan. Before these workshops can be finished there are three essentials required: (1) God's help; (2) my money; (3) your work. Your work and God's help without my money are useless. God's help and my money without your work, and your work and my money without God's help are equally useless."[93] The amir who was generally so strict about the expenditure of money became, on the contrary, generous when the efficiency and expansion of Kabul workshops was in question and was "quite satisfied not to receive a penny in return on the money he had laid on new works."[94] Pyne was given full authority and money to purchase machinery, to make trips to England and India, to keep himself up to date in his profession and to employ British and Indian specialists for various branches of the new industry.

A plant of wood-working machinery and a mint were set up. By 1891, the workshops—which included coining, cartridge making, a cannon foundry, barrel rifling, sawmills, and flour mills with weaving and boot-making machinery—were all in operation.[95] In the last years of the century factories for the manufacture of such nonmilitary items as candles, soap, carpets, and blankets were also added. In the leather factory leather was tanned and dyed and all kinds of items necessary for military use and for use in machinery were made. A spirit distillery in Zindabanan was also set up. Electric lighting, a telephone line connecting the Kotwali with the palace in the city and within the Babur Garden, and lithographic printing presses were also added.

The workshops, occupying an area a third of a mile long and two hundred yards wide, comprised the main shops with "about a hundred machines of sorts."[96] While in other countries such machinery was run by coal fuel, the Afghans were dependent on wood fuel supplied by the landowners of the surrounding areas, especially the Kohistan, in return for the landlord's tax revenue.[97] But the cutting of green trees was so distasteful to the landlords that they spread all sorts of rumors about the workshops. In particular it was said that the British, who had been unable to pacify Afghanistan militarily, were now scheming to deprive the country of mulberry trees, which, because they were the source of *talkhan*, enabled the Afghans to carry on the struggle with the British for a long time. The most difficult problem for the workshops, however, resulted from the landlocked position of the country, since imported iron had to be transported from abroad through India and then by camel to the workshops.[98] Still by 1906 six hundred tons of suitable metals were imported for the construction of cartridges for Martini-Henrys and Sniders.[99] In spite of the odds the machinery was supplied with steam power, and iron and production increased progressively. Within seven months of the setting up of the workshops 11,000 Sniders and Martini-Henrys were produced. In January 1888 the monthly output of the breech-loading rifles reached 200. Rifles of a Russian pattern, which was said to be of the same quality, were also made. During the Hazara War when the machinery was in full operation, about 10 breech-loading rifles and an artillery gun were produced daily.[100] By 1896 2 field guns and 2 "firing guns" were made each week, and 15 rifles, 120,000 coins, and 10,000 cartridges for Martini-Henrys and the same number for Sniders were made daily.[101] To boost the morale of his people the amir announced that war equipment had been supplied for waging a jehad that was "beyond the power of man."[102]

The quality of the Kabul-made arms and ammunition could not match the quantity. In the course of their manufacture sometimes weapons and ammunitions were made that were considered to be either of poor quality or useless. Pyne, who was probably more optimistic than realistic, claimed that "the weapons made by the Amir's own workmen have long been of excellent quality."[103] Similarly, the British agent held that "At the present time Afghanistan equals the European countries in manufacturing arms and other articles of use."[104] Frank Martin, who later succeeded Pyne, on the other hand, believed that the field and machine guns made in Kabul workshops were unreliable.[105] Opinions of the military experts of the British government have not been traced; but the commissioner of Peshawar spoke of the guns and rifles made in Kabul as of "superior quality" constructed after the English model.[106] The author of *The Military Report on Afghanistan*, however, believed that much of the Kabul-made ammunition was "unreliable"[107] and that the cartridges were not up to European standards,[108] but he made no comments on the quality of guns and rifles.

As chief engineer, Pyne was given sole authority over the technical aspects of the establishment, while a separate bureaucracy and military management took care of its other aspects. Gradually, a number of other British experts, such as Walter, Taskar, Wild, Smith, Thornton, Middleton, Collins, Clemence, Stewart, Medlin, and Edwards, were also employed. In 1895 Frank Martin joined the group. With the court's physicians, Dr. John Gray, Lady Lillias Hamilton, and Mrs. Daly they formed a little European community, the first of its kind in Kabul.[109] In 1899, Pyne, whom the amir had treated so well and considered to be a true friend of Afghanistan, was dismissed for no apparent reason. His post was then given to Martin, a rival of Pyne's.

Another group of foreigners whose number fluctuated from twenty to fifty were Indian Muslim mechanics from the Panjab and Bengal commonly referred to as *mistaries*. These "Indians were openly in his [the amir's] service, but secretly they were working for the British government."[110] Ram Singh, a Sikh from the Panjab, supervised the spirit distillery, but this industry was soon dismantled since the spirits made there were not approved by physicians in Bombay.

Afghan artisans and workers formed the largest group in the workshops. Because of the expansion of the workshops the number of Afghan artisans increased rapidly. A large number of artisans of various professions from all over the country were employed there and as a result "very few" tradesmen were left in the rest of the country.[111]

In all works there was one *ustad* (foreman or artificer) who had a few apprentices (*shagirds*) under him. Previously they had worked under rigid conditions similar to those found under the guild system, but the new factory conditions and the amir's pressure on the Afghan artisans to learn modern technology quickly tended to undermine the traditional authority of the masters over their apprentices. In the absence of public courses in technological instruction the masters still trained their apprentices in their special fields, but relations between them were far from cordial. More fundamental was the need for a large number of skilled men to meet the requirements of the expanding workshops. In 1895, for instance, six hundred promising boys were employed to learn skilled work and, after a while, were reported to have become "experts."[112]

At first the Afghan artisans were a little backward; but being, according to Pyne, a people of "an inventive turn of mind"[113] and since various artisan trades had existed in Afghanistan for centuries, they soon became enthusiastic. The frequent visits by the amir to the workshops and his rewarding of the Afghans for their success had a great deal to do with the progress made there. According to Pyne, half a dozen of them once set to work to make a steam engine of one-quarter horse power. No one but Afghans had anything to do with the work, and when the amir saw the result of their labor he was delighted and rewarded them.[114] Ruthless dictator that the amir was, he was sometimes "so overcome with the magnitude of the work that his enthusiasm overcame his kingly dignity, and [he] set to work himself."[115] The Afghan master artisans whose salary varied between 20 and 100 rupees a month gradually took the places of the Indian *mistaries* and at one point fifty of the Afghans replaced an equal number of the *mistaries*.[116] The better known among them were Zaman, Najaf, and Jan Muhammad.

The number of workers in the workshops fluctuated between four and five thousand.[117] According to Martin, the Afghan workman at his best was intelligent and, if he only gave his mind to it, could do work requiring considerable skill in a manner that was highly creditable. They were failures, however, when it came to precision because Afghan workers lacked technical knowledge. It was this lack of exactitude that made the field and machine guns unreliable. Besides, Afghan workers did not like the idea of working together and preferred "to do things off their own bat . . . hoping, thereby, to get all credit from the Amir."[118] The workers were careless of precautions and a series of explosions and deaths occurred until regulations were laid down and strictly enforced. The regulations, however, did not include provisions to improve their conditions. Most of them had "no surplus adipose substance on their bones" because their pay was "mostly fixed at starvation rates," though several of the men, who had their pay increased for doing small things for the amir himself, "got too much" so far as ability was concerned.[119] Manual workers received eight rupees and skilled workers from twenty to thirty rupees per month. At the bottom of the pay scale were the beggars, sometimes employed to do unskilled labor. An adult male beggar received four annas, a female two, and a child one a day. At times, batches of unsupported prisoners were also made to work, presumably at the rates for beggars.

Timber and Building

In architectural styles there were great differences from one part of the country to another, but almost all buildings in Afghanistan were made of mud. Some buildings, mostly in rural areas, were built of pure mud. More common in the cities was a mixture of straw and mud that often produced structures of considerable stability. Sun-dried bricks were also widely used. Baked bricks were used less frequently because their manufacture required large ovens. In the rural areas, almost without exception, baked bricks were never used in house construction. A kind of plaster, known as *gach*, was often used on walls. Stone or wooden houses were almost never found in the large urban or most of the rural areas of Afghanistan. In Badakhshan and some places in the Hazarajat where there were many stones houses were often constructed of this material. In Kafiristan wooden houses were often found. As mentioned previously, some of the Wazirs and Afridays lived in caves.

Wood was used for making roofs in flat-roofed houses. Where houses were topped by *gunbad* (domes) no wood was used. Willow, poplar (*safid dar*), and plane trees (*chinar*) were used most widely. The most striking difference in architectural styles was the division between *gunbad* and flat-roofed zones. The occurrence of one type did not exclude the other, but one or the other tended to predominate in a certain region. While the *gunbad* form appeared to be characteristic of the steppe oases of Khurasan and Turkestan,[120] the flat-roofed form was characteristic of the rest of the country.

In the amir's reign many new buildings were built in Afghanistan.

First and foremost among them were the buildings for the use of the amir and his household. When the amir ascended the throne, there was no suitable residence for him since Bala Hisar, the royal palace, had been demolished in the Second Anglo-Afghan War. After living for three years in the house of Dabir al-Mulk Mirza Muhammad Hasan in the Murad Khani area of Kabul,[121] the amir moved to a building that was built in the Babur Gardens in forty days. In early 1884 construction of the Arg, the new palace, began, and it was completed in one year. The amir took residence there in December 1884. Although expanded and modernized, it has remained to this day the seat of Afghan rulers. The plan of the Arg was modeled on that of a church that the amir had seen in Tashkent. It was a pretentious two-storied square structure, dome-shaped with towers and cupolas on each corner. After the Bala Hisar the Arg was probably the second building in Afghanistan in which glasses and windows of the European style had been used.

The Arg was at once the central domicile of the court and a strong defensive work, although it was commanded by a fort situated on the summit of Asmaie Mountain. The accommodations were divided between the palace quarter occupying the inmost station and the inner and outer fort. A high wall enclosed the entire position. Within the gateway and extending around the wall of the outer fort were the quarters of the troops and in the center there were spacious gardens, which formed an ever green oasis with fresh flowers, green grass, shady trees, and neatly tended paths. The inner fort was separated from the outer by a wide deep ditch and on the remote side there were high battlements. Access to it was gained by a drawbridge that, lowered between sunrise and sunset, was raised at night. The inner work was divided by a farther wall, which was pierced with loopholes and unceasingly patrolled. The massive gates were made of wood and studded with iron; the arches on either side contained quarters for troops. For semi-private or public audiences the amir frequented the Darbar Hall, situated beyond the moat in the garden of the Arg. It was a long, lofty building with a pillared verandah, a roof of corrugated iron and spacious windows on each side, curtained after European fashion.[122]

Adjacent to the Arg were the Gulistan Serai and Boston Serai. The latter was used by the amir as an audience hall, and the former was built for his principal wife in 1896. Other palaces included those of the Bagh-i-Bala, Hindki (Chilsitun), and Qal᾽a-i-Hashmat Khan.

In 1888 a summer palace was built in Paghman where in addition to quarters for the amir's *haram* there were also quarters for government offices. The amir called Paghman the Simla of Afghanistan (after the summer residence of the British viceroy of India, in what is now Pakistan) and ordered his senior officials to build residences there for themselves too. Expanded considerably in the reign of King Aman Allah, Paghman has ever since been a popular summer resort.

A new winter palace was built in the city of Jalalabad. Other noted buildings raised in Kabul during the amir's reign were the Kotwali in the Arg bazar, the Puli Khishti mosque (1895), the ᾽Id Gah mosque, the

Royal mosque, and Shahrara tower. In 1892, for the convenience of travelers and traders caravanserais were built along the principal roads throughout the country. Also the amir ordered all the *hakims* to build suitable quarters for their offices.

Chapter IX
Economic Structure: 2

Trade and Commerce

As a crossroad, Afghanistan, especially before the discovery of seaways, was always an important center of transit trade between India and central Asia. Contrary to general belief, in the reign of Amir 'Abd al-Rahman Khan, the transit trade, as well as Afghanistan's own internal and external trade, suffered greatly. Meanwhile, the government monopolized trade, advanced loans to merchants, and made trade safe from brigandage.

Internal Trade

There was little difference between external and internal trade in Afghanistan before its boundaries were demarcated. Turkestan and Herat were commercially more closely connected with Panjdeh, Merv, Bukhara, and Mashhad than with, say, Kabul, while Badakhshan had closer trade ties with eastern Turkestan, Tashkent, and Chitral than with either Kandahar or Herat. Similarly, the regions south of the Hindu Kush were closer to the regions in northern India. On the whole, before 1880 trade was still not nationally developed and was mainly regional. This situation may account for the existence and circulation of different systems of measurements and currencies in Afghanistan before the amir came to power.

The fact that Afghanistan served as a crossroad for international trade also accounted for the use of a large number of routes, most of which ran across the country. Four main routes connected northern India with Afghanistan. They were the routes through Khybar

(Peshawar-Khybar-Kabul), Bolan (Sind-Bolan-Gomal or Khojak-Kandahar), Dera Isma'il Khan (Panjab-Dera Isma'il Khan-Shuturgar-dan-Ghazni), and Chitral (Panjab-Chitral-Badakhshan). Kabul and Kandahar were the centers where many routes converged and from which they stretched north and west, connecting Herat and other minor cities in northern Afghanistan with Mashhad, Merv, Bukhara, and Kashghar in eastern Turkestan. From all these main routes, smaller routes stretched in many directions so that all regions were connected with the urban centers [1] and through these with the world at large.

None of the routes was suitable for wheeled traffic. Nor were all passable throughout the year, because of snowfall in the winter. Only the Khybar route was fit for camels all the year round, but the caravans generally avoided this route because of its brigandage and lack of security. Except for carriages drawn by horses for the convenience of passengers in cities, wheeled traffic for commercial goods did not exist in Afghanistan. Goods were carried by camels, horses, ponies, and donkeys. Trade was, in consequence, slow, especially when it had to be carried through passes. It took, for instance, twenty days for a caravan or *qafila* to reach Herat from Kandahar[2] and three months to go from Quetta to Mashhad by way of Kandahar and Herat. Merchants had to wait for a fixed date to dispatch their goods. First, a date for the dispatch of a *qafila* was fixed; then, merchants determined the amount they intended to send. Because of the insecurity and the long intervals between the dispatches caravans were large. In the 1830s, for instance, one caravan going from Kabul to Turkestan was made up of 1,600 camels, 600 horses, and 2,000 people.[3] Sometimes one firm alone employed from 2,000 to 3,000 animals for the carriage of goods, between Peshawar and Kabul.[4] All caravans were accompanied by armed guards, since they were open to attack in the Khybar area by Pashtuns (mainly the Afridays), in the Jigdalik area by Ghilzays, in the Bamian area by Dehzangi Hazaras, and, beyond that, between Saighan and Kahmard by Shaykh 'Ali Hazaras. The Lakai Uzbeks on the banks of the Oxus also occasionally raided on the road between Khulm and Mazar. In fact, all main roads before 1880 were frequently infested by organized robbers.[5]

Trade in the urban areas was largely in the hands of the Hindus and Jews. Since as zimmis both were unable to participate in other activities trade was, in fact, the only profession left to them. Also, since the Muslims were prohibited by the Quran from lending money at interest, the Hindus found it profitable to engage in banking activities and money lending. As a consequence, the Hindus everywhere formed a wealthy but despised and humiliated section of the community.[6] Hindu merchants were found in large numbers in all cities and market towns to the south of the Hindu Kush; some were found even in cities to the north of it. Concerned with the safety of their capital they were purely a commercial group.

Among the Muslims, those engaged in trade were the Tajiks, Qizilbashes, and Parachas, the latter a mercantile group living in Kabul as well as Peshawar. Of the Pashtuns it was said, although with much exaggeration, that "The mass of the nation are devoted to arms or plunder." Although it is correct to say that the Pashtuns were, as stated, men of the sword and landed property and that they left commerce to others; yet even among them some were engaged in trading activities. The Pashtun *powindas* are an obvious example; of their commercial activities it was said that "The severity of mountain winter and the insecurity of the commercial roads have given rise to a peculiar class of Afghan traders called Povindas. They possess large numbers of camels. Some are merchants, whilst others are merely carriers or retail agents."[7] Before 1862 every year about 9,400 such agents and traders descended into India in the winter with about 35,000 camels.[8] In addition, every year "hundreds of the Kakar tribe from the Boree valley" by custom collected the wild asafoetida in the hills about Herat and Farah and took it to India for sale.[9] Also, Babi Pashtuns in the south of Kandahar and Sayyeds were engaged in commercial activities.[10] By and large in Afghanistan commerce was held in rather high esteem, but only Muslim merchants were reckoned among "the upper classes of the society."[11] In the reign of Amir ʾAbd al-Rahman, Kabul Muslim merchants considered themselves a "privileged class" of equal rank with the Muhammadzays.[12] This thinking probably had something to do with the fact that members of the royal dynasty had engaged in trade in the past. In the reign of Amir Dost Muhammad, for instance, a significant number of his brothers and nephews invested their capital in trade with India and Turkestan carried on by their agents (*gomashta*). Mainly because of this royal tradition traders were protected from oppression by the officials (*kardars*) and others; the only extortion to which they were subjected was the imposition on them of an enormous duty by the over-valuation of their goods by the customs officials.[13]

In every region there were special market days. Once or twice a week customers thronged the bazars. As happened in most Asian countries, periodic fairs for the sale of commodities were held in Afghanistan. This system existed in full force in the regions north of the Hindu Kush, although it was also known in the Kabul area.[14] A description of Tashqurghan may well illustrate the marketing situation of a flourishing city in Afghanistan. There, bazars were held every Monday and Thursday and, in addition to the produce of Bukhara and India, there was a considerable market in livestock. Horses, mules, cows, goats, and asses were assembled in one quarter for sale. Cotton goods, cloth, and silk-stuff came from India; tanned leather, raw cotton, hides, and wood for fuel from Turkestan; grapes, raisins, pistachio nuts, pomegranates, dried plums from the countryside. Rock salt, Russian boots, indigenous dyes, and indigo from India were exposed, together with chogas from Chitral and raw wool from Badakhshan. Printed chintzes, quilts, and turbans were also brought from Russian Turkestan and coarse saddlery from Kabul was much in demand. One section of the bazar was set aside for the sale of melons, which were raised in large quantities in the neighborhood.[15]

In cities and fairs smaller merchants and peddlers purchased goods and carried them either on their own backs or by animals to remote places, where trade was also conducted in barter. Before their pacification Kafiristan and the Hazarajat were the regions where trade in barter was most prevalent. Of the Hazaras and Aimaqs Arthur Conolly has observed: "Neither among Hazaras nor Aimaks is money current, and sheep form the prime standard of barter with the traders. . . . These merchants establish a friendly understanding with chiefs of different districts, to whose forts they repair and open shops, giving their hosts two and a half yards of coarse narrow cotton cloth for the value of each sheep received in barter; and being furnished, till their bargains are concluded, with straw for their beasts, and generally bread for themselves and their people."[16] Even in remote areas in Afghanistan trade articles were taken. Into the Hazarajat, for example, traders from Herat, Kandahar, and Kabul brought turbans, coarse cotton cloths and chintzes, tobacco, felt and carpet dyes, iron spades and plough ends, molasses, and raisins. Uzbek merchants brought similar articles from their land, with a little rice, cotton, and salt, and, occasionally, horses, all of which they preferred to exchange for slaves. On the other hand, the articles that the Hazaras themselves took to market were women and men, oxen, cows, sheep, ghee, some woven woolens, and patterned carpets; the last two were made from the produce of their flocks, for they exported no raw wool. They also furnished lead and sulphur.[17] In Kafiristan, too, merchandise (woolen goods, cotton pieces, salt, iron) was bartered for hides, honey, sheep, goats, and slaves (from among the *baris*), and peddlers from all the surrounding areas, even as far away as Peshawar, could enter the region in time of peace. The principal peddlers with the Kafirs were from among the Shaykhs (Kafirs converted to Islam), the Isma'ili Shi'as of Munjan, and the Gabars of Kunar.[18]

As noted trade in Afghanistan in the reign of Amir 'Abd al-Rahman suffered much and many merchants became bankrupt. One reason for this was the fall in agricultural production, as has already been discussed in the preceding chapter. The civil war also disrupted the production of manufactured goods; but of more far-reaching consequence were the amir's treatment of merchants and his trade policies.

Although the merchants had not opposed the amir as the sardars and elders had, the amir systematically squeezed the merchants and wealthy people and persons with whom the rich had deposited money before they had either been killed in wars or fled the country. In 1883, the amir forced several bankers of Kabul to deliver 150,000 rupees alleged to have been deposited with them by the former Mustaufi Habib Allah and the late Na'ib Muhammad 'Alam Khan.[19] A famous Kabul merchant 'Abd al-Majid was fined 40,000 rupees for the same charge.[20] In Kandahar debts outstanding against merchants and officials were demanded without any proof.[21] In fact, wealthy people were compelled to deliver any money in their possession that was said to have been the property of the exiled sardars. In addition, they were fined for their failure to volunteer to deliver the money.[22] In recovering the so-called deposits the amir was "exhausting his ingenuity in devising means of extracting money from his wealthier subjects."[23] The means commonly applied was the forgery of letters alleged to have been written by the exiled sardars.[24] This practice continued periodically for the first decade of the amir's reign. During three months of 1890, for instance, 160,000 rupees were recovered from merchants and officials and deposited in the state treasury.[25] In addition, merchants were sometimes asked to make donations for providing medals to troops engaged in wars.[26] Such donations were in addition to large presents that Kabul merchants, following the example of government officials, offered to the amir.[27] Those merchants whose annual income exceeded 1,000 rupees a year were also made to pay 5 percent of their profit as *zakat* to the state.[28] The British agent observed, "If this state of things [confiscation] continues no money will be left with anybody in the whole of Afghanistan, and Government coffers will overflow with money."[29] A result of this highhandedness was that some principal merchants became bankrupt, while many others left Kabul for Bukhara and other regions.[30]

Merchants with medium-sized operations who kept shops in principal cities were likewise hit hard in the reign of the amir. Since these merchants did not possess large sums, the amir's policy was directed at their shops and the incomes from these shops. In 1884, he ordered that shopkeepers should pay one month's income of their shops every year and that this arrangement was to be permanent and retroactive from 1881.[31] In 1890 all shops in the city of Maimana,[32] in the province of Turkestan, and in the Murad Khani section of Kabul were declared state property.[33] It is not known whether this order was applied throughout the country, but the principle that stated that owners must produce deeds of ownership if they claimed their estates applied to shops as well as to lands. Already in Kandahar shopkeepers were deserting the city. In 1884, eighty of them, who were probably Hindus, moved to Quetta and other places.[34] As a consequence of this new government policy many shopkeepers and traders became bankrupt[35] and trade in Afghanistan began to dwindle away.[36] In the background was, of course, the poverty of consumers whose purchasing power had fallen sharply, because they were "robbed . . . of their wealth."[37] Also, for fear of confiscation, those with whom money had been left did not bring it forth.[38] As was the custom in Afghanistan, people preferred to bury their money and so kept it out of circulation.

During the second decade of his reign the amir, on the one hand, supported merchants by granting them loans and, on the other hand, established government monopolies on the sale of major items of trade. Merchants never again, during the reign of the amir, regained their lost position, mainly because the field of activity for traders was reduced and the Afghan state, for the first time, entered the field of trade not on the basis of free competition with merchants but by monopolizing the sale of major items of trade.

Actually the amir first ordered loans (*taqawi*) for traders in 1888.[39] But until after the Hazara War nothing more was heard about the order. The question was taken up again in 1893. In 1894 alone, in Kandahar one million rupees were sanctioned as loans to merchants.[40] For merchants of Kabul and Turkestan somewhat smaller amounts were sanctioned. A loan of from 5,000 to 50,000 rupees was sanctioned to be paid to an individual merchant in accordance with his means, position, and character.[41] Merchants were at first required to give security to the state, but later this requirement was dropped. No time limit was fixed for merchants to repay the borrowed capital, but the government reserved the right to demand its repayment at any time.[42] As to the amount of interest charged, reports are conflicting. Writing in 1893, Dr. John Gray, the amir's physician, held that should a Kabuli wish to start business and not have sufficient money, he could apply to the amir, who, for a certain number of years, would lend him, without interest, a sum sufficient for his purpose.[43] Sultan Mahomed states that the loans were without interest on the capital[44] which is true but does not go far enough. Subsequent writers have taken this to mean that the whole transaction was interest free.[45] In fact, it was not, but the interest was charged on profit and not on the capital itself, which was to be safe regardless of what happened to the business. This kind of partnership in the profit, called *muzaribat*, was sanctioned by Islam and was quite common in Afghanistan.

According to Fayz Muhammad, the official historian, a number of Kabul merchants, who applied for loans, undertook to offer a "present" of 5 percent on the borrowed capital to the state.[46] He also adds that in three years the state doubled the capital it advanced to merchants and that resources for this capital came out of tax levied on the trade the merchants transacted. This procedure seems impossible unless the state had exacted a higher rate of interest than reports from other sources seem to indicate. In 1894, the amir decreed that those merchants who wanted loans should pay two-thirds of their profit to the state.[47] On these terms merchants showed reluctance to receive loans, fearing the government would demand the money too soon to make the transaction profitable. Also, because of government interference in trade in general and the high rate of taxation, they were reluctant to do business with the government.[48] It is not known how many merchants received loans. In 1896 arrangements were made whereby the profit made on the borrowed capital was to be divided evenly between merchants and the state, as was required by the practice of *muzaribat*. From then on the number of borrowers increased.

Other measures that the amir took for the promotion of internal trade included the stationing of a chief of merchants (*tajir bashi*) in every province and the construction of caravanserais along the major roads and in cities.[49] The amir also discontinued the practice of issuing new copper coins in Kandahar, where customarily twice a year new coins had been issued. Since the new coins invalidated the old ones altogether, the custom caused bankruptcy among merchants and hampered trade.[50] Whether the amir abolished interprovincial tolls, as Hamilton[51] and Gregorian[52] assert, is doubtful. In a report to his government, Henry Baker, U.S. consul at Bombay, states that in Afghanistan "On most classes of goods there are also octroi tolls and other special provincial taxes."[53] Unless it can be otherwise established the case for the amir's imposition of interprovincial tolls weighs stronger than does that for their abolition. Such tolls fit well into the amir's system of administration, especially his financial policies, which were aimed at increasing the direct income of the state. For this reason, in the amir's reign the number of toll posts and the rates of dues on import and export were increased.

There is no doubt that in the amir's reign trade was made secure from brigandage. The inhabitants of a region were made accountable not only for banditry, but also for any plundering of caravans in their regions. This accountability contributed greatly to the promotion of trade, but merchants, whether trading inside or outside the country, were still required to obtain passports, as were nonmerchants.

External Trade
The establishment of government monopolies in trade was accompanied by a protectionist policy. This policy, and the amir's rigid fiscal policies, contributed to a fall in trade. In addition, the Russian protectionist policy in central Asia and the imposition by the Afghan government of heavy tolls on transit goods led to a considerable reduction in the volume of international trade, and Afghanistan, thus, lost its traditional role as intermediary between central Asia and India.

The amir argued that because his subjects were poor, the state was obliged to establish monopolies and to lend loans to merchants for the promotion of trade.[54] In fact, because trade was profitable and because at that time all countries of the area used commercial transactions as political weapons,[55] the amir did not intend to leave trade to the merchants alone. He welcomed the suggestion that government monopolies be established when it came from a certain ghee-seller, Muhammad Afzal, who was also the amir's newswriter in Kandahar.[56] At the same time the amir did not conclude trade agreements with other countries, presumably because he intended to have a free hand in the external trade of Afghanistan and in spite of the fact that from time to time agents of Britain and Russia made overtures for free commerce with Afghanistan.[57] He also did not permit the stationing of foreign commercial agents in Afghanistan in spite of the fact that his own agents were stationed in Bukhara, Mashhad, Peshawar, and Bombay.

The first steps with regard to monopolies were taken in the mideighties. Initially, the sale of almonds, lambskins (karakul), wools, and carpets was monopolized and soon afterward, the manufacture of gunpowder, soap, and candles was added. The monopoly of wools and lambskins was temporarily abandoned following the boycott of lambskins by the merchants of Bukhara and Mashhad where many thousands of them had been sent.[58] This failure, however, did not deter the amir, and he soon afterward extended the monopoly to the sale of asafoetida, which grew wild in Herat, Dasht-i-Kafir Qal'a, Gulran, Karatipa, and other places. Customarily, every spring, one thousand Kakar traders from Kakaristan collected asafoetida in Herat and, after paying a light rent for the land on which it had grown and a small tax to government authorities in Herat and Kandahar, exported it by three hundred camels to India, where they sold it at a high price. In 1890 the Kakars were told either to pay half of the proceeds to the government or to sell asafoetida directly to it. The Kakars did not agree and gave up their collection and sale forever.[59] From 1890 onward the government monopoly was widely extended. It came to include the sale of dried fresh fruits, ghee, pistachio, edible pine nuts, tobacco,[60] salt, postins, opium, sugar, *baraks*, timber, and sheep. In fact it became so extensive that not much was left for private merchants to trade in. In 1901 in Herat, for instance, the only articles left for traders were rice, wool, and a few edibles.[61]

The introduction of monopoly did not mean that the government purchased goods from the producers and sold them abroad through its agents. After the fiasco of the lambskins monopoly, the government refrained from taking over the management of a whole transaction, which would have increased government expenses. Instead the sale of monopolized items, such as pistachio nuts and asafoetida, was farmed out. No one but the contractors was allowed to sell the asafoetida of Herat and the pistachio nuts of northern Afghanistan, which were farmed out for 70,000 rupees[62] and 20,000 rupees,[63] respectively, per annum. Similarly, the sale of goatskins and the monopoly of sugar and "other articles" were leased out.[64] In 1895, trade in the monopolized items of Herat and Kandahar was farmed out to "local merchants."[65] As has been pointed out in chapter 4, the rate of the contract was, as a rule, increased every year, sometimes by 50 percent in excess of the former year. Wool, the most important item of trade in Herat, was exported to Panjdeh. Sometimes it was sold to Herat merchants at double its original price. For the sale of fruits, a different arrangement was made. Fresh and dried fruits were customarily taken to markets in northern India. Usually every spring Peshawar merchants advanced large sums of money to *kuchis* who took the commodities there in the autumn and winter.[66] This arrangement had the effect of placing a fruit monopoly in the hands of the Peshawar merchants and the *kuchis*. In order to deprive Peshawar brokers of their hold over the trade of fruits the amir in 1892 granted the monopoly of all kinds of fruits for export to Peshawar to a certain Nur Muhammad Tarakay for 1,200,000 rupees a year. The change, however, had a much wider implication. In theory Nur Muhammad was supposed to purchase the fruits from the merchants at the price of the day and to sell them "at the price agreed upon between both parties."[67] In reality, however, he and his agents compelled the merchants to sell them goods at such prices as they thought fit. If they did not want to purchase a particular item themselves, they imposed a special tax on it and only after this taxation could its owner sell it elsewhere.[68] Also, these agents charged the merchants high brokerage and weighing fees. Consequently, the profit of the *kuchis* and the Kabul merchants was slashed and they paid little to the original producers. Prices that had hitherto been fixed by the supply and demand of a free market were determined by the amir's agents, much to the latter's advantage. Smuggling began to increase and to combat it the amir sent agents to Baluchistan and the Panjab to levy taxes on goods that the Afghan merchants had exported there.[69] Even though the value of fruits exported to India fell as a result of smuggling from nearly 1,300,000 rupees in 1889–1890 to 763,752 rupees in 1891–1892, the amir continued his policy.[70] Neither the complaints of the *kuchis* and the Kabul merchants nor the representation of Mortimer Durand and the British agent persuaded him to give up the monopoly. It remained in force until late 1901 when the amir's son and successor declared that there would be no more monopolies and that trade would be free.[71]

With regard to the export of foodstuffs and certain other goods the amir's policy was prohibitory. When soap was produced in Kabul workshops (1893) and salt extracted in Balkh (1896), the amir prohibited the import of both items into Afghanistan. To carry the salt from Balkh, instead of importing it from Kohat in India, the *kuchis* were exempted from paying toll for the first year and then were to pay two rupees for each camel loaded with salt instead of six as they had when their beasts had been loaded with other commodities. The export of tobacco was also prohibited and a snuff factory was set up in Kabul. Owing to the development of local tanneries international trade in leather suffered.[72] Horses, sheep, camels, and cows were not allowed to be exported.[73] Likewise, the export of ghee and grain was banned, although at one point the amir ordered the export of wheat to Russia, arguing that the Afghan government and people would suffer much if wheat was not sold to the Russians.[74]

Toll posts along the border and main roads were increased. Between Kandahar and India alone the total number of new and old toll posts reached thirty-two. From Kabul to Peshawar there were five toll posts —one each in Buthkhak, Gandamak, Surkhpul, Jalalabad, and Dakka— an increase of one from the former days. In these posts three kinds of tolls were levied on goods destined abroad: the old tolls, the new tolls known as *goshi*, and another known by the name of *rawanagi*. In addition, an escort tax (*badraqagi*) was imposed. Kandahar merchants were, however, exempt from paying the last two taxes. The total amount of tax levied on, say, a camel load, is not known, but the *goshi* tax alone was four rupees a load.[75] Merchants complained that the taxes were higher than they had been at any time previously.

Because of this taxation and the ban on certain items, smuggling continued on all fronts, in spite of the increased number of toll posts and the rigidity that characterized the administration of the amir. In

1893, for instance, from Mazar alone, two thousand horses were smuggled to Panjab via Chitral, in spite of the fact that that route had been declared closed to merchants. Seeing that a total ban on the export of horses was not possible, the amir modified his earlier order to a partial ban. From then on the export of stallions was allowed but that of mares was prohibited under severe penalty.[76] Although, like Badakhshani traders who were prohibited from trading in the Pamirs, Herat merchants were not allowed to trade in Russian territories,[77] the Taimanis, Taimuris, Jamshidis, and Hazaras of Qal'a-i-Nao, went daily to Panjdeh with raisins, ghee, skins, and pistachio nuts.[78] Perhaps a larger volume of goods was smuggled out by the Jews of Herat, who were shrewd speculators and the main dealers in grain and who traded with Bukhara through Murghab, Panjdeh and Merv.[79] Because Panjdeh depended on grain from Herat and Maimana, the Russians, for their part, provided an additional incentive to Afghan exporters. In 1896, they exempted Afghan merchants from paying customs dues in their territory on grain, cattle, and ghee.[80] Along the border with India, smugglers, with the connivance of tax collectors, took goods on hundreds of camels through the Mohmand country, usually to Peshawar.[81] Consequently, customs duties on export goods (items not specified) then fell considerably. Hearing from merchants that the "great fall" of trade was due to heavy taxes, the amir, in 1899, reduced the rate of charge by one-fourth,[82] but exports to India and central Asia were still sluggish since the amir, for political reasons, ordered merchants to boycott British railways at New Chaman and Russian railways at Kushk.[83]

In its imports Afghanistan was a market and a transit point for goods mainly of Russian, British, Indian, and Bukharan origin. After the Russian domination of central Asia British and Indian goods, with the notable exceptions of tea, muslin, and indigo, were banned from entering Russia's markets. Afghanistan itself also did not remain an exclusive market for British and Indian goods, although politically the country was part of the sphere of British influence. Russian goods dominated Afghan markets to the north of the Hindu Kush and British goods those to the south of it, but the volume of the British goods was four times greater than that of the Russian.

Among the principal Indian firms engaged in importing into Afghanistan and central Asia were those of Ahmad Gul, Mir Ahmad, Ilahi Bakhsh of Peshawar, and Makhad and Shahpur of Rawalpindi, which had agencies in Kabul, Mazar, and Khulm. Merchants from Afghanistan and Bukhara too imported goods from India. Among the smaller merchants were the sayyeds of Pisheen, the Kakars of Kakaristan [84] and those from Bajaur and other independent areas. Those from independent areas traded with Badakhshan, and beyond, by the more difficult Chitral route and brought tea, piece goods, and indigo in return for horses, cumin, orpiment, antimony, and postins.[85] These merchants suffered much, since the amir directed them to use only the Kabul-Peshawar route so that they would have to pay tolls.[86] The main commodities which Indian merchants sent to and through Afghanistan consisted of piece goods (European and Indian), spices, indigo, leather, metals, sugar, tea (foreign and Indian), and drugs. From Afghanistan they imported raw silk (which they also brought from Bukhara), wool, felt, postins, furs, horses, fruits, opium, and chogas. Before 1862 about 182 items of goods worth about 1,473,330 Indian rupees were annually exported from India to Afghanistan and central Asia, while in the reverse trade the figures for the number of goods were 130 and for their value 1,945,420 Indian rupees.[87]

Indian trade with Afghanistan and central Asia in the reign of the amir declined progressively. In the background was the competition of Russian against Indian and British goods. Thanks to her domination of central Asia, Russia drove British and Indian goods out of the region's markets by monopolizing them for her own goods. Only tea (including green Chinese tea exported to the area by Indian merchants), indigo, muslin, for which there was a great demand, and certain other items (not specified) that were needed in Russian factories were allowed to be exported.[88] English goods sent to Bukhara via Afghanistan were valued at £750,000 annually. Russian goods had been rare in 1873, but after the Russian railway line reached Bukhara these commodities made great progress and drove out English manufactured goods, except muslin, from central Asian markets.

Merchandise from India, dispatched to Bukhara via Kandahar, Herat, and Kerki, amounted to 3,600 camel loads or 1,025 tons in 1881 but sank in 1884 to 1,700 camel loads or 490 tons. By 1888 trade in these goods (except muslin) with Bukhara vanished altogether.[89] The few items that were allowed to be sent to Bukhara were, in addition, made subject to exorbitant dues in both Afghanistan and Bukhara. It is reported that in Bukhara a rupee per ser of tea was levied in any of the five toll posts set up between the Oxus and that city. In addition a similar tax was levied by the Russian authorities.[90] In 1892, the toll was reported to have been increased to 75 percent on tea and indigo and 200 percent on muslin. A little later in Afghanistan the total amount of transit duty levied on each camel load of tea from Peshawar to the Oxus was 244 rupees[91] and on each camel load of cotton goods, 57. Obviously, even in Afghanistan the new rate was considerably higher than that levied before the amir came to power and that was 2.50 percent on the value of the transported goods.[92] In terms of load per camel of transported goods this toll from Peshawar to Bukhara via Kabul, before 1862, was just over 41 rupees.[93] In the reign of Amir ʾAbd al-Rahman government officials, motivated by self-interest, interfered in the affairs of merchants and the new fiscal policy required them not to remit pure silver currency abroad. All this hit the import and export merchants hard. In consequence, all, except two principal, firms suspended business with Afghanistan and sent goods to central Asia[94] through Bombay, Bandar-i-ʾAbbas, and Mashhad. Also, some Persian merchants who used to import goods from India into eastern

Persia through Quetta and Herat followed suit. Kandahar merchants, in fact, were the first to send "large quantities of indigo to Meshed by way of Bandar Abbas."[95] The Quetta–Herat route, which except for the exorbitant tolls, was much cheaper and shorter than the Bandar-i-'Abbas–Mashhad route, was for several years abandoned.[96] The amir was still unwilling to reduce the tolls, when requested to do so by the British agent, who was acting on instructions from the government of India; the amir refused on the grounds that the agent was interfering in the internal affairs of Afghanistan, arguing that, "I can not abolish the custom which my forefathers [have] established."[97] Leslie Rogers complained that his company, which exported through merchants 30,000 maunds of green tea annually to Afghanistan and central Asia, suffered much and asked for an interview with the amir.[98] Apparently, the interview was not granted. Next year, however, the representative of Walsh, Lovett and Co. succeeded, probably through correspondence, in convincing the amir of the profitability of free trade with minimum taxes. Only then did the amir reduce transit dues, which was to the satisfaction of merchants, who then undertook to send all their goods to central Asia through Afghanistan and to abandon the Mashhad route.[99] The loss to Afghanistan in transit tolls all these years appeared great. Figures are not available, but as early as 1881, when the Russian authorities imposed restrictions on the importation of goods from India to central Asia, the amir complained that this action would cause Afghanistan a loss of some five to six lakhs of rupees a year.[100]

The principle of free trade with the minimum tax imposed on it, however, did not apply as far as trade with India was concerned. Customs duties on export goods have already been discussed. Import duties during the brief period in office of Mir Ahmad Shah, as head of the Kabul octroi department (1880–1883) were not high. But his successor Jan Muhammad, on his own initiative, imposed sixty kinds of seemingly small taxes on merchandise. Contrary to expectation, this imposition of small taxes caused a slight reduction in revenues (which had been about eleven lakhs of rupees a year), mainly because of the diversion of transit trade and a considerable reduction in imported goods.[101] A tax of 199 rupees was levied on a camel load of Chinese tea from Dakka to Kabul and 96 on indigo.[102] Dues on piece goods dispatched by the shortest route to Ghazni were, likewise, high—eighteen rupees on each camel load at the Shuturgardan Pass, and upon arrival at Ghazni a forfeiture of one piece out of every forty and a further eight rupees.[103] The dues were, of course, realized on goods whether imported by foreign or Afghan merchants. There is, however, no doubt that the amir tried to discourage the former and to encourage the latter out of his belief that the little trade that existed in Afghanistan was carried on by foreign merchants and that "This impoverished the country, because these foreigners sent the money that they made, over and above what they required for trading purposes, to their own lands."[104] To combat this, the amir subsidized Afghan merchants and banned the remittance of pure silver currency abroad, but trade with India declined progressively, as the following figures indicate. Goods *exported* from India to and through Afghanistan were valued at:

1882–1883	5,293,529 (Indian rupees)
1883–1884	4,783,587
1884–1885	4,409,130 [105]

The value of goods of Indo–Afghan (export and import) trade:

1886–1887	8,751,184 (Indian rupees)
1887–1888	7,833,296
1888–1889	6,981,132 [106]

Export and import figures given by Hamilton for the last eight years of the amir's reign are exceedingly low and do not follow the general sequence, but for the most part, these figures, like others, indicate a steady decline in Indo–Afghan trade.

1892–1893	1,363,436 (Indian rupees)
1893–1894	1,258,067
1894–1895	1,036,617
1895–1896	1,138,799
1896–1897	1,086,482
1897–1898	876,832
1898–1899	1,105,641
1899–1900	1,156,405 [107]

For 1900–1901 Hamilton's figures are over ten and one half million; these show an incredible jump over the previous year.[108]

By contrast, Russo-Afghan trade showed a slight improvement during the reign of the amir, but the overall volume of Afghan trade with Russia and Bukhara was much less than that of Indo-Afghan trade. Russian goods dominated the markets of northern Afghanistan almost to the exclusion of British goods.

As a result of her domination of central Asia, Russia, by 1889, controlled the area's markets. As late as 1885 one Russian company had its agents in Bukhara, but by 1889 there were, in Bukhara, branch houses of at least a dozen Russian firms of first importance, as well as a branch of the Imperial Russian Bank.[109] This commercial dominance partly reflected the official policy of Russia to dominate the markets of northern Afghanistan, Khurasan, and Seistan.[110] As her finance minister declared, "Northern Afghanistan presents a market in which Russian goods find a ready sale, and compete successfully with Anglo-Indian and other European merchandise."[111] For the promotion of their trade in Afghanistan, Russian merchants appointed Muslims of Tashkent as their agents, paid them passage money, octroi duty, and carriage and food expenses with 5 percent commission on sale of commodities that these agents brought to Balkh, Badakhshan, Herat, Kandahar, and Kabul.[112] The Turkman merchants of Merv and Panjdeh also carried on a constant traffic with the markets of Herat and Maimana.[113] For their part, Herat Jews imported Russian merchandise to Herat in large caravans.[114] Russian Armenians, too, were engaged in trade with Seistan and Sabzwar.[115] From these main markets, Russian goods found their way to smaller towns and villages. In 1889, when the Russian railway line of Merv-Panjdeh was extended to the Kushkinski post on the Afghan border, Russian trade increased considerably. Owing to the proximity of Russian territories, the amir, when in Mazar in 1890, preferred Russian goods to be imported into northern Afghanistan. The most important single factor in establishing the ascendancy of Russian manufactured goods over British goods in northern Afghanistan was their cheapness, although the Russian items were less durable than the British.

This cheapness was owing partly to the comparative cheapness of transport from European Russia, because the Trans-Caspian and Orenburg-Tashkent railway lines carried Russian merchandise at a specially low rate[116] and partly to the lighter rate of customs dues in northern Afghanistan. For instance, a camel load of Russian goods paid only 20 tangas (6 rupees and 8 shahis) if sold in Mazar. On the way to Kabul, it was subject to dues of 15 rupees and 6 shahis if taken via the new road of Bamian-Charikar, and 21 rupees if taken by the old road of Bamian-Argandeh. On entering Kabul it was, in addition, subject to one-fortieth (or 2.50 percent) ad valorem tax.[117] British goods if taken to Turkestan were subject to an assessment of 57 rupees a camel load. Thus Russian goods had the advantage north of the Hindu Kush and British goods south of it. The advantage was increased when the amir, sometime in 1889, lifted restrictions on trade with Russia that he had imposed following the Russian occupation of Panjdeh. Russian goods (piece goods, sugar, iron, trunks, drugs, matches, and leather) then increased in northern Afghanistan and British goods decreased correspondingly.[118] From October 1888 (when the amir arrived in Turkestan) up to May 1890 the value of trade transacted between Afghanistan and Russian territories amounted to five million rubles.[119] Other than this no reliable statistics on trade between Russian territories and Afghanistan are available. Gregorian's figures on Russo-Afghan trade for 1888–1900, taken from both *Statesman's Yearbook* and the Soviet scholar Babakhojzaaevis, are unreliable. Gregorian does not say whether the two sources he has quoted agree with each other. In addition, his peak figures are those for 1888 (7,927,838 rubles),[120] but during that year Russo-Afghan trade, which was still subject to restrictions, was severely hampered as a result of the revolt of Sardar Muhammad Ishaq. In Curzon's words, "While during the autumn of last year [1888], when the rebellion of Ishak Khan agitated Turkistan communication by caravan between Kabul and Bukhara ceased altogether."[121] Furthermore, Gregorian's figures show a downward trend in Russo-Afghan trade, just as there was a declining trend in Indo-Afghan trade. This is also incorrect, because, as stated below, during the second decade of the amir's reign Russo-Afghan trade improved.[122] Customs dues on goods exported from Afghanistan to Russian territories were reduced by Russian authorities by 50 percent and the amir granted a rebate on goods purchased by Afghan merchants in Russian territories that was equal to the tax levied on them.[123] Also, unlike Afghan exports to India, which always lagged behind imports, Afghan exports, especially in lambskins, to Russian territories, exceeded her imports, a profitable situation for Afghanistan in expanding her trade with the latter. Since most Afghan trade was transacted with India and since this trade was progressively declining, it is incorrect to conclude, as a number of Afghan writers have,[124] that the volume of trade in Afghanistan in the reign of Amir ꜥAbd al-Rahman increased. It is also incorrect to hold the view, as Ghobar does, that in the reign of the amir "the promotion of foreign trade turned Afghanistan into a favourable market for international capitalism."[125] On the contrary, in this period internal, as well as external and transit, trade declined; merchants were squeezed; and internal markets shrank, in spite of the advance of *taqawi* to traders and the suppression of brigandage. One can speak of a trade improvement during the second decade only by comparison with the first decade of the amir's reign.

The Financial System

Currency
During the nineteenth century and before, Afghanistan, like other countries of the area, had a complicated, nonstandardized, and nondecimal system of currency. Foreign currencies were also in circulation in Afghanistan. In the reign of the amir, the Afghan currency was standardized, and began to be minted only in Kabul, but it lost its value considerably, owing to repeated debasement and recurring inflation.

The unit of Afghan currency was a rupee, but there were three kinds of rupees: Kabuli, Kandahari, and Herati. One Kabuli rupee was equal to 1.7 Kandahari rupees[126] and divided into 60 paisas and each paisa, into 10 dinars. A *kham* rupee (an "unripe" rupee, said of the Kandahari rupee), as opposed to a *pukhta* ("ripe" or Kabuli rupee), was an informal, nominal unit of account but was widely used and valued at 50 paisas. Different numbers of paisas made different subunits of a Kabuli rupee. For example, 30 paisas made 1 qiran; 20 paisas, 1 'abbasi (or tanga); 10 paisas, 1 sanar; and 5 paisas, 1 shahi. To express these equivalents in relation to 1 Kabuli rupee, 2 qirans, 3 'abbasis, 6 sanars, and 12 shahis each made 1 rupee. Twenty rupees made 1 toman. Except for

rupee (Kabuli)
2 qiran
3 'abbasis
6 sanars
12 shahis
60 paisas

paisas
1 qiran
1 'abbasi
1 sanar
1 shahi
10 dinars

paisas and shahis which were made of copper, these coins were made of pure silver. The qirans and tangas, though integrated into Afghan currency, were essentially Persian and Bukharan currencies. Other foreign coins current in Afghanistan were the Belgian ducat or Venetians (locally known as "boojaglee" or "boodkee"), Bukharan tilla, Russian ruble (known as "sours"), Chinese yamoos, Tabrizi toman, and, of course, Indian rupee (known as "kaldar"). The first two were gold coins and the rest were made of silver.[127]

Before 1880, dies were cut and coins struck by hand in Afghanistan. Although coins were designed and produced by skilled artisans, the pieces of metal used were not always of the same size and shape.[128] The Kabuli rupee was, for instance, an irregularly shaped and hand-stamped coin.[129] A skilled engraver spent long hours before he was able to design and execute each die. Even with the availability of silver bullion, the production of a large number of coins in a short time was not possible then. Coins were regularly issued in Kabul, Kandahar, Herat, and occasionally in other places. The last handmade coins were issued in 1890 in Kabul, in Kandahar in 1889, and in Herat in 1888. In 1890 when a modern mint was set up in Kabul the provincial mints were closed. The amir declared, "for the future only new coins struck by the machinery lately erected at the headmint in Kabul will be allowed currency in Afghanistan."[130] The Kabuli rupee then gradually superseded the Kandahari and Herat rupees until in 1925 when, as a result of the adoption of the decimal system, 11 Kabuli rupees became equal to 10 new Afghanis, and each Afghani was divided into 100 puls.[131]

The minting machinery, consisting of three large machines, had been purchased from A. Slater Savil and Co. and put in the charge of an English specialist named McDermont, a former employee of the Calcutta mint, under whose supervision Kabul workmen learned to cut the die, erect the stamps, and strike off the coins.[132] The mint embarked first on the production of rupees and qirans and then on silver coins, paisas, shahis, and also gold. Gradually copper coins, especially paisas, replaced brass coins, and one-shahi and two-shahi coins ceased circulation. ʾAbbasis and sanars were also widely used. Amir ʾAbd al-Rahman's coinage, which was beautifully designed, became the basis for future coins. The biggest change that these machines made possible and that had far-reaching consequences on the economy as a whole was the result of their capacity for great production. They were then capable of producing from 40,000 pieces[133] to 120,000 pieces a day.[134] Annual production for the first year according to Hamid Hamidi was approximately ten million coins.[135] From this it appears that even the minimum capacity of the machines was not reached in that year. Still at that time this was the largest number of coins issued in Afghanistan in a single year. In time of necessity the mint was used to its fullest capacity. On such occasions it worked day and night without stopping.[136] This overproduction and the debasement of the money caused the Afghan currency to lose much of its value both at home and abroad.

Debasement of the Afghan currency was not the result of a deliberate devaluation of the Kabuli rupee to offset the adverse balance of trade in India; rather, it was the result of adulteration with baser metals. The ratio of debasement was not fixed but kept fluctuating. As early as 1884, qirans and rupees were adulterated with baser metals "by half of their weight."[137] Later, a Kabuli rupee was composed of seven shahis of silver and five of alloy.[138] Still later the ratio of copper to silver became one to eight. Because of the production of a large number of silver coins and the shortage of silver bullion there was a demand for silver. Since the celebrated silver mine of Panjshir was no longer in use, Afghanistan depended on silver from abroad. To keep a reasonably steady flow of silver into Afghanistan, the amir encouraged merchants to import silver from abroad in large quantities and declared it free of customs duties,[139] whereas in 1862 1.0 percent had been charged on its import and 1.5 percent on its export.[140] Through his agents, Martin and Co., the amir, in addition, purchased silver bullion from Europe.[141]

More important, in terms of their immediate effect on prices and trade, were the collection of foreign silver coins and the banning of the remittance of silver coins abroad. First, the amir prohibited dealing in silver and gold and ordered Hindu and Muslim merchants to send to the mint all the silver and gold they possessed,[142] presumably in return for Afghan money. Later, shopkeepers and money dealers were ordered to exchange their old rupees for new rupees[143] and to give three paisas extra for the new rupees. On this basis, efforts were made to collect the old silver coins for recoining purposes throughout Afghanistan. Martin claims that the amir had all the old silver coins collected and reissued with copper alloy.[144] After that, the amir ordered the collection of foreign silver currencies in circulation in Afghanistan. In Kandahar, where Indian rupees were expected to be found in large quantities, a special collector was given the task of procuring the Indian rupees with Kabuli and Kandahari rupees.[145] In Herat, Mashhad qirans and Indian rupees were collected and sent on to Kabul. If a man was known to possess any foreign currency and he had failed to take it to the mint for exchange with the Afghan currency in accordance with the order, his currency was confiscated and he was fined in addition.[146] Indian rupees were turned into Kabuli rupees first at the rate of 122 Kabuli rupees from 100 Indian and then 140 from 100. Still later, two rupees were made out of one qiran. The new Kabuli rupee, made by mixing copper with Persian qirans, had an unusual amount of alloy, since Persia at the time had also debased her coins.[147]

For two reasons the amir banned the remittance of silver currency abroad. India was Afghanistan's biggest trading partner and the latter had a large deficit with the former. The amir argued that because of the fineness of the Kabuli rupees the Indians melted them down for ornaments and Afghanistan, owing to the scarcity of silver, was bound to suffer. With the debasement of the Kabuli rupee, this kind of argument should have lost ground and the ban been lifted; but the amir was still unwilling to remove it mainly because, in spite of the amir's efforts, silver was not coming into Afghanistan.[148] The amir then continued the enforcement of his earlier order that "no cash should be allowed to go to Peshawer. I have closed the mint and I have no mines of silver in my country. If 40 or 50 lakhs [of rupees] go to Peshawer annually, what shall I do?"[149] Merchants were, however, allowed to send Russian and Chinese gold coins and, presumably, Bukharan tilla, to India instead of the rupees. They were told that if they wanted to remit the rupees to India they had to give the amir "the profit" they made on their remittance, in addition to their payment of certain transit duties.[150] Failing this, they were directed to barter merchandise for goods they imported to Kabul.[151] In view of the great disparity in value of import and export, trade on the basis of barter was out of the question for merchants of Indo-Afghan trade. Ultimately, the amir removed the ban on cash remittance abroad, but imposed a duty of 3 percent[152] in the belief that this would serve as a deterrent and that merchants would increase the volume of export from Afghanistan rather than accept cash duty.[153] At the same time duty on cash remittance inside Afghanistan was also levied but was subsequently abolished. Merchants were allowed to import silver coins into Afghanistan free of charge. Printed stamps were issued for cash remittance abroad, but since these stamps required merchants to disclose the total amount of their transaction they were hesitant to use them. Instead, they continued to carry on their business as before, by the use of *hundis* (bills of exchange).[154] Meanwhile, the amir imposed a fee of 6 percent on all cash remittance that passed through Afghanistan.[155]

This fee applied mainly to Indian merchants who dispatched merchandise to central Asia and remitted their cash through Afghanistan. Thereafter these merchants remitted their cash through Moscow, abandoning Afghanistan in the same manner as they had diverted the transit trade from Kabul and sent goods through Mashhad to central Asia. To combat this diversion the amir decided that a register of all merchandise intended for Bukhara should be made. He ordered that should the merchants not return the money and goods they received in exchange by the Kabul route within twelve months the transit fee would be charged on the merchandise. Whether this high transit duty was enforced is not certain. According to one report, the amir later made it optional for merchants to remit their cash from central Asia through either Moscow or Afghanistan.[156] It seems probable that in 1891 with the reduction of duty on merchandise, as described previously, the 6 percent duty on transit cash was lowered to 3 percent. This percentage was, in fact, the tax on cash remittance that continued until the end of the amir's reign.[157]

The debasement of the Afghan silver coins and the imposition first of the ban and later of a duty on cash remittance abroad had many effects. First, it created an inflation that continued for most of the amir's reign. People thought that the new silver coins were spurious and their market value fell gradually. One Kabuli rupee was, for instance, worth 9 sers of wheat flour in Kabul in May 1891. Ten years later in the same month its worth was reduced to 5.50 sers. Second, the ban on the remittance of the Indian rupee tended to paralyze Anglo–Afghan trade, since Afghan coinage was not current in India,[158] presumably, beyond Peshawar and Quetta. The subsequent cash remittance abroad, though still subject to tax, eased the trading situation; but, among other factors described earlier, it also contributed to the decline in the volume of export goods from India to Afghanistan. Third, perhaps the most obvious effect of the debasement was the widening fall in the rate of exchange between the Afghan and foreign currencies, as reflected in the steady decline of the Khybar tolls on goods exported to Afghanistan. For instance, as compared with the first quarter of 1887 the tolls in the first quarter of 1888 fell by 21 percent.[159] Before the amir came to power, Kabuli and Indian rupees were of equal value in Kabul, although the quantitative ratio of silver in the Indian rupee to that in the Kabuli rupee was six to five. Even so, people in Kabul hesitated to accept Indian rupees during the British stay in Afghanistan.[160] Indian rupees were then reissued as Kabuli rupees for circulation.[161] During the amir's reign steady decline began in the value of the Kabuli against the Indian rupee. In 1899, for instance, while the official rate of exchange was 2 Kabuli rupees for 16 annas or 80 paisas (a ratio of three to four)[162] the actual black market rate was two to one in favor of the Indian rupee.[163] The decline in value of the qirans against the ruble in Herat was, however, on a much smaller scale. One ruble that had been the equivalent of five qirans in Herat increased in value to 560 qirans during 1901. Also, a Kabuli rupee that had been worth 3 tangas in Afghanistan was reduced to 2 tangas and 0.50 miri or 11.50 annas in Bukhara in 1883.

Banking

Before the amir's reign, individual bankers in the main cities were exchanging money. For the most part, they were Hindus, who mixed trading with their regular banking activities and made large profits by negotiating bills of exchange. They also made large transactions connected with the fluctuations of the exchange.[164] Among the Muslims, particularly the Tajiks, bankers were also found.[165] In the amir's reign banking activities consisted mainly of the exchange of currencies and, thus, helped to further trade; but at no time was all surplus money in circulation. Perhaps the larger part of it was stagnant, because the tendency to hoard hard cash, which arose from insecurity and government exaction, was strong. Only government officials and influential wealthy people deposited their surplus money with the bankers, presumably on interest.

Information about banking activities by individual bankers in the reign of the amir is not available. Now and then references were made to them in connection with the probable unfavorable effects of the amir's financial policies. For example, the Hindu bankers of Kandahar[166] were forced to deliver the moneys that were said to have been deposited with them by officials of Amir Sher 'Ali Khan and the exiled sardars on the ground that these moneys were state property. The state, in the reign of the amir, performed some banking activities, although no separate bank was set up for this purpose by the government or foreign or private Afghan shareholders. The setting up of the first modern bank where private capital accumulated was to be a phenomenon of the future.

In 1885 the amir announced that the people should deposit all their capital in the government treasury. Traders were especially urged to and to keep back only two hundred rupees to carry on trade.[167] Apparently, there was no favorable response to this suggestion. For one thing, the prospective depositors were not promised any interest. In August 1896 when the wars were over and a period of tranquility began, the amir renewed his earlier appeal, but this time he gave out that the state would pay 2 percent interest annually on the money deposited. Depositors would be free, said the amir, to withdraw their money whenever they desired. He also impressed on them that their surplus money when deposited would be secure and safely transferred to their heirs. Again, the appeal fell on deaf ears. The fact was that people feared to do business with the government, especially when it came to depositing their money in such a novel enterprise where the money could be forfeited under any pretext. Also, the promised rate of interest was much lower than what was common in the country. Merchants, however, took advantage of transferring their money within the country and abroad through the state treasury. Remitting money from

Kabul to Peshawar and vice versa by state draft had begun in 1883.[168] Under this system, merchants sent their money to India through the state treasury and obtained drafts (*barats*) that were cashed in India by the amir's agents.[169] The state charged merchants for the dispatch of their money to India at a rate of 2 percent in 1883 and 3.25 percent in 1896.

The Raising of Capital and Its Investment

Before the amir's reign capital was raised by private individuals and invested through the agency of merchants and usurers. In the amir's reign the state also stepped in and led others in investing capital.

There is no information available to show the mechanism of raising capital for agriculture and industry in Afghanistan. The presumption is that the surplus outputs in both fields were invested in the land and through the agency of traders. In the predominantly agrarian Afghanistan attention was directed more to the land than to either trade or industry.[170] From time immemorial, land in Afghanistan had been a commercial commodity and subject to sale. The ancient custom of *wesh* or the periodic redistribution of land among clans and families, which did not allow its owners to dispose of it as a commodity but only to exploit it for a fixed period, was dying in nineteenth-century Afghanistan.[171]

The safest form of savings investment for the prosperous classes of the population, which included the officials (also the Muhammadzay sardars), mullas, merchants, and caravan leaders was to purchase land beyond the confines of the city and to turn it over to *dehqans* to work as sharecroppers.[172] On the eve of the amir's reign, in the fertile area of Jalalabad first-class land was sometimes sold for three hundred rupees a jarib, average land with a sufficient supply of water for two hundred rupees a jarib, and inferior land for from thirty to fifty rupees a jarib.[173]

The *kuchis'* investment of capital in the Hazara land after the opening of the Hazarajat is an example of an investment by nomadic traders in Afghanistan. To increase grazing lands for their flocks and herds the *kuchis*, after the pacification of the Hazarajat, slowly acquired legal rights to the land in the central uplands. It is reported that close to 20 percent of some of the area's land was owned by the *kuchis*, who acquired the land by their involvement in both trading and money lending. The Hazaras were made to work the poorer lands because of the Pashtun movements in the area.[174] Capital was frequently invested in the land not only as a permanent purchase but also as a temporary purchase in the form of a mortgage (*girawai*). In the latter case the buyers, in fact, acquired only the right to exploit the land and were required to return this right whenever their capital was repaid.

Among those who raised capital and invested it in either land or trade, usurers figured high. As noted earlier, the prohibition in the Quran against Muslims taking interest made most of the business of banking and usury fall into the hands of the Hindus, who lent money to the people at a high interest in Afghanistan;[175] but the Hindus preferred to invest capital in trade and banking rather than in land. Muslims also engaged in usury in spite of the Islamic prohibition. Needy small producers turned to usurers whenever a sudden misfortune, such as the loss of a cow or of a member of the family, befell them. As elsewhere in Afghanistan, in the Hazarajat too, usury was practiced. There in the 1830s an additional factor that drove a cultivator to the usurer was the exactions of the elders and their deputies. "These harpies" writes Josiah Harlan,

✤

luxuriate and fatten upon the cultivator, not unfrequently levying double and selling the surplus under the pretext of obstinacy on the part of the cultivator or ryott [*sic*], as he is called. By this means the ryott is driven to all means and every mode of defence and deprecation, flying ultimately, . . . to some usurer, when that indispensible may chance to be accessible, and paying willingly, . . . at least thirty-three percent to get rid of the vampire or a heavy bonus to buy off the application of a *bastinado* from the sole of the feet! . . . this is the "unknown system" which has existed for ages throughout the whole East.[176]

✤

Another common practice similar to usury was the advance of money by merchants and usurers to small producers before their crops were reaped. The borrowers paid them back in produce at a very cheap rate fixed by the moneylenders at the time of the transaction. An example may suffice. In Kandahar, Herat, and Hazarajat usurers customarily advanced credits for wool to nomads. In 1857 the advances made to nomads for one Kandahari mound of wool were only twelve annas, whereas the price of the same amount at the time of the shearing was one Indian rupee plus four annas. On the other hand, if the same amount of wool was taken at the time of the shearing on credit, the buyer had to pay four annas over and above the actual price.[177] The dominant form of capital remained the usurers' and merchants' capital, but it remained in many hands with no prospect for accumulation.

During the amir's reign, the largest single corporate institution that accumulated capital and invested it in trade and industry was the state itself. As already detailed in the previous chapter, except for taking over the land of the refugees and purchasing some tracts of land and a few *karezes* here and there, the amir did not take over the means of production as a whole. The principle of private property remained the cornerstone of the economy as before. Yet the amir in the name of the state accumulated capital, something which no Afghan ruler had done previously. The amir raised capital principally through revenue and the confiscation of wealth. Practically every person—whether a merchant, a landlord, or an official—who was known to have amassed money was deprived of it in the reign of the amir. The state directly and indirectly invested the accumulated capital in trade. The state purchased commodities through its agents directly from the producers

and sold them through the monopolies described previously. Indirectly, it advanced loans on profit to merchants and farmers and others. At
the same time, it invested a huge amount of capital in the Kabul workshops. By so doing the state extended its control over the economy
and fostered for the first time in Afghanistan what could be termed
state capitalism.

Transportation and Communication

In the amir's reign, as before, animals were the only means of transportation. The amir, for political reasons, did not introduce modern means
of transportation and communication but widened the old paths and
built a network of new roads throughout Afghanistan.

Because of the mountainous nature of Afghanistan, before the reign
of the amir there were "no man made roads in Afghanistan."[178] Even
in the plains of Turkestan only "a few ordinary paths" were in existence.[179] Until widened, even the widest road of all, the one which
ran between Kandahar and Kabul and Kandahar and Chaman, was not
fit for wheeled carriages. Neither were the existent roads maintained
properly. Only when a road became impassable was it repaired and,
then, not by or through the agency of government but by travelers for
their own convenience. Also, rivers were not bridged, but ferries of
floating skins did exist on some of them, a relic of older times.[180]

Nevertheless, all cities and regions were connected with each other
and with the cities in adjoining regions by roads that followed the passable but circuitous, rather than the difficult and straight, lines. Thus,
in addition to the bad and unsafe conditions of roads, they were long
and, thus, caused delays in movements of men, animals, commodities,
and ideas.

In the amir's reign the necessity of widening the old roads and con-
stucting the new ones arose first and foremost out of military considerations. The quick dispatch of army and provisions was considered
essential for pacifying the country and establishing the administration.
The improvement of interprovincial and transit trade through the construction of roads, though important, was of secondary significance.
Hence, the amir's declaration that everyone, particularly elders, should
consider work on roads as "Government business." This statement
was probably the first official pronouncement making the construction
of the new roads and improvement of the old ones and their maintenance a government responsibility.

Generally, building of the roads followed pacification of the country.
With a few exceptions, it was mainly during the second decade of the
amir's reign that a wide network of roads throughout the country was
built. First, all major cities were connected by roads with major villages and summer resorts in their environs. From the city of Kandahar
roads were, for instance, built from the Herat Gate to Kokaran, Topekhana Gate to Baba Wali, ʾId Gah to Kotal-i-Murcha, and Shikarpur
to Zakird, and to other villages frequented by the people. Newly con-

structed roads in Herat that connected the city with its environs were wide enough for the passage of two carriages at a time.[181] In 1883, the amir expressed satisfaction over the construction of roads in Afghanistan by the British during their last campaigns; these roads were said to have been "favourable to traffic."[182] These were, in fact, the roads between Kabul and its environs, Kabul and Jalalabad, and Kandahar and Quetta, all for military use.

In the amir's reign roads inside the cities were not widened, but in 1888 in Kabul a railroad connecting the Arg with 'Alam Ganj was constructed. In 1887, the most important road constructed was that which connected Kabul with Bamian by way of Charikar. Previously, the road from Kabul to Turkestan had followed the long Arghandeh-Unai-Bamian line. The Kabul side of the Bamian Pass was now widened to seven meters to admit loaded animals. Still, in the winter, caravans preferred the old road. The most important road built in the reign of the amir was the Tang-i-Gharu between Kabul and Jalalabad, which took ten years and an expenditure of forty-eight lakhs of rupees to complete. It was completed in August 1896 but only opened officially to traffic in 1899.[183] It was shorter by twelve koses than the old road that went along the Lataband Pass. A traveler on foot could reach Jalalabad from Kabul in three days on the new road joining the old road at Jigdalik. Loaded animals and horses could pass through it. To shorten the road still further, in February 1901 work was started on the road between Jalalabad and Tang-i-Gharu along the Kabul River, but after the amir's death not only was this work stopped but the Tang-i-Gharu was abandoned.

Following the conquest of Kafiristan three main roads were built that connected Badakhshan with Kunar and Laghman through Kafiristan (Chagha Serai-Munjan, Asmar-Badakhshan, and Munjan-Laghman). Although the best of them, that is, Chagha Serai-Munjan, was a mere track, they all were usable by loaded ponies, horses, and mules. In the east, other notable roads, either completed or started, were from Asmar to Mamund, Surkano to the border of Mamund, from Lalpura in the direction of Mamund, and, most important, through the Mohmand country. The road through the Mohmand country, which was started in the last months of the amir's reign and then abandoned, had been intended to supersede the Khybar Pass. In 1892, a new road built between Kabul and Khost shortened the distance by five days for a traveler. While the old road ran through Zarghunshar-Khoshi-Thana-i-Zazay and other places and took nine days, the new one was extended through Zarghunshar, Altimur, Gardez, and so on and took four days.

Herat was connected with Kabul by a new road through the northern Hazarajat by way of Dai Kundi, Dai Zangi, and Dawlatyar.[184] It was two hundred miles shorter than the old road, which connected Kabul with Herat through Ghazni and Kandahar over six hundred miles. The new road, however, unlike the old one, which was macadamized and widened between Kandahar and Herat, was unfit for wheeled traffic. On the other hand, a macadamized road from Kandahar to the southern

Hazarajat was pushed along rapidly after 1891. Simultaneously, from the opposite direction, that is from Dai Kundi and Gizao, work was started on another road that was four yards wide and ran in the direction of Kandahar. Meanwhile, Kabul was connected with Badakhshan by the road that ran along Babaqushqar, Panjsher, and Andarab. On this road, horsemen could reach Khanabad from Kabul in five days and footmen in ten, but caravans preferred the old Kabul-Badakhshan road that ran along the Iraq Pass over a distance of two hundred miles. In 1891 the amir ordered the construction of a road between Badakhshan and Laghman to go through Farajghan, but thereafter no more was heard of this. In Turkestan "many roads" were constructed and macadamized on the patterns of roads in India.[185]

Serais were built and military posts established along the main roads used by caravans. Along the old road to Jalalabad, for instance, there were eight military posts (thahans) in Buthkhak, the Mulla ꞌOmar Caves, Bankan, Jigdalik, Surkhpul, Gandamak, Nimla, and Fathabad, each of which was guarded by a group of six soldiers led by a hawaldar. In addition, the safety of roads was made the responsibility of the people through whose territories the roads passed. It was the strict enforcement of this principle that accounted for the safety of roads in the reign of the amir. The newly built road of Asmar-Badakhshan which ran along the narrow valley of Basghgal in Kafiristan had a special significance. It was generally believed that this road was built for "the use of the Russians, who can . . . enter India without entering Afghanistan proper."[186] With this view in mind the amir sanctioned a large amount of money for the construction of serais and hamlets along the Asmar-Badakhshan road. To popularize it Hindus were encouraged to open shops along it and merchants were exempted from paying tolls on their goods along this road for three years. In the early part of 1897, when the road was open to traffic, merchants used it and also the Chagha Serai–Munjan road. For a time these two roads superseded the Chitral-Badakhshan road, but after the amir's death they were abandoned.

In the reign of the amir a few bridges, such as those over the rivers Helmand, Khashrud, Kockcha, and Fayzabad, were built.[187] The first two, which were built principally for the conveyance of heavy guns to Herat, were made of wood. As before, rivers were still crossed mainly by inflated skins and boats made of inflated skins. One such boat bridge was built over the Kabul River in Besud opposite the city of Jalalabad. Over the Oxus at Kilif ferry boats drawn by a couple of horses across swift and deep waters were used. These boats were heavy and made of logs rather than of planks.[188] Over the Helmand, traffic between Persia and Lash Jowin in Afghanistan was carried on mainly by means of rafts made up of bundles of reeds tied together and punted by a single boat. These rafts were small and carried four passengers.[189]

Principally, roads, bridges, dams, canals, and buildings were constructed by forced labor, although at times laborers were paid wages. To the "lowest class of laborers" engaged in the construction of roads and particularly the road between Chowkay and the Pech Valley the government paid six annas per day.[190] Sometimes a lump sum, say, ten rupees, was paid in advance to each laborer to work on the construction of a project, presumably until it was completed. The general principle applied was to employ laborers who were close to the construction site. Only when the project was on a grand scale were laborers from distant localities also employed. In such a case a large number of prisoners were also made to work. On the Tang-i-Gharu road, for instance, at one time 700 prisoners were employed. They were set free from prison for good to work on the road, presumably until its completion. In March 1894, when the rebellions were over, the amir ordered that 200,000 laborers from all over the country should take part in the construction of the Tang-i-Gharu road. In fact, people from Buthkhak up to Laghman worked on the road for ten days each. The inhabitants of the Kabul environs set one-third of their labor force. The Arg, however, was built exclusively by prisoners. At one time in 1885, all Kabul prisoners were employed there. In Turkestan, laborers were brought from a distance as far as Sar-i-Pul to work without pay on the erection of the fort in Dehdadi and the construction of dams.[191] Similarly the Patab Canal in Kandahar and the cantonment in Bamian were constructed by laborers from the surrounding areas without pay. On the Babaqushqar-Panjsher road 2,500 laborers worked daily.

The employment of large numbers of laborers suggests the lack of mechanical tools for making roads. Locally made spades and pick axes were the only tools that the government was reported to have put at the disposal of the laborers. The number of casualties was high. It is reported that from 1894 to 1896 in Tang-i-Gharu alone three hundred laborers died as the result of sudden torrents, landslides, or extreme cold. Sometimes soldiers, who along with elders supervised the work, beat the laborers to death.

Before the reign of the amir, carriages, whether carrying merchandise or human beings, were pulled by donkeys, horses, ponies, mules, camels, and possibly elephants. For the carriage of machines and iron the amir bought a large number of elephants from India, but improper care and the cold climate of Afghanistan gradually decreased their number. In 1893, the amir had a light railway constructed from Kabul to the gorge of Tarakhel, about five miles northeast of the cantonment, to bring construction stones to the city, but of this project no more was heard. Carts drawn by horses, however, proved of long duration. Carts or *tangas* were used in India. The amir wanted Sardar Muhammad Afzal, the British agent, to ask the British government to send him a few of them as a pattern.[192] They must have been sent, for next year the amir ordered the making of two hundred of them.[193] Later, in Kabul alone there were in use one hundred carts, like the *arabas* of central Asia, drawn by a pony each.[194]

The amir, however, was unwilling to accept the suggestion of Viceroy Lord Dufferin that both a telegraphic line linking Kabul with Peshawar[195] and a railway line connecting Kandahar with Herat be constructed. Apparently, the amir argued that the introduction of these innovations, useful as they might be, might confuse the Afghans to "suppose that he was indebted to the British government for every measure of improvement."[196] In fact, just as he was unwilling to exploit the natural resources of the country on the ground that this would ultimately attract foreign aggression, he was likewise opposed to the introduction of modern means of transportation and communication, fearing that these might create complications and provoke the jealousy of Russia and, thus, jeopardize the independence of Afghanistan. As noted earlier, a telephone line, connecting the Arg with the Kotwali, was set up in the reign of the amir, but the major means of mechanical communication remained the heliograph, which was used exclusively for military purposes. Two hundred artificers knew this art in Afghanistan during the reign of the amir.[197] Through it the amir used to convey messages to Kabul from Paghman and Jalalabad.

Conclusion

In the present study the personality of Amir ʾAbd al-Rahman Khan has been interwoven with the history of Afghanistan during the period under consideration. The amir, who more than any previous Afghan ruler left his imprint on the Afghan society, stands out as the dominant force in shaping the history of the country not as an isolated individual, but as a social figure representing basically conservative forces.

Initially, the internal threats, unleashed by the civil war in the 1860s, convinced the amir of the necessity of a strong central government. This conviction was subsequently reinforced by external threats to the integrity of the country and to the amir's rule. To meet the threats and protect Afghanistan the amir organized a strong standing army and made attempts at mobilizing the human and natural resources at his disposal. To accomplish this he isolated Afghanistan in the belief that it was necessary for a "house to have walls before putting in the furniture and the curtains; otherwise burglars would come in and take the things away."[1] These policies proved of the utmost significance, since they seriously affected government structure and the social groups inside the country, as well as Afghanistan's relations with her neighbors.

The new army necessitated the expansion of the existing bureaucracy to arrange payment, uniforms, and provisions to the army as well as to maintain itself. The necessary expenses were funded from land revenue and a multitude of other taxes, which were increased to an unprecedented degree. Even these, though, were still not enough, for the government structure and the expenses it required for normal functioning gradually grew too huge for the meager internal resources to meet. The army alone, according to the amir, absorbed about 78 percent of the total income of the state. To ease the heavy financial burden the amir, as well as his successors, relied on outside financial help, but by so doing they made themselves dependent on outside powers. Two results followed, both of which undermined the moral posture of the Afghan rulers. First, they lost freedom of action with respect to external affairs, especially relating to the territories that, as a result of the Durand Agreement, were considered to be within the British sphere of influence but that, in Afghanistan, were still looked upon as belonging to Afghanistan. Second, Amir ʾAbd al-Rahman and his successors were looked upon with suspicion by their own subjects for their alleged nonmilitant attitudes toward the British that were presumed to result from their receiving British assistance (pecuniary grants, weapons). This attitude persisted in spite of the official efforts aimed at intensifying xenophobia among the people.

The new army and bureaucracy attracted talented people to these economically unproductive fields. Since this manpower drain limited careers in other areas, the army and bureaucracy became, to a large extent, substitutes for private enterprise. Conditions favorable to the development of the national economy through private enterprise were not created. A contemporary observer writes, "What ruins the country in the first place is its disjointedness and its consequent feuds; in the second place, the fact that the people have no outlet. If a man is clever and ambitious, instead of taking up some work that makes him someone in his own district, he goes to the court and commences an elaborate system of intrigue, by which he endeavours to oust some other man from his position in order that he may occupy it. The government is paternal in the strictest sense, and everything belongs to the head of the state."[2]

The adverse effects of the new army and bureaucracy were especially felt in agriculture, the basis of Afghanistan's economy. The new system of taxation and land revenue enabled the state to appropriate for itself a large portion of agricultural produce that, in a society of predominantly small agricultural producers, left the peasants at a subsistence level. Worse still, these measures undermined the incentive of the small landholders who constituted most of the proprietors, so much so that the amir's policies for improving agriculture (the advance of loans, the construction of irrigation canals, and the program for irrigating the uncultivated lands in parts of Turkestan) proved marginal in their effects. Equally disastrous was the amir's policy concerning the distribution of, and the trade in, agricultural produce. By creating government monopolies and by levying high rates of taxes on manufactured goods without, at the same time, supporting handicraft industries, the amir discouraged the emergence of an enterprising trading class. Although in the end all of these policies failed for being inherently unrealistic and, moreover, mismanaged by incompetent and self-motivated officials and were abandoned in favor of free trade, it was then too late for traders, who had been so battered, to compete successfully with their foreign rivals in the ensuing decades. In sum, although his improvement of the communication and the road systems, suppression of the brigandage and the establishment of Kabul workshops were notable achievements, the overall economic policies of Amir ʾAbd al-Rahman condemned Afghanistan to remain an agrarian country in which even agriculture suffered beyond the hope of immediate recovery.

In evaluating Amir ʾAbd al-Rahman's policies, however, one should not forget general concern at the time in Afghanistan for the safety of the country. The Muslims of Afghanistan, after having fought for over a year against the British, had become seriously concerned about the safety of Islam, of the country of Islam, of women, and of their possessions and feared future encroachment of the approaching Russians and the British. Amir ʾAbd al-Rahman fully appreciated this concern and devised schemes to strengthen the state so that in his words "the country of Afghanistan remain to the people of Islam forever, and that the latter are at no time defeated by a foreign nation."[3] In this the amir went so far that he, in fact, became overconcerned with the state and neglected the real welfare of the people that must be the criterion for real human accomplishments. Consequently, his overconcern caused him to fail to realize that pure military strength was ill founded unless supported by a strong national economy. He made no efforts to develop the economy and natural resources by novel means. That he did not permit the construction of railways and telegraphic lines inside Afghanistan was quite understandable; for there is every reason to believe that this would have jeopardized the integrity of Afghanistan or what was left of that integrity. The xenophobia that he intensified among the people, however, also haunted him to the extent that he became guilty of "culpable neglect in working the rich mines of his country."[4] Frank Martin notes that the amir "often mentioned the benefits to his country which the working of these mines would occasion, and soon after my appointment he gave me written orders to build the necessary works for smelting the copper ores which have been found in the neighborhood of Kabul. When the work was about half completed, however, he sent instructions to me to postpone work on it until further orders, and thereafter left the matter in abeyance." It can only be supposed that the amir "was fearful of adding an incentive to interference with his country on the part of his neighbors by showing the riches it contained."[5] The amir, instead, tried to consolidate the state and his dynastic rule by the well-known harsh traditional methods that left every group of the people at the mercy of the most powerful and repressive state Afghanistan ever had.

Seen from another angle, the policies that the amir adopted helped to bring about an egalitarian society in Afghanistan. The same policies that hindered the increase of wealth led to the leveling of such differences of incomes as existed among the various groups of people. The most effective factor in this respect, the extensive application of the system of *se-kot* that, among other things, entitled landless peasants to one-third of the crops, was an unintentional by-product of the amir's policies, not the outcome of his deliberate efforts. The amir sincerely believed that men were not innately equal among themselves. According to him since "intellect has grades God has granted larger portions of it to big containers [brains, i.e., men] and smaller portions of it to small containers. He has deprived no man of it, and this for the good of the world so that men should be in need of one another."[6] The result of this belief was the amir's deliberate effort to rearrange the society on a hierarchical order topped by the Muhammadzays.

As far as internal politics was concerned, the amir's achievements, thanks to the army he organized, were most successful. The essence of these achievements was the elimination of some and the subordination of others whom he called the "middlemen," that is, those who had the potential of opposing the state and his dynasty. Combined with the country's fear of external threats this subordination of others made it possible for him to establish an absolute monarchy founded on a claim to divine right of authority. The amir's reign also marked the beginning of a nation-state in which individuals realized that, over and above their attachment to their communities, they were members of a larger unit, Afghanistan, with uniform sets of laws and regulations and fairly standardized units of weight and currency and with no barriers to the development of internal trade because of significant improvements in the road system and the opening of new regions. In short, Afghanistan in this period began to emerge as a single economic and political unit. This emergence and the introduction of modern military technology in Afghanistan, which still resembled more an *ancien régime* than a modern state, opened the way for modernization decades later.

In introducing the reforms mentioned above the amir had to choose between becoming a benevolent gradualist or a despotic reformer. He chose the latter and showed little or no concern for the lives of men. To be sure, in Afghanistan human life had been at no time sacred, and in every level of society life was lost for this or that reason; but in the amir's reign violence committed in the name of the state was without parallel in Afghan history. Indeed the state the amir organized was based on force and compulsion. The amir himself, although he clamored so much for the common people, turned, in the words of one of his officials, into a "falcon much fond of flesh."[7] That is why his despotic rule, in spite of his being the real founder of modern Afghanistan, has remained to this day a symbol of terror. It must, however, be remembered that he ruled over a people for whom "Force was the only law,"[8] which might explain why even after his death his harsh methods of administration were followed by his successors. At the same time the state the amir organized has proved a bulwark against the long periods of internal wars that had occurred so frequently in Afghanistan. On balance, Amir ʾAbd al-Rahman's many accomplishments make him stand out as one of the great Afghan rulers. In the words of a specialist on Afghanistan's diplomatic history of this period,

"Afghanistan owes a tremendous debt of gratitude to Abdur Rahman who guided her destiny in an hour of extreme danger with remarkable political perception, diplomatic shrewdness, and perseverance."[9] Nevertheless, even today most of his countrymen, who are entering the iconoclastic period of their history for the first time, hate him the most of all Afghan rulers.[10]

Appendix

Weights and a List of Prices of Agricultural Products and Other Commodities (1880–1901)

(A) In Afghanistan during the reign of Amir 'Abd al-Rahman, there were, as there had always been, a variety of weights in use. The same was true of Persian and Indian weights, which were also used in Afghanistan. The regions where different weights were current were Kabul, Kandahar, Herat, and Turkestan; this situation existed despite the fact that in 1891 the government decreed that transactions should be made only on the basis of the Kabuli ser and that weights were to be standardized throughout the country "for the sake of the welfare of the people, convenience in official registers, and improvement in trade affairs."[1]

One Kabuli ser was declared to be the unit of weight with the following equivalents:

1 ser = "768 Kabuli rupees" in weight (approximately 16.3 lbs.)
1 ser = 4 charaks (approximately 16.3 lbs.)
1 charak = 4 paos
1 pao = 4 khurds
1 khurd = 4 Pukhtabars[2]
1 Pukhtabar = 4 misqals
1 misqal = 24 nakhuds ("peas")[3]
8 sers = 1 maund or man
10 maunds = 1 kharwar.

In Kandahar and Herat:

2 misqals = 1 ser (approximately 0.21 lbs.)
40 sers = 1 Kandahari maund (approximately 8.5 lbs.)
100 maunds = 1 Kandahari Kharwar
1 Herati maund = approximately 7 lbs.

In northern Afghanistan, Mazar-i-Sharif weights were in general use:

1 Mazari ser = 1.75 Kabuli sers (approximately 28.5 lbs.)
15 Mazari sers = 1 Mazari maund
3 Mazari maunds = 1 Mazari kharwar.

Persian weight units were used extensively in western Afghanistan.
The basic units in Persia were also the misqal and the maund, but
the Persian maund varied from region to region. The main Persian
unit in western Afghanistan was the Tabrizi maund:

256 misqals = 1 charak
2.5 charaks = 6 ’abbasis = 1 Tabrizi maund
100 Tabrizi maunds = 1 Tabrizi kharwar (approximately 649 lbs.).[4]

(B) Afghan currency included the following equivalents:

1 rupee = 2 qirans
1 rupee = 3 ’abbasis or tangas
1 rupee = 12 shahis
1 rupee = 60 paisas
30 paisas = 1 qiran
20 paisas = 1 ’abbasi or tanga
10 paisas = 1 sanar
5 paisas = 1 shahi
1 paisa = 10 dinars.

Foreign exchange rates for selected years were as follows:

1880 1 Kabuli rupee = 1 Indian rupee
1899 1 Kabuli rupee = 16 annas or 80 paisas (official rate)
1899 1 Kabuli rupee = ½ Indian rupee (actual market rate)
1883 1 Kabuli rupee = 2 tangas (in Bukhara)
1870s 1 Kabuli rupee = 1 shilling, 1 pence
1890–1914 1 Kabuli rupee = 8 pence.[5]

Kabuli rupees were struck in silver; a few were struck in gold; ’abbasis,
shahis, paisas, and dinars were struck in copper, brass, and bronze.

(C) Prices of agricultural products during the reign of Amir ’Abd al-
Rahman differed from one region to another, and those in Turkestan

were generally the lowest. Also, in one region, three levels of prices were current: the actual, the official (mainly in cities), and those fixed by usurers, who advanced money to needy producers months before crops were reaped. The following list of prices indicates mainly the actual rates, but sometimes it is difficult to differentiate between the official and actual ones. For prices within a locality, weights and money of the same locality are given, unless otherwise indicated. Kabul, Kandahar, Herat, and Jalalabad indicate cities of those names, not regions or other entities.

Abbreviations used include:

A = Annas	M = maund
Ch = Chatak	Misq = misqals
H = Herati	P = pao
Ind = Indian	Q = qiran
K = Kabuli	R = rupees
Kand = Kandahari	S = ser
Kh = Kharwar	

Date	Product or commodity	Amount or unit	Price	Locality
1879	horse	1	100 R	Kabul
1880				
17 July	wheat flour	7 S	1 R	Kabul
5 Nov.	barley	9 KS	1 R	Kandahar
5 Nov.	wheat	7.50 KS	1 R	Kandahar
14 Dec.	flour	4.5 S	1 R	Kabul
10 Dec.	grain (corn?)	8 S	1 R	Kabul
14 Dec.	flour	4.50 S	1 R	Kabul[6]
14 Dec.	barley	7 S	1 R	Kabul
20 Dec.	wheat	6.50 KS	1 R	Kandahar
1881				
23 Dec.	wheat	2 M	1 R	Kandahar
1882				
Feb.	wheat	2 M	1 R	Kandahar
Feb.	wheat flour	1 M+25 S	1 R	Kandahar
Feb.	ghee	1 M	8.50 R	Kandahar
Feb.	grain	1.50 M	1 Q	Ghorian[7]
Feb.	wheat	1 M+30 S	1 Q	Herat
Feb.	barley	2 M+35 S	1 Q	Herat
Feb.	ghee	1 M	7 Q	Herat
Feb.	mutton	1 M	4 Q	Herat
Feb.	rice	20 S	1 Q	Herat
July	wheat	2 M	1 Q	Herat
28 Aug.	grain	3.25 M	1 R	Kandahar

Date	Product or commodity	Amount or unit	Price	Locality
1883				
29 Jan.	chaff	1 Kh	4 KR	Kabul-Jalala-bad road
29 Jan.	barley	2 KS (16 Ind S)·	2 KR	Kabul-Jalala-bad road
Feb.	shoe	1 pair	3	Jalalabad
6 Mar.	land	1 jarib	20 to 80	Jalalabad
1 Nov.	grain	1 Kh	4.50 tomans[8]	Herat
8 Nov.	meat	1 S	4 A	Turkestan
8 Nov.	ghee	1 S	2 R	Turkestan
8 Nov.	rice	1 S	4 A	Turkestan
8 Nov.	wheat flour	1 S	1.50 A	Turkestan
8 Nov.	barley	1 S	9 pies[9]	Turkestan
8 Nov.	barley	21 S	1 R	Turkestan
8 Nov.	cotton	1 S	1 R+8	Turkestan
8 Nov.	oil	1 S	1 A	Turkestan
8 Nov.	tea	1 S	4 R	Turkestan
1884				
Jan.	wheat	13 Ind S	1 R	Kandahar
Jan.	wheat	10 Ind S	1 R	Kandahar[10]
1885				
20 July	flour	0.75 KS	1 R	Kabul[11]
Nov.	flour	15 lbs. (P?)	1 R	Kabul
Nov.	flour	80 lbs. (?)	1 PKR	Turkestan
1886				
6 May	wheat	1 M+17 S	1 R	Kandahar
11 June	grain	2 M (8 Ind S)	1 R	Kandahar
11 June	barley	5 M	8 A	Kandahar
11 June	rice	1 M	1 R	Kandahar
23 Sept.	wheat	2 M	1 R	Herat
23 Sept.	barley	3.50 M	1 R	Herat
4 Oct.	wheat	2 M	1 R	Kandahar
4 Oct.	ghee	1 M	3.50 R	Kandahar
29 Nov.	wheat	6 M+42 lbs. (?)	1 Q	Murghab
29 Nov.	barley	10 M	1 Q	Murghab
13 Dec.	wheat	2 M	1 Q	Herat
1887				
30 Aug.	land	1 jarib	12 tomans	Paghman
2 Dec.	wheat	2.50 M	1 R	Kandahar
2 Dec.	ghee	1 M	1 R	Kandahar[12]
29 Dec.	wheat	1 Kh (100 M)	66 Q	Herat
1888				
8 Mar.	wheat	2 M+8 S	1 Q (6 A)	Herat
8 Mar.	barley	2.50 M	1 Q	Herat
8 Mar.	ghee	1 M	1 Q	Herat

Date	Product or commodity	Amount or unit	Price	Locality
1889				
6 June	wheat	3.50 M+12 S	1 Q	Herat
6 June	barley	5 M	1 Q	Herat
1890				
June	grain	3.50 M	1 R	Kandahar
June	almonds	1 M	7 A[13]	Kandahar
14 Sept.	wheat	3 M+10 S	1 R	Kandahar
——	wheat	5 KS	1 KR	Khost
1891				
8 Jan.	charcoal	6 S	1 R	Kabul
8 Jan.	fuel	1 Kh	30 R	Kabul
20 May	wheat flour	9 S	1 R	Kabul[14]
20 May	wheat	2.25 M	1 R	Kandahar
10 Nov.	flour	7 Ind S	1 R	Kabul
1892				
23 Sept.	wheat	1.50 M	1 R	Kandahar[15]
1893				
17 Feb.	wheat flour	1.25 M	1 R	Kandahar
19 Feb.	wheat	3 M	1 Q	Herat
19 Feb.	barley	3 M	1 Q	Herat
10 Mar.	——	——	——	Kandahar[16]
17 Mar.	——	——	——	Kandahar[17]
31 Mar.	——	——	——	Kandahar[18]
11 May	bread	1 M	1 Q	Herat[19]
3 June	wheat	2 M	1 R	Kandahar
7 June	wheat flour	6.25 Ind M	1 R	Kabul
7 June	corn flour	7.25 Ind S	1 R	Kabul
7 June	barley	12 Ind S	1 R	Kabul
7 June	rice	5 Ind S	1 R	Kabul
11 Oct.	wheat flour	1.25 S (10 Ind S)	1 R	Kabul[20]
14 Oct.	wheat	2 M	1 R	Kandahar
26 Dec.	wheat	2 M	1 R	Kandahar
26 Dec.	wheat	6 Peshawari S	1 KR	Turkestan
1894				
29 Jan.	meat	1 M	2 R	Kandahar
9 Feb.	wheat	3 M	1 R	Kandahar[21]
13 Apr.	raisins	0.50 M	1 R	Kandahar[22]
1895				
4 Jan.	wheat	3.50 M	1 R	Kandahar[23]
4 Jan.	wheat	3 M + 15 S	1 R	
22 Mar.	wheat	3.50 M	1 R	Kandahar
23 May	wheat	1 M+4 S	1 Q	Turkestan
Sept.	wool	1 M	1 Q	Herat[24]
Sept.	wool	1 M	2 Q	Herat[25]

Date	Product or commodity	Amount or unit	Price	Locality
1896				_____ [26]
_____	_____	_____	_____	
1897				
12 Jan.	salt	1 S + 4 Ch	1 R	Kabul[27]
Oct.	salt	12 lbs.	1 R	Kabul[28]
18 Dec.	wheat flour	11 S	1 Ind R	Kabul
1898				
27 Aug.	barley	14 S	12 A	Kabul
Aug.	barley	20 S	12 A	Kabul
Sept.	salt	13 S	1 R	Kabul[29]
5 Nov.	wheat flour	10.25 S	12 A	Kabul
Dec.	salt	12 S	1 R	Kabul
1899				
Mar.	salt	20 S	1 R	Kabul
20 May	gold[30]	1 tola	36 R	Kabul
15 Aug.	gold	1 Misq	21 R	Kabul
2 Sept.	gold	1 Misq	19.50 R	Kabul
18 Nov.	salt	6.75 Peshawari S	1 R	Ningrahar[31]
1900				
31 Jan.	wheat flour	9 S	1 R	Kabul
31 Jan.	wheat	11 S	1 R	Kabul
31 Jan.	maize	15 S	1 R	Kabul
31 Jan.	rice	5.25 S	1 R	Kabul
31 Jan.	meat	3.45 S	1 R	Kabul
31 Jan.	ghee	15 Ch[32]	1 R	Kabul
31 Jan.	salt	7 to 7.50 S	1 R	Kabul
28 Apr.	wheat flour	6 to 7.50 S	1 R	Kabul
28 Apr.	barley	10 S	1 R	Kabul
28 Apr.	corn	11 S	1 R	Kabul
12 May	wheat flour	5.50 S	1 R	Kabul
1901				
12 RS[33]	wheat	2 S+6 P	1 KR	Jaghori
12 RS	corn	2.75 S	1 KR	Jaghori
12 RS	wheat flour	2 S	1 KR	Jaghori
22 RS	wheat	1.75 S	1 KR	Turkmen wa Parsa
22 RS	ghee	3 P	1 KR	Turkmen wa Parsa
JA[34]	wheat	4.50 to 4.75 S	1 KR	Dai Folada[35]
JA	wheat	1.75 S	1 KR	Turkmen wa Parsa
JA	barley	2.25 S	1 KR	Turkmen wa Parsa
JA	ghee	3 P	1 KR	Turkmen wa Parsa

Date	Product or commodity	Amount or unit	Price	Locality
14 JS [36]	wheat	3.50 to 3.75 S	1 KR	Dai Folada
15 JS	wheat	2 S	1 KR	Behsud
15 JS	*mashung*	2.50 S	1 KR	Behsud
6 Rajab	wheat	3.75 S	1 KR	Dai Folada
18 Rajab	wheat	1.50 S	1 KR	Jaghori
18 Rajab	barley	1.75 S	1 KR	Jaghori
13 Shu'ban	wheat	3 S	1 KR	Behsud [37]
13 Shu'ban	barley	3.75 S	1 KR	Behsud
13 Shu'ban	wheat	2 S	1 KR [38]	Behsud
13 Shu'ban	barley	2.50 S	1 KR	Behsud
4 JS	wheat	2 Sangcharak S (8 KS)	2 KR	Sangcharak
4 JS	meat	3 Ch	1 KR	Sangcharak
4 JS	ghee	2 P	1 KR	Sangcharak
19 JS	wheat	1.75 S	1 KR	Mangal
19 JS	barley	2.25 S	1 KR	Mangal
21 JS	wheat	2 S	1 KR	Turkmen wa Parsa
21 JS	barley	2.25 S	1 KR	Turkmen wa Parsa
21 JS	ghee	2.75 P	1 KR	Turkmen wa Parsa
21 JS	wheat	4 S	1 KR	Dai Folada

Note on Sources

Source materials for the period under discussion are considerable and come mainly under four headings: unpublished official records, published official records, contemporary printed works, and modern printed works. Also available are a number of manuscripts in Persian. The unpublished official records are the most comprehensive; and these can be further divided into Afghan and British records, the former in Persian and the latter in English.

Afghan official records are preserved in Kabul in the Ministry of External Affairs, but as yet these are not open to the public. For this reason Afghan historiography, especially that relating to modern Afghanistan, is poor. Indeed, no work based on Afghan archival sources has so far been attempted, and this field has been virtually left to non-Afghan authors, who are mainly nonhistorians. By special permission I was given access to the files relating to the reign of Amir ʾAbd al-Rahman that have not been consulted before. I was, however, disappointed to discover how little was available there about the period covered in this study, despite the fact that this period was once so rich in documents.

This deficiency in Afghan unpublished documents is, however, compensated for, largely, by the availability of such official publications as *Saraj al-Tawarikh* (ST) and numerous other booklets. ST is considered in detail elsewhere. It is to be regretted that not all of the pamphlets can be found in one center at present; they are scattered in private hands and libraries. Fortunately I was able to procure the most important of these booklets from bookshops in the narrow and crowded bazars in the old section of the city of Kabul. The booklets in my

possession are manuals of instruction for government officials; a few
are on jehad.

The official records (published and unpublished) of the British government of India relating to Afghanistan during the reign of Amir ʾAbd
al-Rahman confront the researcher with immense problems resulting
from an abundance of source materials, contradictory in nature and
marked by gaps and discontinuities. First let us compare those records
concerning the period under discussion that today exist in the India
Office Library (IOL) and India Office Records in London with those in
the National Archives of India (NAI) in Delhi.

To begin with, the records in both these archival centers differ only
in number of volumes and arrangement. Delhi is richer than London in
unpublished records for both external and internal history of Afghanistan, whereas the reverse is true of published records. Furthermore,
documents at NAI are properly indexed, and summaries of diaries
are given; but the titles chosen for them do not necessarily represent the contents. In IOL these unpublished documents are included
at random in large volumes entitled "Political and Secret Letters
and Enclosures Received from India" and are not indexed. Some
are not even paginated. In sum, on the whole Delhi can offer more
documents than London can, and these are also more systematically
arranged. Combined, these records constitute the most comprehensive
source materials to exist in any language on the formative period of
modern Afghan history, with which this study is concerned.

Three groups of official diarists—British officials, Indian Muslims,
and local newswriters—have recorded events in Afghanistan from
1880 to 1901.

The diaries of the British officials stationed in Afghanistan cover
only the period of occupation. Brief though it was, the period was of
great importance; and Col. St. John and Lepel Griffin, chief political
officers in Kandahar and Kabul during the occupation period, have left
us on the whole very informative records, not only of political affairs,
but also of social and economic changes. Outside Afghanistan, the PD,
compiled by various deputy commissioners, is another important
source, which covers the whole period of this work. Its information
comes mainly from merchants, Afghan refugees, and informers, who
were occasionally sent to eastern Afghanistan to collect information.
The reports on eastern Afghanistan are fairly reliable, but those on the
rest of the country are mixed with exaggerations and rumors. The
same is true of Mala. D and Kh.D, which were established toward the
end of the amir's reign; but CD and GD, which were compiled mainly
by George Robertson, the well-known writer on Kafiristan, are particularly reliable on Kafiristan. The reports of members of the three ad hoc
commissions (the Boundary Commission, the Durand Commission,
and the mission led by Raja Jahan Dad Khan), which were sent to Afghanistan in 1885, 1893, and 1901, are extensive and, in various degrees, trustworthy. With the diaries of Muslim agents working for the

British government of India inside Afghanistan, however, the story is strikingly different.

To begin with the agents: They were Qazi ʾAbd al-Qadir (1880–1882), Sardar Muhammad Afzal Sadozay (1882–1885), Col. ʾAtta Allah (Rajput) (1885–1891), Afzal Khan Gandapuri (1890–1894), Risaladar Muhammad Akram Khan (1894–1895); and Mawlawi ʾAbd al-Ghafur of Laknow (1896 to beyond the end of the amir's reign). The Kabul Agency had thirty-five men listed as "retinue" and even had a hospital attached to it. In the absence of the agent, the KD was compiled by a secretary.

The agents had a very unpleasant life in Kabul. They were lodged in squalid surroundings and were looked down on by all Afghans with "undisguised contempt,"[1] not only because they were British agents, but also because they were Indian natives who were generally looked down upon in Afghanistan. Of Afzal Khan Gandapuri, Mortimer Durand wrote that he "felt nervous and uncomfortable"[2] not only in the presence of the amir, but also in the presence of Afghan senior officials. The British Agency was under constant guard, and the agents were not allowed to travel unaccompanied by guards, who actually prevented them from talking to the people. The agents were, in fact, treated like "prisoners."[3] But they had free and undisturbed access to the amir's darbar, where he treated them courteously.

Two results were to follow from the amir's treatment of the agents. First, the KD became mainly a record of darbar proceedings, as the agents understood them. Of course, the darbar was the center from which the amir, as an absolute head of the state, exercised his overall power; hence the significance of these reports. Since the agents were under surveillance they were handicapped in their task, and many of their local contacts lost their lives, since passing information to the agents was considered a capital offense. The agents had, therefore, no effective means of verifying the reports they were given, and these reports were mixed with rumors and exaggerations. Second, the reports of all agents, except the qazi and Mawlawi ʾAbd al-Ghafur, were biased. Although they had been instructed to confine their reports to facts and figures only (they were asked to send their own views separately), the agents concentrated on the dark side of events. Of Col. ʾAtta Allah, who of all the agents served for the longest period, it was said that he took "the gloomiest views of the Amir's position and character."[4]

The reports of Qazi ʾAbd al-Qadir, known in Kabul as Qazi Qadiro, and of Mawlawi ʾAbd al-Ghafur, were better balanced and more impartial. The qazi, who acted as a secret newswriter and wrote under the name of A. B., Kabul correspondent, belonged to the respectable Qazi family of Peshawar. He himself was an adviser to Amir Sher ʾAli Khan during the seventies.[5] During this period, especially because of his supervising the taking of a general census in 1876, the qazi acquired a thorough knowledge of Afghanistan. In spite of his service with Amir Sher ʾAli, the qazi entered the service of Amir ʾAbd al-Rahman for two years. While back at Peshawar he worked for ʾAbd al-Rahman as his newswriter and, at the same time, occasionally advised the deputy commissioner on Afghan affairs. Nevertheless, the government of India always suspected him, because he had been known to be the most anti-British of all Sher ʾAli's advisers.[6] Lord Ripon, British viceroy in India, even spoke of him as an "acknowledged scoundrel."[7] The fact was that ever since 1864, when the qazi as a junior revenue officer (naʾib tahsildar) in Peshawar had been imprisoned for his alleged corruption,[8] relations between him and the government of India had remained strained. In spite of this, Lepel Griffin, acting for the government of India, left the qazi in Kabul in 1880 as a secret newswriter, not as an agent, because it was thought inadvisable to send an agent openly so soon after the evacuation and because the government of India wanted to know about the activities of Russian agents in Afghanistan and their treatment by the amir. The qazi, however, was the most intelligent of all the Muslim writers, and his reports on Afghan affairs are the most meaningful. As he wished to remain in the service of the amir, who also paid him, the qazi was cautious and avoided misrepresentation.[9] Mawlawi ʾAbd al-Ghafur's reports were impartial, but they were short and did not contain much significant information.

Mir Muhammad Hashim, Mirza Muhammad Taqi, Mirza Yaʾqub ʾAli, and Sayyed Dilawar Shah, who were stationed at Kandahar and Herat as newswriters during the amir's reign, formed another group of newswriters. For the obvious reason that ʾAbd al-Rahman was the first ruler to break the power of the Qizilbashes, these newswriters, who, except possibly for Sayyed Dilawar, were all Qizilbashes, reported unfavorably on the amir and on the feelings of his subjects toward him. Robert Sandemand's view of Mir Hashim—that he did not report "truly"[10] what happened in Kandahar—applies in varying degrees to others also. The obvious reason for this was that they were all treated with open contempt and scorn. For fear of the amir's spies and because of their service to the British, these newswriters were ostracized not only by other local people, but also by their own relations, some of whom suffered much and were expelled to Persia because of kinship with the newswriters.[11] The amir's officials from whom they obtained information in the darbar did not treat them badly, mainly because the amir had compelled the newswriters to report to him on his own officials. In spite of the restrictions placed on them, their diaries are especially valuable for their recording the firmans of the amir in parts and the system of taxation in detail.

Of the printed works in English about the period under discussion, *The Life of Abdur Rahman* by Sultan Mahomed is by far the best. Until recently it was considered genuine in its entirety and was much quoted. Soon after its appearance in English it was translated into Persian and printed in Mashhad, Lahore, and Bombay. It is, therefore, necessary to describe in some detail the circumstances under which it was composed.

To begin with it is not an autobiography in its entirety, for only the first part, covering the events of the amir's early life up to his reentry into Badakhshan in 1880,[12] was written by the amir himself. The manuscript is undated and preserved in the Manuscripts Department of the Kabul Public Library. It was published in 1886 under the title *Pandnama-i-Dunya wa Din* (A Book of Advice on the World and Religion). Fayz Muhammad, the author of *Saraj al-Tawarikh*, has liberally used it in his book. It is not clear when the amir wrote the *Pandnama*. According to some reports, the amir was engaged in composing his autobiography sometime before 1895. There are, however, some indications that he had started composing this or possibly an early autobiography while he was in exile, since at that time he sent portions of his early autobiographical sketches to the governor-general of Russian Turkestan. These portions were translated into Russian and later from Russian into English. They are quoted in full by Stephen Wheeler in his book, *The Ameer Abdur Rahman*.[13] The two autobiographies are not the same in form and subject matter; but they do not contradict each other in substance, although the earlier one is decidedly pro-Russian in sentiments.

Sultan Mahomed, a Panjabi native of "humble" origin in the service of the amir after 1883 as an interpreter and secretary (*munshi*), claims he wrote the rest of the book as it was dictated by the amir himself,[14] but this is not true. In 1895, John Gray, the amir's former physician, sent his former patient his book, *My Residence at the Court of the Amir*, a collection of personal impressions and observations of rather insignificant matters that is, nevertheless, very important for understanding the state of public health in Afghanistan. The amir was displeased with the book, but it proved a strong stimulus to him to enlarge the *Pandnama* and incorporate the events of his entire reign. The amir commissioned Sultan Mahomed, jobless at the time, to undertake the task and in 1896 made available to him the necessary documents. Sultan Mahomed was instructed to show the manuscript to the amir through Sardar Habib Allah and Sardar Muhammad Yusuf, the amir's son and uncle. How the work actually proceeded in Kabul is not known, for Sultan Mahomed, fearful for his life, "escaped" to India, leaving his family behind. He did so apparently to escape the wrath of the amir who was said to have turned on Sultan Mahomed because of his reported embezzlement of government money and his earlier correspondence with "certain British and Indian officers" to the effect that the amir used harsh language when speaking of the British government of India.[15] In fact, as early as 1887 Sultan Mahomed, as well as Indian artisans working under him, was charged with passing information to the British, but at that time the amir did not accept the charge, saying that he needed their service.[16] Nevertheless, some Indian government officials believed that Sultan Mahomed was sent abroad to spy for the amir. His easy "escape" reinforced the suspicion, although in England Sultan Mohamed engaged himself in academic work, wrote *The Constitution and Laws of Afghanistan*, and became a barrister at law at Christ College at Cambridge. No doubt while in Europe, Sultan Ma-

248 ❖   Note on Sources

homed continued to correspond with the amir. His relations with the
amir appeared good, and Sultan Mahomed was expected to return to
Kabul soon.

With the appearance of the "autobiography" Sultan Mahomed's relations with Kabul became strained. In all probability Amir ʾAbd al-
Rahman himself was dead by the time its publication was known in
Kabul; but his son and successor Amir Habib Allah is said to have
expressed extreme displeasure with Sultan Mahomed, who was not allowed to return to Kabul, despite his repeated pleas and the fact that
he had been Habib Allah's tutor. Even his repeated applications to
work for the new amir in India as his confidential agent were not accepted, and Sultan Mahomed began practicing law in his own home
town. Sir A. H. MacMahon, political officer with Amir Habib Allah
during his state visit to India in 1907, notes that the amir treated Sultan Mahomed disgracefully when he appeared before the ruler in
Sirhind.

Fayz Muhammad, the official historian of Amir Habib Allah, casts
doubts on the reliability of the second part of the autobiography, assert-
ing that it is based on what Sultan Mahomed heard from a number
of people in Kabul and on the information he collected from officials in
the darbar.[17] Even if what Fayz Muhammad claims were correct, this
assertion does not make the book necessarily unreliable, but there can
be no doubt that the portrayal of Amir ʾAbd al-Rahman's views regarding international affairs, particularly his views concerning Anglo-
Afghan relations, are not genuine. I have been worried for some time as
to how one could reconcile the amir's views expressed in his firmans
with those contained in his alleged autobiography, until I discovered
that "all the latter part is made up in England."[18]

To a certain extent this fact of authorship is evident in the monthly
memoranda, prepared by high officials of the government of India. In
one of them, Sultan Mahomed is referred to as "editor and part author
of the amir's so-called Autobiography."[19] It has not been established,
however, whether the author himself changed the manuscript to suit
British views. His interviews with certain officials in India do not re-
veal anything of the sort. Also, his relations with the government of
India remain obscure. There are some expressions of Sultan Mahomed's service to the government of India in the sense that he did his best
"to keep the Amir on good terms with the English"[20] and that according to Sultan Mahomed he was able "to present matters concerning
the British Government to the Amir in a way which the Amir would
accept."[21] British officials in India concerned with Afghan affairs have
described Sultan Mahomed's activities in Kabul as obscure. Only W. J.
Cunningham, foreign secretary to the British government in India, has
stated that Sultan Mahomed had acted "treacherously to the Government of India in 1893."[22]

It then would appear that the second part of the autobiography was
composed in England, when the manuscripts were placed with the
publishers. This supposition, however, will become definite only when

we obtain access to them; they are not available in the British Museum, where Sultan Mahomed claims to have placed them. According to a recent, unconfirmed report, they are in the private collection of Sultan Mahomed's son Fayz Muhammad, a famous Panjabi poet in Pakistan. At any rate, the second part of the autobiography cannot be dismissed altogether as fake, for those sections that deal with internal matters, as opposed to international affairs, tally very closely with reports from other sources. Readers, however, should guard themselves against the many factual mistakes therein.

The second most valuable English-language book on Afghanistan under Amir ʾAbd al-Rahman is Frank Martin's *Under the Absolute Amir*. Frank Martin was the younger brother of Sir A. Martin, through whom the amir employed English specialists for his workshops and bought war materials from England. Frank Martin came to Kabul in 1895. Subsequently he succeeded Salter Pyne as the amir's chief engineer. Martin spoke Persian well and Pashto poorly and was a keen observer of conditions in the city of Kabul, especially those of the workers of Kabul workshops. The amir received Martin in the darbar frequently and lectured to him about the state of the country, especially of his relations with the British government. The main merit of his book is that it gives a good description of the institutions, rather than concentrating on the author's impressions and views.

Also important for the period under discussion is Stephen Wheeler's *The Ameer Abdur Rahman*, a combination of the amir's biography and a concise account of Afghanistan's internal history and foreign relations from the rise of the Muhammadzay dynasty to 1895. Wheeler had not been to Afghanistan; but, like John Kaye, who while in India based his book *The Afghan War* on documents and private correspondence, Wheeler composed his work in India from Afghan official publications and British official records. His scholarly treatment of the subject (Wheeler was once a fellow of the Panjab University) has made his book indispensable for any student working on the period concerned.

Among the printed Persian works on the period under discussion, *Saraj al-Tawarikh* (ST) is the most important. ST is a chronological narrative of the first seventeen years of the amir's rule from his accession to 1896. Its last sentence is incomplete, suggestive of an abrupt ending. The book is a collection of disconnected facts based on Afghan official documents and reports. Fayz Muhammad is, therefore, not its author, but the editor or scribe (*katib, muharrir*) as he prefers to call himself.[23]

As will be seen shortly, however, his imprint on the book is considerable; therefore, a brief biographical sketch of this first known Hazara historiographer and scholar will be given before the book is commented on.

Fayz Muhammad (1861–1931) was born into a wealthy Hazara family. His father, Saʾeed Muhammad, was an elder of the Khwaja Muhammad Hazara of Nahur in Ghazni.[24] Fayz Muhammad studied in Lahore and returned, via Peshawar, to Kabul in 1888. Precisely what subject he studied in Lahore is difficult to tell. Presumably religious science (*fiqh*) was his major theme, since he was also known as Mulla Fayz Muhammad. In addition to Persian, he knew Pashto, Arabic, and probably Urdu. After he settled in Kabul, Fayz Muhammad studied history and literature and showed some interest in politics. In 1893, he entered the service of Sardar Habib Allah on the recommendation of Muhammad Sarwar Ishaqzay, a famous scholar, and employed himself in copying and editing documents and books, among them the first and second volumes of ST.[25] It was only in 1911 that Fayz Muhammad was commissioned to compile the third volume of ST independently.[26] By this time, Fayz Muhammad had made a place for himself in the royal court and received a good salary and occasional presents. It took him four years to complete his work, which was printed in 1915. Subsequently he drafted the fourth volume in the series, covering the reign of Amir Habib Allah, but so far no trace of this manuscript has been found. During the reign of King Aman Allah, Fayz Muhammad taught at Habibiyya High School, until the fall of that king in 1929. During the following civil war the bandit Amir Bacha-i-Saqao sent Fayz Muhammad at the head of a mission to the Hazarajat to bring about the submission of his kinsmen. Apparently he did so; but, being a well-wisher of the former royal dynasty, he secretly urged Hazara elders to oppose Bacha-i-Saqao. The Hazaras, who were grateful to King Aman Allah for having liberated them from the last vestige of slavery, consequently rose and defeated the contingent Bacha-i-Saqao had sent against them. In Kabul the bandit amir became suspicious of Fayz Muhammad and beat him so hard that in 1931, he died of the effects of the beating.[27]

In recording events Fayz Muhammad was honest and cautious. In places where he has made corrections, he also has footnoted the names mentioned in the original documents. On certain subjects, such as the Hazara War, however, his prejudice is obvious. Also, he has used euphemistic expressions throughout the book to cover the extreme harshness with which Amir ʾAbd al-Rahman treated his subjects.

Being an official record of events, ST is selective, in addition to being incomplete. Events which tended to show the amir in an unfavorable light have been either omitted or mentioned briefly. The best examples of this are the amir's correspondence and interviews with Lepel Griffin, his confrontation with Sardar Muhammad Ayyub, and his interviews with Mortimer Durand. These limitations are probably the contribution of Amir Habib Allah, who personally selected documents for publication and in addition made what Fayz Muhammad calls "scholarly improvements,"[28] in going through the final proofs. Rumors have it that Amir Habib Allah once beat Fayz Muhammad for having given a relatively gloomy and detailed picture of the Hazara War. If true, this is not surprising, since of all the topics mentioned in the ST the Hazara War has been treated most extensively.

Poor on foreign relations, ST deals with internal developments in minute detail. It is like a thesaurus of facts about all aspects of life. It deals with high-level politics occasionally and concentrates mainly on what actually happened, carrying the reader to the field of action and giving him a chance to see for himself how history was shaped there. This is probably the most important characteristic of the book, because it enables the reader to make generalizations and patterns from actual events rather than from descriptions of high-level policies, the extent of implementation of which is always difficult to ascertain.

Since ST is a heavy volume (962 foolscap pages) of unindexed facts, the task of a historian is a laborious one. That is why, except for Ghulam Muhammad Ghobar, no historian other than the present author has used the third volume, and it has consequently had little impact on Afghan historiography. An additional factor is the limited number of copies available for scholarly scrutiny. It is reported that all except three hundred copies of it were destroyed on instruction from King Aman Allah, because of the mention in it of the word "service" in the insignia, G.C.S.I., conferred on his grandfather by the British government; Aman Allah considered "service" to be below the dignity of an Afghan king.[29]

A main characteristic of the book is its consistency and continuity—a sharp contrast with the often incoherent, contradictory, and discontinuous statements recorded by the British agents. The latter, however, are far more comprehensive, with the additional merit of their comments on the amir's policies. With both these sources and the numerous Afghan official publications the problem of the amir's reign becomes one of abundant sources, though still not enough. Unless it is indicated otherwise, references to ST in this work are to the third volume.

Another important Persian-language source dealing with the period under discussion is a collection of twelve relatively unknown books, among them ʾAyn al-Waqaiʾ and Ziya al Muʾrafa by Muhammad Yusuf Riyazi, a contemporary of Amir ʾAbd al-Rahman Khan. Riyazi claimed to be a descendant of the royal line of Herat.[30] His mother was an Afshar. It was probably because of this that Riyazi expresses pro-Shiʾite sentiments in his works without being anti-Sunni.

Riyazi had wide interests, ranging from the writing of poetry (not of the first quality) to traditional medicine; but he was mainly interested in politics and history. He was born into a big landholding family with a good literary background. His ambition was to hold an important government position, but in this he failed because he was forced to flee to Mashhad in the late 1880s to spend the rest of his life as a refugee. Although he puts the blame for this exile on certain of his rivals who, according to Riyazi, plotted against him, his own writings indicate that he had made contacts with Persian and Russian officials, and this action was unforgivable to the amir. In spite of this, Riyazi's writings are not marked by hostility to the amir. They are, in fact, serious attempts by an intelligent scholar and observer to write his autobiography and accounts of Afghan events with only that degree of prejudice that is the outcome of upbringing rather than is of a deliberate nature.

His escape to Mashhad still further enriched his experiences, which are well reflected in his writings. He made several journeys for various reasons to northeastern Khurasan, Seistan, Farah, Kandahar, and Hazarajat. His writings, therefore, reflect the sociopolitical conditions of western and central Afghanistan and of eastern Persia in the late nineteenth century. In addition, Riyazi, while in Mashhad, established contacts with officials of the British and Russian consulates, more particularly with Persian officials, in an attempt to receive allowances to maintain his family and a large number of followers. In the beginning he received an allowance from the British in return for a service that he had rendered to them;[31] but this allowance was soon suspended, and Riyazi became bitter on this account. Subsequently he entered the service of the Persian government[32] until he was able to obtain a regular allowance from the Russian consulate.[33] One consequence of these contacts was that he widened his outlook. Probably for this reason we find, side by side with the description of Afghan events, an account of events in other countries of the world, notably Persia, in his most important work, *᾽Ayn al-Waqai᾽*.[34]

Another source, which has been frequently consulted in this work, is *Afghanistan along the Highway of History* by Ghulam Muhammad Ghobar, the foremost Afghan historian of the present day. Ghobar died early in 1978 and is relatively unknown outside Afghanistan, although he had written many works, including numerous articles, and had been writing history for fifty years or so. Of all contemporary Afghan historians, Ghobar is the only one who played an active role in politics at the same time as pursuing scholarship; but, unlike other Afghan scholars, he was not associated himself with the Afghan government and from an early age was an unwavering partisan of the constitutional movement. This attitude brought him into conflict with those who held power, except for King Aman Allah, whom Ghobar, like other constitutionalists, supported. After a long period of imprisonment in the 1930s Ghobar again took a leading part in politics, during the second short-lived democratic experiment in Afghanistan in the early 1950s, by serving as a member of the parliament, editing *Watan* (an independent weekly), and leading a political party also known as Watan. After the suppression of this experimental movement, he took to writing and the result is the 830-page *Afghanistan along the Highway of History* published in 1967, in the middle of the third liberal-democratic movement in the history of the country.

The book, in fact, is a general history of Afghanistan, beginning with its ancient days down to the fall of King Aman Allah in 1929. The greater part of it, however, is devoted to Afghanistan during the past two centuries. Based mainly on printed and original sources in Persian and Arabic, although not satisfactorily footnoted, it is the only history of Afghanistan by a professional Afghan historian, who followed a political line consistently in opposition to the establishment and who composed his work at a time when Afghanistan enjoyed a degree of political freedom that it had never previously experienced. This freedom is well reflected in the book, which surpasses other works of history by Afghan authors in profundity, content, and expression. In it Ghobar with his perceptive personality and sharp views appears at his best. In short, it is the first critical study of the political history of Afghanistan to appear to date. Unfortunately, after about ten copies of it were distributed, the book was banned. These few copies, however, have been circulated widely, and the impact of the book has been most significant. It is fortunate that the new government, which effectively terminated the Muhammadzay rule in April 1978, released Ghobar's book. An attempt will be made here to introduce the book in a general way and to take in the last part of it, which covers the Muhammadzay period.

First, the book is mainly a political history of Afghanistan. Second, unlike other Afghan authors who have interpreted history in terms of individual heroes, Ghobar believes that history is no longer the record of achievements of a few individuals [35] and that the people, whose actions are determined by social conditions, are the real molders of history.[36] In this, however, he is often imprecise and at times dangerously misleading. For instance, Ghobar asserts that the "people" (mardum) fired at Amir 'Abd al-Rahman in 1889 in Turkestan,[37] whereas, in fact, a single soldier whose motives have not been discovered fired the shot. There is no evidence to suggest that the would-be assassin acted in concert with others. Reflecting the relaxed political situation of his own time, Ghobar, unlike other Afghan authors who have more or less followed the official line in promoting the cult of the individual, has vigorously decried this cult. Instead, he has tried, although not always successfully, to describe the history of Afghanistan in terms of social forces represented by such groups as the rulers, sardars, feudal and religious leaders, traders, artisans, and, above all, the people, that is, the peasants and nomads. This new approach in Afghan historiography is Ghobar's contribution.

Third, although Ghobar is profoundly critical of British proceedings and policies towards Afghanistan, he does not hold that external factors were the main factors in shaping the internal history of Afghanistan. An obvious example of this is the downfall of King Amam Allah, which was generally believed in Afghanistan to have been engineered by the British; but to Ghobar his downfall was caused by the alienation of the king from the general populace. The British, according to Ghobar, only exploited the discontent [38] in expediting his downfall.

Fourth, because he has tried to describe the history of Afghanistan in terms of social forces, Ghobar has actually underrated ethnic considerations in the predominantly tribal society of Afghanistan. While he has overrated the role of the Tajiks in opposing the British, Ghobar has kept silent over the pro-British role of some minorities, particularly the Qizilbashes, in the critical periods of Afghan history. Here he has obviously been influenced by the current feelings decrying tribal-ism, regionalism, and religious and linguistic differences in an effort to support national cohesion. By doing this he has reinforced the well-known view that "all history is modern history."

Fifth, Ghobar's work is poor on foreign relations, but his comments about this subject reflect a critical appraisal of Afghan rulers conduct-ing the foreign policies of Afghanistan. This observation brings us to the last main point: Ghobar is not slow in condemning here and vindi-cating there, not so much in accordance with the values of the time in which the events took place, but in accordance with the values of the time in which he composed his work.

Among the Persian sources that shed some light on Afghanistan in the nineteenth century is "Aman al-Tawarikh" (AT), a series of manu-scripts in seven volumes by ʾAbd al-Muhammad Isfahani. Most of the series, hitherto unknown to scholars, deals mainly with the history of Afghanistan from its invasion by the Arabs in the seventh century down to 1924. Portions of the series also deal with the neighboring Muslim lands, as well as with other countries of the Middle East. Fur-ther, it includes biographical accounts of poets, writers, and scholars of Afghanistan, which make it valuable as a source of Persian literature as well; but the series does not treat its subject matter chronologically. In addition, its early parts have been merely taken from the generally known books in Persian, although an admiring reviewer of it claims that Isfahani has based his work on books in French, Latin, Greek, English, German, Russian, Turkish, Arabic, and so on.[39]

Volumes 5 and 6 are relevant to our study. Volume 5 has two parts: Part 1 is an account of the tribes of Afghanistan, originally prepared by Fayz Muhammad, the editor of ST. This part is important, because Fayz Muhammad, who had an intimate knowledge of the tribes of Af-ghanistan and of their relationships with each other and with the cen-tral government, has here freely expressed himself, something he did not do in ST. Part 2 of this volume contains a historical account of Afghanistan from the rise of the Durranis up to Amir Dost Muhammad Khan's confrontation with the Sikhs in the Panjab in the 1830s; but, as with other historical sections, this part is poor. Volume 6 is a sum-mary of a part of ST covering the first eight years of the reign of Amir ʾAbd al-Rahman. Volume 7 contains in part the author's observations of developments in Afghanistan during the reign of King Aman Allah, whom he visited in Kabul in 1922. The last volume also contains a biographical sketch of some Afghan poets and scholars of the nine-teenth and early twentieth centuries.

The author was originally from Isfahan in Persia; but at an early age he settled in Cairo, where he edited a journal, *Chihranuma*, in Persian and from where, at the invitation of the Afghan government, he visited Afghanistan in 1922. I am grateful to Mr. and Mrs. S. C. Ioannidis of Cambridge, Massachusetts for lending me these volumes for consul-tation.

Notes

Abbreviations Used in the Notes

ABC — The 1885 Afghan Boundary Commission charged with delimiting the northwest boundary of Afghanistan with Russia.

AQ — *Asas al-Quzzat* by Mawlawi A. J. Alkozay.

ARAMFA — Past Records and Files, Archives of the Afghan Ministry of Foreign Affairs, Kabul.

AT — "Aman al-Tawarikh" by A. M. Isfahani.

AVI — Memoranda on the Visit of His Highness the Amir of Afghanistan by H. M. Durand, Capt. M. C. Talbot, and others, Nos. 3, 4, 5, 1885, PSLI, vol. 44, pp. 1–20

AW — *'Ayn al-Waqai'* by Muhammad Yusuf Riyazi, in *Kulliyat-i-Riyazi.*

BACA — *Biographical Accounts of Chiefs, Sardars and others of Afghanistan*, publication of the British government of India.

BSOAS — *Bulletin of the School of Oriental and African Studies,* University of London.

CD — Chitral Agency Diary in PSLI.

CLA — *The Constitution and Laws of Afghanistan* by Sultan Mahomed.

DSCD — Dir, Swat, Chitral Agency Diary in PSLI.

EI — Encyclopedia of Islam.

F. — Foreign.

F.L. — Foreign Letter.

For. Dept. Foreign Department.

GAK (1895) Gazetteer of Afghanistan, 1895, publication of the British government of India.

GD   Gilgit Agency Diary in PSLI.

HD   Herat Diary in PSLI.

ID   *Ihtisab al-Din*, publication of the Afghan government.

IGA   Imperial Gazetteer of India, Afghanistan, and Nepal, publication of the British government of India.

IOL   India Office Library, London.

Kand. D Kandahar Diary in PSLI.

KD   Kabul Agency Diary in PSLI.

Kh. D   Khybar Agency Diary in PSLI.

Mala. D Malakand Agency Diary in PSLI.

Merk, W. DA Memorandum regarding Affairs among the Char Aimak Tribes, For. Dept., Secret—F. Pros. July 1886, Nos. 318–449. NAI.

MM   Monthly Memorandum.

Molloy, E. For. Dept., A–Political–E, September, Nos. 312–319, NAI (Reports on the Hazarajat, Tokhi Ghizais, and Kabul Districts and on Herat).

MRA   *Military Report on Afghanistan*, publication of British government of India.

MRA (1925) *Military Report on Afghanistan, History, Geography*, publication of British government of India (1925).

MU   *Mir'at al-'Uqul* by Amir 'Abd al-Rahman, publication of the Afghan government.

NAI   National Archives of India, Delhi.

PD   Peshawar Agency Diary in PSLI.

PSLI   Political and Secret Letters and Enclosures Received from India, India Office Library, India.

QKMH *Qanun-i-Karguzari dar Ma'amilat-i-Hukumati* by Malawi Ahmad Jan Alkozay, publication of Afghan government.

RLMA *Report on a Linguistic Mission to Afghanistan* by Georg Morgenstierne.

RM   *Risala-i-Muwa'izza*, publication of the Afghan government.

SDAA Strength and Distribution and Armament of the Afghan Army, For. Dept., Secret-F., Pros. Feb. 1893, Nos. 224–229. NAI [compiled from information supplied by the Afghan Boundary Commission and other sources by R. W. R. Robertson in Simla in 1893].

SJD   *Sawal wa Jawab-i-Dawlati* [The Amir's interviews with the viceroy of India] by M. Nabi, Kabul: Official Publications, 1885.

ST   *Saraj al-Tawarikh* by Fayz Muhammad.

(T)   Telegram.

TD   *Taqwim al-Din* by Mulla Abu Bakr and other mullas, publication of the Afghan government.

ZM   *Zia al-Ma᾽rrafa* by Muhammad Yusuf Riyazi, in *Kulliyat-i-Riyazi*.

Note: References to records without noting either ARAMFA or NAI indicate records of the India Office Library, London.

❖

Introduction

1. For details see Horace H. Wilson, *Ariana Antiqua*, pp. 119–126. G. M. Ghobar, "Afghanistan and a Glance at Its History," *Kabul* nos. 2, 4, 5, 6, 9, 10, 11, 12 (1931). Idem, *Afghanistan Along the Highway of History.* Considerable confusion has arisen in literature over the names *Aryana* and *Iran.* Briefly the name *Aryana* is older than the name *Iran.* The latter, which was derived from Aryana and which probably appeared for the first time during the early Sasanid period (A.D. 208–561) (Richard Frye, personal communication, 1974), was applied as *Eran shahr* to the land ruled by the Sasanian kings (A. Huart, "Khurasan," EI, vol. 2 (1927): 966).

In the Islamic period, the name Iran lost its political significance, despite its persistence in literature, especially in the *Shahnama* of Ferdausi. It was re-applied to modern Persia probably before the nineteenth century (J. H. Kramers, "Iran," EI, vol. 3 (1936): 1038). It was, however, only in 1935 that Reza Shah asked foreigners to use Iran instead of Persia to refer to the country of which he was the king (Richard Frye, personal communication, 1974).

2. Huart, "Khurasan," p. 966.
3. G. M. Ghobar, *Khurasan.*
4. Mountstuart Elphinstone, *An Account of the Kingdom of Caubul,* 1: 200.
5. Saifi, *History of Herat,* with an introduction and notes by Al-Siddigi, M-2, p. 77.
6. S. M. Durrani, *Tarikh-i-Sultani* [The history of Sultani], p. 10.
7. Elphinstone, *An Account,* 1: 124.
8. Ibid., p. 125.
9. M. Q. Firishta, *Tarikh-i-Firishta* [The history of Firishta], p. 220; B. Dorn's introduction to *History of the Afghans* by Neamatullah, p. 64.
10. Georg Morgenstierne in *An Etymological Grammar of Pashto,* trans. Dr. A. G. R. Farhadi, pt. 1: 211.
11. M. Q. Firishta quoted by Durrani, *Tarikh-i-Sultani,* pp. 20, 21.
12. George Peter Tate, *The Kingdom of Afghanistan,* p. 15.
13. Herodotus, *The Persian Wars,* 3.102; 7.67–68.
14. R. C. Majumdar, *The Classic Works on India,* 4n.
15. C. E. Bosworth, *The Ghaznavids,* p. 113.
16. A. A. Kohzad, *Afghanistan dar Shahnama* [Afghanistan in the Shahnama], p. 288.
17. M. Sprengling, "Shahpuhr I the Great on the Kaabah of Zoroaster (KZ)," *American Journal of Semitic Languages and Literature* 57 (October 1940): 411–412.
18. Varahamira, *Brihat Samhita,* trans. P. S. Sastri and V. M. R. Bhat, 2.61; 16.38.
19. A. Cunningham, *The Ancient Geography of India,* pp. 1–87.
20. M. A. Nayyir, "Aryana, Khurasan, Afghanistan," *Aryana,* nos. 1–2 (1965): 62–90.
21. J. P. Ferrier, *History of the Afghans,* p. 11.
22. G. Morgenstierne, "The Languages of Afghanistan," *Afghanistan* no. 3 (1967): 84.
23. H. F. Schurmann, *The Mongols of Afghanistan,* pp. 42, 45.
24. Herodotus, *The Persian Wars,* 3.91.

25. H. W. Bellew, *The Races of Afghanistan*, p. 58.

26. Ghobar, "Afghanistan and a Glance at Its History," p. 48.

27. Hameed ud-Din, "The Loodis," in *The Delhi Sultanate*, ed. R. C. Majumdar, p. 141.

28. W. Bingham et al., *A History of Asia*, 1: 231.

❖

I. The Central Government: 1

1. Sultan Mahomed, *The Life of Abdur Rahman*, 1; in ST (p. 200) it is also noted that ʾAbd al-Rahman was born in 1844.

2. Lepel Griffin, "The Late Amir and His Successor," *Fortnightly Review* (1901): 748.

3. S. E. Wheeler, *The Ameer Abdur Rahman*, p. 19.

4. Mahomed, *Life of Abdur Rahman*, 1: 4.

5. Ibid., 1: 191.

6. Yaʾqub Ali Khafi, *Padshahan-i-Mutakhir-i-Afghanistan* [The recent kings of Afghanistan], 2: 80.

7. Mahomed, *Life of Abdur Rahman*, 1: 1, 7.

8. Ibid., 1: 1, 8.

9. Ibid., 1: 1, 25.

10. C. C. Davies, "Abd al-Rahman" EI (new edition), p. 87.

11. Amir to Afzal, 26 January 1883, PSLI, vol. 37, p. 159.

12. BACA, p. 16.

13. Autobiographical notes from ʾAbd al-Rahman to Kaufmann, quoted by Wheeler, *Ameer Abdur Rahman*, p. 247.

14. Ibid., p. 245.

15. Ibid., p. 34.

16. Ibid., p. 35.

17. Ibid., p. 37.

18. Ibid., p. 46.

19. Amir to Gordon, amir's visit to India, 1885, PSLI, Encl. 5, p. 18.

20. Wheeler, *Ameer Abdur Rahman*, p. 54.

21. Ibid.

22. Autobiographical notes from ʾAbd al-Rahman to Kaufmann, quoted in ibid., p. 241.

23. Ibid., p. 55.

24. Ibid., p. 54.

25. Ibid., p. 57.

26. Kaufmann to Sher Ali, 28 March 1870, quoted in ibid., p. 56.

27. Ibid., p. 62.

28. Ibid., p. 63.

29. Naʾib Muhammad ʾAlam to Kaufmann, quoted in ibid., p. 65.

30. Ibid., p. 66.

31. BACA, p. 16.

32. Wheeler, *Ameer Abdur Rahman*, p. 59.

33. Eugene Schuyler, *Turkistan*, 0.137.

34. See Hasan Kakar, *Afghanistan: A Study in Internal Political Developments, 1880–1896.*

35. ST, p. 1028.

36. Nikki Keddie, *Sayyid Jamal ad-Din "al-Afghani,"* p. 55.

37. Vartan Gregorian, *The Emergence of Modern Afghanistan*, p. 130.

38. TD, p. 111. The amir claimed that he was the *naʾib* of the Prophet (ST, p. 1088).

39. TD, p. 144; the phrase "shadow of God" was applied in its original sense: "the shadow [protection] provided by God, not the Shadow which God in any anthropomorphic sense Himself cast." It meant that the monarch, in the fashion of the Ottoman Sultans, derived his authority from God (T. W. Arnold, *The Caliphate*, p. 50).

40. TD, p. 112.
41. RM.
42. KD, 19 January 1888, PSLI, vol. 52, p. 917.
43. ST, p. 709.
44. KD, 23 December 1887, PSLI, vol. 52, p. 384.
45. Amir's firman to the people of Afghanistan, HD, 17 January 1882, PSLI, vol. 33, p. 1167.
46. Amir's firman to governor of Kandahar, Jamadi al-Sani, 1319, Unclassified File, no. 26, ARAMFA.
47. Amir to Sayyed Hasan, PD, 10 August 1889, PSLI, vol. 57, p. 1383.
48. Ibid.
49. MM, September 1899, PSLI, vol. 116, no. 978 (18).
50. BACA, p. 21.
51. CLA, p. 33.
52. ST, p. 709.
53. PD, 10 August 1889, PSLI, vol. 57, p. 1383.
54. ST, p. 629.
55. Frank A. Martin, *Under the Absolute Amir*, p. 157.
56. KD, 25 June 1887, PSLI, vol. 49, p. 557.
57. KD, 20–23 June 1893, PSLI, vol. 70, p. 1797.
58. Rennick to Owen, 19 November 1879, Secret Memorandum 28 in IOL.
59. KD, 3 May 1887, PSLI, vol. 50, p. 588.
60. Amir to elders of Katawaz and Zurmut, etc., KD, 21–24 October 1893, PSLI, vol. 72, p. 1280.
61. Amir in darbar, KD, 19 November 1886, PSLI, vol. 48, p. 1231.
62. Amir in darbar, KD, 31 August 1886, PSLI, vol. 48, p. 519.
63. KD, 30 September 1887, PSLI, vol. 51, p. 776.
64. ST, p. 403.
65. ST, p. 890.
66. MM, September 1899, PSLI, vol. 116, no. 978 (18).
67. Amir to 700 prisoners working on the Tang-i-Gharu road, KD, 6 June 1891, PSLI, vol. 63, p. 637.
68. Amir to Ghilzay elders, KD, 25 March 1887, PSLI, vol. 49, p. 1141.
69. MM, September 1899, PSLI, vol. 116, no. 978 (18).
70. ST, p. 1217.
71. MM, September 1899, PSLI, vol. 116, no. 978 (18).
72. KD, 17 July 1891, PSLI, vol. 63, p. 1092.
73. Amir to a gathering of 6,000 in Jalalabad, KD, 19 January 1888, PSLI, vol. 52, p. 917.
74. Mahomed, *Life of Abdur Rahman*, 1: viii.
75. Griffin to Stewart, 4 August 1880, PSLI, vol. 26, pt. 5, p. 963.
76. Griffin, "The Late Amir and His Successor," p. 748.
77. BACA, p. 21.
78. Martin, *Under the Absolute Amir*, p. 39.
79. George N. Curzon, *Tales of Travels*, p. 65.
80. Ibid., p. 60.
81. Amir to courtiers, KD, 31 July 1895, PSLI, vol. 81, no. 29 (3).
82. ST, p. 435.
83. Kh. D, 31 March 1900, PSLI, vol. 122, no. 505.
84. PD, 3 July 1885, PSLI, vol. 45, p. 238.
85. Amir to viceroy, 24 April 1889, PSLI, vol. 57, p. 551.
86. Amir in darbar, KD, 18 February 1887, PSLI, vol. 49, p. 135.
87. Qazi Sayyed Hasan of Qarabagh, news agent with the British mission to Khanabad, June 1880, PSLI, vol. 25, p. 1300.
88. Kand. D, 28 December 1882, PSLI, vol. 35, p. 375.
89. Durand to Cunningham, 3 December 1893, PSLI, vol. 73, p. 17.
90. KD, 15 August 1896, PSLI, vol. 88, F.L. no. 254 F. (96).

91. Amir to his favorite wife, Bibi Halima, KD, 14 March 1891, PSLI, vol. 62, p. 963.

92. Amir in darbar, KD, 27–29 November 1892, PSLI, vol. 68, p. 962.

93. Amir in darbar, KD, 17–24 September 1892, PSLI, vol. 68, p. 36.

94. KD, 26 August 1892, PSLI, vol. 67, p. 1105.

95. Martin, *Under the Absolute Amir*, p. 114.

96. PD, 15 February 1901, PSLI, vol. 131, no. 391.

97. ST, p. 563.

98. ST, p. 1002.

99. For details see Chapter VII of this work.

100. Amir to Muhammadzay sardars, KD, 27 June 1896, PSLI, F.L. no. 2009 F. (96).

101. Amir to British agent, KD, 24–27 December 1892, PSLI, vol. 69, p. 444.

102. Amir to Habib Allah, KD, 28 February 1891, PSLI, vol. 62, p. 917.

103. Kand. D, 26 July 1895, PSLI, p. 81, no. 26.

104. From an anonymous letter attached to five mosques in Kabul. KD, 30 September 1893, October 1893, PSLI, vol. 72, p. 729.

105. An anonymous letter to the amir in a petition box, KD, 18 February 1889, PSLI, vol. 56, p. 771.

106. Mahomed, *Life of Abdur Rahman*, 1: 25, 129.

107. ST, p. 803.

108. British agent, Mazar, 6 May 1890, PSLI, vol. 60, p. 489.

109. Mahomed, *Life of Abdur Rahman*, 2: 24.

110. Durand to Cunningham, 20 December 1893, PSLI, vol. 73, p. 23.

111. KD, 20–22 July 1892, PSLI, vol. 67, p. 315.

112. Mala. D, 16 February 1901, PSLI, vol. 131, no. 365.

113. Mahomed, *Life of Abdur Rahman*, 1: 232.

114. Amir to British agent, KD, 26 May 1892, PSLI, vol. 67, p. 1105.

115. Surgeon Owen, 12 October 1886, PSLI, vol. 49, p. 51.

116. KD, 18 March 1891, PSLI, vol. 62, p. 965.

117. KD, 1 April 1891, PSLI, vol. 63, p. 866.

118. Martin, *Under the Absolute Amir*, p. 37.

119. Memo on the state of health of the amir by Surgeon Major W. A. C. Roe, AVI, Encl. no. 4, 16.

120. Surgeon C. W. Owen, member of the ABC, who examined the amir in Kabul, 12 October 1886, PSLI, vol. 49, p. 51.

121. MM, December 1890, PSLI, vol. 62, p. 7.

122. KD, 25–27 November 1891, PSLI, vol. 64, pp. 16, 22.

123. MM, Pyne, December 1890, PSLI, vol. 62, p. 7.

124. Martin, *Under the Absolute Amir*, p. 125.

125. Kh. D, 17 August 1901, PSLI, vol. 137, no. 1117.

126. According to Mrs. Daly, the amir's physician, 'Abd al-Rahman died on Monday, 30 September 1901, but was buried on 3 October, the day when Habib Allah acceded to the throne. Political officer in Khyber to Peshawar commissioner (T) 10 October 1901, PSLI, vol. 138, no. 130 (13) Encl. 52.

127. Kand. D, 1 November 1901, PSLI, vol. 140, no. 1473a.

128. Kh. D, 19 October 1901, PSLI, vol. 139, no. 1432. G. M. Ghobar, *Afghanistan Along the Highway of History*, p. 699, relates a story from Mirza Muhammad Ibrahim, confidential physician of the amir, that when the amir was in a critical state, a bowl of "medicine" was given to him by the order of Sardar Habib Allah. Shortly after this, so the story goes, the amir died. The story is related in such a way as to suggest that the amir was poisoned, but there is no real reason to believe this.

129. BACA, p. 19.

130. ST, p. 702.

131. Martin, *Under the Absolute Amir*, p. 120.

132. Ibid., pp. 32, 121.

133. Sardar Habib Allah to amir, KD, 9 March 1896, PSLI, vol. 85, F.L. no. 806 F.

134. An anonymous letter to amir, KD, 30 September 1893, October 1893, PSLI, vol. 72, p. 729.

135. MM, February 1891, PSLI, vol. 62, p. 763.

136. Raja Jahand Dad Khan, chief of Indian Muslim delegation to Amir Habib Allah, 27 December 1901, PSLI, vol. 141, no. 215 (1).

137. PD, 23 June 1888, PSLI, vol. 54, p. 314.

138. Elphinstone, *An Account*, pp. 11, 243.

139. On the question of succession, the amir's views are described in detail by Sultan Mahomed. In the first chapter of the second volume of *Life of Abdur Rahman* the amir is quoted as saying "the eldest son [of the Afghan kings] succeeds to the throne, provided he is fitted for the post, and is also approved and selected by the nation." This remark is a correct reflection of the situation and is probably a genuine statement of the amir's. Since the second part of this book, however, is not genuine and more specifically, since on the question of nominating an heir apparent the amir's assertion that no one knew of his "intentions," is in conflict with his firmans (which will be discussed shortly), I have not drawn information on this subject from this book.

140. PD, 23 June 1888, PSLI, vol. 54, p. 314.

141. KD, 29 April 1887, Sec. F., 465–570, July 1887, NAI.

142. John Gray, *My Residence at the Court of the Amir*, p. 323.

143. Durand to Cunningham, 3 December 1893, PSLI, vol. 73, p. 17.

144. PD, 11 January 1892, PSLI, vol. 65, p. 179.

145. KD, 7 March 1891, PSLI, vol. 62, p. 1017.

146. ST, p. 964.

147. Ghobar, *Afghanistan Along the Highway of History*, p. 656.

148. Years later, Amir Habib Allah's principal wife, Sarajal-Khawatin, defaced a Kuchi woman, whom the amir had married for her beauty.

149. BACA, p. 20.

150. Dr. ʾAbd al-Rahman, the amir's physician, PD, 23 June 1888, PSLI, vol. 54, p. 314.

151. PD, 22 December 1890, PSLI, vol. 62, p. 66.

152. KD, 10 July 1895, PSLI, vol. 81, no. 26.

153. ST, p. 703.

154. Amir to British agent at Mazar, 20 January 1890, PSLI, vol. 59, p. 838.

155. Amir's firman to the people of Laghman, Ningrahar, etc., PD, 23 November 1891, PSLI, vol. 64, p. 1449.

156. To make him popular, the amir instructed Habib Allah to be specially lenient with the people whenever the amir treated them harshly. KD, 10–13 June 1893, PSLI, vol. 70, p. 1589.

157. Raja Jahan Dad Khan, 17 December 1901, PSLI, vol. 141, no. 215 (5).

158. PD, no. 11, 1 December 1900, PSLI, vol. 129, no. 1317.

159. Amir to Sardar Habib Allah, PD, 1–30 June 1901, PSLI, vol. 136, no. 1012.

160. PD, 7 August 1896, PSLI, vol. 88, no. 15, FOL, no. 2326, F. (96).

161. Raja Jahan Dad Khan, 27 December 1901, PSLI, vol. 141, no. 215 (2).

162. Khybar political officer to Peshawar commissioner, 9 October 1901, PSLI, Kabul Series, no. 1260, 138, Encl. no. 33 (7).

163. Kh. D, 19 October 1901, PSLI, vol. 139, no. 14329.

164. KD, 5 October 1901, PSLI, vol. 138, no. 1301, Encl. no. 65 (18).

165. Raja Jahan Dad Khan, 27 December 1901, PSLI, vol. 141, no. 215 (5).

166. EI (1965), p. 210.

167. The number of *ghulam bachas* in the service of the amir can be estimated from the number of Kafir boys, which by 1900 reached 210 from the following regions: Lutdeh, 60; Kamdesh and Mujash, 60; Mudugal, 30; Katwar, 20; Veron, 20; Waigal, 20 (CD, 22 May 1900, PSLI, vol. 123, no. 669).

168. ST, p. 852.

169. For details, see Martin, *Under the Absolute Amir*, p. 109; CLA, pp. 151–152.

170. Kh. D, 6 July 1901, PSLI, vol. 135, no. 936.

171. Ghobar, *Afghanistan Along the Highway of History*, p. 716.

172. ST, p. 649.

173. ST, p. 1164.

174. CLA, p. 70.

175. Ghobar, *Afghanistan Along the Highway of History*, p. 595.

176. MU.

177. AQ, p. 6.

178. MM, July 1896, PSLI, vol. 87, F.L. no. 145 (96).

179. Amir to Ahmad Shah, confidential secretary, PD, 23 June 1893, PSLI, vol. 69, p. 738.

180. KD, 13 May 1899, PSLI, vol. 114, p. 565.

181. Ghobar, *Afghanistan Along the Highway of History*, p. 652.

182. CLA, p. 65.

183. CLA, pp. 48, 61, 65. Angus Hamilton, *Afghanistan*, p. 273.

184. CLA, p. 56.

185. CLA, p. 61.

186. CLA, p. 57.

187. Durand to Cunningham, 3 December 1893, PSLI, vol. 73, p. 17.

188. CLA, p. 39.

189. G. Singh, *Ahmad Shah Durrani*, p. 354.

190. Elphinstone, *An Account*, pp. 2, 102.

191. C. M. MacGregor, *Central Asia*, pp. 57, 60.

192. Ibid., p. 60.

193. Keddie, *Sayyid Jamal ad-Din "al-Afghani,"* p. 56.

194. ST, p. 933.

195. CLA, p. 58.

196. Ibid.

197. CLA, p. 55.

198. KD, 12–14 August 1891, PSLI, vol. 63, p. 1302.

199. Ghobar, *Afghanistan Along the Highway of History*, p. 595; Khafi, *Padshahan-i-Mutakhir-i-Afghanistan*, 2: 59.

❖

II. The Central Government: 2

1. The title of *sadr-i-a'zam* was conferred on Mir Abul-Qasim (*dabir al-mulk*), *na'ib al-sultanat* on Na'ib Sarwar (governor of Herat) and on Muhammad Nabi (*dabir al-mulk*), *na'ib al-dawla* on Sardar Ghulam Rasul (governor of Jalalabad), and wazir on Sipah Salar Charkhi.

2. KD, no. 37, 25 September 1895, Sec. F., November 1898, no. 5, nos. 147–82, NAI.

3. KD, 27 December 1890, PSLI, vol. 62, p. 369.

4. Ghobar, *Afghanistan Along the Highway of History*, p. 657.

5. Once in winter the amir ordered a *peshkhidmat*, while in uniform, to throw himself into a tank full of water. Also, Kotwal Muhammad Hyssayn was made to pick up by his mouth gold *mohrs* (a kind of small shell resembling a pearl) inserted in a sweet made of rice and milk. KD, 17 July 1895, PSLI, vol. 81, no. 27.

6. "List of gentlemen on whom military titles were conferred," 11 July 1891, PSLI, vol. 63, p. 1097.

7. KD, 27–30 May 1893, PSLI, vol. 70, p. 1337.

8. Colonel C. E. Yate, 10 April 1893, PSLI, vol. 70, p. 1176.

9. In reply to a demand to render his accounts, Kabul Kotwal Parwana Khan said that he had nothing to do with the accounts as he had only 840,000 rupees with him. He was then told that when it reached 900,000 he should deliver it to the treasury. KD, 9–11 November 1892, PSLI, vol. 68, p. 691.

10. Ghobar, *Afghanistan Along the Highway of History*, p. 657.

11. ST, p. 668.

12. Frank A. Martin, *Under the Absolute Amir*, pp. 246, 250.

13. Ibid., p. 249.

14. Ibid., p. 247.

15. Ibid., p. 248.

16. KD, no. 22, 20 March 1889, Sec. F., May 1889, nos. 530–543, NAI.

17. R. D. McChesney, "The Economic Reforms of Amir Abdul Rahman Khan," *Afghanistan*, no. 3 (1968): 12.

18. ST, p. 379.

19. ST, pp. 419–420.

20. ST, p. 668.

21. ST, p. 438.

22. ST, p. 698.

23. McChesney, "Economic Reforms," p. 23.

24. ST, p. 832.

25. Of the other *sanjishiyyan*, Mirza Sher 'Ali and Mirza Ghulam Hasan were killed for their alleged failure to work honestly. Mirza Sayyed Mahmud resigned his office, and Mirza Sayyed Qasim was appointed *sardaftari* of the eastern region, ST, p. 874. According to Ghobar, *Afghanistan Along the Highway of History*, p. 655, the auditing office came to be known as *shash kulah* (i.e., the six hat) and was charged with examining financial transactions and evaluating the property of those who had been condemned.

26. ST, p. 909.

27. ST, pp. 514, 1032.

28. KD, October 1898, PSLI, vol. 107, no. 1006.

29. ST, p. 653. Among the main deeds for which stamps were issued were the following: power of agency (*wakalat nama*), deed of recognizance (*iltizam nama*), deed of divorce (*talaq nama*), notification (*'ilim nama*), deed of sale (*gabala-i-Shari'a*), deed of acquittance (*ibra nama*), deed of marriage (*nikah nama*), note of clarification (*tasfiyya nama*), lease (*ijarah khat*), legacy (*turuqjat-i-Shari'a*), revenue receipt (*ta'luqa-i-daftari*), deed (*hujjat*), judgment of claim (*faisala da'wa*), order (*hukumnama*), summons to appear (*muhzar nama*), and deed of compromise (*sulh nama*). KD, 18 September 1889, PSLI, vol. 58, p. 315.

30. ST, p. 1032.

31. Ibid.

32. PD, 6 August 1886, PSLI, vol. 48, p. 75.

33. Mahomed, *Life of Abdur Rahman*, 2: 61.

34. MRA (1925), p. 583.

35. Martin notes that "stamps have to be affixed to the letters," but he does not specify whether this was in the reign of Amir 'Abd al-Rahman or of Habib Allah. Martin, *Under the Absolute Amir*, p. 211.

36. MRA (1925), p. 583.

37. PD, 4 July 1881, PSLI, vol. 29, p. 500.

38. HD, 19 October 1884, PSLI, vol. 42, p. 914.

39. Durand to Cunningham, 20 December 1893, PSLI, vol. 73, p. 20.

40. ST, pp. 861, 700.

41. ST, p. 622.

42. ST, p. 752.

43. ST, p. 858.

44. KD, 3 December 1890, PSLI, vol. 61, p. 978.

45. Ghobar, *Afghanistan Along the Highway of History*, p. 644.

46. Wheeler, *The Ameer Abdur Rahman*, p. 212.

47. KD, 9 December 1887, PSLI, vol. 52, p. 88. At one time the officials were compelled to work fourteen hours a day. Ghobar, *Afghanistan Along the Highway of History*, p. 654. This was probably during the time when they were hard pressed to complete the statement of accounts of income and expenditure.

48. ST, p. 833.

49. KD, 24–27 October 1891, PSLI, vol. 64, p. 1086.

50. ST, pp. 668–671.
51. ST, p. 941.
52. ST, p. 699.
53. ST, p. 1011.
54. KD, 11 July 1893, PSLI, vol. 71, p. 107.
55. ST, p. 921.
56. ST, pp. 593, 1055.
57. AQ, p. 98.
58. AQ, pp. 7, 90.
59. BACA, p. 14.
60. KD, 23 August 1887, PSLI, vol. 51, p. 383.
61. KD, 24 August 1889, PSLI, vol. 57, p. 1241.
62. CLA, p. 95.
63. Amir in darbar, KD, 17 March 1885, PSLI, vol. 44, p. 739.
64. AT, 5: 122. The man whom Shah Mahmud had appointed as *khan-i-mulla* was Muhammad Sa'id.
65. BACA, pp. 14, 93, 176.
66. CLA, pp. 97, 98.
67. Col. Haji Gul from Shinwar to Amir, KD, 6 May 1887, PSLI, vol. 50, p. 591.
68. Ghobar, *Afghanistan Along the Highway of History*, p. 655.
69. BACA, p. 138. KD, 2 July 1886, PSLI, vol. 47, p. 900.
70. KD, 27 May 1888, PSLI, vol. 50, p. 875.
71. KD, 13 January 1888, PSLI, vol. 52, p. 869.
72. Amir to Sardar Habib Allah, KD, 27 April 1889, PSLI, vol. 57, p. 353.
73. BACA, p. 138.
74. British agent in Jalalabad, 13 April 1888, PSLI, vol. 53, p. 432.
75. KD, 29 July 1887, PSLI, vol. 50, p. 1701.
76. BACA, p. 138.
77. PD, 23 November 1892, PSLI, vol. 68, p. 694.
78. ST, p. 795.
79. William Jenkyns, *Report on the District of Jalalabad*, p. 17.
80. Martin, *Under the Absolute Amir*, p. 146; Ghobar, *Afghanistan Along the Highway of History*, p. 653.
81. ZM, p. 3.
82. Mala. D, 23 June 1901, PSLI, vol. 135, no. 851.
83. At one time the daily birth average among these prisoners was four or five children, who were done away with. KD, 12 June 1889, PSLI, vol. 57, p. 824.
84. Kand. D, 24 December 1885, PSLI, vol. 46, p. 952.
85. PD, 7 June 1888, PSLI, vol. 52, p. 408.
86. KD, 3 September 1890, PSLI, vol. 61, p. 248.
87. KD, 22 October 1898, PSLI, vol. 109, no. 1073.
88. In 1894 the daily consumption was seven kharwars of grain. KD, 3–5 January 1894, PSLI, vol. 73, p. 340. The food given to each prisoner was two *nans* (flat bread weighing about half a pound each). Martin, *Under the Absolute Amir*, p. 149.
89. KD, 26 June 1889, PSLI, vol. 57, p. 956; Martin, *Under the Absolute Amir*, p. 147.
90. KD, 2 July 1890, PSLI, vol. 60, p. 938.
91. MM, June 1889, PSLI, vol. 57, p. 853.
92. MM, December 1890, PSLI, vol. 62, p. 7.
93. PD, 15 November 1890, PSLI, vol. 61, p. 889.
94. PD, 22 December 1890, PSLI, vol. 62, p. 65.
95. Kand. D, January 1891, PSLI, vol. 63, p. 1191.
96. Warburton to Durand, 21 July 1889, PSLI, vol. 58, p. 145.
97. KD, 4 February 1884, PSLI, vol. 47, p. 569.
98. KD, 23–26 May 1894, PSLI, vol. 74, p. 1291.
99. MM, June 1889, PSLI, vol. 57, p. 853.
100. PD, 7 January 1888, PSLI, vol. 52, p. 408.

101. MM, June 1886, PSLI, vol. 47, p. 841.
102. Martin, *Under the Absolute Amir*, p. 146.
103. PD, 24 October 1885, PSLI, vol. 45, p. 1254.
104. Kand. D, 19 July 1895, PSLI, 81, no. 25.
105. Ghobar, *Afghanistan Along the Highway of History*, p. 654.
106. Martin, *Under the Absolute Amir*, p. 302.
107. Curzon, *Tales of Travels*, p. 73. For graphic examples of punishments see Martin, *Under the Absolute Amir*, pp. 142–172, and Ghobar, *Afghanistan Along the Highway of History*, pp. 653–655. Warburton to Durand, 21 July 1889, PSLI, vol. 58, p. 145.
108. For details, see Mahomed, *Life of Abdur Rahman*, 1: 293.
109. PD, 11 April 1893, PSLI, vol. 70, p. 178.
110. ST, pp. 902, 909.
111. PD, 15 May 1901, PSLI, vol. 134, no. 756.
112. Kh. D, 26 October 1901, PSLI, vol. 140, no. 147a; ST, p. 1158. For text of the firman in Persian and English see Angus Hamilton, *Afghanistan*, p. 370.
113. CLA, p. 101.
114. BACA, pp. 93, 146.
115. ST, p. 1035.
116. ST, p. 815.
117. CLA, p. 104.
118. CLA, p. 61.
119. Negro slaves were brought to Afghanistan from Ethiopia during the Sadozay period and were settled in Kabul and other cities. AT, pp. 5, 120.
120. ST, p. 821.
121. BACA, p. 10.
122. MRA, p. 205.
123. CLA, p. 104.
124. ST, p. 713.
125. BACA, p. 236.
126. A.B., Kabul Correspondent, 26 January 1882, PSLI, vol. 31, p. 733.
127. A.B., Kabul Correspondent, 31 December 1881, PSLI, vol. 31, p. 301.
128. BACA, p. 183.
129. BACA, p. 210.
130. Amir to Pyne, undated, Documents and Records of the Past, nos. 8, 11, ARAMFA.
131. Durand to Lansdowne, Kabul, 26 October 1893, Mss. Eur. D, 727, no. 5.
132. Durand to Lansdowne, Kabul, 9 October 1893, Mss. Eur. D, 727, no. 5.
133. ST, p. 591.
134. Griesbach to Cunningham (Mazar), 25 February 1889, For. Dept. Sec. F., May 1889, nos. 216–225, NAI.
135. Ibid.
136. Ibid.
137. Ibid.
138. Martin, *Under the Absolute Amir*, p. 41.

❖

III. The Local Government

1. Elphinstone, *An Account*, 2: 255.
2. Singh, *Ahmad Shah Durrani*, p. 354.
3. Ibid.
4. Ghobar, *Afghanistan Along the Highway of History*, pp. 418, 574; ST, 1: 250.
5. PD, no. 13, 6 July 1896, PSLI, F.L. no. 1934-F., vol. 87 (96).
6. ST, p. 687.
7. "List of Districts and Governors of Afghanistan," For. Dept. Secret-F. Pros. February 1893, nos. 141–160, 151 NAI.

8. Major Hasting, "A Short Account of the Ghazni District," 1880, PSLI, vol. 26, pt. 3, p. 359.

9. For names of these districts see "List of Districts and Governors."

10. GAK (1895), pt. 4, Appendix A, Afghanistan, p. XLV.

11. ST, pp. 418, 424.

12. CLA, 109.

13. PD, 1 September 1883, PSLI, vol. 37, p. 1302.

14. AQ, p. 119.

15. ST, p. 1060.

16. ST, p. 962.

17. QKMH, p. 13.

18. QKMH, p. 12.

19. QKMH, p. 14.

20. QKMH, p. 44.

21. QKMH, pp. 13, 28.

22. Durrani, *Tarikh-i-Sultani* [The history of Sultani], p. 23.

23. RM, p. 10.

24. Elphinstone, *An Account*, 2: 263.

25. Among the Pashtuns, Pashtunwali or customary laws were adopted by a very large proportion of people for the settlement of their disputes in preference to the Shari'a. H. W. Bellew, *Journal of a Political Mission to Afghanistan in 1857*, p. 67.

26. As experts in the legal knowledge of Islam, the muftis gave *fetwas* and were engaged in the legal profession; but in Afghanistan, as in Muslim Spain, where the institution of the *shura* developed, permanent muftis were attached to the courts as advisers (*mushawer*), EI (1965): 866. Later in the amir's reign the muftis were not supposed to give *fetwas* unless they were asked to do so. AQ, p. 39.

27. RM, p. 10.

28. ST, p. 1120. A number of important persons from Baghdad and Medina who claimed they were sayyeds and were versed in Islamic laws were refused entry into Afghanistan. ST, pp. 1043, 1108.

29. ST, p. 652.

30. AQ, p. 27.

31. AQ, p. 42.

32. AQ, p. 44.

33. AQ, p. 28.

34. ST, p. 961.

35. QKMH, pp. 7, 11, 13.

36. RM, p. 12.

37. ST, p. 1114.

38. ST, p. 1230.

39. ST, p. 1114.

40. AQ, p. 48.

41. AQ, p. 99.

42. AQ, p. 101.

43. AQ, p. 46.

44. The actual phrase was *wallah, billah, tillah.*

45. AQ, p. 67.

46. AQ, p. 61.

47. ST, p. 987.

48. Kand. D, 1 May 1888, Sec. F., 43–62, no. 49, NAI.

49. The Kandahar *kotwal* was actually ordered to arrest people found in groups. Kand. D, 19 January 1884, PSLI, vol. 39, p. 1190.

50. KD, 20 July 1886, PSLI, vol. 47, p. 1050.

51. Most of this information about the *kalantars* comes from *Kitabcha-i-Dastur al 'Amal-i-Kalantarha-i-Guzarha-i-Dar al-Sultana-i-Kabul wa Ghaira Wilayat-i-Afghanistan* [A manual of instruction for the *kalantars* of Kabul and other cities of Afghanistan], p. 19.

52. ST, p. 1061.
53. Martin, *Under the Absolute Amir*, p. 49.
54. KD, 28 January 1884, PSLI, vol. 39, p. 1204.
55. Martin, *Under the Absolute Amir*, p. 49.
56. ST, p. 836.
57. ST, p. 978.
58. Kand. D, 15–18 August 1891, PSLI, vol. 63, p. 1393.
59. CLA, p. 94.
60. Bellew, *Journal*, p. 39.
61. ST, p. 978.
62. In the early Muslim period, the office of the *hisbah* was known as *sahib al-sug*, or *'amil al-sug* (master of the market) after a Greek term. It was in the reign of Caliph al-Ma'mun (d. 833) that the word *muhtasib* was coined. At that time the authority of this office overlapped with that of the judge and of the police agent. In fact, the *muhtasib* was more powerful than the other two. A. F. 'Omar, "Hisbah," *Journal of Muslim World League* 1, no. 9 (1974): 16.
63. My information on the *muhtasibs* comes from *Ihtisab al-Din* [A manual of instruction for the *muhtasibs*], p. 39. Wheeler, *The Ameer Abdur Rahman*, p. 215.
64. ST, p. 710.
65. PD, no. 3, 15 February 1901, PSLI, vol. 131, no. 393.
66. Kand. D, 27 May 1886, PSLI, vol. 47, p. 709.
67. ST, p. 397.
68. ST, p. 709.
69. ST, p. 409.
70. Kh. D, 19 May 1900, PSLI, vol. 123, no. 667.
71. "List of District Governors," For. Dept. Secret-F., Pros. February 1893, nos. 141–160, no. 157, NAI.
72. QKMH, pp. 13, 26.
73. AQ, p. 118.
74. QKMH, p. 2.
75. ST, p. 638.
76. MRA (1925), p. 370.
77. For details, see "Report on the Origin and History of the Ghilzais," by Capt. F. C. Burton, October 1880, F.-No. 4–6, NAI.
78. H. F. Schurmann, *The Mongols of Afghanistan*, pp. 141, 142.
79. Ibid., p. 131.
80. Ibid., p. 142.
81. Ibid., p. 141.
82. Ibid., p. 143.
83. Ibid., p. 119.
84. Ibid., p. 121.
85. Elphinstone, *An Account*, 1: 403–409. B. Kushkaki, *Rahnuma-i-Qataghan wa Badakhshan* [A guide to Qataghan and Badakhshan], p. 338; E. Molly, no. 319, NAI.
86. Josiah Harlan, *Central Asia: Personal Narrative of Josiah Harlan, 1823–1841*, pp. 130, 134, 137. E. Molly, "The Hazarajat," no. 316, NAI. Once Na'ib Yusuf of Heecha Hazara put seven of his tribesmen to death, ST, p. 471.
87. For details see Elphinstone, *An Account*, 2: 100–105. C. Rawlinson, "Report on the Dooranee Tribe, April 1841," quoted by Charles MacGregor, *Central Asia*, pp. 823–869.
88. For details see Elphinstone, *An Account*, 2: 150–154.
89. For details see T. L. Pennell, "The Tribes on Our North-West Frontier," *Asiatic Quarterly Review* 30 (1910): 88–103; C. C. Davies, *The Problems of North-West Frontier of India 1890–1908*, pp. 37–56; and "The Pathans of the North-West Frontier of India," *Blackwood's Edinburg Magazine*, May 1879.
90. Bunyad Khan of Malistan in the Hazarajat collected 660 sheep, 110 sers

of ghee, 137 kharwars of wheat, and 5.5 sers of wool as revenue from his tribe but paid only 400 sheep to the government. ST, p. 515. On ST, p. 417, however, Fayz Muhammad states that the same elder exacted 4,000 sheep from his tribe.

91. MRA (1925), p. 371.
92. Alexander Burnes, *Cabool*, p. 379.
93. Elphinstone, *An Account*, 1: 233.
94. Amir to Shahghassi, KD, 8 November 1887, PSLI, vol. 51, p. 980.
95. Viceroy to secretary of state of India, 16 August 1892, PSLI, vol. 67, p. 389.
96. Kakar, *Afghanistan: A Study in Internal Political Developments, 1880–1896.*
97. ST, p. 592.
98. ST, pp. 491, 492, 605.
99. ST, p. 542.
100. ST, p. 652.
101. ST, p. 630.
102. ST, p. 531.
103. ST, p. 592.
104. ST, p. 430.
105. ST, p. 973.
106. For. Dept. Secret-F., July 1887, nos. 855–868, no. 865, NAI.
107. KD, 30 September 1899, PSLI, vol. 116, no. 979 (2).
108. QKMH, p. 13.
109. QKMH, p. 27.
110. QKMH, p. 28.
111. Fines ranged between 20,000 and 50,000 rupees. Martin, *Under the Absolute Amir*, p. 28.
112. Ibid.
113. The last incident of robbery reported in ST was in 1896, the last year of its coverage. ST, p. 1230.
114. Villagers were made responsible for murders that happened within the circle in which the voice of the *muwazzins* could be heard.
115. QKMH, p. 35.
116. QKMH, p. 47.
117. ST, p. 770.
118. ST, pp. 415, 421.
119. ST, p. 924.
120. C. E. Yate, *Northern Afghanistan*, p. 146.
121. Col. Afzal (Jalalabad), 30 March 1883, PSLI, vol. 36, p. 369.
122. ST, p. 416.
123. ST, p. 541.
124. ST, pp. 1043, 1075, 1233.
125. ST, p. 690.
126. MacGregor, *Central Asia*, p. 59.
127. PD, 21 April 1884, PSLI, vol. 40, p. 937.
128. RM, p. 11.
129. ST, p. 437.
130. ST, p. 570.
131. PD, 28 November 1885, PSLI, vol. 45, p. 1641.
132. Kand. D, 2 December 1885, PSLI, vol. 46, p. 947.
133. Kand. D, 13 June 1884, PSLI, vol. 41, p. 418.
134. Kand. D, 11 January 1884, PSLI, vol. 39, p. 1031.
135. RM, p. 16.
136. ST, p. 589.
137. ST, p. 824.
138. ST, p. 1059.
139. Ibid.
140. MacGregor, *Central Asia*, p. 59.

141. PD, 23 November 1880, PSLI, vol. 26, pt. 7, p. 1933.

142. Kand. D, 6 May 1886, PSLI, vol. 47, p. 295.

143. ST, p. 554.

144. MM, September 1899, PSLI, vol. 116, no. 978 (19).

145. ST, p. 1219.

146. Col. Atta Allah (Mazar), 6 June 1890, PSLI, vol. 60, p. 865.

147. See The System of Taxation, Chapter IV.

148. ST, pp. 956, 1120.

149. A. B., Kabul Correspondent, 9 February 1882, PSLI, vol. 31, p. 740. According to Martin, *Under the Absolute Amir*, p. 151, the amir imitated the Russian spy system.

150. Amir to British agent, KD, 24 January 1884, PSLI, vol. 35, p. 647.

151. The cities abroad where the amir's spies were stationed included Peshawar, Rawalpindi, Lahore, Karachi, Calcutta, Quetta, Mashhad, Tehran, Urganj, Merv, Tashkent, Samarqand. In 1901, the amir added forty informers to his "numerous agents" already stationed in India. Mala. D, 30 April 1901, PSLI, vol. 133, no. 640.

152. Kand. D, 14 April 1884, PSLI, vol. 40, p. 1226.

153. Mahomed also adds that in Afghanistan every house was believed to have had a spy. A wife was afraid, he continues, of her husband having set a spy on her and the husband was afraid of his wife. There were not wanting many instances, continues Sultan Mahomed, where children reported against their parents. *Life of Abdur Rahman*, 1: 259.

154. Ibid. The British agent once complemented the amir by stating that "Your Highness keeps yourself so well-informed that you know what a wife and husband talk about at night." KD, 14 August 1888, PSLI, vol. 54, p. 939.

155. Mahomed, *Life of Abdur Rahman*, 1: 60.

156. PD, 1 June 1883, PSLI, vol. 36, p. 1549.

157. ST, p. 1187.

158. Ghobar, *Afghanistan Along the Highway of History*, p. 625.

159. Ibid.

160. Agha Jan Sahibzada of Kohistan to Peshawar commissioner, PD, 9 October 1891, PSLI, vol. 64, p. 763.

161. Kand. D, 27 April 1890, PSLI, vol. 60, p. 336.

162. ST, p. 990.

163. ST, p. 1008.

164. Ghobar, *Afghanistan Along the Highway of History*, p. 652.

165. The people of Ningrahar told the amir that "They suffered greatly from Government informers, from whose unfounded accusations no one was safe." Mala. D, 23 June 1901, PSLI, vol. 135, no. 851.

166. KD, 12 August 1887, PSLI, vol. 50, p. 408.

167. Lillias Hamilton, *A Vizier's Daughter*, p. 180.

168. ST, p. 383.

169. ST, p. 933.

170. ST, p. 969.

171. ST, p. 593.

172. ST, p. 648.

173. ST, pp. 434–437; for the amir's instructions to governors in general see also ST, pp. 424–426, 720–727, 648.

✣

IV. The System of Taxation

1. Elphinstone, *An Account*, 2: 259.

2. Ibid., 2: 158.

3. Ibid., 1: 408.

4. Ibid., 2: 197.

5. Ibid., 1: 238. The total amount of revenue in this period was, according to Elphinstone (2:258), nearly 30 million rupees and, according to Ghobar, *Afghanistan Along the Highway of History*, p. 358, 31 million.

6. Ferrier, *History of the Afghans*, p. 322.

7. Kand. D, 13 August 1883, PSLI, vol. 37, p. 1088.

8. Amir to British agent, KD, 15 December 1885, PSLI, vol. 46, p. 939.

9. For details see Jenkyns, *Report on the District of Jalalabad*, Major Hasting, "A Short Account of the Ghazni District," PSLI, vol. 26, pt. 3, pp. 357–359.

10. MU, p. 20.

11. ST, p. 945.

12. MU, p. 24.

13. ST, p. 1088.

14. ST, p. 945.

15. ST, p. 787.

16. Amir to Dufferin, 12 Zay al-Qaʾida 1304 [3 August 1887], For. Dept. Secret-F., Pros. September 1887, no. 92, 2, NAI. In MU the rates are *zakat* (animal tax of one out of forty), *ʾushr, se-kot,* and *char-kot,* p. 20. There is no mention in MU of *jamʾbast.*

17. For details see A. N. Poliak, "Classification of Lands in the Islamic Law and Its Technical Terms," *American Journal of Semitic Languages and Literature* 57 (January 1940): 50–62.

18. Amir to Dufferin, 12 Zay al-Qaʾida 1304 [3 August 1887], For. Dept. Secret-F., Pros. September 1887, no. 92, 2, NAI.

19. A. A. Shahristani, "A Short Account of the Forty Years Proceedings of the Ministry of Finance," *Wata*, special issue, 1958, p. 2.

20. Col. Afzal (Jalalabad), 19 January 1883, PSLI, vol. 37, p. 68.

21. KD, 17–21 July 1891, PSLI, vol. 63, p. 1093.

22. KD, 2 September 1884, PSLI, vol. 41, p. 1549.

23. In the district of Jalalabad, as a result of the appraisal, the revenue increased from 5 lakhs to 5 lakhs and 90,000 rupees, KD, 17–21 July 1891, PSLI, vol. 63, p. 1093.

24. Kand. D, 11 December 1884, PSLI, vol. 43, p. 413.

25. Survey officials to amir, KD, 25 November 1884, PSLI, vol. 42, p. 934.

26. In 1889 landowners between Jalalabad and Gandamak were ordered to pay 4 rupees per jarib, while a similar rate had been already imposed on the landowners of Laghman and Chaprihar; but the Shinwars were made to pay only 1.5 rupees per jarib as revenue.

27. A *buluk* is said to be a canal or stream, but actually it is a collection of villages, ranging in number from sixteen (Sabqar) to seventy-three (Anjil) but irrigated from a common canal. The whole region within the *buluks,* situated between the rivers of Herat and Foshanj, had fixed boundaries. This region is known as the oasis (*jilga*) of Herat, as distinct from its dependencies referred to as the provinces (*wilayat*) of Herat. As the most fertile region of Herat, the oasis is known for its vineyards and agriculture. The city of Herat is situated within the *buluk* of Anjil. For details see Hafiz Abro, *Joghrafiyya-i-Hafiz Abro* [The geography of Hafiz Abro], "Herat" and Qasim b. Yusuf A. Herawi, *Risala-i-Tariqi-i-Qismat-i-Ab-i-Qalb* [The irrigation system of Herat].

28. Anjil, Alinjan, Adwan wa Tizan, Khiaban, Ghoran wa Pashtan, Kambaraq, Guzara, Sabqar, and Shafilan. Riyazi mentions Atishan, Kandah, and Karabad instead of the last three. ZM, p. 44.

29. Muhammad Taqi, "Report on Herat," 1885, PSLI, vol. 49, p. 1175.

30. Amir to British agent, KD, 15 December 1885, PSLI, vol. 46, p. 939.

31. McChesney, "The Economic Reforms of Amir Abdul Rahman Khan," *Afghanistan*, no. 3 (1968): 24.

32. QKMH, p. 4.

33. Kand. D, no. 49, 7 December 1889, Sec F., 132–160, no. 65, NAI.

34. In 1889 the taxpayers of Turkestan (Col. Atta Allah, 23 July 1889, PSLI, vol. 57, p. 1289) and in 1890 those of Kandahar (Kand. D, 1 June 1890, PSLI, vol. 60, p. 783) were ordered to pay their tax revenue in advance for one year.

35. ST, pp. 990, 991.

36. HD, 26 July 1894, PSLI, vol. 76, p. 108.

37. QKMH, p. 6.

38. ST, p. 841.
39. ST, p. 942.
40. ST, p. 841.
41. M. Mirza Hussayn (*hakim* of Yakawlang) to Sardar Habib Allah, 17 Rabi al-Sani 1318 [1901], Unclassified File no. 20, ARAMFA.
42. F. Muhammad (*hakim* of Surkh wa Parsa) to Amir Habib Allah, 25 Zay al-Hijja 1318 [1901]. File no. 69, ARAMFA.
43. M. Mirza Hussayn to Sardar Habib Allah, 24 Rabiʾ as-Sani 1318 [1901], Unclassified File no. 20, ARAMFA.
44. Kand. D, 17 March 1893, PSLI, vol. 70, p. 155.
45. Kand. D, 24 December 1885, PSLI, vol. 46, p. 951.
46. ST, p. 841.
47. ST, p. 866, Kand. D, 1 March 1883, PSLI, vol. 36, p. 165.
48. ST, p. 942.
49. ST, p. 841.
50. Ibid.
51. PD, no. 21, 25 October 1893, PSLI, vol. 72, p. 1273.
52. KD, 20 August 1898, PSLI, vol. 106, no. 882.
53. MM, August 1899, PSLI, vol. 115, no. 888.
54. ST, p. 757.
55. PD, 19 December 1884, PSLI, vol. 43, p. 74.
56. Kand. D, 11 December 1884, PSLI, vol. 43, p. 413.
57. KD, 6 September 1890, PSLI, vol. 61, p. 307.
58. ST, pp. 859, 870, 894.
59. ST, p. 859.
60. HD, 12 November 1895, PSLI, vol. 84, no. 47.
61. F. Muhammad (*hakim* of Turkmen and Parsa) to Amir Habib Allah, 25 zay al-Hijja 1318 [1901], File no. 69, ARAMFA.
62. ST, p. 945.
63. Col. Afzal in Mamakhel, 17 April 1883, PSLI, vol. 37, p. 1001.
64. Before the amir's reign, the Jamshidis and Hazaras of Herat collected pistachio nuts for themselves, paying ʾushr to their elders. In 1886 they were made to pay two-thirds to the government and allowed to keep the rest for themselves.
65. MM, June 1888, PSLI, vol. 54, p. 407.
66. Jenkyns, *Report on Jalalabad*, p. 10.
67. Major Hasting, "A Short Account of the Ghazni District," PSLI, vol. 26, pt. 3, p. 358.
68. Kand. D, 4 January 1891, PSLI, vol. 62, p. 615.
69. PD, 14 August 1884, PSLI, vol. 41, p. 1268.
70. Government revenue in wheat and barley for the whole country was computed at 34,000 kharwars. Amir in darbar, Col. Allah (Mazar), 20 September 1889, PSLI, vol. 58, p. 534.
71. Kand. D, 2 February 1894, PSLI, vol. 73, p. 899.
72. MM, December 1890, PSLI, vol. 62, p. 7.
73. MM, March 1900, PSLI, vol. 122, no. 519 (4).
74. Shahristani, "A Short Account of the Ministry of Finance," p. 2.
75. RM, p. 12.
76. KD, 19–22 December 1891, PSLI, vol. 64, p. 237.
77. KD, 2 March 1888, PSLI, vol. 53, p. 420.
78. KD, 24 December 1886, PSLI, vol. 49, p. 150.
79. PD, 2, 8 September 1885, PSLI, vol. 45, p. 1157.
80. PD, 22 September 1893, PSLI, vol. 72, p. 277.
81. Amir to viceroy, 12 Zay al-Qaida 1304 [3 August 1887], For. Dept. Secret-F. Pros., September 1887, nos. 92–103, no. 92, 2, NAI.
82. ST, p. 844.
83. Ibid.
84. GD, 14 October 1895, PSLI, vol. 83 [page not numbered].
85. HD, 15 January 1891, PSLI, vol. 62, p. 767.

86. PD, 20 November 1900, PSLI, vol. 128, no. 1317.

87. ST, p. 1223.

88. ST, p. 702; HD, 21 May 1891, PSLI, vol. 64, p. 661.

89. These taxes were called *rahdari, darwazadari, maidandari, qapanpuli, dagh-i-piezar, qadirkhani, chiraghpuli, piemuri, tangapulie, chehl yaka, dahyaka, shahganji, guzari, sawiyirat,* and other names. Shahristani, "A Short Account of the Ministry of Finance," p. 2.

90. KD, 22 November 1890, PSLI, vol. 61, p. 957.

91. KD, 19 October 1890, PSLI, vol. 61, p. 857.

92. PD, 23 June 1891, PSLI, vol. 63, p. 794.

93. March 1889, PSLI, vol. 113, p. 429 (4).

94. PD, 1 November 1901, PSLI, vol. 140, no. 1471 (a).

95. Kand. D, 28 March 1886, PSLI, vol. 47, p. 7.

96. Kand. D, 6 July 1891, PSLI, vol. 63, p. 1079.

97. KD, 10 July 1895, PSLI, vol. 81, no. 26 (1).

98. KD, 20 May 1899, PSLI, vol. 114, no. 586.

99. KD, 16 May 1896, PSLI, vol. 87, F.L. 1498.

100. PD, 17 October 1883, PSLI, vol. 38, p. 401.

101. KD, 17–20 February 1894, PSLI, vol. 73, p. 1031.

102. ST, p. 653.

103. C. Henry Rawlinson, "Report on the Dooranee Tribe, April 1841," quoted by MacGregor, *Central Asia*, p. 827.

104. RM, p. 7.

105. KD, no. 8, 6 March 1895, PSLI, vol. 79 [page not numbered].

106. PD, 20 February 1885, PSLI, vol. 44, p. 269.

107. KD, 23 January 1885, PSLI, vol. 43, p. 567.

108. HD, 21 October 1886, PSLI, vol. 48, p. 1161.

109. Kand. D, 6 September 1886, PSLI, vol. 48, p. 721.

110. In addition there are references to "poll tax" paid by certain Muslim groups in the reign of the amir. It was reported that in Kandahar "poll tax" was still levied on the Ghilzays and all other tribes, except the Durranis. Kand. D, 14 October 1893, PSLI, vol. 72, p. 1265. Similarly the Taimanis and Aimaqs of Herat were said to be subject to a "poll tax." HD, 8 March 1894, PSLI, vol. 74, p. 973. In all probability this tax is the same as the house tax.

111. MM, April 1887, PSLI, vol. 50, p. 222.

112. Kand. D, 16 November 1890, PSLI, vol. 61, p. 957.

113. Jenkyns, *Report on Jalalabad*, p. 13.

114. ST, p. 475.

115. KD, 13 January 1886, PSLI, vol. 46, p. 1193.

116. MM, April 1898, PSLI, vol. 103, p. 535 (2).

117. KD, 14 January 1887, PSLI, vol. 49, p. 399.

118. RM, p. 9; Jenkyns, *Report on Jalalabad*, p. 13.

119. ST, p. 475.

120. Jenkyns, *Report on Jalalabad*, p. 13.

121. KD, 1 June 1894, PSLI, vol. 74, p. 1275.

122. KD, 9–11 May 1894, PSLI, vol. 74, p. 973.

123. Kand. D, 5 December 1886, PSLI, vol. 49, p. 141.

124. KD, 6–9 February 1892, PSLI, vol. 65, p. 748.

125. PD, 7 March 1888, PSLI, vol. 52, p. 1003.

126. Jenkyns, *Report on Jalalabad*, p. 18.

127. MM, March 1900, PSLI, vol. 122, no. 519 (4).

128. MM, March 1901, PSLI, vol. 132, no. 521 (2).

129. For details see Amir ʾAbd al-Rahman, *Sarrishta-i-Islamiyya-i-Rum* [Arrangements for the Islamic government of Turkey].

130. KD, 4 March 1887, PSLI, vol. 49, p. 1138.

131. Jenkyns, *Report on Jalalabad*, p. 12.

132. HD, 10 May 1894, PSLI, vol. 74, p. 1560.

133. Kand. D, 20 November 1884, PSLI, vol. 43, p. 293.
134. PD, 1 August 1883, PSLI, vol. 37, p. 1006.
135. QKMH, p. 6.
136. PD, 14 April 1898, PSLI, vol. 103, p. 518.
137. HD, no. 21, 23 May 1895, PSLI, vol. 81 [page not numbered].
138. KD, 2–4 August 1893, PSLI, vol. 71, p. 945.
139. Kand. D, 1 June 1891, PSLI, vol. 63, p. 669.
140. ST, pp. 1186, 1226.
141. MM, January 1896, PSLI, F. Dept. no. 131 (96).
142. PD, 8 December 1887, PSLI, vol. 51, p. 1397.
143. Major Hasting, "A Short Account of the Ghazni District," PSLI, vol. 26, pt. 3, p. 358.
144. HD, 30 March 1893, PSLI, vol. 70, p. 439.
145. ST, p. 643.
146. HD, 23 May 1895, PSLI, no. 21, vol. 81 [page not numbered].
147. KD, 25 April 1896, PSLI, F.L. no 1223-E.
148. The revenue derived from the *khalisa* in Kandahar was fifty-five lakhs of rupees per year and in 1896 it was farmed out to Haji Asad Khan. These figures are the highest found for any single province. MM, June 1896, PSLI, F. Dept. no. 131 (96).
149. KD, 2–4 August 1893, PSLI, vol. 71, p. 945.
150. HD, 22 March 1888, PSLI, vol. 53, p. 473.
151. ST, p. 1239.
152. ST, p. 1186.
153. ST, p. 1220.
154. ST, p. 1226.
155. It is to be noted that government share of the revenue is shown here as higher than even the highest rate, which was the *se-kot*.
156. Sardar Sher Ahmad Khan, "Report on Badakhshan," (Khanabad), 29 June 1886, Ridgeway to secretary to government of India, 6 July 1886, PSLI, vol. 47, p. 1258.
157. Kand. D, 27 July 1891, PSLI, vol. 63, p. 1192.
158. KD, no. 24, 31 May 1890, Sec-F., August nos. 82–101, NAI.
159. Kand. D, 21 October 1884, PSLI, vol. 42, p. 874.
160. Elphinstone, *An Account*, 1: 389.
161. ST, pp. 1062, 1086.
162. Sher Ahmad Khan, "Report on Badakhshan," 29 June 1886, Ridgeway to secretary to government of India, 8 July 1886, PSLI, vol. 47, p. 1258.
163. PD, 26 December 1893, PSLI, vol. 73, p. 191.
164. Col. Atta Allah (Jalalabad), 30 April 1887, PSLI, vol. 50, p. 516.
165. MM, August 1899, PSLI, vol. 115, no. 888.
166. Kh. D, 24 August 1901, PSLI, vol. 137, no. 1138.
167. Kand. D, 22 February 1892, PSLI, vol. 65, p. 967.
168. HD, 26 February 1891, PSLI, vol. 62, p. 1057.
169. HD, 21 November 1895, PSLI, vol. 84, no. 47.
170. HD, 18 January 1900, PSLI, vol. 120, no. 345.
171. HD, 4 October 1900, PSLI, vol. 128, no. 1289.
172. ST, p. 788.
173. ST, p. 1019.
174. Kand. D, 22 February 1892, PSLI, vol. 65, p. 976.
175. MM, September 1885, PSLI, vol. 45, p. 875.
176. PD, 26 December 1893, PSLI, vol. 73, p. 191.
177. Sardar Sher Ahmad Khan, "Report on Badakhshan," 29 June 1886, Ridgeway to secretary to government of India, 8 July 1886, PSLI, vol. 47, p. 1258.
178. MacGregor, *Central Asia*, p. 65.
179. For details see J. Lambert, "Statement of Revenue and Expenditure of Afghanistan, 1877–78," 6 March 1884, For. Dept., Secret F., 1886, NAI.
180. PD, 22 December 1890, PSLI, vol. 62, p. 66.

181. KD, 25 November 1884, PSLI, vol. 42, p. 942.

182. Umar Jan (the amir's gardener) to Peshawar commissioner, PD, 7 January 1887, PSLI, vol. 52, p. 408.

183. ST, p. 902.

184. Col. Afzal (Jalalabad), 6 February 1883, PSLI, vol. 35, p. 753.

185. Col. Afzal (Jalalabad), 4 February 1883, PSLI, vol. 35, p. 653.

186. ST, p. 1182.

187. ST, pp. 972–974.

188. ST, p. 990.

189. For details see "Revenue and Expenditure of Afghanistan," 1885, PSLI, vol. 44, p. 1441.

190. ST, pp. 896, 1071, 1087.

191. PD, no. 51, 7 January 1881, Sec. E. 254, 255, NAI.

192. E. Molloy, no. 317, 15.

193. Griesbach (Mazar) to N. Ellas, 5 March 1889, For. Dept., Secret F. Pros., May 1889, nos. 216–225, D. no. 273, NAI.

194. Sahibzada Mir Agha to Peshawar commissioner, PD, 23 October 1891, PSLI, vol. 64, p. 908.

195. Col. Atta Allah (Mazar), 19 November 1889, Sec. F., February 1890, nos. 161–181, 79, NAI.

196. Ghobar, *Afghanistan Along the Highway of History*, p. 648.

197. For the amir's treatment of the mirzas, see "Offices and Methods of Work," Chapter II.

198. For details, see ST, pp. 419, 638–671.

❖

V. The Army

1. Elphinstone, *An Account*, 2: 268.

2. Harlan, *Central Asia: Personal Narrative*, p. 31.

3. Ferrier quoted by MacGregor, *Central Asia*, p. 72.

4. For details see Elphinstone, *An Account*, 2: 266–267; Rawlinson, "Report on the Dooranee Tribe, April 1841," quoted in MacGregor, *Central Asia*, pp. 830–840; Singh, *Ahmad Shah Durrani*, pp. 356–364.

5. For details see M. E. Yapp, "The Revolutions of 1841–42 in Afghanistan," *BSOAS* 27 (pt. 2 1964): 333–381.

6. Ibid., p. 381.

7. Gregorian, *The Emergence of Modern Afghanistan*, p. 84.

8. SDAA, no. 227.

9. Ghobar, *Afghanistan Along the Highway of History*, p. 596.

10. Lambert, "Statement of Revenue and Expenditure of Afghanistan, 1877–78," 6 March 1884, For. Dept., Secret F., 1886, NAI.

11. Ferrier, *History of the Afghans*, pp. 312–313.

12. PD, 31 January 1900, PSLI, vol. 120, no. 323.

13. Amir in darbar, Kh. D, 30 June 1900, PSLI, vol. 125, no. 849.

14. Amir in darbar, PD, 31 January 1900, PSLI, vol. 120, no. 323.

15. Ridgeway to Foreign Office, 20 December 1886, PSLI.

16. ST, p. 642.

17. KD, 20–23 February 1892, PSLI, vol. 65, p. 959.

18. Kandahar to Simla (T), 5 November 1880, PSLI, vol. 26, pt. 8, p. 1945.

19. PD, 20 December 1899, PSLI, vol. 119, no. 179.

20. ST, p. 554.

21. ST, p. 1057.

22. MM, July 1899, PSLI, vol. 115, no. 797 (4).

23. SDAA, p. i.

24. PD, 31 May 1885, PSLI, vol. 44, p. 225.

25. KD, 5 August 1887, PSLI, vol. 50, p. 1843.

26. PD, 8 May 1894, PSLI, vol. 74, p. 709.

27. PD, 20 December 1895, PSLI, vol. 84, no. 24.

28. PD, 27 February 1896, PSLI, vol. 85, no. 4, General no. 695-F.

29. For details see Chapter V.

30. Kand. D, 1 February 1883, PSLI, vol. 35, p. 762.

31. MM, April 1883, PSLI, vol. 36, p. 56.

32. Amir to Capt. Christie (deputy commissioner of Peshawar), 4 July 1887, PSLI, vol. 50, p. 1775.

33. KD, 26 March 1890, PSLI, vol. 59, p. 1241.

34. KD, 11 July 1896, F.L. no. 2090-F. (96), PSLI, vol. 87. According to Ghobar, *Afghanistan Along the Highway of History*, p. 644, the total number in the regular army was 96,000; but he does not say when this figure was reached.

35. For details see "Rough Distribution of Map of the Afghan Army," July 1898, PSLI, vol. 106 [page not numbered].

36. Ghobar, *Afghanistan Along the Highway of History*, p. 644.

37. TD, pp. 101–109.

38. For details see SDAA, p. 2; ST, p. 329; KD, 31 October 1891, PSLI, vol. 64, p. 1097.

39. ST, p. 440.

40. ST, p. 1042. One-third of the payment of those who fell in the battle of Ghaznigak was fixed to be paid to their descendants until "the continuation of the state." ST, p. 618.

41. ST, pp. 687, 1182.

42. ST, p. 681.

43. Soldiers off parade or on sentry duty were sometimes engaged in such trades as shoe repairing, peddling, and shopkeeping; in fact they did anything to supplement their insufficient pay. MRA, p. 196.

44. MM, August 1901, PSLI, vol. 138, no. 1254 (5).

45. KD, 6 November 1901, PSLI, vol. 140, no. 1472a; RM, p. 20.

46. ST, p. 1010.

47. ST, pp. 551, 616, 637.

48. MM, December 1897, PSLI, vol. 99, p. 171 (3).

49. KD, 6–8 June 1894, PSLI, vol. 75, p. 131.

50. KD, 16–19 September 1893, PSLI, vol. 72, p. 373.

51. KD, 6–8 June 1894, PSLI, vol. 75, p. 131.

52. SDAA, p. 1.

53. AW, p. 245. Ghobar, *Afghanistan Along the Highway of History*, p. 655, refers to this incident as the firing of the "people" at the amir.

54. KD, 12 May 1900, PSLI, vol. 123, no. 602.

55. SDAA, p. 1.

56. MRA, p. 202.

57. Durand to Cunningham, 20 December 1893, For. Dept., Secret-F. Pros., January 1894, nos. 193–217, no. 194, I, NAI.

58. Curzon to secretary of state for India (T), 24 March 1901, PSLI, vol. 131, no. 407.

59. MRA, pp. 199, 200.

60. KD, 17 August 1895, PSLI, vol. 81, no. 30.

61. Kh. D, 26 May 1900, PSLI, vol. 123, no. 667.

62. M. A. Babakhodjayev, "Afghanistan's Armed Forces and Amir Abdul Rahman's Military Reforms, Pt. I," *Afghanistan*, no. 2 (1970): 11.

63. MRA, p. 195.

64. Lillias Hamilton, *A Vizier's Daughter*, p. 162.

65. Martin, *Under the Absolute Amir*, p. 214.

66. Ibid.; SDAA, p. 6.

67. Durand to Cunningham, 3 December 1893, PSLI, vol. 73, p. 20.

68. MRA, p. 201–202.

69. MRA, p. 195.

70. M. A. Babakhodjayev, "Afghanistan's Armed Forces and Amir Abdul Rahman's Military Reform, Pt. II," *Afghanistan*, no. 3 (1970): 12.

71. SDAA, p. 7.

72. MRA, p. 216.
73. Martin, *Under the Absolute Amir*, p. 104.
74. KD, 15 October 1898, PSLI, vol. 108, p. 1051.
75. MRA, p. 197.
76. ST, p. 422.
77. ST, p. 580.
78. ST, p. 1112.
79. For names of forts along the border with India, see ST, p. 1037.
80. ST, p. 438.
81. ST, p. 467.
82. ST, p. 458.
83. Ibid.
84. SJD, p. 3.
85. AW, p. 226.
86. Elphinstone, *An Account*, 2: 215.
87. ST, p. 466; SJD, p. 15.
88. AVI, p. 3.
89. The Kabul division included the garrisons of Kabul, Parwan, Logar, Jalalabad, Dakka, Kahi, Peshbolak, Asmar, Barkot, Chaghan Serai, Surkanay, Shewa, Kafiristan, Laghman, Matun, Hariob, Ghazni, Zurmut, Birmal, Mugur, and Qalat and the garrisons in the Hazarajat.
90. It garrisoned the city of Kandahar, Girishk, Farah, Chakhansur, Lash-Juwain, Speen Boldak, and others.
91. It included the garrisons of the city Ghorian and a large number of small posts along the Persian and Russian borders.
92. It included the garrisons of Mazar, Fayzabad, Zebak, Andarab, and Maimana.
93. For details see MRA, p. 191; BACA, pp. 77–79; SDAA, p. 4.
94. Martin, *Under the Absolute Amir*, p. 219.
95. MRA, p. 198.
96. Ibid.
97. KD, 15 April 1884, PSLI, vol. 40, p. 815.
98. Ibid.
99. ST, p. 1153.
100. ST, p. 1046.
101. KD, 29 June–1 July 1892, PSLI, vol. 66, p. 1727.
102. Mir Agha Sahibzada to Peshawar commissioner, PD, 8 October 1891, PSLI, vol. 64, p. 764.
103. MM, February 1901, PSLI, vol. 131, no. 387.
104. SDAA, p. 7.
105. ST, pp. 1014, 1016, 1064.
106. ST, p. 1014.
107. ST, p. 642.
108. Ibid.
109. ST, p. 997.
110. The *khassadars* stuck to their old titles, but their organization and titles did not always match. They were composed of separate companies, each one hundred strong and independent of all others. A commander of ten was called *dahbashi*, of one hundred *sadbasi* or *yuzbashi*. A *sartip* commanded a company of four hundred. A *sarhang* was the superior of all, but how many men worked under him is not known. C. E. Yate, *Northern Afghanistan*, p. 216.
111. PD, no. 23, 9 December 1898, PSLI, F.L. no. 3376-F. (96), vol. 88.
112. KD, 14–16 March 1894, PSLI, vol. 74, p. 119.
113. According to one report, the total number of the Herat horsemen was 3,900; for the Herat and Ghorian districts, 2,500; the Jamshidis, 500; the Hazaras, 500; the Firozkohis, 300; and the Jamshidis of Karrukh, 100. SDAA, p. 7. The figures noted by Fayz Muhammad do not agree with these. According to him, the Hazaras of Herat provided 2,000 cavalry, at the rate of one horseman per family. The same author goes on to

say that this rate was in line with the rest in the province of Herat. The Hazaras had also one elder per one hundred families. ST, p. 527.

114. SDAA, p. 7.
115. ST, p. 622.
116. PD, 19 July 1890, PSLI, vol. 60, p. 992.
117. KD, 18–20 April 1894, PSLI, vol. 74, p. 531.
118. Sardar Afzal (Jalalabad), 31 May 1882, PSLI, vol. 33, p. 273.
119. Mahomed, Life of Abdur Rahman, 1: 283. According to M. Y. Riyazi the total number of eljaris was 60,000. AW, pp. 2–5, 8.
120. PD, 9 March 1893, PSLI, vol. 69, p. 1342.
121. MRA, p. 191.
122. PD, 29 October 1895, PSLI, vol. 83, no. 20.
123. KD, 28 April–1 May 1894, PSLI, vol. 74, p. 757.
124. KD, 21–24 April 1894, PSLI, vol. 74, p. 647.
125. KD, 28 April–1 May 1894, PSLI, vol. 74, p. 757.
126. KD, 18–20 April 1894, PSLI, vol. 74, p. 531.
127. KD, 7–10 April 1894, PSLI, vol. 74, p. 531.
128. ST, p. 1172.
129. Ibid.
130. MM, March 1900, PSLI, vol. 122, no. 519 (2).
131. KD, 11 July 1896, F.L. no. 2090-F. (96), PSLI, vol. 87.
132. MM, July 1899, PSLI, vol. 115, no. 797 (4).
133. KD, 27 August 1898, PSLI, vol. 106, no. 904.
134. PD, no. 4, 1 March 1901, PSLI, vol. 132, no. 452.
135. PD, 9 April 1897, F. Sec. Letter no. 7 (97), PSLI, vol. 91.
136. KD, 10 June 1899, PSLI, vol. 114, no. 667.
137. AW, p. 279.
138. MM, September 1901, PSLI, vol. 138, no. 1254 (5).
139. MRA, p. 191.
140. AW, p. 245.
141. AW, p. 227.
142. KD, 24 May 1887, PSLI, vol. 50, p. 874.
143. ST, p. 1116.
144. Yate, Northern Afghanistan, p. 370.
145. MRA, p. 203.
146. Martin, Under the Absolute Amir, p. 226.

❖

VI. Social Structure: 1

1. Rawlinson, "Report on the Dooranee Tribe, April 1841," quoted in MacGregor, Central Asia, pp. 823, 924.
2. See Elphinstone, An Account, 1: 389.
3. For details see M. Athar 'Ali, "The Passing of Empire: The Mughal Case," Modern Asian Studies (July 1975): 394.
4. Elphinstone, An Account, 1: 378.
5. Ibid., p. 389.
6. MacGregor, Central Asia, p. 34.
7. A. K. Lambton, Landlord and Peasant in Persia, p. 263.
8. Norman Brown, The United States and India, Pakistan, and Bangladesh, p. 32.
9. Theodore Shanin, "Peasantry as a Political Factor," p. 247, in T. Shanin, Peasants and Peasant Society.
10. Ibid., p. 240.
11. E. R. Wolf, Peasants, p. 3.
12. L. Mair, An Introduction to Social Anthropology, p. 11.
13. For the opposite view, see Louis Dupree, Afghanistan, p. 250.
14. G. R. Amiri, "Notes on Afghan Seistan."
15. Elphinstone, An Account, 2: 117.

16. H. F. Schurmann, *The Mongols of Afghanistan*, p. 314.

17. Ibid., p. 303.

18. Quoted in ibid.

19. Elphinstone, *An Account*, 1: 228; 2: 14, 27–30. Schurmann, *Mongols of Afghanistan*, pp. 302–303. Klaus Ferdinand, *Nomadism in Afghanistan*, p. 144. Davies, *The Problems of North-West Frontier of India*, pp. 38–41.

20. Quoted in Schurmann, *Mongols of Afghanistan*, p. 311n.

21. Davies, *Problems of North-West Frontier*, pp. 38–41.

22. Ferrier, *History of the Afghans*, p. 323.

23. Ibid., p. 319.

24. Ibid., p. 320.

25. Quoted in Schurmann, *Mongols of Afghanistan*, p. 303n.

26. Elphinstone, *An Account*, 1: 228; 2: 27.

27. Ibid., 2: 27.

28. Ibid., 2: 28.

29. Ibid., 2: iii.

30. Doms were originally a low caste of entertainers and musicians in India. A. L. Basham, *The Wonder That Was India*, p. 513. From an early date the doms were found in eastern and central Afghanistan. In the rural areas one household of doms was (and still is) attached to a *ulus*, and all members of the household performed varieties of services for it.

31. Schurmann, *Mongols of Afghanistan*, p. 298.

32. Ferdinand, *Nomadism in Afghanistan*, pp. 143–46.

33. Schurmann, *Mongols of Afghanistan*, p. 301.

34. Ibid., p. 300n.

35. For details see Ferdinand, *Nomadism in Afghanistan*, pp. 143–146.

36. Ferrier, *History of the Afghans*, p. 304.

37. Karl Marx quoted in Shanin, *Peasants and Peasant Society*, p. 230.

38. For a list of names of Pashtun nomads see ST, p. 715.

39. Elphinstone, *An Account*, 2: 42.

40. Ibid., 2: 80.

41. Ibid., 2: 160.

42. Ibid., 2: 174–177.

43. Ibid., 2: 156.

44. MRA (1925), p. 1.

45. J. A. Robinson, *Notes on the Nomad Tribes of Eastern Afghanistan*, p. 3.

46. Ferdinand, *Nomadism in Afghanistan*.

47. Ibid., p. 133.

48. Elphinstone, *An Account*, 2: 159.

49. For details see ibid., 2: 174–176.

50. Robinson, *Notes on Nomad Tribes*, p. 3.

51. Ibid., p. 9.

52. C. E. Bruce, *Notes on Ghilzais and Powinda Tribes*, p. 1.

53. Robinson, *Notes on Nomad Tribes*, p. 2.

54. Ibid., p. 9.

55. Ferdinand, *Nomadism in Afghanistan*, p. 138.

56. ST, p. 714. According to Ferdinand the *powindas* had opened up the Hazarajat proper for the first time during the reign of Amir Sher 'Ali Khan, but he does not indicate his source. *Preliminary Notes on Hazara Culture*, p. 19.

57. ST, p. 925.

58. ST, p. 925.

59. ST, p. 926.

60. ST, p. 1100.

61. ST, p. 986.

62. Ferdinand, *Nomadism in Afghanistan*, p. 137.

63. For details see Ferdinand, *Preliminary Notes on Hazara Culture*, pp. 18–22.

64. Christine L. Jung, *Some Observations on the Pattern and Processes of Rural-Urban Migrations to Kabul*, p. 9.

65. For details and information on the opening of annual markets in the Hazarajat and Ghor by the *powindas*, see Ferdinand, *Nomadism in Afghanistan*, pp. 138–143.

66. For. Dept., Secret-F., July 1887, nos. 855–868, no. 865, NAI.

67. KD, 13 July 1888, PSLI, vol. 54, p. 657.

68. ST, p. 540.

69. ST, pp. 540, 561. In PD there is a report to the contrary: "During the rebellion they remained not only loyal to the Amir, but also fought with the Andars and Tarakis." PD, 30 June 1888, PSLI, vol. 54, p. 369A.

70. ST, p. 540.

71. ST, p. 550.

72. KD, 29 June 1888, PSLI, vol. 54, p. 435.

73. ST, p. 672.

74. ST, p. 649.

75. ST, p. 660.

76. ST, p. 679.

77. Kand. D, 28 June 1889, PSLI, vol. 57, p. 994.

78. ST, pp. 686, 699.

79. MM, August 1889, PSLI, vol. 58, p. 71.

80. Schurmann, *Mongols of Afghanistan*, p. 47.

81. For details, see Elphinstone, *An Account*, 2: 111–120; Ferdinand, *Nomadism in Afghanistan*, pp. 146–150.

82. Jenkyns, *Report on the District of Jalalabad*, p. 5.

83. According to Ferdinand, *Nomadism in Afghanistan*, p. 129, the Arabs and some Tajiks also used variations of yurts.

84. Elphinstone, *An Account*, 2: 206.

85. E. Molloy, p. 9; C. E. Yate, *Northern Afghanistan*, p. 4.

86. Yate, *Northern Afghanistan*, pp. 217, 219.

87. Ibid., p. 122. For a description of tents and their varieties, see Schurmann, *Mongols of Afghanistan*, pp. 335–353.

88. MRA, p. 105.

89. E. Molloy, p. 9.

90. ZM, p. 44.

91. Yate, *Northern Afghanistan*, p. 339.

92. MRA, p. 105.

93. AT, pp. 5, 104.

94. Yate, *Northern Afghanistan*, p. 135.

95. Merk, W. DA, 15, 22.

96. Ferdinand, *Preliminary Notes on Hazara Culture*, pp. 9, 10.

97. E. Molloy, p. 10.

98. Yate, *Northern Afghanistan*, p. 135.

99. Ibid., p. 267.

100. Ibid., p. 342.

101. IGA, p. 83; Nancy Tapper, "The Advent of Pashtun Malders in North-Western Afghanistan: A Preliminary Note," *BSOAS*, 1973, pp. 55–79.

102. Yate, *Northern Afghanistan*, p. 320.

103. Ibid., p. 232.

104. On this the amir went so far as to declare that "I devise a plan to root out from Afghanistan the enmity of cousinship and domestic quarrels, which are mixed up in the nature of this people." KD, 29 August 1885, PSLI, no. 12, For. Dept. Sec. F., March 1886, nos. 128–191, no. 142, NAI.

105. HD, 25 March 1883, PSLI, vol. 36, p. 881.

106. Tapper, "The Arrival of Pashtun Malders," pp. 55–79.

107. Merk, W. DA, p. 19.

108. Merk, W. DA, p. 20.

109. E. Molloy, p. 10.

110. ST, p. 495; HD, 15 January 1891, PSLI, vol. 62, p. 768.
111. KD, 29 June 1886, PSLI, vol. 47, p. 901.
112. MM, April 1886, PSLI, vol. 47, p. 74.
113. MM, May 1886, PSLI, vol. 47, p. 328.
114. HD, 16 September 1886, PSLI, vol. 48, p. 957.
115. ST, p. 511.
116. ST, p. 562.
117. ST, p. 567.
118. Tapper, "The Arrival of Pashtun Malders," pp. 55–79.
119. Ibid.
120. KD, 10 September 1890, PSLI, vol. 61, p. 309.
121. HD, 7 June 1892, PSLI, vol. 65, p. 651.
122. Kand. D, 9 December 1893, PSLI, vol. 73, p. 186.
123. ST, p. 567.
124. ST, p. 1237.
125. Schurmann, *Mongols of Afghanistan*, pp. 338–340.
126. MM, September 1885, PSLI, vol. 45, p. 875.
127. PD, 24 October 1885, PSLI, vol. 45, p. 1253.
128. MM, December 1885, PSLI, vol. 46, p. 221.
129. PD, 28 November 1885, PSLI, vol. 45, p. 1640.
130. MM, January 1886, PSLI, vol. 46, p. 668.
131. Kand. D, 11 December 1885, PSLI, vol. 46, p. 950.
132. KD, 29 June 1886, PSLI, vol. 47, p. 902.
133. PD, 13 February 1886, PSLI, vol. 46, p. 1547.
134. KD, 10–13 October 1891, PSLI, vol. 64, p. 861.
135. Amir's firman to governors of Jalalabad, Laghman, and Kohistan, KD, 16 April 1890, PSLI, vol. 60, p. 155.
136. KD, 11 October 1890, PSLI, vol. 61, p. 727.
137. KD, 22 October 1890, PSLI, vol. 61, p. 733.
138. KD, 10 September 1890, PSLI, vol. 61, p. 309.
139. PD, 20 September 1890, PSLI, vol. 61, p. 412.
140. Ptolemy, *Ancient India as Described by Ptolemy*, pp. 86, 124. Ghulam Muhammad Ghobar, "Shar-i-Kabul" [The city of Kabul], *Kabul* 1 (1931): 44–48. Hafiz N. Muhammad, "A Glance at the History of Kabul" in *Kabul* 3 (1931): 36–58.
141. For details, see Angus Hamilton, *Afghanistan*, pp. 376–380.
142. ZM, pp. 38–39. Hamilton, *Afghanistan*, pp. 376–399.
143. Surgeon E. Tully (Quetta), 1 June 1881, PSLI, vol. 29, p. 1103.
144. Hamilton, *Afghanistan*, p. 194. ZM, p. 41. Elphinstone, *An Account*, 2: 133.
145. Elphinstone, *An Account*, p. 197.
146. IGA, p. 72.
147. Ibid.
148. Surgeon E. Tully (Quetta), 1 June 1881, PSLI, vol. 29, p. 1103.
149. ZM, p. 41.
150. Hamilton, *Afghanistan*, p. 198.
151. Elphinstone, *An Account*, 2: 216.
152. Hamilton, *Afghanistan*, p. 157. In the tenth century Herat had four gates: Firozabad, Saraiyum, Khosh, and Qunduz. Sayf ibn Ya'qub al-Harawi, *Tarikh Nama-i-Harat* [The history of Herat], p. 36.
153. Hamilton, *Afghanistan*, p. 166.
154. Quoted in Ptolemy, *Ancient India*, p. 310.
155. ZM, p. 42.
156. IGA, p. 79.
157. ZM, p. 42.
158. HD [undated], 85, PSLI, vol. 49, p. 1125.
159. Hamilton, *Afghanistan*, p. 1969.
160. Ibid., p. 173.

161. ZM, p. 44.

162. Major Hasting, "A Short Account of the Ghazni District," PSLI, vol. 26, pt. 3, pp. 355–364. Hamilton, *Afghanistan*, pp. 343–345.

163. Schurmann, *Mongols of Afghanistan*, p. 361.

164. Hamilton, *Afghanistan*, p. 256.

165. Harlan, *Central Asia*, pp. 28–29.

166. ZM, p. 47.

167. Yate, *Northern Afghanistan*, p. 281.

168. ZM, p. 49. Yate, *Northern Afghanistan*, pp. 280, 319. Harlan, *Central Asia*, p. 32. Hamilton, *Afghanistan*, p. 257.

169. RLMA, p. 6. Morgenstierne's survey was undertaken in 1924.

170. Georg Morgenstierne, "The Languages of Afghanistan," *Afghanistan*, no. 3 (1967): 81.

171. Ibid., p. 83.

172. Ibid.

173. The name *Ghilzay* covers a great variety not only of tribes, but also of dialects. RLMA, p. 11.

174. Georg Morgenstierne, "Pashto Literature," EI (1961), p. 220.

175. Morgenstierne, "Languages of Afghanistan," p. 84.

176. A. G. R. Farhadi, "Languages," *Kabul Times Annual*, p. 121.

177. Morgenstierne, "Languages of Afghanistan," p. 85.

178. RLMA, p. 7.

179. R. Frye, "Dari," EI (1965), p. 142.

180. Morgenstierne, "Languages of Afghanistan," p. 86. According to Dr. D. N. MacKenzie of the University of London (personal communication, 1975), the language recorded by Zarubin was Yazghulami.

181. Morgenstierne, "Pashto Literature," p. 225.

182. RLMA, p. 5.

183. Some of the older men among the Jawanshir of Chindawal (a division of the Qizilbashes) spoke "Turki" in 1880. Howard Hensman, *The Afghan War of 1879–80*, p. 414.

184. RLMA, p. 6.

185. Morgenstierne, "Pashto Literature," p. 225.

186. Farhadi, "Languages," p. 123.

❖

VII. Social Structure: 2

1. AW, p. 198.

2. AT, pp. 5, 113.

3. Ibid., pp. 5, 102.

4. ST, p. 664.

5. *Report on the District of Jalalabad*, p. ix.

6. Morgenstierne, "Pashto Literature," EI, p. 225.

7. J. Bidulph, *The Tribes of the Hindoo Koosh*, pp. 118–123. Bidulph was a major in the British army and political officer at Gilgit. For text of *Kalam-i-Pir* in Persian and English see *Kalami Pir*, edited and translated by I. Ivanov, Bombay, 1935. The original text in Persian had been acquired from Shighnan in Badakhshan.

8. *Kalami Pir*, pp. xlvii. According to M. Y. Riyazi, some Berbers (Hazaras) considered Caliph ʾAli a deity. ZM, p. 46.

9. Burhan al-Din Kushkaki, *Rahnuma-i-Qataghan wa Badakhshan* [A guide to Qataghan and Badakhshan], p. 239.

10. S. H. Nasr, *Ideals and Realities of Islam*, p. 105.

11. From the "Covenant of the Hindus of Kabul," File of the subjects of Afghanistan addressed to Amir ʾAbd al-Rahman Khan, 1896, ARAMFA. AT, pp. 5, 116.

12. ST, p. 833.

13. PD, 1–30 June 1901, PSLI, vol. 136, no. 1012.

14. ST, p. 696.

15. After 1917, Soviet Jews emigrated to Afghanistan, especially in the period between 1932 and 1933, when about 1,600 of them arrived. Among them, however, were some Soviet agents. This fact led the Afghan government to transfer the old colonies of the Jews from Mazar and Kndkhui to Kabul.

16. Squire (Kabul) to Eden (London), 29 December 1944, Political External Dept., Coll., 3/93, Encl., Note on the Jews in Afghanistan.

17. RM, p. 9.

18. AW, p. 328.

19. AT, pp. 5, 120.

20. John Gray, *My Residence at the Court of the Amir*, p. 209.

21. AT, pp. 5, 120.

22. *Asiatic Quarterly Review* 2 (1896): 184.

23. ST, p. 799.

24. HD, 17 December 1890, PSLI, vol. 62, p. 564.

25. Ibid.

26. RM, p. 11.

27. ST, p. 858.

28. RM, p. 23.

29. KD, no. 31, 14–17 April 1894, Sec. F., July 1894, pp. 245–271, no. 211, NAI.

30. ST, p. 847.

31. George S. Robertson, *The Kafirs of the Hindu Kush*, p. 376.

32. MM, February 1898, PSLI, vol. 101, no. 372 (4).

33. KD, 13 November 1897, PSLI, vol. 98, p. 1191.

34. Kh. D, 20 April 1901, PSLI, vol. 133, no. 644.

35. Mala. D, 9 February 1901, PSLI, vol. 131, no. 36993.

36. ZM, p. 50.

37. ST, p. 1190.

38. ST, p. 787.

39. ST, p. 1158.

40. Hamid Algar, "The Naqshbandi Order: A Preliminary Survey of Its History and Significance," pp. 21, 39.

41. Jenkyns, *Report on Jalalabad*, p. 14.

42. Rawlinson, "Report on the Dooranee Tribe, April, 1841," quoted in MacGregor, *Central Asia*, p. 867.

43. Davies, *The Problems of North-West Frontier of India*, p. 40.

44. Harlan, *Central Asia*, p. 144.

45. Jenkyns, *Report on Jalalabad*, p. 11.

46. Ibid., p. 17.

47. Harlan, *Central Asia*, p. 68.

48. Keddie, *Sayyid Jamal al-Din "al-Afghani,"* p. 55.

49. Qazi Abd al-Khaliq to Peshawar commissioner, PD, 7 April 1887, PSLI, vol. 50, p. 242.

50. Ibid.

51. MM, November 1885, PSLI, vol. 45, p. 1490.

52. Amir to Mulla Najm al-Din, PD, 23 December 1892, PSLI, vol. 69, p. 9.

53. Amir to Mulla Khosa, KD, 23–26 September 1893, PSLI, vol. 72, p. 671.

54. KD, 18 December 1883, PSLI, vol. 39, p. 333.

55. Col. Afzal (Jalalabad), 4 May 1883, PSLI, vol. 36, p. 904.

56. KD, 29 October 1886, PSLI, vol. 48, p. 1173.

57. Amir in darbar, KD, 18 January 1887, PSLI, vol. 48, p. 493.

58. PD, 11 April 1893, PSLI, vol. 70, p. 176.

59. Kand. D, 11 January 1887, PSLI, vol. 49, p. 631.

60. HD, 16 September 1886, PSLI, vol. 48, p. 959.

61. PD, 7 April 1887, PSLI, vol. 50, p. 244.

62. PD, 16 August 1887, PSLI, vol. 51, p. 254.

63. Col. Atta Allah (Mazar), 18 January 1889, PSLI, vol. 56, p. 615.

64. Col. Atta Allah (Mazar), 15 January 1889, PSLI, vol. 56, p. 534.
65. MM, August 1889, PSLI, vol. 58, p. 73.
66. PD, 10 August 1889, PSLI, vol. 57, p. 1385.
67. Kand. D, 22 February 1892, PSLI, vol. 65, p. 967.
68. KD, 6–9 February 1892, PSLI, vol. 65, p. 748.
69. KD, 9–12 January 1892, PSLI, vol. 62, p. 533.
70. KD, 12–15 June 1894, PSLI, vol. 75, p. 280.
71. KD, 12 July 1887, PSLI, vol. 50, p. 1539.
72. AW, p. 338.
73. Amir to courtiers, KD, 12 July 1887, PSLI, vol. 50, p. 1539.
74. KD, 19 July 1887, PSLI, vol. 50, p. 1669.
75. BACA, p. 146–147.
76. PD, 13 August 1887, PSLI, vol. 50, p. 1887.
77. PD, 10 August 1889, PSLI, vol. 57, p. 1384.
78. PD, 20 June 1889, PSLI, vol. 57, p. 887.
79. PD, 22 December 1894, PSLI, vol. 78, p. 174.
80. PD, no. 3, 8 February 1896, F.L. no. 473-F. (96), PSLI, vol. 84.
81. PD, 24 June 1893, PSLI, vol. 70, p. 1598.
82. Izah al-Bayan, 1897, Kabul, PSLI, vol. 96, no. 1043, Encl. 376, 3.
83. ST, pp. 1209, 1218.
84. Kh. D, 4 August 1900, PSLI, vol. 126, no. 969.
85. Kh. D, 6 January 1900, PSLI, vol. 119, no. 232 (2).
86. Col. Atta Allah (Mazar), 15 January 1889, PSLI, vol. 56, p. 534.
87. Col. Atta Allah (Mazar), 23 June 1890, PSLI, vol. 59, p. 810.
88. KD, 31 August–2 September 1892, PSLI, vol. 67, p. 1167.
89. Charles Masson, *Narrative of Various Journeys in Baloochistan, Afghanistan and the Panjab, 1826–1838*, 2: 298.
90. Kand. D, 23 April 1882, PSLI, vol. 32, p. 985.
91. They were supporters of the former Sipah Salar Hussayn ʾAli who was allied with Sardar Muhammad Ayyub Khan.
92. MM, June 1886, PSLI, vol. 47, p. 841.
93. AT, pp. 5, 118.
94. They were ordered to wear these turbans because the literal translation of their Turkish name is redhead, referring to the special red turban (the *taj* or crown) worn as a distinguishing insignia by the followers of the Safavid cause. The term is extended loosely to the Safavid ideology as a whole, to its specific institutions, and to groups and individuals formally linked to the Safavid cause. The translation red for Qizilbashes would be ideal were it not for the modern connotation of communist. Martin B. Dickson, "Shah Tahmasb and the Uzbeks," p. 6.
95. KD, 10 February 1885, PSLI, vol. 43, p. 975.
96. PD, 12 October 1886, PSLI, vol. 48, p. 827.
97. MM [undated], 1886, PSLI, vol. 49, p. 79.
98. AW, p. 276.
99. Amir to viceroy, 21 October 1892, PSLI, vol. 68, p. 1053.
100. Amir to viceroy, 27 October 1892, PSLI, vol. 68, p. 1053.
101. ST, p. 848.
102. KD, 17 April 1889, PSLI, vol. 57, p. 127.
103. PD, 10 October 1894, PSLI, vol. 77, p. 925.
104. KD, 14 June 1890, PSLI, vol. 60, p. 779.
105. Ibid.
106. Sardar Habib Allah to Jalal al-Din, 14 July 1890, PSLI, vol. 60, p. 779. Jalal al-Din was the son of Shahabal-Din.
107. KD, 9 May 1896, F.L., No. 1431-F., PSLI, vol. 86.
108. Kand. D, 6 August 1892, PSLI, vol. 67, p. 467.
109. AW, p. 253.
110. KD, 20 August 1890, PSLI, vol. 60, p. 1364.
111. KD, 6 August 1890, PSLI, vol. 60, p. 1307.

112. KD, 1–4 August 1891, PSLI, vol. 63, p. 1236.
113. KD, 9–11 September 1891, PSLI, vol. 64, p. 186.
114. PD, 8 June 1891, PSLI, vol. 62, p. 376.
115. Amir to Sunni mullas, KD, 6–9 August 1892, PSLI, vol. 67, p. 498.
116. KD, 11 April 1896, F.L. no. 2, 1072-F. (96), PSLI, vol. 86.
117. KD, 24 October 1896, F.L. no. 3176-F. (96), PSLI, vol. 89.
118. KD, 13 June 1896, F.L. no. 1795-F. (96), PSLI, vol. 87.
119. ST, p. 1065.
120. Kand. D, 6 August 1892, PSLI, vol. 67, p. 467.
121. Kand. D, 18 January 1892, PSLI, vol. 65, p. 737.
122. AW, p. 257.
123. HD, 15 September 1896, PSLI, vol. 68, p. 195.
124. HD, 6 October 1896, PSLI, vol. 68, p. 463.
125. MM, October 1896, PSLI, vol. 68, p. 473.
126. HD, 3 November 1892, PSLI, vol. 68, p. 712.
127. Amir to viceroy, 13 April 1893, PSLI, vol. 70, p. 323; ST, p. 848.
128. HD, 23 May 1901, PSLI, vol. 134, no. 899.
129. Amir's newswriter in Mashhad to Amir [no date], PSLI, vol. 68, p. 1055.
130. The Qizilbash tribes who survived the persecution were the Afshar, Kacharlu, Namarlu, Osmanlu, Jawanshir, Sipahi-Mansur, Shah-sevan, Shirazi, Khawafi, Kurts, and others. AT, pp. 5, 115.
131. AT, pp. 5, 114, 119.
132. For how children were instructed in the schools, see Martin, *Under the Absolute Amir*, p. 64.
133. For the state of education in preindustrial societies, see Gideon Sjoberg, *The Pre-Industrial City.*
134. Gregorian, *Emergence of Modern Afghanistan*, p. 150.
135. Amir to mullas, British agent in Mazar, 30 February 1890, PSLI, vol. 59, p. 840.
136. PD, 12 May 1886, PSLI, vol. 47, p. 205.
137. ST, p. 951.
138. ST, p. 1153.
139. MM, June 1886, PSLI, vol. 47, p. 841.
140. ST, p. 587; AW, p. 257.
141. HD, 8 May 1901, PSLI, vol. 137, no. 1169.
142. Ghobar, *Afghanistan Along the Highway of History*, p. 560.
143. KD, 16–19 July 1892, PSLI, vol. 67, p. 191.
144. Ludolph Fischer, *Afghanistan: A Geomedical Monograph*, p. 94.
145. Ibid., p. 85.
146. Ibid.
147. Gray, *My Residence*, p. 123.
148. Fischer, *Afghanistan*, p. 85.
149. Gray, *My Residence*, p. 186.
150. Fischer, *Afghanistan*, p. 85.
151. Surgeon E. Tully (Quetta), 1 June 1881, PSLI, vol. 29, p. 1079.
152. Gray, *My Residence*, p. 51.
153. Ibid., p. 42.
154. Gregorian, *Emergence of Modern Afghanistan*, p. 148.
155. Gray, *My Residence*, p. 127.
156. Ibid., p. 126.
157. Ibid., p. 43.
158. Ibid., p. 127.
159. Ibid., p. 469.
160. Ibid., p. 125.
161. KD, 16 November 1889, PSLI, vol. 58, p. 890.
162. KD, 11 August 1900, PSLI, vol. 126, no. 965.
163. CLA, p. 126.
164. G. B. Scott, *Afghan and Pathan*, p. 154.

165. Elphinstone, *An Account* 1: 219. For details on Pashtunwali, see Davies, *The Problems of North-West Frontier of India*, pp. 49–53.
166. For details, see S. H. Nasr, *Ideals and Realities of Islam*, pp. 93–118, and N. J. Coulson, *A History of Islamic Law*, p. 106.
167. CLA, p. 126.
168. Ibid., pp. 126, 127, 130.
169. Coulson, *History of Islamic Law*, p. 133.
170. CLA, p. 132.
171. Ibid., p. 133.
172. Coulson, *History of Islamic Law*, p. 132.
173. Martin, *Under the Absolute Amir*, p. 67.
174. CLA, p. 142.
175. ST, p. 1064.
176. CLA, p. 142.
177. ST, p. 1065.
178. KD, 21–24 April 1894, PSLI, vol. 74, p. 649.
179. Coulson, *History of Islamic Law*, p. 91.
180. CLA, p. 148.
181. Ibid., p. 150.
182. Ibid., p. 155.
183. Ibid., p. 152.
184. Ibid., p. 131.
185. For details, see ibid., pp. 161–162, 131.
186. Ibid., p. 128.
187. Ibid., p. 143.
188. Schurmann, *The Mongols of Afghanistan*, p. 200.
189. Hamilton, *Afghanistan*, p. 380.
190. Martin, *Under the Absolute Amir*, pp. 60–62.
191. KD, 22 January 1884, PSLI, vol. 37, p. 938.
192. Schurmann, *Mongols of Afghanistan*, p. 211.
193. Ibid., p. 210.
194. Martin, *Under the Absolute Amir*, p. 97.
195. Elphinstone, *An Account*, 1: 237.
196. CLA, p. 150.
197. AW, p. 328.
198. Erika Knabe, "Afghan Women," in *Afghanistan in the 1970s*, ed. Louis Dupree and Linette Albert, p. 145.
199. ZM, p. 45.
200. Harlan, *Central Asia*, p. 139.
201. Ibid., p. 86.
202. Schurmann, *Mongols of Afghanistan*, p. 213.
203. G. Robertson, "Confidential Report on Kafiristan," 14 January 1890, PSLI, vol. 59, p. 1013 (11).
204. Ernest and Annie Thornton, *Leaves from an Afghan Scrapbook*, p. 10.
205. Martin, *Under the Absolute Amir*, p. 227.
206. Amir's firman to the people of Ningrahar and Kunar, PD, 25 October 1893, PSLI, vol. 72, p. 1271.
207. Ibid.
208. Amir ʾAbu al-Rahman, *Nasaʾih Namcha* [A book of advices], p. 8.
209. KD, 16 December 1887, PSLI, vol. 52, p. 93.
210. Although in these references the amir singled out only the British, on other occasions he spoke of the Russians in the same tone. Amir in Izah al-Bayan, PD, 24 September 1897, PSLI, vol. 96, no. 1043, Encl. 376; see also *Nasaʾih Namcha*, p. 8.
211. ST, p. 1078.
212. KD, 5 April 1887, PSLI, vol. 48, p. 539.
213. CLA, p. 148.
214. For a detailed account of the legal aspects of slavery and its practices in the Muslim world see E. Brunschvig, "ʾAbd," EI, vol. 1 (1960), pp. 24–40.
215. Elphinstone, *An Account*, 1: 318.

216. Ibid.

217. KD, 11 January 1884, PSLI, vol. 39, p. 1032.

218. Col. Afzal (Jalalabad), 9 March 1883, PSLI, vol. 36, p. 197.

219. Viceroy to secretary of state for India, 22 April 1896, F.L. no. 77 (96), PSLI, vol. 85.

220. Committee of the British and Foreign Anti-Slavery Society (London) to secretary of state for India, 12 March 1874, PSLI, vol. 37, p. 651.

221. HD, 1 February 1894, PSLI, vol. 73, p. 1228.

222. Elphinstone, An Account, 1: 318.

223. Ibid., p. 320.

224. ST, p. 385.

225. ZM, p. 45.

226. Sayyed Shah of the Peshawar mission, who had been sent to Kafiristan, quoted by A. Durand in The Making of a Frontier.

227. Shah Yusuf Ali Shah, while the mir of Roshan for three years during the reign of the amir, sent him slaves as presents. Burhan al-Din Kushkaki, Rahnuma-i-Qataghan wa Badakhshan [A Guide to Qataghan and Badakhshan], p. 338.

228. Elphinstone, An Account, 1: 319.

229. KD, 6 March 1884, PSLI, vol. 40, p. 1102.

230. CLA, p. 152.

231. Col. Afzal (Jalalabad), 27 March 1883, PSLI, vol. 36, p. 262.

232. KD, 13–15 July 1892, PSLI, vol. 67, p. 187.

233. CLA, p. 151.

234. KD, 4 November 1884, PSLI, vol. 42, p. 847.

235. HD, 18 January 1894, PSLI, vol. 73, p. 828.

236. Ibid.

237. MM, April 1899, PSLI, vol. 114, no. 586.

238. CD, 18 June 1901, PSLI, vol. 135, no. 877.

239. On the accession of Amir Habib Allah, the hakim of Farah presented him with seven slave boys. KD, 11 December 1901, PSLI, vol. 141, no. 178.

240. TD, p. 8.

241. Ibid., p. 72.

242. Ibid., p. 8.

243. Kalimat-i-Amir-al-Balad fi Targhib alal jehad [The words of the amir of the land toward the encouragement of jehad], p. 9.

244. Ibid.

245. EI, vol. 1 (1965), p. 539.

246. For details, see TD, pp. 67–74, RM, pp. 59–60. Kalimat-i-Amir, pp. 25–26.

247. ST, pp. 537–541. Rabats were large buildings of burnt bricks, some sixty or seventy yards square with a double row of domed corridors all round and an open courtyard in the center. C. E. Yate, Northern Afghanistan, p. 53.

248. TD, pp. 7, 74; RM, p. 58.

249. ST, p. 74.

250. TD, p. 13.

251. Ibid., p. 7.

252. Kalimat-i-Amir, p. 34.

253. RM, p. 61.

254. EI, vol. 4 (1934), p. 1086.

255. For details see R. C. Majumdar, "Wahabi Movement: 881–899," The History and Culture of the Indian People, British Paramountcy and Indian Resistance, ed. R. C. Majumdar, p. li.

256. For details, see TD, pp. 187–203.

257. EI, vol. 1 (1960), p. 301.

258. Martin, Under the Absolute Amir, p. 203.

259. Ibid., p. 300.

260. Ibid., p. 276.

❖
VIII. Economic Structure: 1

1. For approximations of the population of Afghanistan before 1880, see Mac-Gregor, *Central Asia*, pp. 28–32.

2. Col. Afzal (Jalalabad), March 1883, PSLI, vol. 35, p. 930.

3. Kand. D, 18 July 1891, PSLI, vol. 63, p. 1190.

4. ST, p. 1217.

5. Curzon, *Tales of Travel*, p. 72.

6. GAK (1895), Appendix A, p. 35.

7. Ibid., p. 36.

8. MRA, p. 111.

9. "Improvement in Sanitary Conditions in Kandahar (Quetta)," 1 June 1881, PSLI, vol. 29, p. 1103.

10. Kand. D, 7 October 1880, PSLI, vol. 26, pt. 8, p. 1963.

11. C. M. Cipolla, *The Economic History of World Population*, p. 81.

12. Schurmann, *The Mongols of Afghanistan*, p. 214.

13. MacGregor, *Central Asia*, p. 30.

14. A. D. Baker, *British India with Notes on Ceylon, Afghanistan, and Tibet*, p. 560.

15. T. L. Pennell, *Among the Wild Tribes of the Afghan Frontier*, p. 43.

16. KD, 7–10 May 1892, PSLI, vol. 66, p. 605.

17. IGA (1906), p. 83.

18. PD, 9 June 1892, PSLI, vol. 66, p. 1263.

19. Amir to British agent, KD, 29 June 1892, PSLI, vol. 66, p. 1676.

20. A Shinwar murdered an Uthman Khel in 1895 in revenge for the murder of his kinsmen fifty years previously. ST, p. 1180. The Wazirs, unlike other Pashtuns, avenged a murder only on the person of the murderer, and not on any other relative. This restriction was imposed to lessen blood feuds. G. B. Scott, *Afghan and Pathan*, p. 154.

21. For details, see Davies, *The Problems of North-West Frontier of India*, pp. 49–52.

22. Perhaps an extreme example of the blood feud is found among the Mohmands. In three generations, of the seventeen Lalpura (a leading family) males who lived to manhood eight were killed by brothers and cousins. Scott, *Afghan and Pathan*, p. 97.

23. Yate, *Northern Afghanistan*, p. 320.

24. MacGregor, *Central Asia*, p. 29.

25. KD, 19 November 1889, Sec. F., February 1890, nos. 161–181, 79, NAI.

26. Cipolla, *Economic History*, p. 83.

27. KD, 23 May 1884, PSLI, vol. 40, p. 1383.

28. Klaus Ferdinand, *Nomadism in Afghanistan*, p. 133.

29. N. I. Vavilov and D. D. Bukinich, *Agricultural Afghanistan*, p. 547.

30. Amir 'Abu al-Rahman, *Nasa'ih Namcha* [A book of advices], p. 8; Martin, *Under the Absolute Amir*, p. 137.

31. Vavilov and Bukinich, *Agricultural Afghanistan*, p. 548.

32. Ibid., p. 550.

33. For more details, see Elphinstone, *An Account*, 1: 396–402. MacGregor, *Central Asia*, pp. 37–39. Vavilov and Bukinich, *Agricultural Afghanistan*, p. 547. Schurmann, *Mongols of Afghanistan*, pp. 325–333.

34. For details, see MacGregor, *Central Asia*, pp. 39–45. For varieties of fruits, see Angus Hamilton, *Afghanistan*, p. 298.

35. Elphinstone, *An Account*, 1: 402.

36. Vavilov and Bukinich, *Agricultural Afghanistan*, p. 549.

37. Major Hasting, "A Short Account of the Ghazni District," PSLI, vol. 26, pt. 3, p. 357.

38. W. Jenkyns, *Report on the District of Jalalabad*, p. 10.

39. Schurmann, *Mongols of Afghanistan*, p. 305.

40. The Hazara population was divided into two classes, the military and the husbandmen; the former, constituting the landed gentry, was provided for by an allotment in *jagir* and the latter subsisted upon a fixed portion of their labor. Harlan, *Central Asia*, p. 124.

41. Schurmann, *Mongols of Afghanistan*, p. 313.

42. Ibid., p. 136.

43. For details, see Monic quoted in ibid., pp. 405–408.

44. A. K. Lambton, *Landlord and Peasant in Persia*, p. 348.

45. Jenkyns, *Report on Jalalabad*, p. 11.

46. KD, 7 November 1896, F.L. no. 3219-F, PSLI, vol. 89.

47. MM, October 1898, no. 1088 (3), PSLI, vol. 109.

48. Kand. D, 17 March 1893, PSLI, vol. 70, p. 155.

49. KD, 6 June 1896, F.L. no. 1721-F (96), PSLI, vol. 86.

50. KD, 9 July 1886, PSLI, vol. 47, p. 997.

51. KD, 1 December 1885, PSLI, vol. 46, p. 383.

52. Martin, *Under the Absolute Amir*, p. 298.

53. Ibid., p. 87.

54. Ibid., p. 97.

55. Ibid., p. 98.

56. Ibid., pp. 197–198.

57. PD, 26 August 1886, PSLI, vol. 48, p. 75.

58. PD, 11 May 1893, PSLI, vol. 70, p. 675.

59. KD, 28 January 1899, PSLI, vol. 111, no. 272.

60. Col. Atta Allah (Mazar), 20 September 1889, PSLI, vol. 58, p. 535.

61. HD, 8 August 1901, PSLI, vol. 138, no. 1328.

62. Kh. D, 5 October 1901, PSLI, vol. 138, no. 1328.

63. KD, 25 June 1898, PSLI, vol. 104, p. 714.

64. ST, p. 875.

65. Yate, *Northern Afghanistan*, p. 353.

66. ST, p. 954.

67. ST, p. 1194.

68. ST, p. 1202.

69. ST, p. 880.

70. ST, p. 997.

71. MacGregor, *Central Asia*, p. 50.

72. ST, p. 864. Vavilov and Bukinich, *Agricultural Afghanistan*, p. 549.

73. MacGregor, *Central Asia*, p. 48.

74. R. H. Davies, *Report on the Trade and Resources of the Countries on the North-Western Boundary of British India*, p. 41.

75. Vavilov and Bukinich, *Agricultural Afghanistan*, p. 549.

76. Harlan, *Central Asia*, p. 116.

77. MacGregor, *Central Asia*, p. 50.

78. Ibid., pp. 45–47.

79. Ibid., p. 48.

80. For a list of Kabul artisans and trades see Elphinstone, *An Account*, 1: 336.

81. Hamilton, *Afghanistan*, p. 378.

82. M. A. Nayyir, "Sanaiʾ wa ʾImranat-i-Afghanistan" [Industries and constructions in Afghanistan], *Aryana* 4 (1969): 52.

83. Hensman, *The Afghan War of 1879–80*, p. 323.

84. Ibid.

85. Nayyir, "Sanaiʾ wa ʾImranet-i-Afghanistan," p. 53.

86. Hensman, *Afghan War*, p. 326.

87. Nayyir, "Sanaiʾ wa ʾImaranet-i-Afghanistan," p. 53.

88. Hensman, *Afghan War*, p. 71.

89. Twenty-eight of these guns are today in Fort Museum at Lahore. Their metal composition is copper (84 percent), iron (10 percent), zinc, and tin.

90. Mahomed, *Life of Abdur Rahman*, 2: 20; PD, 20 January 1881, PSLI, vol. 27, p. 841.

91. M. A. Babakhodjayev, "Afghanistan's Armed Forces and Amir Abdul Rahman's Military Reforms, Pt. I," *Afghanistan*, no. 2 (1970): 17.

92. Mahomed, *Life of Abdur Rahman*, 2: 28.

93. Pyne to Reuter's agent (India), 19 January 1894, PSLI, vol. 73, p. 127.

94. Pyne quoted in *The Times of India*, 17 February 1892, PSLI, vol. 65, p. 515.

95. MM, September 1891, PSLI, vol. 64, p. 278. For a full description of the machines, see Martin, *Under the Absolute Amir*, p. 234.

96. Martin, *Under the Absolute Amir*, p. 234.

97. AW, p. 305.

98. The amir's import agents were Walsh-Lovett and Co. (Calcutta).

99. MRA, p. 202.

100. PD, 8 October 1891, PSLI, vol. 64, p. 756.

101. Pyne to Reuter's agent (London), 20 January 1896, PSLI, vol. 84, no. 66-F.

102. RM, p. 21.

103. MM, February 1889, PSLI, vol. 56, p. 743.

104. KD, 17 August 1895, PSLI, vol. 81, no. 30.

105. Martin, *Under the Absolute Amir*, p. 235.

106. PD, 8 May 1896, PSLI, F.L. no. 1276-F, vol. 86, no. 9.

107. MRA, p. 195.

108. MRA, p. 202.

109. According to the amir, twenty-two Austrian ladies lived in Ghazni. They were given allowances, but how and when and why they came to Afghanistan is not known.

110. KD, 22–25 April 1893, PSLI, vol. 70, p. 600.

111. Martin, *Under the Absolute Amir*, p. 239.

112. KD, 7 August 1895, PSLI, vol. 81, no. 30.

113. Pyne quoted in *The Times of India*, 17 February 1892, PSLI, vol. 65, p. 515.

114. Ibid.

115. Pyne to Reuter's agent, 19 January 1894, PSLI, vol. 73, p. 127.

116. KD, 17 August 1895, PSLI, vol. 81, no. 30.

117. Martin, *Under the Absolute Amir*, p. 236.

118. Ibid.

119. Ibid., p. 238.

120. For details, see Schurmann, *Mongols of Afghanistan*, pp. 357–359.

121. ST, p. 379.

122. Hamilton, *Afghanistan*, pp. 347–353. Ghobar, *Afghanistan Along the Highway of History*, p. 650. Martin, *Under the Absolute Amir*, p. 51.

✤

IX. Economic Structure: 2

1. For details see MacGregor, *Central Asia*, p. 51. Curzon, "British and Russian Commercial Competition in Central Asia." *Asiatic Quarterly Review* 8 (1889): 449. Angus Hamilton, *Afghanistan*, p. 289. Davies, *Report on the Trade of the Countries on the North-Western Boundary of British India*, p. 46.

2. "Report on the trade routes and custom duties on goods from India to Meshed from Kandahar via Afghanistan, December 1888," pp. 102–103, Frontr-A no. 102, 7, NAI.

3. Harlan, *Central Asia*, p. 70.

4. Col. R. Warburton to Peshawar commissioner, 23 August 1888, For. Dept. Frontier-A, January 1889, nos. 114–120, no. 120, NAI.

5. Harlan, *Central Asia*, p. 136. Davies, *Report on Trade*, Appendix 23.

6. Hamilton, *Afghanistan*, pp. 198, 379, 344.

7. Davies, *Report on Trade*, p. 42; the earlier quotation in this paragraph is also from Davies, p. 8.

8. Ibid.

9. Ibid., p. 40.

10. Ibid., p. 7.

11. Elphinstone, *An Account*, 1: 335.

12. Covenants of Kabul merchants, file of the covenants of the subjects of Afghanistan addressed to His Majesty 'Abd al-Rahman Khan, 130, ARAMFA.

13. M. A. Nayyir [Herawi], "Tujarat-i-Afghanistan dar Qarn-i-Nuzdahnan" [Afghanistan's trade in the nineteenth century], *Aryana* 1 (1967): 18. For names of Amir Dost Muhammad's relatives engaged in trade, see Davies, *Report on Trade*, Appendix 23. Sardar Muhammad Afzal, Amir Dost Muhammad's eldest son, was the largest trader in the province of Balkh. He bought up at cheap rates "all the cotton and silk" produced in that province and sold them at his best advantage to traders.

14. Burnes, *Cabool*, p. 283.

15. Hamilton, *Afghanistan*, p. 255.

16. Conolly quoted in Davies, *Report on Trade*, p. 7; Harlan, *Central Asia*, p. 133.

17. Davies, *Report on Trade*, p. 7.

18. G. S. Robertson, *The Kafirs of the Hindu Kush*, p. 53.

19. PD, 17 October 1883, PSLI, vol. 38, p. 401.

20. KD, 19 October 1883, PSLI, vol. 38, p. 420.

21. KD, 26 October 1890, PSLI, vol. 61, p. 858.

22. MM, September 1885, PSLI, vol. 45, p. 877.

23. Kand. D, 6 August 1884, PSLI, vol. 41, p. 1593.

24. MM, September 1885, PSLI, vol. 45, p. 877.

25. KD, 26 October 1890, PSLI, vol. 61, p. 858.

26. PD, 21 September 1883, PSLI, vol. 38, p. 131.

27. PD, 4 February 1882, PSLI, vol. 31, p. 747.

28. KD, 17–20 February 1894, PSLI, vol. 73, p. 1031.

29. KD, 27 November 1885, PSLI, vol. 46, p. 381.

30. Kand. D, 6 August 1884, PSLI, vol. 41, p. 1593.

31. KD, 20 March 1884, PSLI, vol. 40, p. 267.

32. HD, 14 August 1890, PSLI, vol. 61, p. 301.

33. KD, 20 September 1890, PSLI, vol. 61, p. 509.

34. Kand. D, 21 June 1884, PSLI, vol. 41, p. 419.

35. KD, 7 December 1889, PSLI, vol. 58, p. 1006.

36. KD, 18 March 1892, PSLI, vol. 62, p. 964.

37. PD, 22 December 1890, PSLI, vol. 62, p. 65.

38. PD, 25 July 1889, Sec. F., 99–100, August 1889, NAI.

39. KD, 27 November 1888, PSLI, vol. 55, p. 1342.

40. Kand. D, 21 June 1894, Sec. F., nos. 284–314, no. 205, NAI.

41. ST, p. 746.

42. Ibid.

43. John Gray, "Progress in Afghanistan," *Asian Review* 7, pt. 1 (1893): 308.

44. Ibid., pt. 2, p. 76.

45. Gregorian, *Emergence of Modern Afghanistan*, p. 147; Ghobar, *Afghanistan Along the Highway of History*, p. 649; McChesney, "The Economic Reforms of Amir Abdul Rahman Khan," *Afghanistan*, no. 3 (1968): 27; Hamidullah Amin, *Nazari-ba Tarikh-i-Tujarat-i-Afghanistan* [Afghanistan's foreign trade].

46. ST, p. 853.

47. KD, 21 July 1894, PSLI, vol. 75, p. 1159.

48. Ibid.; MM, August 1894, PSLI, vol. 76, p. 45.

49. In Herat alone, eight new caravanserais were built. ST, p. 405.

50. Kand. D, 15 June 1888, PSLI, vol. 54, p. 38.

51. Hamilton, *Afghanistan*, p. 290.

52. Gregorian, *Emergence of Modern Afghanistan*, p. 144. The sources he gives do not indicate that the amir abolished these tolls.

53. A. D. Baker, *British India with Notes on Ceylon, Afghanistan, and Tibet*, p. 554.

54. Durand to Cunningham, For. Dept., Secret-F., Pros. January 1894, nos. 193–217, no. 194, NAI.

55. Gregorian, *Emergence of Modern Afghanistan*, p. 147.

56. Kand. D, 6 July 1891, PSLI, vol. 63, p. 1079.

57. Durand to Cunningham, For. Dept., Secret-F., Pros. January 1894, nos. 193–217, no. 194, 9, NAI. Russian political agent at Bukhara to Afghan commercial agent, MM, April 1900, PSLI, vol. 123, no. 594.

58. MM, May 1890, PSLI, vol. 61 [page not numbered].

59. HD, 27 November 1890, PSLI, vol. 61, p. 1011.

60. MM, April 1893, PSLI, vol. 70, p. 397.

61. HD, 8 August 1901, PSLI, vol. 137, no. 1169.

62. KD, 12–14 August 1891, PSLI, vol. 63, p. 1301.

63. PD, 21 August 1891, PSLI, vol. 63, p. 1286.

64. PD, 23 January 1893, PSLI, vol. 69, p. 739.

65. HD, 11 July 1895, PSLI, vol. 81, no. 28.

66. Peshawar commissioner to chief secretary of Panjab, 30 September 1892, PSLI, vol. 70, p. 463.

67. Amir to 30 Peshawar merchants, KD, 14 December 1892, PSLI, vol. 70, p. 474.

68. "Note on the Amir's monopolies," Sec. F., October 1895, nos. 454–497, 631, no. 488, 14, NAI.

69. Ibid.

70. MM, April 1893, PSLI, vol. 70, p. 397.

71. Kh. D, 19 October 1901, PSLI, vol. 139, no. 1432A.

72. Hamilton, *Afghanistan*, p. 297.

73. ST, pp. 592, 593.

74. Col. Atta Allah (Mazar), 10 March 1890, PSLI, vol. 59, p. 1217.

75. ST, p. 1204.

76. ST, p. 1211.

77. MM, February 1901, PSLI, vol. 131, no. 387.

78. MM, December 1900, PSLI, vol. 129, p. 181.

79. HD, 13 July 1893, PSLI, vol. 71, p. 746.

80. ST, p. 1169.

81. MM, January 1902, PSLI, vol. 142, no. 325.

82. MM, March 1899, PSLI, vol. 113, p. 429 (4).

83. MM, June 1899, PSLI, vol. 114, no. 704 (2). Martin, *Under the Absolute Amir*, p. 114.

84. Hamilton, *Afghanistan*, p. 204.

85. PD, 19 December 1884, PSLI, vol. 43, p. 72.

86. For details see Davies, *Report on Trade*, Appendix 18.

87. MM, December 1887, PSLI, vol. 52, p. 63.

88. G. Scalof, "The Development of Russo-Afghan Trade through Central Asia," trans. Mandaizay, *Aryana* 2 (1970): 55–61.

89. Curzon, *Tales of Travels*, pp. 444–446.

90. PD, 1 January 1882, PSLI, vol. 31, p. 218.

91. "Note on the Amir's monopolies," Sec. F., October 1895, nos. 454–456, no. 471, 631, NAI.

92. Harlan, *Central Asia*, p. 71.

93. Davies, *Report of Trade*, Appendix 17, p. cii.

94. PD, 25 July 1889, Sec. F., August 1889, nos. 99–100, NAI.

95. Kand. D, 29 October 1884, PSLI, vol. 42, p. 837.

96. "Report on the trade routes and customs duties on goods from India via Afghanistan," December 1888, nos. 102–103, Frontr. A, nos. 102, 7, NAI.

97. "Refusal of the Amir to reduce customs dues," February 1886, no. 331, Sec. F., NAI.

98. Rogers to Amir, 31 July 1890, Sec. F., nos. 114–129, no. 129, NAI.

99. PD, 23 September 1891, PSLI, vol. 64, p. 227.

100. A. B., Kabul correspondent, 31 December 1881, PSLI, vol. 31, p. 301. In the 1830s such annual transit tolls amounted to 50,000 rupees. Harlan, *Central Asia*, p. 71.

101. "Restriction put upon trade in Afghanistan," KD, 20 March 1889, Sec. F., May 1889, nos. 530–543, NAI.

102. KD, 31 May 1890, Sec. F., August 1890, nos. 82–101, 39, NAI.

103. Curzon, *Tales of Travels*, p. 449.

104. Mahomed, *Life of Abdur Rahman*, 2: 76.

105. For. Dept. Frontr. A., December 1885, nos. 3–8, 2, NAI.

106. Curzon, *Tales of Travels*, pp. 449, 450.

107. Hamilton, *Afghanistan*, p. 293.

108. Gregorian's figures for the last eleven years of the amir's reign have been taken from the *Statesman's Yearbook* (London), the reliability of which is doubtful. Unlike all other figures these are based on each Christian year and seem too high. For instance, the figures of trade with India alone for *northern and eastern* Afghanistan for 1890 are 11,118,000 Indian rupees. Even these figures show a downward trend in Indo–Afghan trade.

109. Curzon, *Tales of Travels*, p. 445.

110. Scalof, "Development of Russo-Afghan Trade," p. 57.

111. Curzon, *Tales of Travels*, p. 448.

112. PD, 14 July 1882, PSLI, vol. 34 [page not numbered].

113. HD, 22 January 1891, PSLI, vol. 62, p. 768.

114. HD, 13 July 1893, PSLI, vol. 71, p. 746.

115. Hamilton, *Afghanistan*, p. 179.

116. Ibid., p. 296.

117. "The progress of foreign trade in Afghanistan," KD, 25 June 1890, Sec. F., August 1–11, 3, no. 33-M, NAI.

118. Col. Atta Allah (Aibak), 21 June 1890, PSLI, vol. 60, p. 943.

119. "The progress of trade in Afghanistan," Sec. F., 1–11 August 1890, 2, NAI.

120. Gregorian, *Emergence of Modern Afghanistan*, p. 146.

121. Curzon, *Tales of Travels*, p. 446.

122. The import into northwestern Afghanistan of Russian goods, including textile fabrics, was on the increase but had not assumed large proportions. IGA, p. 35.

123. Hamilton, *Afghanistan*, p. 296.

124. Amin, *Nazar-i-ba Tarikh-i-Tujarat-i-Afghanistan*, p. 26. Nayyir [Herawi] "Afghanistan's Trade during the Nineteenth Century," p. 57.

125. Ghobar, *Afghanistan Along the Highway of History*, p. 648.

126. ST, p. 614.

127. Hamid Hamidi, *A Catalog of Modern Coins of Afghanistan*, p. 8; Gregorian, *Emergence of Modern Afghanistan*, p. 402; MacGregor, *Central Asia*, p. 55; Baker, *British India*, p. 539; MRA, p. 188; Davies, *Report of Trade*, Appendix 1.

128. Hamidi, *Modern Coins of Afghanistan*, p. 5.

129. Martin, *Under the Absolute Amir*, p. 252.

130. Amir to Kandahar governor, Kand. D, 18 January 1891, PSLI, vol. 62, p. 707.

131. Hamidi, *Modern Coins of Afghanistan*, p. 9.

132. Baker, *British India*, p. 539.

133. MRA (1925), p. 589.

134. Pyne to Reuter's agent in London, 20 January 1896, PSLI, vol. 84, opposite p. no. 66-F.

135. Hamidi, *Modern Coins of Afghanistan*, p. 5.

136. Martin, *Under the Absolute Amir*, p. 251.

137. KD, 12 February 1884, PSLI, vol. 39, p. 1018.

138. KD, 12 July 1890, PSLI, vol. 60, p. 1000.
139. Col. Atta Allah (Aibak), 21 June 1890, PSLI, vol. 60, p. 943.
140. Davies, *Report on Trade*, Appendix 1, p. i.
141. MM, January 1895, PSLI, vol. 78, p. 687.
142. KD, 30 April 1885, PSLI, vol. 44, p. 897.
143. PD, 12 March 1891, PSLI, vol. 62, p. 993.
144. Martin, *Under the Absolute Amir*, p. 252.
145. Kand. D, 8 June 1891, PSLI, vol. 63, p. 883.
146. Kand. D, 8 June 1890, PSLI, vol. 60, p. 784.
147. Martin, *Under the Absolute Amir*, p. 252.
148. Kand. D, 4 May 1889, PSLI, vol. 57, p. 514.
149. KD, 16 January 1883, PSLI, vol. 35, p. 531.
150. Ibid.
151. PD, 27 January 1883, PSLI, vol. 35, p. 613.
152. Col. Afzal (Jalalabad), 19 June 1883, PSLI, vol. 37, p. 68.
153. KD, 28 August 1892, PSLI, vol. 67, p. 187.
154. Kand. D, 10 September 1892, PSLI, vol. 68, p. 41.
155. KD, 27 November 1885, PSLI, vol. 46, p. 382.
156. PD, 21 January 1888, PSLI, vol. 52, p. 471.
157. KD, 21 March 1900, PSLI, vol. 121, no. 464.
158. Col. Atta Allah (Aibak), 21 January 1890, PSLI, vol. 60, p. 943.
159. R. Warburton to Peshawar commissioner, 23 August 1888, For. Dept., Frontr-A., Pros. January 1889, nos. 120–140, no. 120, NAI.
160. Hensman, *The Afghan War of 1879–80*, p. 409.
161. Ibid., p. 407.
162. KD, 25 November 1899, PSLI, vol. 118, no. 1130.
163. Martin, *Under the Absolute Amir*, p. 253.
164. Elphinstone, *An Account*, 1: 333.
165. Haji Muhammad Hasan was the famous banker of Herat. AW, p. 219.
166. ST, p. 564.
167. KD, 10 February 1885, PSLI, vol. 43, p. 974.
168. Col. Afzal (Jalalabad), 22 June 1883, PSLI, vol. 37, p. 74.
169. MM, September 1899, PSLI, vol. 116, p. 978 (12).
170. Hamilton, *Afghanistan*, p. 298.
171. The custom of *wesh* survived until the 1880s in the Jalalabad area in Girday Kach, Basawal, and Hazarnao; among the Khawazay Mohmands (Jenkyns, *Report on the District of Jalalabad*, p. 10); and in a modified form in Kadanoi among the Bareches of Shorawak (George Peter Tate, *The Kingdom of Afghanistan*, pp. 7, 204). By contrast, *wesh* prevailed widely among the Yusufzays in Buner, Dir, Swat, Bajaur, and Uthman Khel. According to a tradition, when the Yusufzays entered these valleys as conquerors, Shaykh Mali, a respected saint among them, divided their newly conquered land into regions corresponding to the number of subtribes. Unlike Ahmad Shah, who centuries later divided the Kandahar land among the Durrani tribal septs on a permanent basis, Shaykh Mali decreed that the land should be periodically redistributed. For details see Davies, *The Problems of North-West Frontier of India*, p. 54. Fredrik Barth, *Political Leadership Among Swat Pathans*, pp. 9, 65.
172. Monic quoted by Schurmann, *The Mongols of Afghanistan*, p. 405.
173. Jenkyns, *Report on Jalalabad*, p. 10. One jarib of first-class land in Laghman is sold for about 80,000 Afghanis today.
174. Jung, *Some Observations on the Patterns and Process of Urban-Rural Migrations to Kabul*, p. 10.
175. Martin, *Under the Absolute Amir*, p. 251. As moneylenders the Hindus exacted exorbitant interest in Tashqurghan. Hamilton, *Afghanistan*, p. 255.
176. Harlan, *Central Asia*, p. 134.
177. Davies, *Report of Trade*, Appendix 8.
178. MacGregor, *Central Asia*, p. 57.
179. MM, August 1900, PSLI, vol. 127, no. 1071.
180. MacGregor, *Central Asia*, p. 57.

181. AW, p. 275.
182. Col. Afzal (Surkhpul on way to Jalalabad), 29 January 1883, PSLI, vol. 36 [page unnumbered].
183. KD, 29 April 1899, PSLI, vol. 113, p. 528.
184. ST, p. 439.
185. MM, August 1900, PSLI, vol. 127, no. 1071. For details see "Information Regarding Roads in Afghanistan," Frontr., November 1898, 150–157, Pt. B., NAI; Hamilton, *Afghanistan*, pp. 329–341.
186. DSCD, 7 March 1900, PSLI, vol. 121, no. 409 (2).
187. ST, pp. 439, 739.
188. Yate, *Northern Afghanistan*, p. 252.
189. Ibid., p. 147.
190. PD, 20 September 1890, PSLI, vol. 61, p. 421.
191. KD, 24 September 1890, PSLI, vol. 61, p. 511.
192. KD, 25 December 1885, PSLI, vol. 39, p. 417.
193. KD, 8 July 1884, PSLI, vol. 41, p. 732.
194. MRA, p. 198.
195. "Amir's Visit to India, 1885," PSLI, vol. 44, Encl. nos. 3, 7, 15.
196. Ibid.
197. AVI, p. 15.

❖

Conclusion

1. Amir quoted by W. Pyne, the advocat of India (Bombay), PSLI, Frontr. Journal, p. 156, pt. B.
2. Hamilton, *A Vizier's Daughter*, p. xv.
3. RM, p. 22.
4. Martin, *Under the Absolute Amir*, p. 305.
5. Ibid., p. 306.
6. MU, p. 14. See also the amir's words on a sheet of a map in Curzon, *Tales of Travels.*
7. Na'ib Kotwal Mir Sultan, PD, 12 February 1887, PSLI, vol. 49, p. 576.
8. Lepel Griffin, "The Late Amir and His Successor," *The Fortnightly Review* (1901): 757.
9. Dalip P. Singhal, *Afghanistan and India*, p. 178.
10. In Afghanistan there is hardly a family today that does not have stories about Amir 'Abd al-Rahman Khan. Members of any significant family will relate stories of how their fathers or grandfathers or relations suffered at his hands. The period still arouses strong passions and is yet to become history.

❖

Appendix

1. QKMH, p. 18.
2. QKMH, p. 19.
3. Gregorian, *Emergence of Modern Afghanistan*, p. 404.
4. Ibid., p. 405.
5. Ibid., p. 402.
6. During the winter, prices rose.
7. The cavalry at Ghorian compelled shopkeepers to sell them 2.50 M of grain for 1 Q.
8. One Tabrizi toman is equal to twenty rupees.
9. A pie was a subunit of the Indian rupee.
10. Prices rose when the governor began to store grain.
11. Kabul experienced severe scarcity at this time.
12. The government sold its own wheat at this rate.
13. This was the official rate.
14. The reason for this rise in late spring is not known.
15. Because of the Hazara War, prices went up. Grain became "very scarce"

because of government purchase of grain throughout Kandahar and the spread of rumors of an impending jehad.

16. Grains disappeared from markets in Kandahar, and the situation was said to have been near famine.

17. In Kandahar scarcity reached such a point that in most villages grain could not be procured and most people subsisted on green fodder.

18. Grain had become abundant.

19. Scarcity also had appeared in Herat. To alleviate it the government offered grain to markets for sale and continued to do so until 11 May. After that date bread could not be found in bazars.

20. Official rate.

21. The fall in price is ascribed to the collection of revenue in cash.

22. The low rate is ascribed to an increase in export duty of two annas per M.

23. The fall in price is ascribed to government sale of wheat to merchants.

24. The government purchased wool at this price.

25. The government sold wool at this price.

26. Throughout the year there were reports of scarcity and high prices, but the rates were not recorded.

27. Salt was scarce because of the rise in price of Kohat salt.

28. Two markets for salt had been opened in Kabul.

29. Salt was brought to Kabul from Turkestan in large quantities at this time, and Kohat salt was imported very little.

30. Imported in large quantities from Bukhara.

31. Imported from Turkestan free of duty to evade the ban on Kohat salt.

32. The equivalents of one chatak are not known.

33. The month of Rabi al-Sani.

34. The month of Jamadi al-Awwal.

35. This rate was fixed by moneylenders.

36. The month of Jamadi al-Sani.

37. On instruction from the amir, the *hakim* of Behsud sent these reports to Kabul, but his rates were actually lower than those reported. By filing false reports he was able to make a profit for himself in selling government grain.

38. This was the actual rate.

❖

Note on Sources

1. Durand to Cunningham, 3 December 1893, PSLI, vol. 73, p. 16.

2. Durand to Cunningham, 6 October 1893, no. 79, Kabul Mission diaries; from 3 October to 22 November 1893, Sec. F., December, 71–158, 63, NAI.

3. Curzon to Amir, 17 November 1899, File no. 1, no. 6 (Persian), ARAMFA.

4. MM, August 1888, PSLI, vol. 55, p. 135.

5. BACA, p. 5.

6. BACA, p. 6.

7. Singhal, *Afghanistan and India*, p. 69.

8. BACA, p. 4.

9. For a critical view of the proceedings of the qazi in Kabul, see Ghobar, *Afghanistan Along the Highway of History*, p. 457.

10. Sandemand to foreign secretary of India, 19 May 1885, PSLI, vol. 44, p. 893.

11. ST, p. 752.

12. ST, p. 656.

13. S. E. Wheeler, *The Ameer Abdur Rahman*, pp. 235–247.

14. Mahomed, *Life of Abdur Rahman*, 1: viii.

15. KD, 4 January 1896, PSLI, vol. 84, no. 156. Riyazi holds that Sultan Mahomed was in the employment of the British. AW, p. 296.

16. KD, 29 November 1887, PSLI, vol. 51, p. 1344.

17. ST, p. 656.

18. Kitchener to Curzon, 20 April 1903, Mss Eur., F. 111, Curzon Collection, vol. 207, Letter no. 117, 109, IOL. I am indebted to Miss Lal Baha of Peshawar University for this reference.

19. MM, December 1901, PSLI, vol. 141, no. 199.

20. Interview of Sultan Mahomed by Donald Stewart, 28 March 1898, PSLI, vol. 102, p. 416.

21. Memo by Lee-Warner, 26 June 1900, Proceeding of Sultan Mahomed while in England and India, Frontr., January, 156 Pt. B, NAI.

22. Cunningham to Lee-Warner, 2 May 1898, PSLI, vol. 103, p. 551.

23. ST, pp. 378, 588.

24. In 1894 the father of Fayz Muhammad, Sa'id Muhammad, was imprisoned for having talked about politics, but soon he secured his release by bribing the general in whose custody he was. ST, p. 984.

25. ST, p. 1196.

26. ST, p. 869.

27. Abd al-Hakim Rustaqi, *Bahar-i-Afghani* [Biographical accounts of poets and writers], pp. 113–14.

28. ST, p. 1236. Actually ST (1: 2) started with the words of Amir Habib Allah Khan (1901–1919). Amir Habib Allah intended to compose a work on the events and biographies of Afghan kings (Wagai' wa sawnih-i-Padshahan-i-Afghani) from Ahmad Shah Durrani to his own reign but could not do so because he was busy with state affairs. He then commissioned Fayz Muhammad for the job but went through every part of it personally before it went to the press.

29. Amir 'Abd al-Rahman actually objected to the word "service" when the title was offered to him, saying that it should be replaced by the word "friendship." Amir 'Abd al-Rahman did not use the insignia.

30. *Bayan al-Waqai'* [An autobiography] in *Collected Works* by Muhammad Yusuf Riyazi, 1324 HQ. *Bayan al-Waqai'* will be called BW hereafter.

31. BW, p. 7.

32. BW, pp. 7, 15.

33. BW, p. 15; AW, p. 157.

34. For details, see BW.

35. Ghobar, *Afghanistan Along the Highway of History*, p. 1.

36. Ibid., p. 2.

37. Ibid., p. 655.

38. Ibid., pp. 789, 790.

39. Fayz Muhammad quoted by Abd al-Mohammad Isfahani in AT, 7: 116.

Glossary

abi: land irrigated by surface water.
ahl al-kitab (*ahl-i-kitab*): people of the revealed books.
ahl-i-diwan: officials of the diwan (q.v.).
Ahmadiyya: follower of Mirza Ghulam Ahmad (b. 1839) of Qadian in
       Pakistan who rejected the notion of the seal of prophecy.
ʾ*amil*: revenue worker responsible for registration work.
ʾ*amil al-suq*: master of the market.
amin-i-mohr: custodian of the royal seal.
amir: originally meant commander, as part of the phrase *amir al-
       muʾminin* (commander of the faithful); in Afghanistan, the
       title of the Muhammadzay rulers from Amir Dost Muham-
       mad Khan to King Aman Allah (1918–1929).
Amir-i-Kabir: the great amir; title by which Amir Dost Muhammad
       Khan was known.
amlak-i-sarkari: crown lands; *khalisa*; *zamin-i-zabti*.
andarun-i-khas: royal household guards.
aqsaqal: elder; greybeard (among the Turki speakers).
arbab: head of a village; landlord.
ashar (*hashar*): cooperation in agricultural work among peasants.
ashik aghasi (*shah ghasi*): gentleman usher; minister of the royal
       court.
asnaf: artisans; classes of artisans.

badal: the principle of retaliation in defense of honor.
badar: master; landlord.

baqiyat-i-wijuh: arrears of revenue.
barat: draft; assignment.
Bardurranis: the Upper Durranis; name given by Ahmad Shah Durrani
to the Pashtuns occupying the region between the Indus
River and Kabul.
bari: skilled craftsmen among the Kafirs of Kafiristan who were treated
as slaves by tribal Kafirs.
bashi: head of a department of service.
bast: seeking refuge by aggrieved persons in sanctuaries.
bayt al-mal: public property.
bazgar: crop-sharing tenant.
beg: head of a village or tribe.
buluk mushr: lieutenant in the artillery and infantry.

chabutara: customs house.
chalwaishtays: among the Sulaiman Khel Pashtuns, groups of forty
men led by a capable leader in times of emergency.
char-kot: see *kot*.
charras: unskilled Ghilzay nomadic laborers working in northern
India.
charsu(q): center of a town.
chehl wa yak: one out of every forty; Muslim rate of *zakat* (q.v.).
Chistiyya: a Muslim mystic order.

dabir: secretary.
dabir al-mulk: chief secretary of the royal secretariat.
dafadar: sergeant in the cavalry.
daftar: register; office; department.
daftari: head of a financial office.
daftar-i-imza: office of the signature in the central diwan (q.v.).
daftar-i-sanjish: auditing office in the central diwan (q.v.).
dahbashi: leader of a group of ten, especially in the militia.
dar al-insha: royal secretariat.
darbar-i-khas: special court, or darbar.
darugha: assistant to a malik (q.v.).
darwesh: mendicant; follower of a Muslim mystic order.
dawatalab: volunteer for a military campaign.
dehgan: crop-sharing tenant; peasant.
devshirme: term for the Ottoman system of collecting subject Christian boys for training, conversion to Islam, and eventual use
in the palace and branches of government.
Dharma Shastre: Hindu religious law.
diwan: office; register; bureau.
diwan-i-aʾla: supreme financial office; central financial department.
doms: those attached to an *ulus* (q.v.) and performing varieties of
services to it.
dunbalapur: double-barreled breach-loading rifles.

durrah: whip of a *muhtasib* (q.v.).

eljari (elajari): foot levies of tribal and nontribal peasants and artisans.

fanah: a form of severe torture by which pieces of hard sticks are
        placed between the fingers and then pressed hard.
feringee: Europeans; infidels.
fetwa: opinion on legal questions issued by the ʾulama.
fiqh: religious science.
firman: royal proclamation.

ghar: name of a traditional faction among some Pashtuns.
gharibkar: seasonal agricultural laborer.
ghat mushr: military rank of general.
ghulam: male slave.
ghulam bacha: page boy; slave boy.
ghulam-i-shah: king's slaves; royal bodyguards.
gomashta: trade agent of individual merchants.
gund: faction; party; bloc.

hakeem: traditional physicians.
hakim: administrator of a district.
hamsaya: poor agricultural laborer of an outside tribe or community
        living in an inferior position in another tribe or
        community.
haq Allah: literally, "God's right"; a basketful of the produce of the
        land granted to a village *imam* (q.v.).
hasht nafari: system of recruitment by which one able-bodied man out
        of eight was enlisted in the army.
hawaldar: corporal (military rank).
hazarbashi: leader or commander of one thousand.
hazirbash: military force formed during the second reign of Shah
        Shujaʾ Sadozay under the supervision of the British officers;
        bodyguards.
hundis: bills of exchange.

ijara: contract.
ijaradar: contractor; *mustaʾjir*.
imam: leader in prayer; chief of the Muslim community. Originally
        the imam was the Prophet himself, and his successors
        filled the office. To the Shiʾas, imams must be from among
        the descendants of the Prophet through his daughter, Fa-
        tima, while the Sunni concept of imam requires that an
        imam must be elected.
Ismaʾili: follower of a Shiʾite sect that holds that the imamate passed
        from ʾAli to his descendants through a seventh imam,
        Ismaʾil.

jamadar: lieutenant in the cavalry.

jam'bandi (*jam'bast*): a fixed quota of revenue assessed on either a region or a specific tract of land.

janbaz: a standing military force formed during the second reign of Shah Shuja' Sadozay under the supervision of the British officers as a counterpoise to the old feudal cavalry.

Janissary: a corruption of the Turkish *yeni cheri* (new troops) that refers to the Ottoman infantry recruited through the *devshirme* (q.v.).

jarchi: town crier.

jarib: measurement of agricultural land equaling one-fourth of an acre.

jazya: poll tax paid by non-Muslims to the state.

jehad: holy war.

jirga: council attended by men of a village, a tribe, or a community for the settlement of disputes in accordance with conventional codes.

kadkhuda: assistant to a malik (q.v.).

kalantar: head of a professional group; elder of a city's quarter.

kalla minar: heap made of skulls of men fallen in battle.

kara nokar: horseman provided by the non-Durrani tribes on feudal terms during the Sadozay period.

kardar: government official.

karez: subterranean canal for irrigation.

karnail: colonel.

keniz: female domestic slave.

khabarchi: newscarrier.

khalifa: caliph; successor to the Prophet; master.

khalisa: see *amlak-i-sarkari*.

khan: head of a tribe or community with many maliks (q.v.) or *arbab* (q.v.) working under him. The khan was usually a big land-lord and enjoyed feudal privileges.

khanadodi: family tax on originally foreign Muslim colonists in Kandahar during the reign of Ahmad Shah Durrani.

khanaqa: cell where followers of mystic orders assemble for the performance of rites.

khanawari: see *khanadodi*.

khan-i-mulla (*khan-i-'ulum*): chief justice.

khan khel: a ruling section, house, or clan among some tribes.

khanzada: son of a khan (q.v.).

kharaji: lands of non-Muslim owners that were subject to a heavy tax.

khassadar: militia.

khatib: preacher of Islam.

khawand: master; possessor; name by which Pashtun wives call their husbands.

khilwat: private court, or darbar.

khirga: building where the mantle of the Prophet is kept in Kandahar.

khirgah: tent of Persian-speaking nomads.

khums: one-fifth; a rate of land revenue.

khutba: Friday sermon in which the name of the Muslim sovereign was mentioned as a sign of obedience to him.

kiftan: captain.

kishtmand: crop-sharing tenant; peasant.

kohna nokar: horseman provided on feudal terms by the landlords of Baldh during the Sadozay period for the defense of frontiers.

kot: system under which a fined share of the gross produce of land was assessed as revenue to the government. Taken by the government in the *nem-kot* were one-half the shares; in the *se-kot*, one out of three; in the *char-kot*, one out of four; in the *panj-kot*, one out of five; and in the *shash-kot*, one out of six.

kotdafadar: sergeant major in the cavalry.

kotwal: minister of home affairs.

kotwali: ministry of home affairs.

kufr: state of unbelief.

kuchis: Ghilzay nomads; *powindas*.

kumaidan: colonel.

lalmi: land irrigated by rain; dry farming.

landakwar: sergeant in the artillery and infantry.

madrasa: center for higher learning in Sunni Islam.

mahr: money or something of value paid by the husband to his wife at her request as a part of the marriage contract.

maijir: major (military rank).

malang: mendicant; beggar.

malik: head of a village or tribe.

mazhab (*madhnab*): the four Sunni legal schools: Hanafi, Hanbali, Maliki, and Shafi'i.

millat: nation.

mingbashi: commander of one thousand militia.

mir: corruption of the term amir (q.v.); head of a tribe or village.

mir akhor: chief of government stables.

mir munshi: chief secretary of the royal secretariat in subordinate position to the *dabir al-mulk* (q.v.).

mir wa'iz: chief preacher.

mirza: junior secretary, especially of the financial department.

muhassil: *khassadar*; militia responsible for the collection of government taxes.

muhtasib: market inspector who was also responsible for the upkeep of public morality.

mujtahid: one who has attained such preeminence in religious scholarship that he may issue opinions on matters of faith.

mulk: private property.

munshi: secretary in the royal secretariat.
murid: follower of a religious leader, especially of a mystic order.
mushawer: adviser on legal affairs.
mushr: elder; greybeard.
musta'jir: contractor; *ijaradar*.
mustaufi: chief of the central diwan (q.v.); minister of the financial department.
mutawalli: guardian of a shrine.
muwazzin: caller for prayers.
muzaribat: partnership in trade based either on doing the actual work of the business or on lending money.

na'ib: lieutenant; vicar; viceroy.
na'ib al-hukuma: governor of a province with much authority; viceroy of the government.
na'ib al-sultanat: honorary title for viceroy to the kingdom.
nam girak: literally, name calling; in fact, the elimination at night of people by special executioners.
nan-khora: fees that tax collectors exacted from taxpayers.
nap: adjutant (military rank).
naqis al-'aql (*naqis-i-'aql*): intellectually deficient; term which men employ for women.
nazim: private tutor.
nazir: overseer; superintendent; chief of a service department.
nazrana: presents offered to Amir 'Abd al-Rahman Khan.
nem-kot: see *kot*.

opra: derogatory term used by the Durranis to refer to the non-Durrani inhabitants of Kandahar.

padshah (*shah*): king.
padshah-i-islam: ruler in Islam.
paira: the lowest subdivision of a company in the infantry.
panchayat: commercial court.
panchayat bashi: chief of the commercial court.
panj-kot: see *kot*.
panza mushr: brigadier general.
parcha nawi: informer; spy.
park mushr: sergeant major in the artillery and infantry.
Pashtunwali: Pashtun codes of conduct.
peshkhidmat: chief servant in attendance upon the amir.
pinjabashi: leader of a group of fifty, especially in the militia.
pir: religious leader, especially of mystic orders.
pishqabz: dagger.
piyada: infantry.
powindas: see *kuchis*.
pultan: regiment in the army.

Qadiriyya: a Muslim mystic order.
qafila: caravan.
qafila bashi: chief of public transport.
qal'a: fort; village surrounded by high walls.
qalander: mendicant; follower of a mystic order.
qarawal khana: feudal horsemen stationed along the frontiers.
qari: reciter of the Quran on certain special religious occasions.
qasm-i-mir: tribe of the mir (q.v.); ruling house or a clan among some Hazara tribes.
qawm: tribe.
qular aghasi: officer of a group of *ghulam-i-shah* (q.v.) during the Sadozay period.
qutb-i-zaman: saint of the time.

rahdari: travel permit.
ra'iyyat: subjects of a ruler.
razanama: letter of contentment that government officials obtained from the people.
reeshsafid: elder; greybeard (among Persian speakers).
risala: cavalry regiment.
risala-dar: captain in the cavalry.
risala-i-shahi-Kandahari: a privileged royal cavalry unit.
rusum: fees paid to government officials.

sadaqa: fees paid to mullas at end of the month of fast; *sarsaya*.
sadbashi: leader of a group of one hundred
sadr-i-a'zam: chief adviser to the king; prime minister.
safar mina: corruption of English phrase *sappers and miners*.
sahib al-suq: master of the market.
samil: traditional faction among some Pashtuns.
sandoq-i-'adalat: literally, justice box; a box in which people cast their complaints against government officials.
sanjish: department of auditing in the central diwan.
sanjishiyyan: name that was used for six enterprising *mirzas* (q.v.) in the auditing office of the central diwan (q.v.) in the reign of Amir 'Abd al-Rahman Khan.
sardaftari: head of a main bureau in the central diwan (q.v.).
sarghala: cattle tax.
sarhaddar: frontier office.
sar-i-marda: family tax paid by the Ghilzay Pashtuns before 1880; *tawan-i-sar*.
sarrishtadar: head of the financial department in provinces and of a bureau in the central diwan (q.v.).
sarsaya: see *sadaqa*.
sartip: commander of one hundred militia.
sawara: cavalry.
sawara-i-kushada: feudal cavalry.

sayyed: a real or assumed descendant of the Prophet Muhammad
 through his daughter, Fatima.
se-kot: see *kot*.
shabnama: leaflet secretly distributed at night for political propaganda
 by opponents of the government.
shaf': the Islamic principle that requires that a piece of land for sale be
 offered first to that landlord whose lands are adjacent to it.
shagird: apprentice; student; beginner.
shah ghasi: see *ashik aghasi*.
shakhshumari: bureau in charge of the cattle tax.
sharik-i-dawlat: partner in state; title bestowed on the Muhammadzay sardars by Amir 'Abd al-Rahman Khan.
shash-kot: see *kot*.
shura: council.
siah chah: deep pit for the imprisonment of serious offenders.
siahkhana: tent of Persian-speaking nomads.
sil mushr: captain in the artillery and infantry.
sipahi: soldier.
sipah-i-ghair-i-munazzam: irregular army.
sipah-i-munazzam: regular army.
soyurghal: grant of land or its revenue in lieu of salary or pension.
speen gund: traditional faction or bloc among some Pashtuns.
Suhrawardiyya: a Muslim mystic order.
suq al-dawab: cattle market.
surati: female slave.

tahsil: revenue department (Mughal period).
tahsildar: chief of the revenue department (Mughal period).
tajir bashi: merchants' chief.
takya khana: enclosed place where the Shi'as commemorate the martyrdom of the Prophet's grandson, Hussayn, during the
 month of Muharram.
talib: student of Islamic studies.
talkhan: dried bread made of mulberry flowers.
tapa: district within a province with boundaries fixed on ethnic lines.
taqawi: governmental loans to people in business and agriculture.
taqqiya: the Shi'ite doctrine of concealment which allowed the Shi'as
 to convert, or to appear to convert, in times of danger.
tariqa: path; mystic order in Islam.
tawachi: assistant to a malik (q.v.).
tawan-i-sar: see *sar-i-marda*.
thahans: small military posts.
tiyul: land assignment in return for military service.
tol-i-sardar: descendant of a sardar; ruling house or clan among some
 Hazara tribes.
topkhana: artillery.
tore qund: traditional faction or bloc among some Pashtuns.
turburi: literally, cousinhood; keen competition among cousins.

ulus: Mongol word for clan or tribe; in Afghanistan, nation or portion of a mixed community or a tribe.

ʾ*ushr*: tithe; the Islamic rate of revenue on land.

ustad: master; professor; skilled artisan; artificer.

wahhabi: disciple of Muhammad b. ʾAbd al-Wahhab (1703–1787) whose aim was to do away with all innovation later than the third century of Islam.

waqf (*awqaf*): religious foundation.

watan: fatherland; also one's own region.

wazifa: allowance paid to religious persons.

wesh: periodical redistribution of land among some Pashtun tribes.

wilayat: province.

yurt: round dome-shaped felt tents used mainly by the Turkish-speaking nomads.

yuzbashi: leader of a group of one hundred.

zabit: military officer of relatively low rank responsible for the collection of government revenue.

zakat: legally obligatory alms paid by Muslims.

zamindar: landlord.

zamin-i-zabti: see *amlak-i-sarkari*.

zar mushr: colonel (military rank).

zawwar: Shiʾite Hazara who has visited the sacred shrines in Karbala (Iraq) and Mashhad; a religious elder.

zimmi: non-Muslim.

Bibliography

Unpublished Sources

Algar, Hamid. "The Naqshbandi Order: A Preliminary Survey of its History and Significance." Typescript. University of California at Los Angeles, 1974.

Amiri, Gul R. "Notes on Afghan Seistan." Smithsonian Institution, Washington, D.C., 1975.

Delhi. Foreign and Political Department, the National Archives of India.

Dickson, Martin B. "Shah Jahmasb and the Uzbeks, the Duel for Khurasan with Ubayd Khan: 930–940/1524–1540 [sic]." Ph.D. dissertation, Princeton University, 1958.

Isfahani, 'Abd al-Muhammad. "Aman al-Tawarikh" [A general history of Afghanistan]. Private Collection of Mr. and Mrs. C. S. Ioannidis, Cambridge, Massachusetts.

Kabul. Ministry of Foreign Affairs. Files Relating to the Reign of Amir 'Abd al-Rahman Khan.

London. India Office Library and India Office Records. Political and Secret Letters and Enclosures Received from India. Vols. 25–141, 1878–1902.

Rahman, Amir 'Abd al-. "Pandnama-i-Dunya wa Din" [A book of advice on the world and religion]. Manuscripts Department, Public Library, Kabul.

❖

Afghan Government Publications

Alkozay, Mowlawi Ahmad Jan. Asas al-Quzzat [The judicial system of Afghanistan]. Kabul, 1899.

———. Qanun-i-Karquzari dar Ma'amilat-i-Hukumati [Regulations concerning government affairs]. Kabul, 1892. [The full text of this work is also found in ST, pp. 762–771.]

Bakr, Mulla Abu, and other mullas. Taqwim al-Din [The calendar of the religion]. Kabul, 1889.

Ihtisab al-Din [A manual of instruction for the muhtasibs]. Kabul, 1889.

Kalimat-i-Amir al-Bilad fi Targhib Illal Jehad [The words of the amir of the land toward the encouragement of jehad]. Kabul, 1886.

Kitabcha-i-Dastur al-ʾAmal-i-Kalantarha-i-Guzarha-i-Dar al-Sultana-i-Kabul wa Ghaira Wilayat-i-Afghanistan [A manual of instruction for the *kalantars* of Kabul and other cities of Afghanistan]. Kabul, 1918.

Kitab-i-Qanun-i-Afghanistan [Regulations concerning payment to the army]. Kabul, n.d.

Qadir, Qazi Abd al-. *Tuhfat al-ʾUlama* [Gift from the ʾulama]. Kabul, 1875.

Rahman, Amir ʾAbd al-. *Mirat al-Ugul* [The mirror of wisdom]. Kabul, 1894.

————. *Nasaʾih Namcha* [A book of advices]. Kabul, 1886.

————. *Pandnama-i-Dunya wa Din* [A book of advice on the world and religion]. Kabul, 1886.

————. *Risala-i-Muwaʾizza* [A book of advice]. Kabul, 1894.

————. *Sarrishta-i-Islamiyya-i-Rum* [Arrangements for the Islamic government of Turkey]. Kabul, 1887.

The British Government of India

Biographical Accounts of Chiefs, Sardars and Others of Afghanistan. Calcutta, 1888.

Gazetteer of Afghanistan. Part 4, *Kabul*, 1895.

Imperial Gazetteer of India, Afghanistan and Nepal. Calcutta, 1908.

Military Report on Afghanistan. Calcutta, 1906.

Military Report on Afghanistan, History, Geography, Ethnology, Resources, Armed Forces, Forts and Fortified Posts, Administration and Communication. Delhi, 1925.

✢

Books

Abro, Hafiz. *Joghrafiyya-i-Hafiz Abro* [The geography of Hafiz Abro]. Ed. Mayil Herawi. Tehran, 1970.

Amin, Hamidullah. *Nazar-i-ba Tarikh-i-Tujarat-i-Afghanistan* [Afghanistan's foreign trade]. Kabul: Kabul University Press, 1971.

Arnold, Thomas W. *The Caliphate.* London: Routledge and Kegan Paul, 1965.

Bacon, Elizabeth E. *Central Asia Under Russian Rule.* Ithaca, N.Y.: Cornell University Press, 1966.

Baker, A. D. *British India with Notes on Ceylon, Afghanistan and Tibet.* Washington, D.C., 1915.

Barth, Fredrik. *Political Leadership Among Swat Pathans.* London: Uthlone Press, 1959.

Basham, A. L. *The Wonder That Was India.* New York: Grove Press, 1959.

Bellew, Henry W. *Afghanistan and Afghans.* London, 1879.

————. *Journal of a Political Mission to Afghanistan in 1857.* London: Smith, Elder and Co., 1862.

————. *The Races of Afghanistan.* Calcutta: Thacker, Spink and Co., 1880.

Bidulph, J. *The Tribes of the Hindoo Koosh.* Calcutta, 1880.

Bingham, Woodbridge, et al. *A History of Asia.* Vol. 1. 2d ed. Boston: Allyn and Bacon, 1974.

Bosworth, Clifford E. *The Ghaznavids.* Edinburgh: Edinburgh University Press, 1963.

Brown, Norman. *The United States and India, Pakistan, and Bangladesh.* Cambridge, Mass.: Harvard University Press, 1972.

Bruce, C. E. *Notes on Ghilzais and Powinda Tribes.* Peshawar, 1929.

Burnes, Alexander. *Cabool.* London: John Murray, 1842.

Caroe, Olaf. *The Pathans.* London: Macmillan and Co., 1958.

Cipolla, C. M. *The Economic History of World Population.* Hammonsworth: Pelican Books, 1967.

Coulson, N. J. *A History of Islamic Law*. Edinburgh: Edinburgh University Press, 1964.

Cunningham, Alexander. *The Ancient Geography of India*. London: Trubner and Co., 1871.

Curzon, George N. *Tales of Travels*. London: Hodder and Stoughton, 1923.

Darmestater, James, et al. *Tarikh-i-Talafuz wa Sarf-i-Pashto* [An etymological grammar of Pashto]. 2 vols. Trans. Abd al-Ghafur Rawan Farhadi. Kabul: Kabul University Press, 1977.

Davies, C. C. *The Problems of North-West Frontier of India, 1880–1908*. Cambridge: Cambridge University Press, 1932.

Davies, R. H. *Report on the Trade of the Countries on the North-Western Boundary of British India*. Lahore, 1862.

Dupree, Louis. *Afghanistan*. Princeton: Princeton University Press, 1973.

———, and Albert, Linette, eds. *Afghanistan in the 1970s*. New York: F. Praeger, 1974.

Durand, A. *The Making of a Frontier*. London: John Murray, 1900.

Durrani, Sultan M. *Tarikh-i-Sultani* [The history of Sultani]. Bombay: privately published, 1880.

Elphinstone, Mountstuart. *An Account of the Kingdom of Caubul*. London: Richard Bentley, 1839.

Ferdinand, Klaus. *Nomadism in Afghanistan*. Budapest: Akademiai Kaido, 1969.

———. *Preliminary Notes on Hazara Culture*. Copenhagen: I Kommission hos Munksgaard, 1959.

Ferrier, J. P. *History of the Afghans*. Trans. William Jesse. London: John Murray, 1858.

Firishta, Muhammad Qasim. *Tarikh-i-Firishta* [The history of Firishta]. Kanpur, 1884.

Fischer, Ludolph. *Afghanistan: A Geomedical Monograph*. Heidelberg, 1968.

Ghobar, Ghulam Muhammad. *Afghanistan dar Masir-i-Tarikh* [Afghanistan along the highway of history]. Kabul: Books Publishing Institute, 1967.

———. *Khurasan*. Kabul: History Association, 1946.

Gray, John. *My Residence at the Court of the Amir*. 2d ed. London: Macmillan, 1901.

Gregorian, Vartan. *The Emergence of Modern Afghanistan*. Stanford: Stanford University Press, 1969.

Hamidi, Hamid. *A Catalog of Modern Coins of Afghanistan*. Kabul, 1967.

Hamilton, Angus. *Afghanistan*. London: William Heinemann, 1906.

Hamilton, Lillias. *A Vizier's Daughter: A Tale of the Hazara War*. London, 1900.

Harawi, Sayf ibn Ya'qub al-. *Tarikh Nama-i-Harat* [The history of Herat]. Ed. Muhammad Z. al-Siddiqi. Calcutta: Khan Bahadur, 1944.

Harlan, Josiah. *Central Asia: Personal Narrative of Josiah Harlan, 1823–1841*. Ed. F. E. Ross. London: Luzac and Co., 1939.

Hensman, Howard. *The Afghan War of 1879–80*. London: W. H. Allen and Co., 1881.

Herawi, Qasim b. Yusuf A. *Risala-i-Tariqi-i-Qismat-i-Ab-i-Qalb* [The irrigation system of Herat]. Ed. Mayil T. Herawi. Tehran, 1968.

Herodotus. *The Persian Wars*. Trans. G. Rawlinson. New York: Random, 1942.

Jenkyns, William. *Report on the District of Jalalabad, Chiefly in Regard to Revenue*. Calcutta: Government of India Publications, 1879.

Jung, Christine L. *Some Observations of the Patterns and Process of Rural-Urban Migration to Kabul*. Occasional Paper no. 2. New York: Afghanistan Council, The Asia Society, 1971.

Kabul Times Annual. Kabul: Kabul Times Agency, 1970.

Kakar, Hasan. *Afghanistan: A Study in Internal Political Development, 1880–1896.* Lahore: Educational Press, 1971.

Kalami-i-Pir [The words of the *pir*]. Trans. I. Ivanov. Bombay, 1935.

Keddie, Nikki. *Sayyid Jamal ad-Din "al-Afghani."* Berkeley: University of California Press, 1972.

Khafi, Ya'qub Ali. *Padshahan-i-Mutakhir-i-Afghanistan* [The recent kings of Afghanistan]. 2 vols. Kabul: History Association, 1945.

Kohzad, Ahmad Ali. *Afghanistan dar Shahnama* [Afghanistan in the Shahnama]. Kabul: Baihagi Book Publishing Institute, 1976.

Kushkaki, Burhan al-Din. *Rahnuma-i-Qataghan wa Badakhshan* [A guide to Qataghan and Badakhshan]. Kabul: Afghan Government Publication, 1924.

Lambton, Ann K. *Landlord and Peasant in Persia.* Oxford: Oxford University Press, 1956.

McGovern, W. M. *The Early Empires of Central Asia.* Chapel Hill: University of North Carolina Press, 1939.

MacGregor, Charles. *Central Asia Pt. II: A Contribution Toward the Better Knowledge of the Topography, Ethnology, Resources and History of Afghanistan.* Calcutta: Government of India Publication, 1871.

Mahomed, Sultan. *The Life of Abdur Rahman.* 2 vols. London: John Murray, 1900.

Mair, Lucy. *An Introduction to Social Anthropology.* Oxford: Oxford University Press, 1965.

Majumdar, R. C., ed. *The History and Culture of the Indian People, British Paramountcy and Indian Resistance.* Bombay: Bharatiya Vidya Bharan, 1970.

Martin, Frank. *Under the Absolute Amir.* London: Harper and Brothers, 1907.

Masson, Charles. *Narrative of Various Journeys in Baloochistan, Afghanistan, and the Panjab, 1826–1838.* 3 vols. London: Richard Bentley, 1842.

Mohammad, Sultan. *The Constitution and Laws of Afghanistan.* London: John Murray, 1900.

Morgenstierne, Georg. *Report on a Linguistic Mission to Afghanistan.* Oslo: H. Aschehoug, 1926.

Muhammad, Fayz. *Saraj al-Tawarikh* [The lamp of histories]. 3 vols. Kabul: Afghan Government Publication, 1915.

Nasr, Sayyed Hussain. *Ideals and Realities of Islam.* Boston: Beacon Press, 1966.

Neamatullah. *History of the Afghans.* Trans. B. Dorn. London, 1914.

Pennell, Theodore L. *Among the Wild Tribes of the Afghan Frontier.* London: Seeley, 1909.

Ptolemy. *Ancient India as Described by Ptolemy.* Ed. Sastri S. Majumdar. Calcutta: Chatterjee and Co., 1927.

Riyazi, Muhammad Yusaf. *Kulliyat-i-Riyazi* [The collected works of Riyazi]. Mashhad: privately published, 1907.

Robertson, George S. *The Kafirs of the Hindu Kush.* London: Lawrence and Bullen, 1895.

Robinson, J. A. *Notes on the Nomad Tribes of Eastern Afghanistan.* London, 1935.

Rustagi, Abd al-Hakim. *Bahar-i-Afghani* [Biographical accounts of poets and writers]. Delhi: privately published, 1932.

Schapera, I. *Government and Politics in Tribal Societies.* New York: C. A. Watts and Co., 1967.

Schurmann, H. F. *The Mongols of Afghanistan.* The Hague: Mouton, 1962.

Schuyler, Eugene. *Turkistan.* Reprint. New York: F. Praeger Publishers, 1966.

Scott, G. B. *Afghan and Pathan.* London: Mitre Press, 1929.

Shanin, Theodore. *Peasants and Peasant Society.* Hammonsworth: Penguin, 1971.

Singh, Ganda. *Ahmad Shah Durrani*. Bombay: Asia Publishing House, 1959.

Singhal, Dalip P. *Afghanistan and India*. Melbourne: University of Queensland Press, 1963.

Sjoberg, Gideon. *The Pre-Industrial City*. New York: Free Press, 1960.

Sykes, Percy. *Sir Mortimer Durand*. London: Cassell and Co., 1926.

Tate, George Peter. *The Kingdom of Afghanistan*. Reprint. Karachi: Indus Publication, 1973.

Thornton, Ernest and Annie. *Leaves from an Afghan Scrapbook*. London: John Murray, 1910.

Varahamira. *Brihat Samhita*. Trans. P. S. Sastri and V. M. R. Bhat. Banglore, 1947.

Vavilov, N. I., and Bukinich, D. D. *Agricultural Afghanistan*. Leningrad, 1929.

Warburton, Robert. *Eighteen Years in the Khyber, 1879–1898*. London: John Murray, 1900.

Wheeler, Stephen E. *The Ameer Abdur Rahman*. New York: Frederick Warne and Co., 1895.

Wilber, Donald. *Afghanistan*. New Haven: HRAF Press, 1963.

Wilson, Horace H. *Ariana Antiqua*. London: East India Co. Publication, 1841.

Wolf, Eric R. *Peasants*. Englewood Cliffs, N.J.: Prentice-Hall, 1963.

Yate, Charles E. *Northern Afghanistan*. London: William Blackwood and Sons, London, 1888.

✤

Articles

'Ali, M. Athar. "The Passing of Empire: The Mughal Case." *Modern Asian Studies* 9, no. 3 (July 1975): 385–396.

Babakhodjayev, M. A. "Afghanistan's Armed Forces and Amir Abdul Rahman's Military Reforms, Pt. I," *Afghanistan*, no. 2 (1970), pp. 8–20; Pt. II, *Afghanistan*, no. 3 (1970), pp. 9–23.

Curzon, George N. "British and Russian Commercial Competition in Central Asia." *Asiatic Quarterly Review* 8 (1889): 438–451.

Davies, C. C. "Abd al-Rahman." *Encyclopedia of Islam* (1961).

Farhadi, A. G. Rawan. "Languages [of Afghanistan]." *Kabul Times Annual*. Kabul: Kabul Times Agency, 1970.

Frye, Richard. "Dari." *Encyclopedia of Islam* (1965).

Ghobar, Ghulam Muhammad. "Afghanistan wa Nazar-i-ba Tarikh-i-An" [Afghanistan and a glance at its history], pt. I, *Kabul*, no. 2 (1931), pp. 39– 51; pt. II, *Kabul*, no. 4 (1931), pp. 44–57; pt. III, *Kabul*, no. 5 (1931), pp. 30–50; pt. IV, *Kabul*, no. 6 (1931), pp. 46–66; pt. V, *Kabul*, no. 9 (1931), pp. 41–64; pt. VI, *Kabul*, no. 10 (1931), pp. 41–58; pt. VII, *Kabul*, no. 11 (1932), pp. 44–61; pt. VIII, *Kabul*, no. 12 (1932), pp. 45–60.

———. "Shahr-i-Kabul" [The city of Kabul]. *Kabul*, no. 1 (1931), pp. 44–48.

Gray, John. "Progress in Afghanistan." *Asian Review* 7 (1893).

Griffin, Lepel. "The Late Amir and His Successor." *Fortnightly Review*, 1901, pp. 748–759.

Hameed ud-Din. "The Loodis." In *The Delhi Sultanate*, ed. R. C. Majumdar. Bombay, 1967.

Huart, A. "Khurasan." *Encyclopedia of Islam* (1927).

Kramers, J. H. "Iran." *Encyclopedia of Islam* (1936).

McChesney, Robert D. "The Economic Reforms of Amir Abdul Rahman Khan." *Afghanistan*, no. 3 (1968), pp. 11–34.

Morgenstierne, Georg. "The Languages of Afghanistan." *Afghanistan*, no. 3 (1967), pp. 81–90.

———. "Pashto Literature." *Encyclopedia of Islam* (1961).

Muhammad, Hafiz N. "A Glance at the History of Kabul." *Kabul*, no. 3 (1931), pp. 36–58.

Nayyir [Herawi], Muhammad Anwar. "Aryana, Khurasan, Afghanistan." *Aryana*, nos. 1–2 (1965), pp. 62–90.

———. "Sanai' wa 'Imranat-i-Afghanistan" [Industries and constructions in Afghanistan]. Pt. I, *Aryana*, no. 3 (1969), pp. 24–37; pt. II, *Aryana*, no. 4 (1969), pp. 39–55; pt. III, *Aryana*, no. 5 (1969), pp. 29–41.

———. "Tujarat-i-Afghanistan dar Qarn-i-Nuzdahuar" [Afghanistan's trade in the nineteenth century]. Pt. I, *Aryana*, no. 1 (1967), pp. 18–36; pt. II, *Aryana*, no. 2 (1967), pp. 49–59; pt. III, *Aryana*, no. 3 (1967), pp. 22–29.

Omar, A. F. "Hisbah." *Journal of the Muslim World League* 1, no. 9 (1974): 16.

"The Pathans of the North-West Frontier of India." *Blackwood's Edinburg Magazine*, May 1879, pp. 595–610.

Pennell, Theodore L. "The Tribes on Our North-West Frontier." *Asiatic Quarterly Review* 30 (1910): 88–103.

Poliak, A. N. "Classification of Lands in the Islamic Law and Its Technical Terms." *American Journal of Semitic Languages and Literature* 57 (January 1940): 50–62.

Rawlinson, C. Henry. "Report on the Dooranee Tribe, April 1841." In *Central Asia*, ed. C. MacGregor. Calcutta: Government of India, 1871.

Scalof, G. "Da Afghanistan aw Rusiyag da Tujarati Rawabito Piralchta da Markazi Asia la Laray" [The development of Russo-Afghan trade through central Asia. Trans. Mandaizay]. *Aryana*, no. 2 (1970), pp. 55–61.

Shahristani, Ali Akbar. "A Short Account of the Forty Years Proceedings of the Ministry of Finance." *Wata* [Kabul], 1958.

Sprengling, M. "Shahpuhr I the Great on the Kaabah of Zoroaster (KZ)." *American Journal of Semitic Languages and Literature* 57 (October 1940): 341–429.

Tapper, Nancy. "The Advent of Pashtan Malders in North-Western Afghanistan." *BSOAS*, 1973, pp. 55–79.

Yapp, Malcolm Edward. "Disturbances in Eastern Afghanistan, 1839–42." *BSOAS* 25, pt. 3 (1963): 499–523.

———. "Disturbances in Western Afghanistan: 1839–41." *BSOAS* 26, pt. 2 (1965): 288–313.

———. "The Revolutions of 1841–42 in Afghanistan." *BSOAS* 27, pt. 2 (1964): 333–381.

Index